A BROKEN TRUST

A Broken Trust

Herbert Samuel, Zionism and the Palestinians
1920–1925

Sahar Huneidi

Foreword by Walid Khalidi

I.B.Tauris *Publishers*
LONDON • NEW YORK

Published in 2001 by I.B.Tauris & Co Ltd
6 Salem Rd, London W2 4BU
175 Fifth Avenue, New York NY 10010
www.ibtauris.com

In the United States of America and in Canada distributed by
St Martins Press, 175 Fifth Avenue, New York NY 10010

ISBN 1 86064 172 5

A full CIP record for this book is available from the British Library
A full CIP record for this book is available from the Library of Congress

Library of Congress catalog card: available

Typeset in Aldus by Hepton Books, Oxford
Printed and bound in Great Britain by MPG Books Ltd, Bodmin, Cornwall

Contents

For
Yasmin and Tariq

Foreword

It is sometimes assumed in the West that Zionism is largely a post-Holocaust phenomenon and that the origins of the Palestine problem (and its derivative, the Arab-Israeli conflict) lay in the 'invasion' by the neighbouring Arab countries of the nascent Jewish state in May 1948. Sahar Huneidi's work is an apt reminder that Zionism and the Palestine problem long predated the Holocaust and the Israeli-Arab war of 1948.

The bulk of this work deals with Sir Herbert Samuel's tenure as high commissioner in Palestine (1920–25) against the background of Great Britain's espousal of the Balfour Declaration and the mandate.

To the best of my knowledge, this is the first book on this subject to pull together such a wide and rich variety of primary sources: documentation from the Foreign, Colonial, and War Offices as well as from the British Cabinet, the private papers and published memoirs of the principal British actors, published and unpublished archival material of the Palestinian national movement, and contemporary British and Arabic newspapers. In addition, the author has successfully integrated into her work the findings of generations of scholars on her topic.

Samuel was the first of seven high commissioners to govern Palestine during the fateful years of the mandate, culminating, as the Palestinians feared from the beginning of the Zionist enterprise at the end of the 19th century, in the Zionist domination of their country in 1948. Samuel's administration was the formative period in the mandate, serving as the pivotal link between pre- and post- Balfour Declaration Zionism and providing the latter with the momentum that made ultimate statehood possible. For it was under Samuel's direction that the support of the paramount imperial power of the day was translated into operative policy and legislation and into the necessary institutional infrastructures and economic and demographic realities.

The choice of Samuel by Lloyd George—the arch-Zionist among Britain's inter-war prime ministers (1916–22) before Churchill—was in itself indicative of British intentions. It was not so much that he was a leading member of the Anglo-

Jewish elite (many of them were anti-Zionist) but that, as a Cabinet minister in the previous Asquith government (1906–16), he had been the first British politician to broach to his colleagues the idea of the creation of a Jewish state in Palestine as early as 1914.

Nevertheless, the author does not rush to judge Samuel. Indeed, the major theme of her work is the dynamics between Samuel's deep Zionist convictions, his self-image as a British proconsul, his learning experience on the job, his changing perceptions of Arab fears and reactions, and the convergence of pressures on him from London, his principal British aides on the spot (Zionist and anti-Zionist) and, above all, from the formidable Chaim Weizmann, his mentor and virtual co-decision maker.

In her thorough mining of the Public Records Office, Huneidi brings to life not only the roles of the principal actors in London (foreign secretaries Balfour and Curzon, colonial secretaries Churchill and Devonshire), but also Samuel's British subordinates (Deedes, Bentwich, Clayton, Keith-Roach and Richmond). Particularly vivid is her portrayal of the thought process of Sir John Shuckburgh, the senior official in the Colonial Office in charge of the Middle East and the quintessential imperial civil servant who, notwithstanding, seemed mesmerized by Chaim Weizmann.

Samuel's tenure witnessed the completion of the process of international 'legitimization' of the Balfour Declaration: the Treaty of Sèvres (August 1920) by which Turkey relinquished its sovereignty over Palestine, and which incorporated the Declaration, and the ratification in July 1922 by the League of Nations of the Mandate for Palestine, whose cornerstone was the Declaration. The assumption by Samuel of his office came hard on the heels of the expulsion, with British connivance, of King Faisal from Damascus the previous month, and the implementation, by force, of French mandates in Lebanon and Syria—developments that generated shock waves that still reverberate in the Arab psyche. It was during Samuel's tenure as well that Iraq was established as a mandatory kingdom under Faisal and that Transjordan, excluded from the scope of the Balfour Declaration, was set up in 1921 as a client emirate under Faisal's brother Abdallah. Also during Samuel's tenure, in 1924–25, King Hussein and his successor King 'Ali of the Hijaz were abandoned to the mercy of Ibn Sa'ud because of Hussein's insistence on the applicability to Palestine of the pledges conveyed to him via McMahon. The ensuing Hashemite-Sa'udi dynastic rift continued to plague inter-Arab relations for the greater part of the 20th century.

A major sub-theme in Huneidi's work is the diligent pursuit by the Palestinian leadership of diplomacy in London to persuade the British government to revise its Palestine policy. Through successive delegations, it lobbied the government, the House of Lords, and the press, only to be met with the hauteur and dismissiveness that Churchill (then colonial secretary) reserved for Afro-Asian leaders, and with the granite posture that the Balfour Declaration was a *'chose jugée'* (Samuel's phrase) and irreversible. An intriguing part of Huneidi's treatment of these early Palestinian diplomatic efforts is her speculation about the Declaration's *reversibility*: in June 1922, the House of Lords passed a motion (by 60 to 25 votes) rejecting the Palestine mandate on the grounds of its inherent injustice to the Palestinians and its violation of the McMahon pledges. The influential Northcliffe press was blasting away at Churchill's Palestine policy. And in October 1922, the Lloyd George government resigned, to be succeeded by a Conservative government less committed to Zionism and willing to 'review' its Palestine policy.

In Palestine itself, Samuel proceeded apace in consolidating the Jewish national home. With Jewish immigration regulated solely by economic criteria ('economic absorptive capacity') as laid out in the 1922 White Paper (Samuel's work), the Third Aliyah (1919–23) brought in 35,000 settlers, doubling the size of the Yishuv to about 100,000 and the number of the colonies to about 100. Newly arrived Jewish immigrants were granted provisional Palestinian citizenship to enable them to participate in local elections, pending their acquisition of full citizenship following only two years of residence. The Keren Hayesod (established in 1920) provided the funds, largely from American Jewish sources, to the Keren Kayemeth (established in 1901) enabling the latter to play an increasing role in centralized colonization and the acquisition of land as the exclusive property of the Jewish people. The economic separatism of the Yishuv (so ably researched by Barbara Smith) was given a tremendous push by the monopoly rights granted in 1921 to Pinhas Rutenberg.

In the civil area, it was thanks to Samuel's persistence that the representative assembly of the Yishuv, the Assefat HaNivharim, and its executive, the Va'ad Leumi, were granted, through the Jewish Community Ordinance approved in 1925, lay powers, including the right to levy taxes. These powers had been denied the Supreme Muslim Council established in 1922. Together with the preferential status accorded the international Jewish Agency in the mandate instrument itself, this Ordinance made possible a vast accretion of autonomous political power in the Yishuv. Meanwhile, in 1920, the Histadrut, which had been established that year, spawned the Yishuv's military organization, the Haganah, with Samuel looking the other way. Thus, by the end of his tenure, the Yishuv was well on its way to becoming an *imperium in imperio*.

To her credit, Huneidi does not paint all this in black and white. She devotes a great deal of space to the various formulae (the Advisory Council, the Legislative Council, the 'Arab Agency') devised by Samuel to co-opt the Palestinian community. All these efforts, however, were premised on Palestinian acceptance of the Balfour Declaration while leaving all executive and legislative powers solely in the hands of the high commissioner—hence their rejection by the Palestinians.

The main underlying question with which Huneidi conscientiously grapples throughout most of her work is the extent to which Samuel, given his Zionist convictions and imperial responsibilities, conducted himself with the impartiality and even-handedness expected of one in his position. Her final conclusion, from which it is difficult to dissent, is that he was neither impartial nor even-handed, though he seems consciously or unconsciously to have convinced himself not only that he was both, but that Zionism as he understood it was somehow good for the Palestinians, even if it led to a Jewish majority and to Jewish statehood.

Huneidi does not duplicate the work of other scholars (Bowle, Friesel, Mossek, Porath, Shepherd, Smith, Stein and Wasserstein), but adds new insights to their findings and provides a fresh look at the period. She joins a growing number of Palestinian historians of a younger generation writing in English (Doumani, Khalaf, Masalha, Mattar, Rouhana, Saikaly and Sayigh) who are contributing notably to a fuller understanding by the West of the Palestinian people and of the genesis and evolution of the Palestine problem.

Walid Khalidi
Cambridge, Massachusetts

Preface

My initial aim in this study was to focus on Herbert Samuel's administration in Palestine in view of its importance in shaping later developments. As research went on, however, it became clear that the relationship between Samuel and the Palestine Arabs had never been examined in depth, and that it deserved a measure of attention that corresponds to its historical importance.

Although Samuel was instrumental in interpreting the Balfour Declaration in such a way as to lead ultimately to the establishment of a Jewish state, the prevailing view, taken by several British officials during the period under study,[1] as well as by some recent scholars,[2] has been that he was an impartial administrator. In this book it will be argued that, as high commissioner, Samuel had in mind the gradual founding of a state with a predominantly Jewish majority. Although in his public statements, as well as in his correspondence with the Colonial Office, Samuel stressed his 'impartiality', in fact his actions were in a diametrically opposite direction. It should be noted at the outset that turning Palestine into a Jewish state was not expressly stated either in the Balfour Declaration, or in the Mandate for Palestine. Both stressed that favourable conditions were to be encouraged with a view to the establishment of a Jewish national home *in* Palestine, on condition that the 'civil and religious rights' of the country's inhabitants were protected. It was therefore Samuel's deliberate policy to interpret the term 'Jewish national home' used in both documents in a radical Zionist sense by making it equivalent to a Jewish state.

By the end of Samuel's five-year term in Palestine, the major foundations of a future state were firmly laid down. Herein lies the importance of studying this period, for what happened after 1925 was only an unfolding of what had been securely established during the first crucial years.[3]

According to Samuel, the mandate was to be implemented through action in five key areas. Legislation was needed on immigration and land, the two essential components for the formation of the Jewish national home; and political, economic and administrative measures had to be taken to encourage and protect the rapidly growing settler community. This book revolves, therefore, around the policies in these five areas, which were implemented by Samuel with a view to bringing about a Jewish state. It argues that these measures, especially in the political sphere, were calculated to block Palestinian Arab aspirations of achieving national independence.

Although this constitutes the main thrust of the book, I have always taken into account that the Palestine problem was a 'triangle' whose three sides were the British, the Jews and the Arabs, and the study therefore takes into consideration British and Zionist policies and also the nascent Arab nationalist movement in Palestine. Emphasis is also laid on Samuel's motives, his thinking and reasoning, how he viewed the Palestine Arabs, and how they viewed him.

Born in Liverpool in 1870 to Jewish parents, Herbert Samuel rose to assume a position of power and influence in the British establishment. As a Liberal MP from 1902 to 1918, Samuel gained appointments as under-secretary of state at the Home Office in 1905, chancellor of the Duchy of Lancaster in 1909, postmaster-general in 1910, president of the Local Government Board in 1914, chancellor of the Duchy of Lancaster in 1915 and home secretary in 1916. In July 1920, Samuel became the first high commissioner in Palestine. As he wrote in his memoirs, he was only the second Jew, after Disraeli, to have reached such a high position in the British government. It is essential, therefore, to explore to what extent Samuel's religious and ethnic background influenced his official decision-making process. In other words, to what extent did Samuel identify with Zionism despite his self-image as a British statesman and empire builder?

Further, as a distinguished ex-cabinet minister, who was rated highly among his colleagues, with a reputation of being an able administrator, was Samuel less amenable to guidance from London than an ordinary colonial governor? Still more importantly, did he have any previous experience to qualify him to govern an eastern country? How susceptible was he to Jewish pressure? Were his views different from or similar to those of the Colonial Office, and those of the Zionist organizations? What were Samuel's attitudes to the obligations to the Arabs set out in the Balfour Declaration and the mandate? And what policies did he adopt to implement these obligations? Was he sensitive to Arab criticism? Was he aware of the negative impact of his policies on the Arabs? And what was his perception of the Arab aspirations and reactions?

It will be shown that the Palestine Arabs saw Samuel as a Zionist, and tended, particularly towards the second half of his term, not to give him the benefit of the doubt. They made the worst assumptions about his motivations, fearing that he would be under Zionist influence and would merely be an instrument of Zionist policy. The book will also trace the course of Samuel's relations with the Arab community, detailing the high and low points as seen by the Arabs: Did Arab opinion swing from approval to disapproval? If so, why and for how long? What did the Arabs think and why? Was the Arab attitude towards Samuel uniform, or were

there differences between them? Were there any sectors of society, Muslim or
Christian, closer to him? Who, amongst the Palestine Arabs, were the most critical
of his policy, and on what issues? Was Samuel successful in playing off one side
against the other, if so, to what extent? Finally, as a devoted Zionist, was Samuel
able to convince the Palestine Arabs that he was not favouring his co-religionists?
Such questions constitute the underlying theme of this work.

The structure of the book is both topical and chronological. The approach is
basically historical and political. The book is divided into two parts. Part I provides
the background essential for an understanding of the period under study. Part II
deals with the way the mandate was actually implemented on the political, administrative and economic levels, showing how Samuel put into practice his own
understanding of the Balfour Declaration, as well as Article 2 of the mandate, and
how he dealt with questions relating to land and immigration (Article 6 of the
mandate). In both parts light will be shed on the measures that were taken, either
by the Palestine Administration, or by the Colonial Office, which may be described
as having gone 'beyond' the League of Nations mandate, focusing attention on
aspects of the British mandate which far exceeded what was expected of a mandatory government, thus posing the question: was this policy in conformity with the
letter and spirit of the Mandate for Palestine? Hence, Chapter 3 puts in focus the
views of the Middle East Department, responsible for formulating Palestine policy
from 1921, when responsibility was transferred from the Foreign to the Colonial
Office. In Chapter 6 light will be shed on Samuel's policy regarding the illicit Jewish para-military organizations at their inception. It will also be shown that in
order to achieve his Zionist goals, Samuel carefully chose his staff in a way that
served only the Zionist cause. His administration was seen by the Arabs, as well as
many British officials, as having been largely a Zionist administration, disguised
as a British one.

Acknowledgements

I should like, first of all, to express my gratitude to Professor C. E. Bosworth and to Dr Feroz Yasamee who supervised my research at the University of Manchester and gave generously of their time and scholarship. This work also owes much to Professor Walid Khalidi, who inspired and provided much needed advice along the way.

I remain particularly grateful to Professor Fouad Zakaria for his keen insights and critical comments on the parts he had read; and to Dr Sulaiman al-Askari, former Secretary General of the National Council for Culture, Arts and Letters in Kuwait, who gave me his moral support from beginning to end.

In different stages throughout the completion of this work, I am indebted to the following: to Professor Muhammad I. Salhiah, for offering generous advice and encouragement in the initial stage, especially after a long interval in which I was absent from academic life; to Dr David Brady of the John Rylands University Library whose help was indispensable as I shuttled back and forth between London, Manchester and Kuwait; to Dr Anis F. Kassim for kindly making available from his private collection the microfiche copies of the *Official Gazette* of the Government of Palestine; to Dr Barbara Smith, first for allowing me access to her unpublished PhD thesis, and at a later stage for reading and making helpful suggestions on this present book, and to Dr Salman Abu-Sitta who always listened to me patiently and offered his help whenever I needed it. My thanks are due to James Hackett for helping out in proof reading, and to Latif Amara, Huda Houry Webster, Issam Dahmash and Imad Dajani for their assistance in a number of different ways.

I would also wish to thank the Institute for Palestine Studies for providing microfilm copies of the newspapers *Filastin* and *al-Karmel*, the staff at the Public Record Office, Kew, the librarian of Pembroke College, Cambridge, the staff of the Royal Commonwealth Society, Cambridge, the staff of the *Illustrated London News*, and the staff of the *Sphere* where I found the pictures of the book.

As this work was transformed from bulky thesis into more manageable book, it benefited from sharp-eyed copy-editing skills by Margaret Owen. Linda Butler was helpful in adapting the part that was published in the *Journal of Palestine Studies*, which now figures in parts of chapter three of this book. My editor Sarah Graham-Brown helped reshape the manuscript, conscientiously cutting without losing understanding, and to her I am most grateful. All shortcomings are mine alone. Special thanks are also due to my publisher, Anna Enayat for her patience and encouragement throughout.

I am deeply obliged to my husband, Azzam Fidda, who heard me endlessly and tolerated my state of distraction; his patient understanding made the completion of this book possible. My children, Yasmin and Tariq, have literally grown up with it, and have admirably and patiently endured my seemingly infinite preoccupation with this work. This book is therefore dedicated to them.

Historical Prologue

The complexity of the Palestine problem means that it is essential to begin this narrative with a brief background about Zionism, British imperialism and early interests in Palestine, and the Palestinian nationalist movement. Nor can any discussion of the Palestine problem be complete without drawing attention to the problem of East European Jewry and the rise of anti-Semitism from the end of the 19th century. It was the plight of East European Jewry that caused the Palestine problem; had there been no anti-Semitism in Europe there would have been no Palestine problem today. Indeed, to early Zionists, there was a 'role' for Palestine to play in the 'solution of the Jewish problem'.[1] It is here that the 'religious' and 'historic' arguments were fully exploited.[2] And it is here that Zionism stepped in to take advantage of powerful emotions rooted in the Jewish religion, which traces its origin to the beginning of the second millennium BCE when God appeared to Abraham and made a covenant with him—in a vision, as the followers of this faith believe—promising him that his seed would inherit the land 'from the river of Egypt to the Euphrates'.

Developments on the European continent over two centuries were, however, far more important in shaping the Zionist movement than these ancient sentiments. In Eastern Europe, anti-Semitism was on the rise after the pogroms in Czarist Russia in 1881.[3] Zionist leaders preached that the solution to the problem of anti-Semitism in Europe could only be found in the Zionist movement, and stressed the need to solve this problem in Palestine; many Jews therefore adopted Zionism as an answer to their growing frustrations.[4]

Hitler's rise to power in the 1930s, and his contribution to the Jewish problem in the 1940s, merely accelerated a process that was in the making; Weizmann himself remarked that the phenomenon of Nazi anti-Semitism was 'already visible' in 1923, when Hitler made his first appearance on the German scene. As the Zionist leader observed, it was in 1924 that *Mein Kampf* was published.[5] This early reference to Nazi anti-Semitism is of direct relevance to the period under study, since it suggests that this concern was foremost in the minds of Weizmann and other Zionist leaders during the early 1920s when the Mandate for Palestine was established, and not from the late 1930s and mid-1940s when the Holocaust was in earnest, as is commonly held.

Political Zionism was founded by the Vienna-educated Theodor Herzl, a Hungarian by birth, and journalist by profession, after the publication of his *Judenstaat* in 1896. Herzl defined the Jews as a people whose assimilation was impracticable, and whose social and economic condition would continue to deteriorate. The solution was to be found in a Jewish state guaranteed by international agreement.[6] The distress of East European Jewry was the *raison d'être* of Zionism itself, and Zionists from all schools of thought tried to solve this problem: political Zionists, (Herzl), cultural Zionists, (Ahad Ha'am) 'practical' Zionists (Ruppin and Otto Warburg), 'territorialists' (Israel Zangwill) 'Palestinophiles', religiously observant, secularists, atheists and socialists.[7] Despite warnings presented to the first and second Zionist Congresses in 1897 and 1898 from Jewish sources that Palestine was inhabited by 650,000 Arabs, the Zionist leadership went ahead, pretending that the problem did not exist.[8]

The programme of the first Zionist Congress in 1897 was to create 'a home for the Jewish people in Palestine to be secured by public law.'[9] A Jewish state, however, was the real Zionist objective. Max Nordau's (one of Herzl's close associates) coining of the phrase *Heimstatte* (national home) at the first Zionist Congress was merely designed to camouflage this intention in order not to offend the Ottoman Turks.[10]

Prior to the First World War eleven Zionist congresses were held,[11] with the eleventh convened in Vienna in 1913. Dr Arthur Ruppin, director of the Palestine Office in Jaffa (which opened in 1908), pointed out in this congress that the prevalent opinion in the early days of the Zionist movement was that Palestine was a land empty of people. He suggested that this 'incorrect assumption' may have guided the movement's entire policy from its early beginnings.[12] Chaim Weizmann mentioned the need to enlighten the Arab population and expressed, together with Otto Warburg, the chairman of the Actions Committee,[13] optimism concerning future relations with the Arabs. However, despite Ruppin's ominous warnings, Zionist congresses between 1911 and 1913 deliberately avoided addressing this 'difficult political situation', apart from general expressions hoping for 'friendly relations' with the Arabs.[14]

At this stage nothing much came out of the Zionist movement, and Herzilian dreams were kept in check until the advent of the First World War and the Balfour Declaration in November 1917, which the Zionists considered their charter for colonizing Palestine.[15] It was during the course of the First World War that Chaim Weizmann (1897–1952) emerged as the new Zionist leader. He had migrated to England and had become a British subject in 1910. Still a secondary figure in 1914, he had rapidly emerged by the end of the war as the undisputed Zionist leader.[16]

Born in Poland, Weizmann belonged to the Russian-Polish concentration; he was a scientist with an academic career in chemistry,[17] and, according to one scholar, was 'nothing but an east European nationalist' who spoke for East European Jews.[18] He envisaged the dismemberment of the Ottoman Empire, and like Herzl before him, he believed in the special status of Jews in 'Eretz-Israel' under the auspices of a great power. In 1914, Weizmann began to act on his own initiative and in all directions, believing that it was in Great Britain that the Jews would find their champion.

When in 1917 (between February and April), the question of the definition of Zionists came up in the course of negotiations with the Zionists, paving the way for the Balfour Declaration, it was Mark Sykes who gave the British government the answer. In his view, it was Chaim Weizmann, Nahum Sokolow and Vladimir Jabotinsky who best represented the Zionists, and after his first meeting with Weizmann in January 1917, Sykes directed his attention to him.[19] However, Weizmann emerged as the undisputed Zionist leader on the international level following his appointment as head of a Zionist Commission that sailed to Palestine immediately after the war ended to advise the military authorities on Zionist policy. He represented the Zionists in the Paris Peace Conference in 1919, and thus the way was paved for him to assume the presidency of the World Zionist Organization in 1920.

For the next thirty-one years, Weizmann pursued Zionist interests with unrivalled diplomatic skill and political force, mastering the art of the 'face to face' contact and direct confrontation with men at the very top of the decision making.[20] He was truly the 'presiding genius' of the Zionist movement, as one British official once described him. His inexhaustible energy and determination finally secured the establishment of the Jewish state in 1948.

On the Arab side, from the earliest days of Jewish colonization towards the end of the 19th century, clashes occurred between Zionist settlers and the Arab population of Palestine. The immediate causes were disputes over grazing rights and Jewish access to land. The largest area of Petah Tikvah, the oldest Jewish colony in the north of Palestine, was set up in 1878 (then abandoned and resettled in 1882) on land which belonged to the adjacent Arab village of al-Yahudiyya (Abbasiyya). This led to the first violent attack on the colony by Arab peasants, inflicting considerable damage, and resulting in the death of one Jewish settler and the injury of four others. Similar incidents over land disputes happened frequently wherever a Jewish colony was set up, and there was hardly any Jewish colony with which the neighbouring Arab village did not clash.[21]

As early as 1891, the notables of Jerusalem demanded of the Ottoman authorities that Russian Jews should be prohibited from entry into the country and prevented from buying land.[22] However, despite Arab opposition to Zionism, and despite official restrictions from 1882 to 1908, the Ottoman state was ineffective in halting Jewish immigration and land sales. The Jewish community in Palestine grew from approximately 24,000 to something between 70 to 80,000, and twenty-six colonies were established.[23] In 1901, Arab officials protested to the Ottoman government in writing against the entry of Jews into Palestine and the sale of land, and between 1909 and 1914 an anti-Zionist Arab movement started to take shape. During the months preceding the First World War, organized opposition to Zionism became evident. In February 1914, youth societies (nationalist and welfare), both Muslim and Christian, which preached patriotism and the importance of education, and were intent on fighting the Zionist threat, emerged in Jaffa and Jerusalem.[24] On the eve of the First World War, Palestinians viewed the Zionists and the ruling Turkish nationalists of the Young Turks as allies against Arab nationalist revival, and hence began to contemplate violent means to overthrow Turkish rule. Palestinian army officers joined secret societies such as al-'Ahd and al-Fatat which promoted an Arab revolt.[25] The futility of Palestinian anti-Zionist efforts in the Ottoman parliament further encouraged the Palestine Arabs to join secret societies to work for Arab autonomy, and later independence. The role of Palestinian members in these secret societies became known when in 1916 Jamal Pasha, the Ottoman supreme military commander in charge of the Arab provinces, hanged a number of Arab leaders for conspiring against the Empire; three of them Palestinians. During the war (1914–17), Palestinian elements in Palestine, then known as Southern Syria, continued to conspire against the Ottoman Empire.[26]

By 1914, Jews possessed about 2 per cent of the land in Palestine, and the basic Arab demands then, as later throughout the period under study and beyond, were to end Jewish immigration and land sales.[27] However, land purchase took a new turn with the opening in 1908 of the Palestine Office in Jaffa[28] under the direction of Arthur Ruppin, assisted by a small staff of Russian Zionists, among them Yehoshua Hankin (both were active in land purchasing during the period under study). Ruppin and his colleagues had as their main purpose the purchase of every tract of fertile land that was available.[29] Consequently, between 1911 and 1913, violent articles in the Arab press and speeches in the Ottoman parliament made the Zionists acutely aware of the need to establish better relations with the Palestine Arabs.[30]

As far as foreign interests in Palestine are concerned, the period from the beginning of the 19th century until 1917 can be divided into two distinct phases with the turning point in the 1860s, when Palestine began to feel the effects of Ottoman reform and centralization on the one hand, and European economic penetration, on the other.[31] As important, in the longer term, was the opening of the Suez Canal in 1869, which prompted a growth of British political and strategic interests in the region. In 1875, upon hearing that the Khedive Isma'il was negotiating with the French to sell Egypt's shares in the Suez Canal Company, the British prime minister, Benjamin Disraeli, persuaded his government to purchase the Khedive's shares for 4,000,000 pounds, arguing that it was 'vital' to Her Majesty's 'authority and power at this critical moment, that the canal should belong to England'.[32]

Thus, a new imperial age began. In 1882, a British protectorate was established in Egypt following a national uprising led by 'Urabi Pasha the previous year.[33] Egypt had become too strategically important to be left alone, and the necessity of safeguarding the lines of communication between Europe and the East through the Suez Canal, 'Britain's lifeline to India', became a permanent concern in the minds of British imperial strategists.

In 1906, a relatively minor incident on Egypt's loosely defined border with Ottoman Palestine awoke the British for the first time to the possibility of a threat from Egypt's eastern border to the Suez Canal. This crisis, known as the 'Aqaba incident', marked the beginning of Britain's strategic interest in Palestine and adjacent regions in Syria. This later developed into a conviction that these regions were vital to the defence of Egypt, and led, a few years later, to the British occupation of Palestine and adjacent regions.[34]

During the First World War, Britain became increasingly aware of the strategic potentialities of Palestine.[35] The country was viewed as a shield for Egypt and the Suez Canal, a fact that was admitted by such personalities as Leopold Amery, Conservative MP and assistant secretary in the War Cabinet in 1917, and General Jan Christian Smuts, South African statesman and member of the War Cabinet 1917–1919, who pointed out that, in conjunction with Mesopotamia, Palestine could give Britain a land route from Egypt to India and bring together the British empires of Africa and Asia.[36]

In November 1914, soon after Britain declared war on Turkey, and again in January 1915, Herbert Samuel, then a cabinet minister, submitted a memorandum to the prime minister, Herbert Asquith, advocating the establishment of a Jewish state in Palestine under British protection[37] on the grounds of its strategic importance to Britain, and urged large-scale Jewish settlement there.

However, Britain's interest in Palestine was much older than the strategic considerations which became manifest during the latter part of the 19th century. This interest was deeply rooted in the British intellectual history and a millenarian concept of the 'restoration of the Jews' to the Holy Land. By the beginning of the 19th century, this millenarian doctrine, which had been developed by Anglican messianism and evangelism, and accepted by non-governmental movements whose efforts in this direction played a role in shaping the Palestine policy, had almost crystallized and no new additions to this idea were added in the course of the century. The basic millenarian concept can be summarized as follows: an integral element for the fulfillment of the prophecies about the Last Day was the 'return' of the Jews to the 'land of their fathers', to which they had an 'inalienable right'. The end of their Diaspora, their physical and religious restoration, and their gathering in Palestine and acceptance of the Christian gospel, was thought to be an essential part of the divine plan for human redemption, which would prepare the way for the 'second coming' of Christ and the establishment of His Kingdom on earth. The question of whether the conversion of Jews to Christianity must take place before or after their 'repatriation' was not settled.[38]

As early as 1840, after Britain had assisted the Ottoman sultan in regaining control of Palestine from his rebellious vassal Mohammad 'Ali Pasha, the ruler of Egypt, the foreign secretary, Lord Palmerston, had appointed the first British vice-consul in Jerusalem, and instructed him to protect the Jews inhabiting Palestine.[39] Towards the end of the 1870s, the idea of the 'restoration of the Jews' combined with pure imperialist interests to produce all kinds of 'secular' projects for colonization. As the concept of the 'conversion' of Jews to Christianity lost its attraction, the vision of the 'return' of the Jews to the land of their fathers lingered, and was a common feature of English literature on Palestine during the last quarter of the 19th century. During the First World War, fascination with this secularized concept of the restoration, together with short-term political considerations and imperial strategies, combined to produce the Balfour Declaration of 1917.[40]

PART ONE

Zionism and British Policy in Palestine

1

The Balfour Declaration and the Mandate System

In November 1914, Great Britain abandoned its traditional Eastern policy of maintaining the integrity of the Ottoman Empire when Prime Minister Asquith announced, four days after Britain declared war on Turkey, that the dismemberment of the Turkish empire had now become a war aim. This was a turning point in British policy towards the Ottoman Empire. What was known as the Eastern Question had been governed by the need to safeguard the routes to India by keeping the Ottoman Empire intact. This policy also meant that Britain could not afford to lose the Arab provinces of the Ottoman Empire.[1]

In April 1915, on the instructions of Asquith, a 'Committee on Asiatic Turkey' was formed under Sir Maurice de Bunsen to advise the Cabinet on British desiderata in the Near East. It was composed of representatives of the government departments which were immediately concerned.[2] In addition, it included one unlikely figure, Sir Mark Sykes, neither a civil servant nor a military man. A member of parliament, Sykes had travelled widely in the Near East, and when war broke out he came to be considered as an 'expert' on Asiatic Turkey. His only merit was that he had first hand knowledge of the region.[3] The committee submitted its report on 30 June 1915. Its chief concern was to strengthen Britain's existing military and naval presence in the eastern Mediterranean, in addition to securing her land communications from the eastern Mediterranean to the Persian Gulf.

Apart from Haifa harbour, which would be needed as the Mediterranean terminal of the oil lines from Iraq, Palestine was of little concern to the de Bunsen Committee. The question of Jewry and Zionism was not discussed at any point. Maps for annexation plans were drawn and the possibilities of dividing spheres of influence were studied in detail. A new Middle East was being envisaged.[4] In 1916

9

the secret Sykes-Picot Agreement proposed the division of greater Syria into British and French spheres of influence.

The idea that, as part of the new order in the former Ottoman territories, Palestine should become a national home for the Jews, was mooted early in the war by Herbert Samuel, then a cabinet minister. After private conversations with the secretary of state for foreign affairs, Sir Edward Grey, on 9 November 1914, Samuel submitted a draft Cabinet memorandum to the prime minister, Herbert Asquith, advocating the establishment of a Jewish state in Palestine under British protection.[5] He argued the case on the grounds of its strategic importance to Britain, and urged large-scale Jewish settlement there. Upon reading it, Asquith observed that Samuel's memorandum read 'almost like a new edition of *Tancred* brought up to date'.[6]

Although Samuel's proposal was not treated seriously at the time, Mark Sykes, in his capacity as adviser to the Foreign Office on Middle Eastern affairs, subsequently initiated negotiations with leading proponents of Zionism. In the course of 1916, Sykes 'discovered' Zionism and got in touch with Herbert Samuel, then home secretary, hoping to learn more about it. Sykes was convinced that the Jews were a power in many countries and might sabotage the Allied cause. In April 1916, Sykes met Rabbi Moses Gaster, Chief Rabbi of the Sephardic Jewish community, who 'opened [his] eyes to Zionism'.[7] Throughout 1916–17, Sykes became the chief advocate of Zionism among British politicians. However, his vision of what Zionism implied seems to have been at variance with the more extreme Zionist interpretations. In February 1916, he wrote to Samuel: 'I imagine that the principal object of Zionism is the realization of the ideal of an existing centre of nationality rather than boundaries or extent of territory.'[8]

On 7 February 1917, Sykes met Lord Rothschild, Chaim Weizmann, president of the English Zionist Federation, and other Zionist leaders, in order to arrive at some understanding on the future of Palestine.[9] It will be recalled that, from February to November 1917, the British government was discussing some form of pro-Zionist declaration. The Zionists were desperate for such a declaration. Upon hearing that a hesitant War Cabinet had once more postponed discussion of the declaration, on 19 September 1917 Chaim Weizmann wrote to Philip Kerr[10] of the Prime Minister's Secretariat:

> This declaration when it is given to us will allow us to get along with the real work, viz. consolidating Jewish opinion all over the world and preparing the framework of a Palestinian organization. We can do nothing of that sort without the declaration … I feel we have reached a critical point and I feel I am not making an appeal in vain to you. Do help us![11]

On 4 October 1917, Balfour and Edwin Montagu, secretary of state for India, argued their cases in the War Cabinet. Montagu strongly advised against a pro-

Zionist declaration, describing Zionism as a 'mischievous political creed' that would promote anti-Semitism. Lord Curzon, the foreign secretary, asked how it was proposed 'to get rid of the existing majority of Mussulman inhabitants and to introduce the Jews in their place?' and what was 'to become of the people of the country?'[12]

The Zionists, both in Britain and further afield, campaigned energetically to gain British support for a state, or at the least a national home, in Palestine. They became heavily involved during the months when the Balfour Declaration was under discussion, and drafts of it were shown to American Zionists for approval.[13] On 31 October 1917, British forces occupied Beersheba in southern Palestine and General Sir Edmund Allenby made his official entry into Jerusalem in December of that year. Despite continuing misgivings on the part of some members of the War Cabinet, on 2 November the British foreign secretary, Arthur James Balfour, made what became known as the Balfour Declaration, promising world Jewry a national home in Palestine.[14]

There is general agreement that the Balfour Declaration was a deliberately vague document. It contained two pledges, which were later judged by the Royal Commission of Inquiry in 1937 (the Peel Commission) to have been incompatible. The first pledge, that the British government 'view[ed] with favour' the establishment of 'a Jewish national home in Palestine', was ambiguous as to the character of that 'national home'. The term 'national home' could be construed to mean anything from a Jewish cultural centre in Palestine, such as a Hebrew University, to a full-fledged state. The national home, however, was to be established on condition that the civil and religious rights of 'existing non-Jewish communities' would be safeguarded. Reference by name to the Arabs of Palestine, who then constituted 93 per cent of the population, was cunningly avoided. This 'dual obligation' to the Jews and the existing population did not clarify how far the existing population could have a say in the extent or character of the Jewish national home.

This inherent ambiguity allowed British officials throughout the first half of the 1920s to interpret the commitments given in the Balfour Declaration in different ways, causing much confusion.[15] Sir Herbert Samuel, as high commissioner in Palestine, made the first public attempt to interpret the declaration in a speech on 3 June 1921. He claimed that there was 'an unhappy misunderstanding' about the declaration. It did not mean that the country would be taken away from its Arab owners to be given to Jews. Samuel also drafted the first official and written interpretation of the Balfour Declaration, the 1922 Statement of Policy, sometimes known as the Churchill White Paper. It asserted that Jews were in Palestine 'as of right and not on sufferance', and that the British government 'did not contemplate the subordination or disappearance of the Arab population, language or culture'.

The White Paper thus confirmed the ambiguity of the Balfour Declaration, since it did not resolve the question of how the Jews could be in Palestine by right, without infringing on the rights of the local inhabitants. In September 1922, Eric

Mills, acting principal in the Colonial Office, minuted that the declaration 'may have been primarily intended to give effect to a policy which should solve the Jewish problem', adding: 'To my mind it was certainly so intended by Zionists … rightly or wrongly.'[16] He spoke of the new 'structure of the society' that was being created in Palestine. Mills observed:

> … although the Jews have not made a physical conquest of Palestine in war, yet the Balfour Declaration and the severance of Palestine from the Ottoman Empire do have an effect in Arab psychology not far remote from that which would have been present had the Jews been in fact a conquering nation … if national as opposed to religious satisfaction demands Palestine, then inevitably the Balfour Declaration meant in the minds of the Jews for whom it was altered, nothing less than a Jewish State. Mr. I. Zangwill[17] was perfectly logical when he stated that this led to the view that the non-Jewish inhabitants of Palestine must be sent elsewhere…. However logical such a solution might be, in its ethical aspects it is repugnant to all fair-minded men and of course has never been contemplated by His Majesty's Government.[18]

Weizmann, as President of the World Zionist Organization, gave unqualified approval to the White Paper. However, an official in the Palestine administration, Edward Keith-Roach, recorded in his diary that his doubts grew shortly afterwards, during a private conversation between Weizmann, Wyndham Deedes, the chief secretary, and himself: 'after giving a picture of the international plight of Jewry … [and] the ever-growing anti-Semitism in Europe, he [Weizmann] said: 'I accept the White Paper because when the time is ripe, I shall make it a blue paper. The Arabs must go elsewhere.'[19]

Keith-Roach was not unsympathetic to the Zionist cause at the time, but he recorded in his memoirs:

> My misgivings about Palestine became deeper. The more I read the official papers of 1914–20 the sharper grew my doubts. Every standard seemed to have been sacrificed to expediency. I had known little of international or political matters. But I was certain that the standard of rectitude established by, and expected from, bankers and manufacturers, was far higher.
>
> I asked myself the questions: Is Great Britain being really honest to the Arabs? To the Jews? To herself? The questions gnawed at my conscience and refused to be silenced.[20]

Lloyd George, one of the 'fathers' of the Balfour Declaration, under whose premiership it was published, told the Peel Commission in 1937 that, at the time the declaration was made, the idea was that

> a Jewish State was not to be set up immediately by the Peace Treaty without reference

to the wishes of the majority of the inhabitants. On the other hand, it was contemplated that when the time arrived for according representative institutions to Palestine, if the Jews had meanwhile responded to the opportunity afforded them by the idea of a national home and had become a definite majority of the inhabitants, then Palestine would thus become a Jewish Commonwealth.[21]

The Peel Commission concluded that His Majesty's Government 'evidently realised that a Jewish State might in the course of time be established, but it was not in a position to say that this would happen, still less to bring it about of its own motion'. The Zionist leaders, on their part, according to the Peel Report, 'recognised that an ultimate Jewish State was not precluded by the terms of the Declaration'.[22]

The Balfour Declaration was often referred to by the Palestine Arabs as 'sinister', and 'a black spot' in the history of the British government in particular and the Allies in general. It was contrary to the previous pledges given to the Arabs during the war (the McMahon pledge to Sharif Hussein in 1915), to official statements proclaimed by Lord Allenby when he occupied Palestine, to the right of self-determination, and to the policy of liberation of small nations, in whose defence the Allies claimed to have entered the war.[23] The declaration, Arab leaders pointed out, created in Palestine a 'strange form of Government, which is rather Zionist than British', and the government worked 'day and night' in order to fulfil this declaration and to 'kill the national spirit'. Article 2 of the mandate was applied 'no matter if that may lead to the ruining of the Arabs as is the case at present'. They furthermore pointed out the intrinsic contradiction in the declaration: 'how could foreign Jews enjoy political rights in Palestine without prejudicing the rights of the Arabs?'[24]

THE MANDATORY SYSTEM

The Balfour Declaration was an expression of intent on the part of the British government of the day, but after the war had ended the fate of the territories of the former Ottoman Empire became the subject of international negotiation. The international mandate system became the legal framework within which the conflicting commitments made in the Balfour Declaration were to be played out. The mandates originated in the treaties made at the end of the First World War. During the war, Allied powers occupied all the German colonies and overseas possessions in Asia, Africa, and Oceania (Pacific islands), in addition to the Arabic-speaking provinces of Ottoman Turkey. The Allies decided after the war that these territories would not be returned to the Germans and the Turks. Opinions varied greatly as to the fate of these conquered territories. An imperialist party among the Allies proposed that German colonies should be annexed in the regular imperialist fashion after wars, but Allied statesman had already declared during the war that there would be no annexation of colonies. The American president, Woodrow Wilson, insisted on making this condition one of his fourteen points on which the USA would insist in the terms of peace. Arab peoples sought autonomy or independence, and Allied statesmen had already entered into understandings with them during the course of the war, recognizing their right as a nation for self-determination. Wilson also demanded that the wishes and interests of the peoples concerned should be a principal consideration in the settlement. The introduction of the system known as 'International Mandates' was a compromise between those conflicting aims. It was put forward at the Peace Conference in January 1919 by General Smuts of South Africa, and adopted by the Council of Ten at the Peace Conference.[25]

The mandatory system was embodied in the Covenant of the League of Nations as Article 22[26] which stipulated that it was to be applied to territories detached from Germany and Ottoman Turkey, and 'inhabited by peoples not yet able to stand by themselves' as a 'sacred trust of civilization'.[27] The mandatory was to be responsible for the integrity of the country and its administration for the benefit of its people, and was subject to the scrutiny of the League of Nations, acting through a special instrument, the Permanent Mandates Commission, whose function was to see that the mandate was faithfully conducted (i) on behalf of the inhabitants of the country, and (ii) on behalf of international society. The mandatory power's obligation was to supervise the improvement of the conditions of the mandated territories, and to improve the moral and material well-being of its people. Any dispute arising as to the application of the mandate was to be submitted to an arbitral tribunal in accordance with the Covenant of the League of Nations, and could come before the Permanent Court of International Justice.

Mandates fell into three classes. Class A was limited to territories detached from the Ottoman Empire, which were populated by 'civilized peoples', but were 'unable for a time to stand by themselves'. The function of the mandatory in this case was to give administrative advice and assistance. Class B and C mandates were assigned to the overseas possessions of Germany in Africa and Oceania, which were inhabited by 'less civilized peoples'.

However, in the case of the Mandate for Palestine, the Zionists were to impose their own understanding of the principle of self-determination and of Article 22 of the Covenant of the League of Nations. According to Norman Bentwich, who became legal adviser to the Palestine government, the function of the mandatory in Palestine 'did not conform' with the above conditions:

> The principle of self-determination had to be modified because of the two national selves existing in Palestine, and the majority Arab population could not be allowed to prevent the fulfilment of the Mandate in relation to the minority Jewish population.[28]

Bentwich further asserted: 'It is the application in law of the idea that "memory also gives a right".'[29]

Some attempt was made during the Peace Conference to ascertain the views of the people in the Middle East region on future forms of governance. Since the wishes of the people were to be the principal consideration in the choice of the mandatory, an American commission, at the insistence of the Peace Conference, visited Syria and Palestine in 1919 and endeavoured to assess the opinion of the population. The idea of a Commission of Inquiry was first mooted by Amir Faisal[30] during the Paris Peace Conference on 6 February 1919. On 25 March, it was agreed between President Wilson, Lloyd George, Clemenceau and Orlando that an International Commission of Inquiry would be sent to the Near East to ascertain the wishes and aspirations of the local inhabitants.[31] However, the two major powers that were involved—Britain[32] and France—were reluctant to join the Commission of Inquiry. On 2 and 3 June 1919, they finally refused to take part. Without French and British participation, the Italians, having no direct interest, also declined to join and the commission became solely an American venture.

The commission therefore consisted of H. C. King, president of Oberlin College, Ohio and C. R. Crane, an American businessman and a prominent member of the Democratic Party, both men of intelligence and independence 'whose honesty and impartiality were unassailable'.[33] Before leaving Paris for Palestine, they sent a statement to President Wilson on 1 May 1919 in which they said that if the partition of the Ottoman Empire was to be based on 'selfish interests' of the Great Powers, 'there would be great difficulties in the Near East, little gain for the Allies, and serious dangers for the world at large … such a division would be forced upon the people and not chosen by them'.[34]

On 5 April 1919, the military authorities publicly announced the arrival of the Commission of Inquiry, reassured the Arabs that this was a 'precious opportunity' to be seized, and appealed to them to ignore the rumours that were being circulated in unofficial (Zionist) papers regarding the political and economic future of Palestine.[35] Immediately, and in preparation, the leaders of the Palestinian nationalist movement (the Muslim-Christian Association) authorized two of its members, Muhammad 'Izzat Darwazeh and Dr Hafiz Kana'an, to proceed to Jaffa where the commission was to arrive by sea, and to prepare the way for a united Arab stand. The broad guidelines to be submitted to the commission were: (i) Palestine was an integral part of Syria; (ii) the Arabs demanded absolute and complete independence for the whole of Syria, and (iii) they completely rejected the Balfour Declaration and the policy of Jewish immigration. By 'mandatory', the Arabs understood technical and scientific advice, and in no way political domination, or military or even administrative presence. If the commission asked how the existing Jews were to be treated, the answer would be that they would continue to enjoy their rights according to Ottoman law and would be treated equally as in other Arab countries.[36]

On 24 May, the Muslim-Christian Association called for a general meeting, which was attended by Muslim and Christian notables, by the heads of the different religious communities, as well as by representatives of the urban centres. They unanimously demanded: (i) absolute independence for Syria from the Taurus mountains in the north, up to Rafah in the south; (ii) Palestine, which was southern Syria, was to remain an integral and inseparable part of Syria with a decentralized form of government; (iii) total rejection of Jewish immigration and the national home policy with safeguards for minorities.[37]

The King-Crane Commission began its work on 16 June, and met the Muslim-Christian Association delegation from Jerusalem, which was composed of forty members, twenty representing Jerusalem and the other twenty representing the surrounding villages. Ten of the Jerusalem representatives were Christians: five Catholics and five Greek Orthodox. They began by reminding the commission of the services rendered by the Arabs to the British army during the war: the Arabs had refused to join the Turkish army, and their volunteers had joined Faisal's forces to the detriment of the Turks; they had refrained from selling vital material and foodstuffs to the Turks, and they had refused to accept paper money which contributed to the depletion of Turkish gold reserves. Arab officers in the Ottoman army had fled with their maps, battle plans and military documents to the other side, which was of great value to the Allied war effort. On the question of Jewish immigration, the delegation said that it would have the most grave consequences on their unity and on the rest of Syria. If the Jews came there, 'they would not live with us in peace as they claim, but would wipe us out and build their home on the ruins of ours'. Expressing their fear, they declared: 'there is no place for us both ... our land is not empty so that Jews from everywhere can come and colonize it; God forbid that one day we will come under a Jewish administration.'[38]

The Arabic documents reveal that the delegations were highly representative,[39] and that their demands were unanimous, although the statements of the village delegations tended to be more emotional than those of the city delegations.[40] The King-Crane Commission toured all the major cities and everywhere its members heard the same three demands until they could, according to Arabic sources, repeat them by heart whenever they met a new delegation.

THE RESOLUTIONS OF THE SYRIAN CONGRESS

The Syrian Congress, meeting on 2 July 1919 with Muslim, Christian and native Jewish representatives from all over Syria[41] (OETA South, East and West) submitted to the King-Crane Commission the following demands: (i) full and absolute political independence to be granted for the whole of geographical Syria (describing the exact frontiers from the north, south and east); (ii) the government should be a constitutional monarchy, based on democratic principles and on broad decentralization where the rights of the minorities would be guaranteed. Amir Faisal was chosen as monarch; (iii) the Arabs of Syria were in no way less civilized than the Bulgarians, the Serbs, the Romanians and the Greeks who were granted independence, and therefore they strongly protested against Article 22 of the Covenant of League of Nations which regarded them as insufficiently developed races requiring tutelage of a mandatory power; (iv) they understood the mandate to mean technical and economic assistance 'which in no way encroaches on our political independence'. The congress therefore asked the USA to grant them this kind of assistance because it had no colonialist past and no ambitions, on condition that this period would not exceed 20 years; (v) should the USA refrain, the second choice was Great Britain, on condition that the political unity and independence of Syria would be preserved, the period also not exceeding 20 years; (vi) the congress proclaimed that France had no rights whatever in Syria, and that any connection with France was strongly rejected; (vii) the congress strongly rejected a Jewish home in Southern Syria (Palestine), and opposed immigration which they considered a grave danger to their national, economic and political life. Native Jews would enjoy equal rights; (viii) there should be no dismemberment of Syria and no separation of Palestine, also the littoral (Lebanon) should remain part of Syria; (ix) the congress demanded complete independence for Iraq, and opposed any economic barriers between the two countries; (x) the congress declared that President Wilson's emphatic denunciation of secret treaties caused them to strongly condemn secret agreements designed to divide Syria, especially Zionist designs.[42] These resolutions were signed by fifteen delegates, including three from Palestine: 'Abd al-Fattah al-Sa'adi (Acre), Jubran Kuzma (Nazareth) and Muhammad 'Izzat Darwazeh (Nablus).[43]

The King-Crane Commission submitted its main recommendations to the League of Nations on 28 August 1919: first, that any foreign administration brought into Syria should be a mandatory power under the aegis of the League of Nations and second, that the mandate should be for a limited term and its administration should be characterized from the beginning by a strong emphasis on education. Democratic institutions should be set up. The Arab fears that their country would become a colonial possession should be completely allayed.

The commission strongly recommended the unity of Syria: 'the territory concerned is too limited … to make the setting up of independent States within its boundaries desirable … The country is very largely Arab in language, culture, traditions, and customs'. The commission recommended the placing of the whole of Syria 'under one single mandate', and proposed a constitutional monarchy along democratic lines, with Faisal as ruler, for this seems 'naturally adapted to the Arabs, with their long training under tribal conditions'. On Zionism, the commissioners had been 'predisposed in its favour' but the facts in Palestine had driven them to recommend 'serious modification of the extreme Zionist program'. The commission had found that definite encouragement had been given to the Zionists by the allies in Mr Balfour's 'often quoted statement', and that if the terms of the Balfour Declaration were strictly adhered to then the Zionist programme must be 'greatly modified'. They concluded:

> ... a national home for the Jewish people is not equivalent to making Palestine into a Jewish State; nor can the erection of such a Jewish State be accomplished without the gravest trespass upon the civil and religious rights of existing non-Jewish communities in Palestine.

In spite of these findings—or, more likely, because of them—the report remained a secret document until 1922 when parts of it were published. Oddly, Bentwich asserts that the commission 'obtained no definite results',[44] though its recommendations were not secret when he wrote his book in 1930.

THE PALESTINE MANDATE

Between June 1919 and April 1920, it became increasingly evident to western leaders that a peace treaty with Turkey would not be signed in the near future. At the San Remo Conference, in April 1920, the Allies consequently decided that, in the Arabic-speaking part of the Ottoman Empire, they would 'implement the provisions of such a treaty as they envisaged', although their action, as one commentator argued, was 'highly illegal'.[45] It was the Supreme Council of the Allies, and not the League of Nations, which actually conferred the mandates, because the League of Nations did not yet exist when the transfer of the territories was made. The Council was the highest international authority, representing the principal Allied and associated powers.[46]

It was in San Remo, therefore, that the future of the Middle East was decided.[47] As far as Palestine was concerned, Lloyd George, the British prime minister, and Georges Clemenceau, the French prime minister, decided that its internationalization was impractical and that the mandate over Palestine would be entrusted to a single power.[48] Thus, on 25 April 1920, it was agreed that the Mandate for Palestine would be assigned to Great Britain, and that the military administration would be brought to an end, and replaced by a civil one under Sir Herbert Samuel. For the Zionist movement, which had lobbied hard to secure a British mandate over Palestine,[49] the San Remo decision was a great victory.[50]

On 10 August 1920, the Treaty of Sèvres laid down the 'legal' basis for the mandatory system. The Ottoman Empire was dissolved, obliging Turkey to renounce all her remaining rights over Arab Asia and North Africa.[51] Under Article

95 it was agreed to entrust, by application of Article 22 of the Covenant of the League of Nations, the administration of Palestine to a mandatory who would be responsible for putting into effect the Balfour Declaration of 2 November 1917. The provisions of the declaration were embodied in Article 95 of the Treaty of Sèvres.[52] The draft Mandate for Palestine was submitted to the Council of the League of Nations in December 1920, but had been the subject of negotiations between the Zionists and the British government since at least March 1920.

The manner in which the mandate was drafted, for which Curzon was ultimately responsible, and the fact that so little was altered in the draft mandate, did not reflect the strong view among some members of the British political establishment that the mandate was 'fundamentally flawed'.[53] Article 2 of the draft gave the mandatory power the authority to place the country under such political, economic and administrative conditions 'as will ensure the establishment of the Jewish National Home'. (See Appendix A) When this was circulated to the Foreign Office for comment in March 1920, the foreign secretary, Lord Curzon, commented that the phrase 'development of a self-governing Commonwealth' was 'surely most dangerous', and that it was a 'euphemism for a Jewish State, the very thing they accepted and that we disallow'. In a subsequent minute he added: 'I at any rate cannot accept it.'[54] When the term 'self-governing institutions' was adopted in the draft mandate (to replace 'self-governing Commonwealth' as had been previously proposed), Curzon wrote on 20 March 1920:

> It all turns on what we mean. The Zionists are after a Jewish State with the Arab as hewers of wood and drawers of water. So are many British sympathisers with the Zionists … That is not my view. I want the Arabs to have a chance and I don't want a Hebrew State. He admitted that he had not been consulted as to the Mandate at an earlier stage, that he greatly disliked the idea that the draft was continually shown to the Zionists. [55]

During the San Remo Conference, Curzon told Balfour that he intended to carry out the pro-Zionist policy in Palestine in line with 'the narrower and more prudent rather than the wider interpretation of the Balfour Declaration'. He once again expressed his rejection of Zionist attempts to go beyond the aspiration of the declaration itself in the wording of the mandate by referring to 'the historic connection of the Jewish people with Palestine'.[56] Though Curzon tried to prevent this phrase from being inserted in the draft mandate, it was eventually included without his knowledge. Curzon commented at the time: 'I objected to the phrase *in toto*, as certain to be the basis upon which the Zionists would for all time found their most extreme pretensions and I told Dr. Weizmann in an interview that I could not accept it.'[57]

There was, at the time, little public discussion on the draft. Nevertheless, in a House of Lords debate in April 1921, the Marquess of Crewe pointed out that the

British parliament had been kept in the dark, and that there was a 'thick veil' thrown on the proceedings of the Palestine mandate in the League of Nations. This view was shared by 'not a few members' of the House.[58]

On the international level, American, French and Italian objections delayed ratification of the Palestine mandate until July 1922. American opposition basically revolved around commercial concession rights.[59] When the French were first shown the draft mandate in June 1920, Robert Vansittart, secretary to Curzon, reported that President Millerand 'nearly jumped out of his skin' when he saw it, adding that he was himself 'surprised and alarmed' by it. In a letter from Paris to Hubert Young at the Foreign Office, Vansittart noted that the president and Philippe Berthelot, secretary-general of the French Foreign Ministry, thought it 'much too Judaised and Judaising—full of red flags indeed', though Berthelot told Vansittart 'if we liked to run ourselves into trouble, that seemed to him our affair'.[60]

However, the French later raised objections on legal grounds. In May 1922, while in Geneva attending the session of the Council of the League of Nations, Balfour reported that the French delegate had raised legal difficulties, arguing that all A-mandates derived from the Treaty of Sèvres which had not been ratified 'but was actually in the process of transformation'. The French delegate also stated that the ministers for foreign affairs in Paris had recently made such radical changes that it was 'impossible to regard the treaty as ever having been signed'. How was it possible then to put into force one part of it? He pointed out that 'even if the League of Nations thought it in the interests of peace and prosperity to ignore strictly [sic] legal difficulty', there were actually three different versions of draft A-mandates in existence, two English and one French; there was no reason why the League should treat the two nations 'otherwise than on a footing of complete equality'.[61]

The Vatican raised objections on moral grounds which were spelled out on 6 March 1922 by Cardinal Gasparri, the cardinal secretary of the state at the Vatican. He declared that the Holy See did not oppose the acquisition by Jews in Palestine of equal civil rights as enjoyed by other nationalities and confessions, but it could not consent to the Jews being given a preponderant position over other nationalities and confessions. The Holy See noted that

> although the draft in its preliminary considerations with reference to the establishment of a national home for the Jews, guarantees that 'rien ne pourra être fait qui puisse porter préjudice aux droits civils et religieux des communautés non-juives existant en Palestine' in the actual articles it establishes an absolute economic, administrative and political preponderance of Jews over other nationalities.[62]

Commenting on the articles of the draft mandate, Gasparri went on to say that recognition as a public body was given to a Jewish commission which was no other than the powerful Zionist Organization (Article 4 of the mandate); this Jewish commission was placed alongside the Palestine administration and had been given a powerful voice in all questions relative to the development of the country, and a favoured position was provided for the Jews in regard to immigration (Article 6) and naturalization (Article 7). Close settlement was to be provided for them on the land, including state lands and waste lands (Article 6). They were given a privileged position with regard to the construction of public works (Article 11). Gasparri continued:

> The Draft Mandate, therefore, in aiming at the absolute preponderance of Jews over all other peoples in Palestine is not only seriously damaging to the rights acquired by other nationalities, but is also contrary to article 22 of the Treaty of Versailles, which establishes the idea and aim of each mandate.[63]

Gasparri pointed out that Article 22 of the Covenant of the League of Nations stated that the mandate was a temporary tutelage which one power assumes over peoples who were not yet capable of governing themselves, and had for its object 'une mission sacrée de civilisation', that is, 'le bien-être et le développement de ces peuples'. He pointed out that a mandate would be 'contrary to all of this were it the instrument for subordinating native populations to the advantage of other nationalities'. While Weizmann assured him that Zionism did not wish to have a privileged and superior position in Palestine over other nationalities, at a conference with him on 4 April 1922 at the Collegio Romano, Weizmann 'expounded the Zionist programme as aiming at the constitution of a real *Jewish State* in Palestine, as liberal as could be desired towards other nationalities and confessions, but sovereign in its own territory'.[64]

Another dimension to the 'peculiar character' of the Palestine mandate was raised by Ronald Storrs, the governor of Jerusalem from 1917 to 1926, who wrote that, while in all other cases it was 'the actual inhabitants of the countries in question' who were the 'beneficiaries' of the mandates, under the terms of the Palestine mandate, it was the Jewish people as a whole who were the beneficiaries 'jointly with the existing population of Palestine'.

> This distinction is one of paramount importance, both in principle and fact. It means that while the rights of the Arabs are based on their residence in the country, the rights of the Jews are independent of this qualification, for the Trust being held by Great Britain for the Jewish National Home to be established in Palestine for the benefit of the Jewish people, it does not depend on the numerical strength of the present Jewish population of Palestine. By virtue of this Trust any Jew no matter where he lives is a potential colonist and beneficiary of the Trust.[65]

LEGAL PROBLEMS

The hiatus between the end of the military administration and the ratification of the mandate presented British administrators with an immediate problem as to the legal status of the new civil administration, set up in July 1920. It remained a de facto administration, since the mandate was not ratified by the League of Nations until July 1922,[66] coming into force as late as September 1923. From a strictly legal point of view, it could further be argued that the mandate could not be considered operative until peace with Turkey had been ratified in August 1924. This implies that the status quo of the country, still legally bound by wartime restrictions, was being inequitably prejudiced in favour of a small Jewish minority.

Legally speaking, Palestine was, from 1917 until 1924, a British-occupied territory, the war with Turkey having been officially declared as terminated only on 6 August 1924. Hence, during the foregoing period, Great Britain was still legally bound by restrictions of the Hague Convention of 1907.[67] Samuel, as the first high commissioner of a civil administration was well aware that he was treading on precarious ground, and continually pressed the Colonial Office for a 'regularization' of the situation in Palestine, through the granting of the mandate, for political reasons that were, in his opinion, vital for the progress of the Jewish national home.

Samuel wrote to Churchill in April 1921 that since he had assumed office,

> the circumstances of the country have called for considerable measures of legislation which goes far beyond the powers vested in the ordinary Military occupant. It is submitted however, that although in theory the Government has rested all this time upon Military occupation, in substance Military occupation had passed into conquest before my arrival and the agreement of the Allied Powers at San Remo to confer the Mandate for Palestine on Great Britain justified the Administration in assuming sovereign rights. Care has indeed been taken not to interfere more than was urgently necessary with the established law of the country pending the promulgation of the Mandate, but a number of important Ordinances such as those dealing with immigration, antiquities, co-operative societies, companies, the police, etc., have been enacted.[68]

This seems to be an understatement. In spite of his comments to Churchill, Samuel did pass ordinances vital to the Zionists immediately after he took office, as a first step in the establishment of the Jewish national home. Palestine was open for Jewish immigration through the Immigration Ordinance, and land was allocated to Jews for closer settlement by means of the Land Transfer Ordinance and a host of other ordinances connected with the land. Hebrew was recognized as an official language alongside English and Arabic; the Sabbath was recognized as an official day of rest; credit banks were introduced to facilitate the transfer of immovable property, and cooperative societies were established for the sole benefit of Jews. On the political level, a National Council for the Jews, the Va'ad Leumi, was recognized in October 1920. No less than 150 ordinances were enacted between 1920 and 1925. Some laws and ordinances passed during the first two years, not to mention the first two months of Samuel's term as high commissioner, were of such magnitude that no military administration could have undertaken them without being convicted of a breach of international law.

One year after the beginning of the civil administration, in October 1921, Samuel was still insisting to the Colonial Office that a settlement of the question of the mandate was an 'absolute necessity'. The administration had been placed at a great disadvantage through not having been properly constituted, and because of this he could not enact a constitution for the country. Even more important were the serious consequences of this long delay in the economic sphere.[69] Samuel was well aware of the 'diplomatic complication' which surrounded this question, but pointed out that there had been a British administration in Palestine for nearly three years (i.e. since the military administration), and that the regularization of the position could not 'be further suspended'. He strongly emphasized the need to bring this matter to a 'speedy issue', adding:

> If no Turkish Government is in a position to ratify the Treaty of Peace, and if the League of Nations refuses to approve the Mandate pending such ratification, then I submit that the League should be pressed to signify its approval of the terms of the draft Mandate, with modifications, if modifications be necessary, and to authorise its execution *de facto* until formal approval be given.[70]

The leaders of the Palestine Arab Executive were fully aware of this situation and pointed it out in their petitions. When martial law was proclaimed in Jerusalem after the disturbances on 2 November 1921, an Arab delegation which had been in London since August wrote to Samuel that the framing of this law was 'illegal' as the country was 'technically still governed by pre-war laws', and that the legal status of Palestine was still 'undefined'.[71] Indeed, before the mandate was ratified in July 1922, they still hoped to convince the British government to re-evaluate its Palestine policy.

This uncertainty was to continue throughout 1922. A Colonial Office memorandum in January 1922 asserted that the administration 'resting on the basis of military occupation suffers constraints imposed by the maintenance of the status quo,' and that these constraints were being 'with difficulty reconciled with the principles of the Covenant of the League of Nations'.[72] When the draft mandate was submitted to the League of Nations for approval in July 1922, Balfour made a speech at the Council of the League of Nations meeting on 18 July in which he stated that he was indeed aware that to ask for an issuance of the mandate was 'impracticable so long as the political status of the country remains indeterminate'.

He urged the Council to at least 'signify their approval of the terms of the draft mandate and to intimate their readiness to issue a mandate in these terms as soon as the position has been regularised'.[73] Balfour went on to reassure the international community, saying that 'certain elements' in the population (referring to the vast majority) took exception to the draft mandate, but that the British government was 'most anxious to give them every reasonable guarantee that their interests will be fully safeguarded'. He referred to the White Paper of June 1922 (copies of which had been communicated to the Council) indicating that this policy clearly defined the limitations placed by the British government on the conception of the Jewish national home, 'repudiating' the more 'extravagant' Zionist claims. Balfour went on to say that the Zionist Organization 'officially identified' themselves with this policy. As a 'particular safeguard', special arrangements were to be made to deal with the question of immigration into Palestine; a 'standing committee on which elected Arab representatives will always be in the majority', was to be set up for the purpose of advising the government on immigration. Balfour hoped to convince the Council that 'this procedure will afford a most effective safeguard against the risk of any injury to the non-Jewish population through the indiscriminate immigration of Jews'.[74] A few days after this assurance, the Council of the League of Nations ratified the mandate.

The second legal issue arising out of the Balfour Declaration was the fact that because of Zionist policy in Palestine, the country was administered as a B-mandate, although it was classified by the League of Nations as an A-mandate, like all the other mandated Arabic-speaking areas of the Middle East. Hubert Young, joint assistant secretary in the Middle East Department of the Colonial Office, described the situation in May 1924:

> The whole position in Palestine, where we are B-mandating an A-mandate territory is so anomalous that the less we try to define it the less likely we shall be to run our heads against one of the many stone walls in which the Middle East abounds.[75]

The Palestine Arabs likewise argued that all the mandated Arabic-speaking territories were classed as A-mandates, and that the League of Nations recognized in principle the independence of all Arab countries which were separated from the Ottoman Empire, and were to be subject to temporary advice and supervision from a mandatory government in the selection of which the public opinion of the people concerned was a determining factor.

This point was closely analysed by an unnamed member of the Arab Higher Committee who affirmed in evidence to the Peel Commission in 1937 that the terms of the mandate were inconsistent with the provisions of Article 22 of the Covenant of the League of Nations. His argument, as the Peel Report presented it, was as follows:

> Paragraph 4 of that Article recognizes the existence of two juristic persons—one the community which should govern independently and the other the foreigner who is to assist and advise until the former is able to stand alone. But in Palestine there is one person who governs and who assists himself. Your Majesty is the Mandatory and your Majesty's Government and their nominees are the Government

of Palestine and, while the Preamble speaks of a Mandate, Article I denies the existence of a Mandate in the proper sense by conferring upon what is called 'the Mandatory' full powers of legislation and administration. The community which is to be provisionally recognized as independent has no existence. This, it was argued, does not meet the provisions of Paragraph 4 and is contrary in principle to the treatment of other territories which were, like Palestine, released from the Government of Turkey. The Arabs maintain that all 'A' Mandates were or are being governed by this section with the exception of the Mandate for Palestine; and they claim that the Arabs of Palestine are as fit for self-government as the Arabs of 'Iraq and Syria. They think that Article 22, and particularly Paragraph 4 of that Article, is really their charter and the Mandate represents—or should represent—its by-laws. They submit that the by-laws are inconsistent with the charter. They complain that the terms of the Mandate are drafted in such a manner that the student might understand that there existed in Palestine a Jewish majority and a non-Jewish minority, the other sections of the population. On the contrary the Arab inhabitants of Palestine form the overwhelming majority and are the owners of the territory for the welfare of which the mandate system was created; yet throughout the Mandate they are referred to as the 'non-Jewish' population—a misleading and humiliating term. The Jews, in fact, are to live in Palestine, to quote the words of the Churchill Statement of Policy [of June 1922] 'as of right and not on sufferance'; while the Arabs, on the other hand, are to live in Palestine as on sufferance and not of right. Again, in Article 2 [of the Mandate] the country is to be placed under such administrative, economic and political conditions as will secure the establishment of a Jewish National Home, while the Arab owners and inhabitants of the land are merely to have their religious and civil rights safeguarded. Under Article 4 a Jewish Agency is to be established to assist the Mandatory in all Jewish affairs. This provision has not only created a state within a state, but has formed a Mandate over a Mandatory in that country.[76]

The legal and political ambiguities created by the Balfour Declaration, and efforts to embody its substance in the Mandate for Palestine, left a good deal of room for political interpretation. Consequently, until the mandate finally came into force in 1923, there were disputes as to how, and if, the pledges in the Balfour Declaration could be accommodated with other commitments made by British governments to the Arab peoples of Palestine and the surrounding region. The early 1920s therefore witnessed a political struggle between, on the one hand, the Zionists and their supporters who sought to incorporate the most 'extensive' interpretation of the Balfour Declaration into the mandate, and on the other, the Palestinian Arab political leadership and its British supporters to prevent the declaration being included in the mandate at all. Successive British governments varied in their enthusiasm for the Zionist project and it is argued that, until September 1923, when the Palestine mandate was finally conferred on Britain, there was no *fait accompli* as to Palestine's future, and a different outcome was conceivable.

2

The Military Administration, 1918–1920: Arabs and Zionists

From the moment the Balfour Declaration was signed, the British government's policy toward Palestine revealed the tensions between its commitment to a Jewish national home and the rights of the indigenous population of Palestine. The legal ambiguities of Palestine's status further muddied the waters. These problems surfaced almost immediately in the administration of Palestine, long before the mandate was finally confirmed.

After the British occupation in December 1917, a military administration under martial law was established under the command of General Allenby, the supreme commander of the Egyptian Expeditionary Force, guaranteeing the protection of religious sites and property of Christians, Jews and Muslims in Palestine. The Occupied Enemy Territory Administration, with its headquarters in Jerusalem, administered southern Palestine (OETA South) until October 1918, after which, following the occupation of the remainder of Palestine and the armistice with the Turks, its authority was extended to the whole of the country until July 1920.[1] Three chief administrators held office in Palestine during this period: Major General Sir Arthur Money, General H. D. Watson and Major General Sir Louis Bols. They took orders from Allenby through General Sir Walter Congreve, general officer commanding, Egypt and Palestine. The War Office was responsible for the execution of policy, acting on instructions from the Foreign Office.[2]

The OETA was guided throughout its two and a half years in Palestine by two major objectives: the preservation of the status quo,[3] and the prohibition of any agreement for the transfer of immovable property until the land registries were re-established.[4] Allenby took the view that the fulfilment of the promises made in the Balfour Declaration could only be fully addressed after the conclusion of peace with Turkey. He therefore sought to apply 'rigorously' the principles of military law in regard to occupied enemy territory, the main objective being the maintenance of order and the treatment of all sections of the community with complete impartiality.[5] Nonetheless, Herbert Samuel, defending the Zionist point of view, sent a letter to the British delegation at the Peace Conference in Paris on 5 June 1919, claiming that the military administration, which was then being vehemently attacked by Weizmann, was not implementing the Balfour Declaration.[6]

When Palestine came under British control in December 1917, the military authorities, well aware of the depth of Arab hostility towards the Balfour Declaration, withheld its publication for fear of an uprising. It was not until May 1920,[7] in the final days of the military administration, that the text of the Balfour Declaration was officially read out in Nablus by Sir Louis Bols.[8] The report of the 1920 Palin Commission of Enquiry revealed that both Generals Money and Watson, and presumably the High Command, had agreed 'that there were military dangers in the publication of the declaration during their tenure of office: General Bols considered that the announcement would awaken antagonism'.[9]

In September 1919, Colonel Richard Meinertzhagen, at that time chief political officer to the Egyptian Expeditionary Force, wrote to Lord Curzon expressing concern at the effects of 'strong local opposition to Zionism in Syria and Palestine, which is frequently being voiced by all communities and classes'. He also observed that the personal views of officials of the military administration, 'incline towards the exclusion of Zionism from Palestine'. The situation had been exacerbated by the 'lack of patience' of local Zionists, who at times were unreasonable in their demands. Furthermore, he argued that stating the 'bare facts' of British policy towards Zionism would be inadvisable. 'The people of Palestine are not at present in a fit state to be told openly that the establishment of Zionism in Palestine is the policy to which H.M.G., America and France are committed. They certainly do not realise this fact.' He therefore proposed a draft document to form the basis of a declaration by the British government 'giving in the most moderate language what Zionism means'.[10]

Lord Curzon's response made clear that he did not regard his government's commitment to Zionism as implying that Palestine would become a Jewish state. He did not approve Meinertzhagen's draft document because it appeared to 'prejudge the decision of the Peace Conference as to the mandate' and 'commits His Majesty's Government further than desirable in the direction of endorsing Zionist aspirations and guaranteeing their future conduct'. He sent Allenby his own draft statement which ascribed the growing hostility in Palestine towards Zionism in part to 'the deliberate fomenting of trouble between the races' by irresponsible people and those who thought the British government could be influenced by such agitation; but partly also to 'a genuine misconception of the nature of the policy of the Allies ...'

The statement emphasized that the endorsement of the Balfour Declaration did not mean that the Allies contemplated any interference with custody of the Holy Places or 'the flooding of Palestine with Jewish immigrants'.

As is recognised by the Zionists themselves, the foundation of a National Home for the Jews must necessarily be a gradual process and it is not anticipated that Jewish immigration will do more than keep pace with the general improvement in the prosperity of the country, which is to be expected from the introduction of the capital and technical skill at the disposal of the Zionists.

There was no intention, Curzon went on to say, of allowing 'spoliation or eviction of the present landowners in Palestine or the grant of profitable concessions to individuals, or the Government of a majority by a minority. Those who profess to apprehend this consequence overlook the fact that the Administration of Palestine will be controlled by a great Power or a combination of Powers under the Mandate'.[11]

The OETA's policy of maintaining the status quo naturally brought it into direct conflict with Zionist leaders who, following the publication of the Balfour Declaration, looked at Palestine only through the spectacles of the Jewish national home. Their motto was, according to the Palin Commission: 'We want the Jewish State and we won't wait'.[12] The Palin Commission also stated that the Jews

> did not hesitate to avail themselves of any means open to them in this country and abroad to force the hand of an Administration bound to respect the 'Status Quo' and to commit it, and thereby future Administrations, to a policy not contemplated in the Balfour Declaration.[13]

Throughout the period from 1917–1922, the British Army filed highly accurate reports on the situation in Palestine, and some officers became overtly sympathetic with the Arabs. This made the Colonial Office, after it took charge of Palestine in 1921, dismiss their reports as unsubstantiated.[14]

During the early days of British rule in Palestine, it was Samuel who took it upon himself to defend the Zionist point of view, sending a letter to the British delegation at the Peace Conference in Paris on 5 June 1919 in which he claimed that the military administration, then being vehemently attacked by Weizmann, was not implementing the Balfour Declaration.[15]

THE ZIONIST COMMISSION AND THE PALESTINE ARABS (1918–20)

Early in 1918, while British military operations in the Middle East were still in progress, and while the northern half of Palestine was still in Turkish hands, Mark Sykes, at the Foreign Office, informed Reginald Wingate, the high commissioner of Egypt, that a Zionist Commission had been created and would soon be despatched to the Middle East. It was to be headed by Chaim Weizmann, with William Ormsby-Gore attached to the commission as the British liaison officer. The British government defined the commission's objectives as carrying out 'subject to General Allenby's authority, any steps required to give effect to the Government's declaration in favour of the establishment in Palestine of a national home for the Jewish people'. It was to 'form a link between the Jewish community and the British authorities in Palestine' and to help to establish 'necessary political connections' with the Arabs.[16] In practice, the commission's recognized representative status upset the Arabs, and caused the military authorities to suspect Zionist motives.

The arrival of the Zionist Commission took the military administration by surprise,[17] and its subsequent activities were regarded by the military authorities as completely contrary to the principle of maintaining the status quo in the occupied territories.[18] The Zionists, on the other hand, regarded the commission as an advisory body that was to act on all questions relating to Jewish settlement, with a clear political purpose: to prepare the grounds for the expansion of a Jewish Palestine.[19] The appointment of Chaim Weizmann as its chairman confirmed him as the pre-eminent leader of the Zionist movement. It was, in the opinion of one historian, 'the first fully public and therefore crowning confirmation of Weizmann's new status as the man of the hour'.[20]

The commission immediately opened offices in Jaffa to replace the former Palestine Office,[21] as well as a centre in Jerusalem to handle food supplies, immigration, education and supply relief work.[22] On 27 April, Storrs held a reception in Jerusalem for the commission to which he invited Weizmann and Muslim and Christian notables.[23] Weizmann 'pronounced an eloquent exposition of the Zionist creed', stating that the Jews had never renounced their rights to Palestine, that they were 'brother Semites', not so much coming but 'returning' to Palestine. After Storrs translated Weizmann's speech into Arabic, the Mufti of Jerusalem replied 'civilly'.[24]

Muhammad 'Izzat Darwazeh, a leader of the pan-Arab movement in Damascus from 1919, reported that Weizmann's manner was 'insolent, deceptive and arrogant' although he tried to reassure the Arabs that the Zionists did not intend to encroach upon their rights, and that they would live with them in peace.[25] Weizmann said that the Jews were in Palestine by right and not on sufferance,[26] and that they were 'returning' to their ancient land to establish there a political, social and economic centre.

The Jerusalem notables were greatly annoyed by Weizmann's statement, and their immediate reaction was to organize themselves politically against this threat. They demanded an end to Jewish immigration and the establishment of a free national government, and firmly opposed land sales to Jews. They intended to call their organization al-Jam'iyya al-'Arabiyya al-Wataniyya (the National Arab Party) but the military authorities persuaded them to name it the Muslim-Christian Association in order to demonstrate to the world that opinion was unanimous in Palestine against Zionism.[27] 'Aref Pasha al-Dajani became its president, and the association immediately started to write memoranda and petitions against Zionist claims in Palestine, and against the Balfour Declaration, and sent copies of these to the military authorities. They also held public gatherings to warn against the dangers of Zionism.

On 8 May 1918, Weizmann gave another speech in Jaffa in the presence of an Arab audience, in which he repeated what he had said in Jerusalem, informing his listeners that he had especially come to Palestine to remove any misunderstandings between the Jewish community on one hand, and Muslim and Christian communities on the other. He assured them, on behalf of the fourteen million Jews, that the Zionists had no intention of 'seizing control of the higher policy of the province of Palestine', nor was it their intention to deprive anyone of his land. Palestine, he said, was a rich country which could support many times its present population, ensuring a life of happiness for all. The Jews considered Palestine their 'sole homeland', and they intended to invest in it, with a view to raising its living standards for the benefit of all its inhabitants. Their objective was to invigorate education and the sciences through the establishment of public institutions that would promote better education. 'Together,' Weizmann told his audience, 'we hope to achieve that aim.'[28]

Shaykh Raghib Effendi al-Dajani made a mild reply to Weizmann's speech on behalf of both Muslims and Christians, in which he stressed that over 350 million Muslims, 750 million Christians and 14 million Jews looked towards Jerusalem as their Holy City. He said that the Jews would get equal treatment in Palestine, and thanked Great Britain which was certain, he thought, to guarantee the rights of all three peoples.[29]

Weizmann soon revealed a different attitude towards the Arabs, as well as his open hostility to the military administration, in a letter to Balfour on 30 May in which he explained the problems which confronted the Zionist Commission. He told Balfour that Arab hostility to Zionism was caused by all sorts of 'misconceptions' and 'misinterpretations', and that the military administration was 'distinctly' hostile to the Jews. He did not particularly like the way the British ran the country because their 'only guide in this difficult situation was the democratic principle, which reckons with the relative numerical strength, and the brutal numbers operate against us, for there are five Arabs to one Jew'. He concluded that the present state of affairs 'would necessarily tend towards the creation of an Arab Palestine, if there were an Arab people in Palestine'. He did not, however, expect an Arab Palestine to materialize because 'the fellah was at least four centuries behind the times, and the effendi … is dishonest, uneducated, and as unpatriotic as he is inefficient'.[30]

In the same letter Weizmann attacked the OETA's policy of maintaining the status quo of the country on the grounds that this policy 'automatically militates against any progress' in the development of the national home policy. Having thus seen with his own eyes the extent of Arab opposition to Zionism, Weizmann's solution was to pretend that the Arab 'problem' did not exist: 'from the political point of view the Arab centre of gravity is not Palestine, but the Hedjaz, really the triangle formed by Mecca, Damascus and Baghdad'. The problem in Palestine was 'not a political one', merely an economic one, and, therefore, the 'only relations' that were necessary with the Arabs of Palestine were economic.[31] In a letter to his wife, Weizmann wrote that, after explaining the Zionist point of view to the Arabs, 'we have done everything that was required of us' and they [the Arabs] should 'take it or leave it'.[32]

It was not until November 1918, when the Zionist Commission held a parade on the occasion of the second anniversary of the Balfour Declaration, that the Arabs sensed real danger. On 1 and 2 November, the Muslim-Christian Association protested to the military governor about Zionist banners, which had made their first appearance. The Arab leaders wrote that Jews had recently been carrying 'white and blue banners with two inverted triangles in the middle'. Was this Jewish emblem 'religious' or 'political'? They drew the attention of the authorities to the serious consequences of any political implications in raising the banners.[33]

Following these Zionist festivities, the tone of Arab protests became sharper. On 7 November 1918, Storrs found it expedient to assure an audience of Arab notables that the Allies did not intend to force a government on the people of the land against their wishes, and that the British government aimed at enhancing the education and economic well-being of the inhabitants of Palestine. Palestine, he added, was free to choose its own government.[34] On 16 November 1918, on the occasion of the first anniversary of the entry of the British army into Jaffa, the Muslim-Christian Association sent a lengthy memorandum to the military governor of Jaffa protesting once more against Zionist intrusion.[35] It was widely representative, signed by all spiritual leaders, landowners, workers, as well as the notables of the Jaffa vicinity. Noting that the latest announcement by Lloyd George and President Wilson in July 1918, had assured them that Great Britain would not have a hand in oppressing the Arabs the signatories rejected Zionist arguments, stating that Palestine was an Arab country and has been so for the last twelve centuries. The number of Jews did not exceed 12,000, half of whom were colonizers. If the Jews were 'returning' to their land, then by the same logic the Arabs would have the 'right' to claim Spain, which they ruled for over 400 years.[36]

On the question of the Balfour Declaration, they wrote that there had been much talk about the meaning of the 'national home', *al-wataniyya al-qawmiyya*.[37] They rejected any preferential position or any political rights for the Jews, whom they did not consider to be citizens in the country. They strongly objected to allowing into Palestine millions of Jews who came to monopolize the resources of the country, and reminded him that it was their 'very livelihood' that was at stake. The memorandum pointed out that some Zionist papers advocated that the Arabs should be driven out of the country, and allocated another land in order to make room for the Jews. The Arabs took such talk seriously and were greatly agitated. They said: 'the Jews must know very clearly that Palestine belongs to us, and we have decided to die in it'. Finally, the memorandum declared: 'we hope that we shall be consulted before the future of Palestine is decided, and that Britain, which saved us from the Turks, will not hand us over to the Jews'.

Unimpeded by this Arab opposition, the Zionist Commission meanwhile continued its practical work. After carrying out initial surveys for the purpose of settlement, it established departments of agriculture, settlement, education, land, finance, immigration and statistics. The commission acted as a semi-official organization, laying the foundations of what later became known in the history of the period as the 'state within a state'.[38] It pressed for Jewish representation in government ranks, equality of Hebrew with Arabic and the appointment of a Land Commission to ascertain the resources of Palestine, its experts to be nominated by the Zionist Organization. It also claimed the right to select and supplement the pay of Jewish candidates for the police force, and began to train its own military force.

Throughout 1919 and 1920, the activities of the Zionist Commission continued to antagonize the Arab population as well as the military authorities in Palestine. With the arrival of Menachem Ussishkin, the hard-line Russian Zionist, in October 1919, and his assumption of charge of the Zionist Commission, the situation deteriorated further.[39]

A 'STATE WITHIN A STATE': THE FINAL DAYS OF THE OETA

Matters came to a head between the Zionists and the military authorities following the first serious outbreak of violence between Arabs and Jews in Jerusalem in April 1920. There followed mutual accusations by the military administration and the Zionist leadership in Palestine, assigning blame for the incidents.

Weizmann demanded the dismissal of the Mayor of Jerusalem, Musa Kazim al-Husseini, and the punishment of what he called the Arab 'ring leaders'.[40] Allenby reported that, after the riots, he had received Weizmann who was 'in a state of great nervous excitement, shedding tears, accusing Administration of Palestine as being anti-Zionist and describing recent riots as pogrom'.[41] David Ben Gurion, the Zionist Labour leader, told a meeting of the Va'ad Zmani (the provisional council of the Yishuv, the Jewish community in Palestine), immediately after the April 1920 riots that direct guilt lay not with the 'inciters', but with Bols and Allenby. Other Zionist leaders expressed similar views.[42]

David Yellin, chairman of the Zionist Commission, wrote from Beirut to the British prime minister on behalf of Weizmann on 12 April 1920, saying that '... wild pogroms, massacres, looting ... did not happen since [the] crusades ...' He demanded 50 per cent Jewish gendarmes, the dismissal of the mayor of Jerusalem who 'always manifested public anti-Jewish feelings', the severe punishment of Arab ring leaders, and the closure of the Arab Club and 'propaganda centres'.[43]

Major General Bols, the last of the three military administrators, noted that strong protests were made by Muslim religious leaders against an attack on the Grand Mufti's house by 'Jewish troops', and that the Zionist Commission had gradually grown into an administration, a situation which could not continue in OETA South.[44] Bols submitted a report on 21 April 1920 to General Headquarters in Cairo, advocating the abolition of the commission and the demobilization of the Jewish Battalion (the Jewish unit in the British army founded in 1917). By this time the Zionist Commission was an organization comprising 100 individuals, 'dealing with the self-same administrative questions and problems as my own administration'. Bols wrote that the Jewish idea of fair treatment implied treatment which was fair to the Jews, but not necessarily to the other party, and that his own authority and that of every department of his administration 'was impinged upon by the Zionist Commission'.[45] This state of affairs could not continue 'without grave danger to the public peace' and without being detrimental to his administration. The Zionists were 'bent on committing the temporary Military Administration to a partialist policy before the issue of the Mandate'. It was 'impossible to please partisans who officially claim nothing more than a National Home but in reality will be satisfied with nothing less than a Jewish State'.

> It is no use stating to the Moslem and Christian elements of the population that our declaration as to the maintenance of the 'status quo' made on our entry into Jerusalem, has been observed. Facts witness otherwise, the introduction of the Hebrew tongue as an official language, the setting up of a Jewish Judicature, the whole fabric of Government of the Zionist Commission of which they are well aware, the special privileges given as regards travelling and movement to members of the Zionist Commission, has firmly and absolutely convinced the non-Jewish elements of our partiality.[46]

On 27 May 1920, O. A. Scott at the Foreign Office minuted:

> The whole account gives one the impression that the Zionist Commission starting with the best motives have 'grown too big for their boots' and are defeating their own ends by excess of zeal. I quite agree that it is impossible for two administrations, one official and one Zionist, to work side by side, and when a Civil Administration is set up I should like to see the Zionist Commission disappear and its place be taken by a Council which would work not independently but in close touch with the Administration.[47]

It is interesting to note that the minutes on this despatch reveal that it was intended that Herbert Samuel should see it, but the official who reported on it did not recommend the dissolution of the Zionist Commission before Samuel reached Jerusalem.[48] Bols noted that it was Samuel, during his visit to Palestine early in 1920, who had drawn his attention to the size and growth of the Zionist Commission, and informed him that the organization comprised one hundred individuals.[49] Samuel also strongly criticized the policy of the commission towards the Arabs during his tour of the country, saying that it had not recognized 'the force and value of the Arab nationalist movement', which was 'very real and no bluff'.[50]

The Palin Commission, the first in a long line of commissions of inquiry on Palestine during the next twenty-five years, investigated the origins of the April 1920 disturbances though its findings were not published.[51] It placed the blame for the riots on the Zionists, 'whose impatience to achieve their ultimate goal and indiscretion are largely responsible for this unhappy state of feeling'; it also drew attention to the fact that they were 'ready to use their powerful foreign and home influence to force the hand of this or any future Administration'. If not carefully checked, the commission's report went on, 'they may easily precipitate a catastrophe, the end of which it is difficult to forecast'.[52]

The Palin Commission sat for fifty days, and examined some 152 witnesses speaking no less than eight languages (English, French, Arabic, Hebrew, Yiddish, Jargon,[53] Russian and Hindustani) which necessitated the assistance of interpreters and lengthened the process. A main feature of the inquiry was a 'vigorous attack' made upon OETA by the Zionist Commission, who were keenly interested and were legally represented.[54] The case of the Arabs, who lacked interest and rarely attended the court, was 'by no means so well prepared'.

The Palin Report reviewed the history of Palestine in its various stages, up to the announcement of the Balfour Declaration, including the previous promises and pledges given to the Arabs during the war, calling them 'fitful essays' which tended to confuse and exasperate the people.[55] As late as 1918, active recruiting was carried out in Palestine for the Sherifian army, 'the recruits being given to understand that they were fighting in a national cause and to liberate their country from the Turks'. There was no question but that this was encouraged by the War Office during the war 'with every kind of propaganda available', and that pamphlets were dropped from aeroplanes, promising peace and prosperity under British rule. The recruits actively took part in the offensive against the Turks, and the report noted that Captain C. D. Brunton, who recruited them, acted in cooperation with a 'Sherifian officer named Hagg Ameen el Husseini, who was described at the time as being very pro-English'. It also noted that, at the time of writing, Hajj Amin was a fugitive from British justice, accused of complicity in the Easter riots.

Since the Balfour Declaration was 'undoubtedly the starting point of the whole trouble', the report quoted its text, saying that it was a carefully worded document, 'but for the somewhat vague phrase "A National Home"'. Its effect was to leave Muslims and Christians 'dumbfounded', when, after three to four months, its true meaning filtered through the minds of the people: 'It is impossible to minimise the bitterness of the awakening. They considered that they were to be handed

over to an oppression which they hated far more than the Turks and were aghast at
the thought of this domination.'

In 1919, Amin al-Husseini had commented on British policy with 'surprise and
anger'. The thought that, had the Arabs left the Turks alone, they would never
have done to them what the British had done was often repeated. Rightly or wrongly,
the report stated, the Arabs 'fear the Jew as a ruler, regarding his race as one of the
most intolerant known to history'. The Arabs did not fear the native Orthodox Jew
who was regarded as inoffensive, dependent for existence on foreign charity. But
they noticed that the latest immigrants from Eastern Europe were men of a very
different type, 'imbued with all shades of political opinions which have plunged
Russia into a welter of anarchy, terrorism and misery during the past few years'.
Nevertheless, it was the Jew as an economic competitor which really inspired 'the
profoundest alarm' in the minds of the native, who was now able to note that
'where the Jew became a landed proprietor, the Arab and Christian fellah peasant
proprietor was reduced to the position of a wage labourer'.[56]

The ability of the Jew as a merchant, agriculturist and administrator, backed
with 'inexhaustible funds', was not doubted, and the prospect of extensive Jewish
immigration inspired a 'panic fear':

> Such a fear cannot be said to be entirely unreasonable. There is certainly evidence
> to show that the tendency of the native small proprietor is to sink into the condition
> of a wage labourer where he comes into collision with Jewish colonial enterprise
> and combination ... .[57]

According to the report, the Zionist Commission was gradually developing into
a body 'bearing a distinct resemblance to an independent administration apparently able to control the administration', and was able to obtain knowledge through
its private intelligence department, thus gaining access to the 'most secret official
documents'. The report observed that all this happened when the mandate had not
yet been given, and the 'threatened' immigration was merely in the preparation
phase. This confirmed Arab fears, and the belief was growing among them that
'room can only be made for the Jews in their country by their own subjection or
eviction'. Because of all this, it was evident that a full comprehension of the Balfour
Declaration created a situation of 'great tension, calling for the exercise of the greatest delicacy and tact' on the part of the Zionists, who were the sole beneficiaries of
that declaration. The rest of the report examined in detail the activities of the Zionists during the previous two years.

From the very beginning, according to the report, the extremists among the
Zionists, both in their writings and in their speeches, had adopted one interpretation of the Balfour Declaration: 'There was no question of moderate colonisation
or a National Home, but a declaration of Palestine as a Jewish State' and Palestine
was to become 'as Jewish as England is English' (Mr Joseph Cowen in a letter to the

Times on 19 September 1919). Other Zionists had added their 'literary gifts to fan the flames'. Leon Simon had written an article in the *Zionist Review*, which, in spite of its apparently moderate conclusions, was 'hardly calculated to pacify a panic-stricken people'. He began by saying: 'There will be a state in Palestine containing a number of Arab inhabitants'. The report remarked: 'one might almost imagine he was referring to a handful of gypsy nomads ... rather than to the great majority of the population of the country'.

Although Weizmann exercised a moderating influence whenever he was personally able to intervene, the report showed that he was unable to control the extremists of his party. Under Ussishkin, a Russian refugee, the Zionist Commission had become 'more aggressive and autocratic'. For the measures taken by the Zionists towards establishing their own autonomous institutions, the report referred to an earlier despatch by Sir Louis Bols which dealt with this question in greater detail. Briefly, however, it concluded that 'every department' of the official administration was 'duplicated' in the Zionist Commission, whose organization consisted of no less than a hundred individuals. It was clear that a 'complete administrative machine is in active operation'. For example, the Peace Courts, an ancient Jewish system of arbitration, had been developed into a complete judicial system 'entirely independent of the Civil Courts of the country'.

Other areas of Jewish autonomy described in the Palin Report included policing, defence, intelligence and public health. Of particular interest is what the report revealed about the Intelligence Department of the Zionist Organization, which it described as 'extremely efficient', and as having access to all postal and telegraphic matter: 'no documents of the Administration are secret from it', and 'the Zionists' system of intelligence evidently knew a great deal more about the inner working of the Administration than the corresponding department of the Administration did about the Zionists'.

The report concurred with the conclusions of the chief administrator, Sir Louis Bols, that 'this state of affairs cannot continue without grave danger to the public peace and to the prejudice of the Administration', and that the situation was 'in truth, intolerable':

> It is not to be wondered at that the Arab population complained of bias on the part of the Administration in favour of the Jews. They see the Administration repeatedly overruled by the Zionist Commission; they see the Zionist Commission intermeddling in every department of Government, in Justice, Public Health, Legislation, Public Works, and forcing the Administration ... to interfere in their favour, in a purely business transaction. They see Jews excluded from the operations of the Public Custodian with regard to enemy property: they have seen the introduction of the Hebrew language on an equality with Arabic and English: they have seen considerable immigration not effectively controlled: they see Zionist stamps on letters

and Zionist young men drilling publicly in open spaces of the town. Finally they have seen them proceeding to the election of a Constituent Assembly.

More examples of the growing irritation of the military administration towards the Zionist Commission were cited. Following the latest disturbances, for example, the administration had received a series of letters from Zionist sources. Bols complained that the tone of these letters was 'peremptory and dictatorial, and such as no Administration could be expected to tolerate.' The extent to which the Zionists 'ultimately carried their autocratic method of dealing with the Administration' was demonstrated on page 32 of the report: the Mayor of Jerusalem, Musa Kazim Pasha al-Husseini, had been present at the second demonstration in the previous March. It was not exactly known what he did, but 'the Zionists strongly resented his action, with the result that a letter was sent to him directly, signed by Mr David Yellin, head of the Zionist Commission in Palestine, practically dismissing him from his post'. Subsequently al-Husseini was dismissed 'without inquiry by Colonel Storrs, the Military Governor of Jerusalem' which 'had a profound effect on his co-religionists, definitely confirming the conviction they had already formed from other evidence that the Civil Administration was the mere puppet of the Zionist Organization.'[58]

However, the report did not advocate a reversal of the policy of the Balfour Declaration which, it said, was a *chose jugée*, and would most inevitably be executed. The solution lay in a firm government which would be able to

> hold the scales as between all parties with rigid equality: that the Zionists must be content to exercise patience and gain their National Home by gradual and reasonable methods ... and that the native population must cease from allowing themselves to become the catspaw of anti-Allied and anti-Christian conspirators and learn to acquire a perfect confidence in the Administration's firm resolution to protect them and their interests in the country which they have an undoubted right to consider their own.[59]

The Palin Commission ended its report by listing the reasons for the disturbances as submitted by its witnesses. (See Appendix B)

In any case, under the civil administration the Zionist Commission continued to function but was renamed the Palestine Zionist Executive in 1921.[60] This organization was recognized by the civil administration as the official 'Jewish Agency' mentioned in Article 4 of the Palestine mandate, though its name was not changed until 1928.[61] With an annual budget of more than £600,000 during the 1920s (excluding funds for land purchase held by the Jewish National Fund), the Zionist Commission became virtually a parallel system of government. It had its own bank, it organized Jewish immigration and directed Jewish settlement, and operated its own schools and health service. It had regular access to the high commissioner and government officials.[62] This body, described by one historian as 'the embryo of the future government of Israel'[63] flourished during Samuel's period, ceaselessly attacking those British officials who opposed its policy in Palestine.

This period also saw the initiation of another Jewish institution in Palestine, the Haganah. The April 1920 disturbances allowed those in the Zionist movement who advocated a more aggressive approach towards opposition to their presence in Palestine to seize the initiative. Following the disturbances, the Muslim-Christian Association of Jaffa wrote to the military governor complaining that 'the Zionist Committee [sic, Zionist Commission] was training their young on military grounds, which fact was observed on the same day when thousands of them demonstrated in a military way, carrying arms and sticks of every description.'[64] They pointed out that the government had collected all arms and ammunition from Christians and Muslims but 'the said law was never put in force on the Jews'.[65] The letter claimed that the British authorities had recruited an army 'all composed of Jews and these have misused the confidence placed in them and used their arms against the Moslems and Christians', adding that several complaints had previously been made against Jewish soldiers at Jaffa, Ludd and Ramleh. The Muslim-Christian Association therefore called on the government, in the interest of peace and to safeguard their 'lives' and 'property', to initiate the 'immediate expulsion' of all Jewish soldiers from the country, 'retaking their arms' as well as those found in the possession of other Jews. It called for a thorough search for arms in Zionist institutions, confiscation of the same and 'severe punishment' of the Jews, who were the cause of the trouble. Should the government not wish to expel Jewish soldiers, 'an army of Arabs under the British flag should be recruited to defend the Moslems and Christians against the Jews'.[66]

The Palin Report gave a detailed account of what it described as a 'singular' incident during the April 1920 disturbances—the offer by Vladimir Jabotinsky[67] and Pinhas Rutenberg (see Chapter 9) to place at the disposal of the local authorities the Jewish volunteer forces which they had recently raised.[68] They went to the military governor of Jerusalem and 'offered the services of themselves and the force they had raised to assist in restoring order'. In the course of the conversation, 'both men admitted having arms'. A discussion ensued in which Rutenberg and Jabotinsky 'refused to surrender the arms their men possessed but asked for the men to be armed by the Administration and used'.[69] They both insisted that the Arab police should be 'disarmed and the Jewish youth ... armed under their responsibility if the Administration considered it necessary'. As a compromise, Colonel Bramley, director of Public Security, suggested the formation of a body of special constables to which Rutenberg and Jabotinsky agreed, but Ronald Storrs refused. However, the events of the following two days prompted the authorities to use the Jewish force, and Rutenberg was called in and asked how many men he could produce because the administration 'had decided to use his men'. One hundred men were immediately produced and it was explained by the government that they were to be used as special constables, 'not armed'. The report adds that Jabotinsky selected the men and was 'in constant consultation' with the officials up to the point of his arrest on 7 April.

Ten days later, after the disturbances were over, Rutenberg wrote to Colonel Storrs saying that calm having been restored to the city, he had 'demobilised the Self Defence', to which Colonel Storrs replied, in a 'decidedly disingenuous' letter, that 'the Administration had no cognisance of such a body!' Rutenberg admitted that in arming the corps 'the wishes of the Administration were disregarded for the reasons already alleged—but subsequent events proved we were right'.[70] In addition, a secret telegram from General Headquarters in Egypt to the War Office on 18 April 1920 indicated that 'no doubt Jews possessed large numbers of fire-arms', and that inspection of casualties bore this out. Consequently, the military administration had carried out a search for arms in Jerusalem including the houses of Jabotinsky and members of the Zionist Commission, who were arrested and tried on several charges of 'inciting disturbances'.[71]

Just before the arrival of Herbert Samuel in Palestine as first high commissioner, Jabotinsky was tried by the military courts and was sentenced to fifteen years penal servitude. He was convicted of possession of firearms; instigation to disobedience by arming the populace; and conspiracy and preparing means to carry out riot acts.[72] On 14 June 1920, a fortnight before Samuel assumed his new responsibilities,[73] Allenby telegraphed to the War Office from Cairo saying that a modification of Jabotinsky's sentence, which had been suggested by Samuel, 'could only undermine authority' and would do no good. General Headquarters in Egypt also telegraphed the War Office two days later to report the 'lenient treatment' accorded to Jabotinsky. Commenting on these telegrams, Hubert Young minuted on 22 June: 'Colonel Deedes says that Jabotinsky is really a lunatic and should be kept under medical surveillance—If he were at large in Palestine now he would certainly cause trouble'. Sir John Tilley wrote: 'We must see that Sir Herbert Samuel realizes this before he includes Jabotinsky in his amnesty'.[74] On 24 June, and with the consent of Lord Hardinge and Lord Curzon, the following despatch (drafted by Young) was sent to Sir Herbert Samuel through the British Embassy in Rome:

> Lord Allenby considers release of Jabotinsky or any modification of his sentence would undermine authority and prestige of Palestine administration—Deedes is of opinion that Jabotinsky should not in any case be set at large in Palestine as he is not responsible for his actions. We repeat these views to you for what they are worth.[75]

All the same, Samuel did include Jabotinsky in his amnesty. And in his first week in office, as he set about 'cleaning up the legacy' of the former administration, he decreed an amnesty of all those convicted of crimes during the latest riots and informed the War Office that the Palin Report should best be forgotten.[76]

On 8 September 1920, when OETA had already ceased to exist, Allenby wrote again to Curzon drawing his attention to the forthcoming campaign for the 'quashing' of the sentence on Jabotinsky, which he said was 'bound to reflect unjustly' on the military administration and hence advised the publication of the Palin Report, which would 'clear' the military.[77] However, on Samuel's advice, the Palin Report, which was submitted in Port Said on 1 July 1920, as already described, was never published and remained a secret document whose contents were kept from the public. On 9 September 1920, Allenby wrote to Curzon:

> This report has reviewed, with great ability and in extensive detail, the whole circumstances which led to the troubles in Jerusalem. Naturally, the Zionists are opposed to such publication; and Sir Herbert Samuel, in the interest of the local situation, has urged H.M.G. to refrain from it. I know that you agree with him; and, having regard to the great desirability of keeping things quiet in Palestine, I agree that it is the desirable course. If, however, this document is to be kept from the public, in the interest of the Zionists—and of them alone—a document which establishes an almost unanswerable case for the Military Administration in Palestine, and certainly removes from their shoulders most of the blame for the riots; the Zionists should be made to observe some restraints on their side too ... I feel strongly in the matter; and I am not prepared to admit, quietly, that any Military Administration was in any way to blame.[78]

Even more revealing than Allenby's letter to Curzon was Clayton's comment on it in Colonial Office minutes. On 9 September, he summed up the whole British position in Palestine during that period in a few, but precise, words. He argued that the Zionist policy was merely a manifestation of British policy and hence it would have been unwise to 'threaten' the Zionists with publication of the report. He said:

> It is true that the Zionists deprecated the publication of the report of the Court of Enquiry as being somewhat damaging to their cause, but I venture to think that publication is also undesirable, if it can be avoided, in the interests of H.M.G. It would tend to revive anti-Zionist feeling, and reflections on the Zionists are to some extent reflections on the policy of H.M.G.[79]

The Palin Report characterized the whole history of the Haganah as 'extremely unsatisfactory' and continued:

> It seems scarcely credible that the fact that these men had been got together and were openly drilling at the back of Lemel School and on Mount Scopas [sic] should have been known as it undoubtedly was, to the population during the month of

March—it was organised after the demonstration of the 8th—and yet no word of it reached either the Governorate or the Administration until after the riots.[80]

The report blamed the intelligence system for this serious defect, which resulted in the British being 'ignorant of the Zionists' duplication of Government until informed by Mr. Herbert Samuel', adding that there was not even an 'attempt to secrecy' and that Mr Rutenberg actually went to Brigadier General Waters-Taylor (who was a strong opponent of the Zionist policy) and asked permission 'to arm the force'.[81] The result of this interview was that Rutenberg 'appears to have understood' that he 'must not arm his force'. Jabotinsky thereupon asked Colonel Storrs for permission to arm his force. According to the report, Jabotinsky misled the administration, leaving Colonel Storrs 'under the impression that what he wanted was arms for outlying colonies', and that he failed to make it clear that he had raised a defence force. Dr Eder (of the Zionist Commission), backing this application, 'apparently made it no clearer' what was the intended use of the weapons. The commission of enquiry concluded: 'The organisers decided to arm their men in spite of the Administration.'[82]

Meanwhile, to counter the repeated assaults and charges of anti-Semitism against OETA's staff by the Zionists, Sir Walford Selby,[83] a senior staff member at General Headquarters in Cairo who had toured Palestine in June 1920, wrote to Sir William Tyrell, under-secretary of state at the Foreign Office, that the 'campaign of calumny' conducted by the Zionists was grossly unfair to General Bols and his chief of staff as well as to the other governors subordinate to them. He also wrote that it was on Colonel Storrs, the military governor of Jerusalem, and the other governors that the whole brunt of the Zionist attack fell after the disturbances in Jerusalem, adding that it was

> little realised how insulting and truculent were the communications with which our authorities had to deal from certain of the members of the Zionist Commission in Jerusalem, who had by then practically constituted themselves a separate administration—in fact a Soviet.

Pointing out that the 'insolence' and 'arrogance' of the Zionist Commission 'surpassed all bounds', Selby went on to say that 'the only matter of surprise' was that the authorities concerned 'succeeded in keeping their heads as well as they did'.[84]

MOVING TOWARDS A CIVIL ADMINISTRATION

As relations between the military authorities and the Zionists continued to deteriorate, many hands were involved in bringing the military administration to an end. Herbert Samuel himself later commented that since the Balfour Declaration had been embodied in the terms of the mandate, 'It became necessary to set up in

Palestine a Civil Administration of the normal kind, in succession to the administration by the Army of Occupation which, in 1920, was still functioning'.[85]

On 19 April, the role of General Bols, and that of Colonel Richard Meinertzhagen, one of the officers of Allenby's Intelligence Staff, and their relations with the military authorities in Egypt, was the subject of discussion in the War Office. Two alternatives were considered: either that Allenby should be regarded as the representative of both the War Office and the Foreign Office for Palestine, or that Palestine should be completely severed from Egypt both as regards military command and political control. After some discussion, it was decided that the first alternative was preferable, provided that the Foreign Office was represented in Palestine itself and not only in Cairo. The appointment of an experienced administrator of high standing was also suggested, and the name of Lord Meston (James Scorgie, an Indian civil servant), was put forward by the Foreign Office, to take charge from General Bols, and that this was to be considered 'in the near future.' It was also proposed that a definitive interpretation of the Balfour Declaration should be laid down by the British government and communicated to Lord Allenby, Faisal and the Zionists, because the root of all difficulty appeared to lie in the fact that different interpretations were being made.[86]

On 24 April 1920, during the San Remo Conference, according to Samuel's account, the British prime minister, Lloyd George, informed him that 'he was convinced that things could not go on as they were'. He was apparently 'much impressed' by a letter from Colonel Richard Meinertzhagen, which claimed that Allenby was not carrying out in Palestine the policy of the Foreign Office in pursuance of the Balfour Declaration.[87] Samuel added that he had convinced Lloyd George that 'the Military Administration must give place to a civilian'. Consequently, Lloyd George, Balfour and Curzon decided that Samuel was the right man for the post of administrator; it was essential to have someone who was genuinely interested in making the Zionist policy a success. 'Would [Samuel] undertake it, say for two or three years, to give them a start?' [88]

When news of Samuel's appointment as first high commissioner reached Palestine, General Bols addressed the representatives of all communities in Acre on 28 April, informing them that the mandate to Great Britain and the Balfour Declaration would probably be incorporated in the peace treaty with Turkey. He stated that the country would be governed by the British government for the good of all the inhabitants.[89] In an interview with a Jerusalem newspaper, Bols elaborated that the Balfour Declaration was endorsed by the Allies on condition that all rights of the native population would be safeguarded. Jewish immigration would be strictly limited to the numbers which the country could economically support, and the Zionist Commission had given assurances that only useful and self-supporting members of society would be admitted, while the interests of the native land-holders would be safeguarded. A strong mandatory power would bring into effect a just and impartial administration in which a native government would be proportionately representative of the entire population and the officials of the mandatory power would train the population to self-government.[90]

However, both Allenby and Bols questioned the wisdom of appointing a Jew as head of the first civil administration, causing Lord Curzon to ask Samuel (on 12 May) to reconsider accepting the post. He read to Samuel a 'very disturbing' cable from Allenby which stressed that the appointment of a Jew would be 'highly dangerous'. The Arabs would regard this appointment 'as handing country over at once to a permanent Zionist Administration', and anticipated that when Samuel arrived, there would be 'outrages', 'murders' and 'raids' against Jews.[91] Samuel considered these reports unduly alarmist, but said he would consult a delegation representing the Palestine Jewish community which was in London at the time. After the Zionists confirmed to Samuel that these 'alarmist' reports were not justified, he decided to accept the offer. His term of office would be four years, with a possible addition of a fifth.[92]

Early in the afternoon of the second day after Samuel's arrival in Palestine, the chief administrator formally handed over the administration to the high commissioner. At the hostel on the Mount of Olives, which had been known as 'Headquarters, Occupied Enemy Territory Administration South' and now became Government House, Bols, about to leave, told Samuel that he wanted him 'to sign a receipt'. When Samuel asked for what, Bols replied: 'For Palestine'. The conversation, as Samuel recorded it in his memoirs, proceeded in the following manner: 'But I can't do that. You don't mean it seriously', to which Bols replied, 'Certainly I do, I have got it typed out here'. After this, Bols produced a slip of paper saying: 'Received from Major-General Sir Louis J. Bols, K.C.B.—One Palestine, complete', with the date and a space for Samuel's signature. Samuel objected, but at Bols' insistence, he signed, adding 'E & O.E.', meaning 'Errors and Omissions Excepted'.[93] As Bols drove past the gate-house and down the hill, Ronald Storrs remarked: 'OETA, as OETA, ceased to exist'.[94]

The wisdom of Samuel's appointment as high commissioner and the Jewish national home policy were debated in the House of Lords only one day before Samuel's arrival in Palestine. In response to concerns expressed about the vagueness of the commitments made under the Balfour Declaration, Lord Curzon gave assurances that the government did not intend to allow 'indiscriminate mass immigration', whether of Jews or non-Jews, and whether of Jews from Russia or elsewhere. He also gave assurances that 'non-Jewish landowners will not be expropriated or compelled to give up their property for the benefit of the Jews'. He conceded that in the Zionist Commission there had been some 'hot-heads who have said and perhaps done foolish things'.[95]

Although it was true that no 'disparaging' remarks had been made about Sir Herbert Samuel during the debate, 'very grave doubts have been expressed as to the wisdom of sending a Jewish Administrator to the country at this moment'. Curzon continued:

> That is a perfectly tenable view. It is a perfectly tenable view to say that—an Arab, of course, not being available, and the Zionists, as representing the minority, being disqualified—you ought to have sent somebody else. That was not the view taken by the Government, and in their search for someone who would loyally carry out the policy to which Mr. Balfour had committed us, with the consent of our Allies, it was thought that no more competent person could be found than Sir Herbert Samuel … I think we must trust Sir Herbert Samuel to carry out the broad principles of policy which I have laid down, and which I believe, the mandate having been accepted and the national home having been taken as one of the principles of our action, will be broadly endorsed by both sides of your Lordships' House.

Curzon assured the Lords that Samuel was 'a judicially-minded and sensible and experienced man', and that from previous experience of serving with him in Asquith's administration he knew him as a man 'of singular impartiality and fairness'. However, Curzon anticipated that Samuel would have a difficult time with the Arabs during the initial period. 'A great authority on the country' had recently told him that in six months' time, Samuel would be equally unpopular with the Jews, noting that this in itself was testimony to the character of Sir Herbert Samuel. Curzon added that if there was any part of the world where the pace should be 'extremely staid', he would name Palestine.[96]

The Lords had great reservations about the national home policy because of the vagueness surrounding its meaning, but some members were reassured by what they had heard about Samuel's personal qualities. The Archbishop of Canterbury had come with a very anxious hope for 'elucidation of the subject', which he admitted, was to most people 'exceedingly perplexing':

> The terms which have been used—the term 'Zionism' itself, or the term 'A Jewish Home'—are equally elusive, and it is extraordinarily difficult to find out what those who use those terms really mean by them, either when they emanate from government authority or from critics of that authority.

The Archbishop was, however, reassured by what he had heard about Samuel's qualities, stating that this had given him the 'greatest confidence in his judgement, his common sense and his largeness of view'.

On the other hand, Lord Sheffield warned that he had no doubts about the meaning of 'national home'. He told the Lords that 'a great deal of mischief' had been done by using such ambiguous words and that this term

> might be interpreted in a harmless way, but it has also been interpreted as giving priority to a small minority of Jews over the mass of people in Palestine. It is idle to

propose that preference should be given to one-tenth who have gone to the country only lately over the nine-tenths who have been there, from father to son, for generations.[97]

He also noted that many people suspected that the government was trying to 'smooth the way so that when things ripen the Jews can step in and take possession of their "Promised Land". That would be a thoroughly vicious principle.' The government

should administer Palestine under the mandate for the benefit of all the people there. The Jews comprise only one-tenth of the inhabitants. They are not an important part of the people ... There ought to be perfectly fair play. No doubt Sir Herbert Samuel will try to be perfectly fair, but there is no doubt that the people of the country, when you select a man of the religion and race of only one-tenth of the inhabitants and send him to rule the whole country, must feel suspicious. I hope that Sir Herbert Samuel will disappoint the hopes of his co-nationalists and co-religionists.[98]

Not only were the military authorities on the spot apprehensive of the appointment of a Jew as first civil administrator in Palestine. Parliamentary questions at that period show a deep concern about the choice of Herbert Samuel. One such question, by Brigadier-General Surtees, in June 1920, asked the under-secretary of state for foreign affairs

whether, in view of the appointment of a High Commissioner for Palestine belonging to the Jewish faith, and the fact that he is about to enter upon his duties, he will state what action has been taken to placate the Arab population, which is greater than the Jewish, and thereby put an end to racial tension.

To which Young suggested a reply that if an assurance was needed that Sir Herbert Samuel would carry out his duties 'with the strict impartiality which is characteristic of British Administration throughout the world', then it would be found in the statement recently made by him and published by the press.[99] The British press was equally apprehensive. The *Morning Post* wrote on 13 September 1920, in an article entitled 'The ferment in Palestine—angry Moslems', that 'Sir Herbert Samuel's appointment as High Commissioner was regarded by everyone, except Jews, as a serious mistake.'[100]

In Palestine, General Bols reported how the news of Samuel's appointment as first high commissioner was received: 'Consternation, despondency, and exasperation express the feelings of the Moslem Christian population ... They are convinced that he will be a partisan Zionist and that he represents a Jewish and not a British Government.'[101]

Intelligence reports in June and July 1920, as well as the many petitions sent to the British government from Palestinian leaders, confirm the view that Samuel's appointment was looked upon with deep suspicion, if not open hostility. One such report reveals that anti-Zionist feeling was 'extremely bitter', and that it was aggravated by the announcement that Samuel would take the appointment of high commissioner, and that both Christians and Muslims feared that this merely foreshadowed a 'camouflaged Jewish Government'. Consequently, the feeling was anti-British, but according to the same report, this anti-British feeling appeared to be directed against the 'actual British Mandate, but only in so far as it is connected with the Zionist programme'.[102] On 23 June, one week before Samuel's arrival, the Muslim-Christian Association protested against his appointment. The telegram, delivered to General Bols, read:

> Sir Herbert Samuel regarded as a Zionist leader, and his appointment as first step in formation of Zionist national home in the midst of Arab people contrary to their wishes. Inhabitants cannot recognise him, and Moslem-Christian Society cannot accept responsibility for riots or other disturbances of peace.[103]

British policy, according to the Palestinians, indicated that Palestine was to be handed over to the Jews, and declared that the appointment of Samuel was evidence of this policy.[104]

3

Britain and Palestine, 1921–1924: Could the Balfour Declaration Have Been Reversed?

Despite the Lloyd George government's firm adherence to the Balfour Declaration as the basis of official policy on Palestine, the first years of British rule were marked by a degree of uncertainty as to its future direction. By mid-1921, the outbreak of violence in Jaffa indicated the extent of Palestinian Arab hostility to the development of the Jewish national home. The British army, which remained in Palestine as a security force after the establishment of the civil administration under Sir Herbert Samuel in July 1920, was openly anti-Zionist. The British press, initially favourable to the Jewish national home policy had, by the early 1920s, become increasingly sceptical, if not hostile, and a movement opposed to the Balfour Declaration gained ground in parliament.

By the time a Conservative government came to power in late 1922, there seemed to be a real possibility that the policy favouring pursuit of the Balfour Declaration could be reversed. However, a year later, the Mandate for Palestine, enshrining the its key provisions, came into force, effectively ending any serious lobby for a different approach to the Palestine issue. This chapter examines various aspects of this debate as it unfolded in London. From the point of view of British interests alone, was the pro-Zionist policy universally considered to have been in the best interests of the British Empire? What justification was there for persisting with such a policy in the face of widespread British opposition, both at home and from the military establishment, as well as from some British officials in Palestine? Was the Middle East Department of the Colonial Office responsible for imposing a policy hated by nine-tenths of the population of Palestine? And what were its motives?

FORMATION OF THE MIDDLE EAST DEPARTMENT

Arguably a key factor in maintaining pro-Zionist policies under several successive governments was the role played by the Middle East Department in the Colonial

Office. After the First World War ended, the War Office handled territories captured from the Turks, while the India Office dealt with Mesopotamia. However, in 1919, the newly-formed Eastern Department of the Foreign Office was assigned to deal with British policy in Turkey, the Caucasus, Persia, Syria, Mesopotamia, Arabia and Egypt. The Foreign Office was therefore competing to some extent with the other two departments, since captured land was considered legally to be foreign territory.[1] In view of widespread trouble in the Middle East towards the middle of 1920 (there were violent upheavals in Mesopotamia and Palestine as well as in Egypt after the nationalist leader, Sa'ad Zaghlul, was exiled), the British government concluded that this system of divided responsibility should come to an end, and jurisdiction be transferred to a single department under the control of one secretary of state. The choice, following an argument between the Foreign Office and the Colonial Office, fell on the latter.

For the first nine months of the civil administration, from July 1920, Palestine remained under Foreign Office control, with Lord Curzon, the only member of Lloyd George's Cabinet with anti-Zionist views, as foreign secretary. But in February 1921, a Middle East Department was created in the Colonial Office,[2] with staff drawn from different government offices, to handle the affairs of the Arabic-speaking mandated areas. In March 1921, Weizmann told Sir Herbert Samuel that these changes might prove 'of great importance' for Palestine.[3] The handing over of responsibility for Palestine to a new committee 'under the aegis' of the Colonial Office had terminated the direct Zionist connection with the Foreign Office, and marked 'the beginning of a new period in which it will be our aim to be in contact with the new authorities'.[4] In fact this proved to be the beginning of a long and fruitful alliance between the Zionists and the Middle East Department, into whose hands the fate of Palestine was entrusted.

The colonial secretary, Winston Churchill, brought Sir John Evelyn Shuckburgh[5] from the India Office to head the department, with Roland Vernon from the Treasury and Hubert Young as joint assistant secretaries. Young was an Arabist from the Foreign Office's Eastern Department who had served during the war with T. E. Lawrence. Lawrence himself was attached to the department as a political adviser, with Colonel Richard Meinertzhagen as its military expert.[6]

With the exception of Meinertzhagen, the department's staff were career civil servants. In contrast to the civil administration in Palestine, where the three most important positions were held by avowed Zionists, only Meinertzhagen came to the department as a convinced Zionist.[7] His support of the Zionist cause was so vehement that the Palin Commission, set up to look into the causes of the 1920 Easter riots in Jerusalem, described him in its report as the 'chief support of the Zionists'. Meinertzhagen, the report concluded, had 'arrived with a definite anti-Arab bias and a prejudice in favour of Zionism and took his views from the Zionists alone'. There seemed to be an element of truth in his being regarded as 'Dr.

Weizmann's nominee', and his own indiscretions 'reveal him as an agent who, however capable of doing good work in other spheres is singularly out of place in the East'.[8]

Throughout his years in the Colonial Office, Meinertzhagen certainly made no secret of his allegiances. He stated:

> Zionism has come to stay. To attempt to interfere with Jewry is to interfere with history. His Majesty's Government and enemies of Zionism can delay the ultimate destiny of Palestine, but they cannot prevent its ultimate fulfilment.'[9]

Meinertzhagen later claimed that after joining the department he had succeeded in converting Hubert Young and John Shuckburgh from Arabists to Zionists,[10] a claim both of them would certainly have disputed. Nevertheless, it is true that in August 1921, Young, apparently influenced by Meinertzhagen's ideas, drew up a memorandum which Churchill circulated to the Cabinet, advocating that all anti-Zionist civil officials, however highly-placed, should be removed from the Palestine administration.[11] The memorandum also advised that the Palestine military force should be separated from the British army in Egypt,[12] and recommended the establishment of a separate reserve force of Jewish police, as well as closer ties with the Zionist Organization.[13] However, Young was apparently shaken by witnessing, during his visit to Palestine in autumn 1921, the extent to which the Palestinian Arabs had lost confidence in the 'straightforwardness' of the British government.[14]

As for Shuckburgh, he was no Zionist, but from the beginning was driven by the conviction that Britain was duty bound to uphold the terms of the Balfour Declaration, although he insisted that this policy would not lead to a Jewish state. There was no doubt that he was strongly influenced by Weizmann, who was a frequent visitor to the department. Weizmann's considerable diplomatic skills were used to best effect in private interviews, which often took place in Downing Street, with successive prime ministers, and with Shuckburgh in the Colonial Office.[15] By Shuckburgh's own testimony, he saw Weizmann 'constantly' when the latter was in England [16] and Weizmann's biographer speaks of Shuckburgh's 'unusual deference' to him.[17] The evidence from the first two years of the Middle East Department's operation suggests that the exceptional relations between Weizmann and the staff of the department were a significant factor in preventing the British government's pro-Zionist policy from being revoked or modified.

During these years, debate and conflict continued within the British political establishment on the desirability of pursuing a policy for the Palestine mandate as laid down in the Balfour Declaration. Despite the conviction on the part of the Zionists and their supporters, and of many British officials, that this was a *chose jugée*, there were significant sections of the political and military establishment where doubts were expressed. The department's reactions to pressures for a change of policy, and its relationships with the various protagonists in the debate, were to be key factors in determining the outcome of this debate.

THE MIDDLE EAST DEPARTMENT AND THE MILITARY

Immediately after the establishment of the Middle East Department, the colonial secretary, Winston Churchill, held a conference in Cairo in March 1921, attended by major political and military officers from the territories with which the newly-formed department was to deal. The colonial secretary's main concern was to find ways and means of reducing imperial expenditure in the Middle East.[18] Although Mesopotamia and Transjordan were his two main preoccupations at the Cairo conference, Palestine, too, was on the agenda. The Middle East Department, however, insisted that nothing in Palestine required any particular attention.[19] Yet the department had been privy to earlier warnings about the danger of disorder, including a December 1920 report to the War Office by the director of military operations in Palestine, stating that riots were likely to break out in Jerusalem, Jaffa, Haifa and Nablus.[20]

The Jaffa riots, the intensity of which shocked the civil authorities, broke out only a few months later in May 1921. The Middle East Department had thus far ignored the advice of the military authorities in Palestine who were seen as opposed to the pro-Zionist policy of the British government. Some officers had indeed displayed overt sympathy with the Arabs and this encouraged the Colonial Office, after it took charge of Palestine in 1921, to play down or discount their reports as unsubstantiated.[21] This attitude was evident in the department's response to military views on the causes and consequences of the Jaffa riots. On 30 May 1921, General Congreve, commander of the British armies in Egypt and Palestine, sent a report to Samuel, which was forwarded to Churchill on 5 June, in which he expressed his fear that 'unless some change is made we may be confronted with a situation beyond our power to cope with'. Although the country seemed 'outwardly calm, the discontent and irritation throughout the whole of the Moslem and Christian population is very grave'. The principal cause of this discontent, in Congreve's view, was Jewish immigration which the Muslims 'take great exception to ... in its unrestricted form, and are prepared to resist it by every means'. Furthermore, the Muslims 'distrust the present Administration of the Law and claim that the whole Legal Administration is tainted with pro-Jewish sympathies'. Congreve warned that if an insurrection resulted, the forces at his disposal were insufficient to quell it. He concluded that three alternatives existed: an alteration of policy; an increase in garrison numbers, or the acceptance of a great danger to the Jewish population. [22]

In a private letter to Hubert Young in June 1921, Congreve wrote that the riots had been neither organized nor premeditated, but warned that 'unless Arab aspirations are attended to ... and Zionist aspirations ... greatly curbed', it would not be surprising if something yet more serious developed. Herbert Samuel had 'seen and heard only what he wanted to see and hear', and resented warnings of growing Arab discontent. He concluded:

> What we have got to face is the fact that as long as we persist in our Zionist policy we have got to maintain all our present forces in Palestine to enforce a policy hateful to the great majority—a majority which means to fight and to continue to fight and has right on its side.

The Middle East Department received a similar letter from Air Vice-Marshal Salmond.[23] It was not only Samuel who refused to listen to the advice of the military authorities in Jerusalem. Shuckburgh argued that General Congreve's letter 'restates the case from the local point of view, against our Zionist policy in Palestine. The real answer is that we are committed to this policy and have got to make the best of it'. The following day, Churchill initialled his name in agreement with Shuckburgh.[24] Meinertzhagen, dismissing Congreve as a 'partisan provocateur', commented:

> It is the old argument against the futility of the Zionist policy. I decline to be influenced by it, as the authors will not realise that (a) Zionism is the avowed policy of H.M.G. and is not merely the whim of individuals. (b) The objects and benefits of Zionism are ignored: it is prejudged before it has a chance. [25]

T. E. Lawrence, the department's political adviser was not impressed by General Congreve's argument, and conjectured that there was 'a personal bias behind the opinions'.[26]

A report from Military Intelligence, passed from the War Office to Churchill, and dated 15 August 1921, informed the Colonial Office that the civil administration in Palestine was 'unpopular'. Gerald Clauson of the Middle East Department wrote in a minute dated 24 August: 'it is most objectionable that "poison gas" of this nature should be produced in Palestine and reach other Cabinet Ministers without this office or the Palestine Government seeing it first'. Not surprisingly, the department labelled the report as 'inaccurate', and it quickly passed into oblivion.[27] A month later, Meinertzhagen accused Military Intelligence of 'in effect "spying" upon the Government [i.e. the Palestine administration]', adding that the 'sooner this department becomes a branch of the Civil Administration, the better'.[28] Hubert Young had already counselled that the British military force in Palestine be separated from the British army in Egypt.[29]

Tension over the military's views came to a head when Samuel forwarded to Churchill a copy of a circular dated 29 October 1921 from the general officer commanding-in-chief, Egyptian Expeditionary Force, to the general officer commanding troops in Palestine. The circular noted, *inter alia*, that while the army officially was supposed to have no politics:

> In the case of Palestine these sympathies [of the British troops] are rather obviously with the Arabs, who have hitherto appeared to the disinterested observer to have been the victims of an unjust policy, forced upon them by the British Government.[30]

Although the circular noted that whatever the justice or injustice of the policy, the government's intentions had been honest, officials in the Middle East Department, as well as the Zionists, found its tone offensive. Meinertzhagen wanted to make an issue of it with the War Office, and Weizmann, who had obtained a copy and sent it to Lloyd George, commented bitterly that it was the worst of all the 'wicked' things that had been done to the Zionists in the last six months. Shuckburgh, on the other hand, counselled against confronting the War Office with this matter:

> The latter would be sure to ask us what were the particular passages to which we objected and what were the precise grounds of our objections. I do not think that it would be very easy to answer. It is the general tone rather than any particular expressions in the Circular that seem to me exceptionable. One cannot read it without forming the impression that it is a document written by an anti-Zionist to anti-Zionists. It is unfortunately the case that the Army in Palestine is largely anti-Zionist and will probably remain so whatever may be said to it. This Circular does at least impress upon officers the necessity for loyal adherence to the policy of the British Government, and to that extent it should have a salutary effect. I should be inclined to leave it at that. [31]

In any event, these were the final days of British military opposition to the pro-Zionist policy. Shortly thereafter, Churchill invited the Air Ministry to assume responsibility for the defence of Palestine, a step that prevented any future friction between the military and the civil administration.[32] Air Vice-Marshal Salmond was already reported to be 'very anxious that his officers should not interfere unduly in political matters.'[33]

ARABS AND ZIONISTS: THE ATTITUDE OF THE MIDDLE EAST DEPARTMENT

In the wake of the Jaffa disturbances in May 1921, Samuel gave an important speech on 3 June, in which he asserted that the Balfour Declaration did not mean that Palestine would be taken away from Palestine's Arabs and 'given to strangers'. This induced a Palestinian Arab delegation to proceed to London in the hope of bringing about a change of policy. However, after a year of unsuccessful discussions, the Palestine White Paper, announced in June 1922, confirmed the policy of the Balfour Declaration. Shortly afterwards, the mandate was ratified by the League of Nations. The Arab Delegation returned to Palestine, having failed to convince the Colonial Office to repeal the Balfour Declaration. Nevertheless, it had been successful in gaining the support of significant sections of the English public for the Palestinian Arab cause and that year witnessed the first major re-evaluation of British policy in Palestine since the declaration in 1917.

In the aftermath of the Jaffa disturbances, some doubts were expressed within the Colonial Office about the wisdom of the government's pro-Zionist policy. The colonial secretary, Winston Churchill, expressed his doubts in a memorandum to the Cabinet on 9 June 1921, 'I do not think things are going to get better in this part of the world, but rather worse'.[34] However, the Colonial Office eventually took up the Zionist argument and the Middle East Department launched a successful counter-attack on the pro-Arab lobby among British politicians.

Even before the Arab Delegation arrived, Shuckburgh had spelled out, in a memorandum dated August 1921, the line that was to be taken. The Arabs 'must accept as the basis of all discussion' that it was the 'fixed intention' of the British government to fulfil its pledges in the matter of the establishment of a national home for the Jews.[35] Given these assumptions, it is not surprising that the talks did not make strong headway. Although Shuckburgh was willing to conciliate the Arabs on trivial issues,[36] he did not alter his position on the interpretation of the Balfour Declaration. In an exhaustive draft statement dated 7 November 1921, he asserted that since the Arabs failed to realize that abandonment of the Balfour Declaration was 'out of the question', any discussion with them in London was 'a mere waste of time'. It had been explained to the Arab Delegation 'over and over again' that the present policy was a *chose jugée*. He noted that the government was 'deeply pledged to the Zionists and have always made it clear to the Arabs that there is no prospect of our wavering on this point. To waver now, in the face of renewed Arab violence, would be absolutely fatal.'[37]

The only course of action Shuckburgh recommended was to 'find some way of repeating the story which, if it does not carry conviction, will at least compel acquiescence'. Experience had shown, he continued, that the Arab Delegation was 'a hopeless body to deal with': firstly, hardly any of them could speak English, and everything had to be translated by an interpreter, and secondly, they were 'very slow of understanding, and probably rather suspicious of one another'. After much inconclusive talk, 'they go back to their Hotel and wait till one of their English advisers comes and tells them what to say'. He concluded that 'the time has come to leave off arguing and announce plainly and authoritatively what we propose to do. Being Orientals, they will understand an order; and if once they realise that we mean business, may be expected to acquiesce'.[38]

The department's treatment of the Zionists was quite a different matter. There were certainly, on occasion, concerns about 'leaks'. In June 1922, for example, Weizmann was discovered to have gained access to secret telegrams and despatches coming in and out of the department.[39] Yet there was a constant flow of information from the Middle East Department to the Zionists.[40] At the same time that Shuckburgh was dealing so sternly with the Arab Delegation, he was keeping Weizmann 'privately informed' of the dealings and 'solicited his views' on how the Colonial Office should respond to Arab demands.[41] And, in autumn 1921, when a review of immigration policy was called for, Shuckburgh confidentially sent Weizmann a Colonial Office memorandum summarizing the findings of a report by the head of the Immigration Department in Palestine who had refused to show it to the Zionists. The Zionist Commission in Jerusalem succeeded in obtaining a copy anyway and promptly sent it their offices in London.[42] Indeed, Weizmann was given the draft memorandum to 'comment' on before it was sent to Samuel.[43]

A clue as to how Shuckburgh could reconcile his conduct at this time with his later claim to 'complete impartiality and detachment'[44] can be found in his memorandum of 7 November and the 'Statement of Policy' which he drafted at the same time. This was to be delivered by the secretary of state for the colonies defining British policy in Palestine. Although it was never adopted,[45] the views expressed in these documents shed more light on how Shuckburgh thought. British policy in Palestine, he wrote, was directed to promote the interests 'not of any particular section' but of the Palestinians as a whole, 'Palestinians' being understood to mean 'not only the existing population of Palestine, but also those future citizens of the country to whom the Balfour Declaration has promised a National Home'.[46]

He dismissed as 'groundless' Arab fears of 'Jewish political ascendancy'. He praised the Twelfth Zionist Congress at Carlsbad held in September 1921 for its 'wise and statesman-like' language. This congress, he stated, had called on its executive 'to redouble its efforts to secure a cordial understanding with the Arab people on the basis of this declaration and in strict accordance with the Balfour Declaration'. It had also declared that Jewish colonization would 'not affect the rights and needs of the Arab working population'. Yet the Carlsbad conference was also the first at which the aim of establishing a Jewish state rather than a Jewish national home was made explicit.[47] There was evidently irritation in the Colonial Office at the tendency of 'extreme elements in the Zionist movement' openly to declare their intention to have a Jewish state. Shuckburgh himself alluded to 'less responsible' utterances made by some Zionists at Carlsbad, but added:

> Provocative language is bad, but provocative action is far worse. And it is here that I have a plain word to say to the Arab leaders. As you all know, there has recently been a further outbreak of violence in Palestine, after a lapse of six months since the Jaffa disturbances. These outbreaks must stop; and I must hold the Arab leaders responsible for seeing that they stop.[48]

In his 7 November 1921 memorandum, Shuckburgh complained that no sooner had the British given the Arabs 'reassuring promises' than somebody 'gets up at the Zionist Congress and talks about the privileged position of the Jews in a Jewish State', thereby 'neutralizing' 'the effect of our language' and giving the Arabs cause to believe 'that our measured statements are mere empty language ...' He evidently had reservations about the ultimate Zionist programme:

> We should make plain to the Zionists, in the presence of the Arabs, the limitations which we attach to the conception of a Jewish National Home and should disavow before both parties the more extravagant claims of the Zionist extremists.[49]

Despite the months of fruitless discussions with the Colonial Office, the Arab Delegation did nonetheless succeed in developing extensive contacts with members of the British establishment. The Middle East Department did what it could to inhibit such interactions, sending numerous letters to highly placed British statesmen whom the Arabs were trying to contact. Letters sent at the end of October 1921 to Lord Robert Cecil, parliamentary under-secretary for foreign affairs, and the Duke of Atholl, for example, stated that negotiations with the Arab Delegation were at a 'standstill' and that meanwhile, 'the Delegation has been canvassing various persons of influence in the hope of receiving their help or support' and Mr Churchill did not advise that they should be granted 'any interviews as they ask for'.[50] A letter to Lord Southborough carried the same message.[51]

Around the same time, following a story in the *Times* on 16 November 1921 about a luncheon given by the Arab Delegation at which Lord Sydenham had said that 'the Jews had no more right to Palestine than the descendants of the ancient Romans had to this country',[52] Meinertzhagen dispatched a minute to Shuckburgh recording the names of the luncheon guests, all high ranking British officers and administrators, and then commented:

> It is idle to suppose that they were not aware of the political significance of the luncheon party, where their presence constituted an act of sympathy with the Arab Delegation, and does in fact constitute an act of obstruction to the Government policy.[53]

Shuckburgh, while remarking in a memorandum to the colonial secretary that there was 'nothing criminal' in accepting an invitation to lunch, added that the presence of high ranking officers 'at what was, in effect, a meeting to protest against the policy of H.M.G. is certainly unfortunate and cannot fail to produce an undesirable impression'.[54]

POLITICAL OPPOSITION

Although Shuckburgh and the Middle East Department consistently maintained that Britain's commitment to the Balfour Declaration was a closed issue, a '*chose jugée*', scepticism within the government had accompanied the policy from the outset. As early as March 1920, when Palestine was still under Foreign Office control, a minute by Hubert Young demonstrated that the possibility of 'abandoning' the government's pro-Zionist policy was a recurring theme in official circles.[55] Domestic opposition to Britain's policy in Palestine focused on two main themes: its tax implications, and the promises made by Britain (as represented by Sir Henry McMahon) to the Arabs (as represented by Sharif Hussein of Mecca) in the famed 1915 correspondence. These promises were argued to be in direct contradiction to the Balfour pledge made two years later.

It was the potential tax burden that was the earlier focus of public scrutiny, being taken up by the press within months of the July 1920 establishment of the civil administration in Palestine. On 5 February 1921, for example, the *Daily Express* wrote that the terms of the mandate made clear the extent of the financial burden at a time when the British people were already 'crushed by taxation, oppressed by restricted trade and widespread unemployment', and that there was no reason why Britain should squander resources in the 'arid wastes of the Middle East'.[56] Despite the March 1921 conference convened by Churchill in Cairo which aimed to reduce imperial expenditure in the Middle East,[57] the press continued on this theme. The *Times*, which initially had supported the Balfour Declaration, by 1922 was raising the question of whether Britain could afford to implement it.[58] Lord Northcliffe, the proprietor of the *Times* and the *Daily Mail*, visiting Palestine in early 1922, observed that Palestine Zionists 'seemed inclined altogether to overestimate the amount of interest taken by the British public in Zionism'.[59]

Lord Milner, Churchill's predecessor in the Colonial Office, and one of the strong advocates of the Balfour Declaration in 1917, gave a Palestinian Arab delegation which had met him in April 1922 confidential assurances to the effect that the national home policy was no more than an experiment:

if practical experience will show it to be impossible, there will be no escape from altering the policy. I consider the entry of Jews into Palestine an experiment, and if they do not succeed and failure follows I shall recognize that a mistake has been made.[60]

With domestic opposition to the government's involvement in Palestine increasing, Churchill telegraphed to Samuel on 25 February 1922 requesting a cut in the expenditure on the new Palestine gendarmerie and noting:

In both Houses of Parliament there is growing movement of hostility, against Zionist policy in Palestine, which will be stimulated by recent Northcliffe articles. I do not attach undue importance to this movement, but it is increasingly difficult to meet the argument that it is unfair to ask the British taxpayer, already overwhelmed with taxation, to bear the cost of imposing on Palestine an unpopular policy.[61]

In an effort to quell opposition to the pro-Zionist policy both in Palestine and at home, and in preparation for the vote on the mandate by the League of Nations scheduled for July, Churchill issued the White Paper of 3 June 1922, written by Samuel in collaboration with Shuckburgh. The White Paper, even while stating that the Jews were in Palestine 'as of right and not on sufferance' placed limits on the definition of the Jewish national home and stated that the British government did not contemplate the 'disappearance or subordination' of the Arab population.

Neither the Arabs nor their supporters in England were mollified, and less than three weeks later, on 21 June, a motion was introduced in the House of Lords rejecting a Mandate for Palestine that incorporated the Balfour Declaration. Lord Islington argued that a mandate based on the Balfour Declaration directly violated the pledges made by the British in 1915 to Sharif Hussein as well as those made by General Allenby in his Declaration to the Palestinian People in 1918. Noting that the great majority of the inhabitants was opposed to the Balfour Declaration, he urged that acceptance by the League of Nations be postponed until modifications complying with those pledges were made.[62] The motion carried by a vote of 60 to 25, causing Young to minute on 23 June:

> Yesterday's debate in the House of Lords will have encouraged the Arab Delegation to persist in their obstinate attitude, and unless the Lords' resolution is signally over-ruled by the House of Commons and the Council of the League of Nations, we must be prepared for trouble when the Delegation gets back to Palestine.[63]

In the event, the Lords' resolution was 'signally overruled'. Although opposition in the House of Commons had been mounting, and a number of passionate speeches against the pro-Zionist policy were made during its debate on 4 July, Churchill managed to carry the day by convincing the members of parliament that he had cut the cost of maintaining Palestine from £8 million in 1920 to an estimated £2 million in 1922.[64] With the Commons voting in favour of the policy, the way was open for the League of Nations formally to ratify Britain's Mandate for Palestine on 24 July. This ratification marked the beginning of a new chapter in British policy in Palestine and gave Britain the necessary 'legal' authority to carry out the national home policy. One scholar rightly asserts that, prior to that date, although committed to a pro-Zionist policy, the British government could have easily abandoned it.[65] The granting of the Palestine mandate to Great Britain was one of Weizmann's 'crowning political achievements'. It was the first international recognition of the World Zionist Organization as the 'legitimate representative' of the Jewish people. Moreover, by incorporating the Balfour Declaration in the writ of the mandate, immediate practical and political meaning was given to what was in 1917 'no more than a letter of intent'.[66]

The ratification of the mandate came at a critical moment for the Zionists. Only three months later, in October 1922, Lloyd George's pro-Zionist government resigned and a new government headed by Bonar Law was installed, following the

Conservatives' overwhelming electoral victory in November. The change of government meant that not only Lloyd George, but also Balfour and Churchill, 'the two fathers' of the Balfour Declaration, were out of office. Balfour and Lloyd George in particular had remained staunch supporters of the Zionist project. Three months before, on 22 July 1922, Lord Balfour had convened a small conference in his house at Weizmann's request, at which the Zionist leader strongly attacked Samuel's speech one year earlier (on 3 June 1921) as an abrogation of the Balfour Declaration. Present at this meeting were Churchill, Lloyd George, Maurice Hankey and Edward Russell of the Colonial Office. In response to Samuel's explanation of the Jewish national home in his speech, Balfour and Lloyd George stated that 'by the Declaration they always meant an eventual Jewish State'.[67] Then they discussed Samuel's proposal for representative government in Palestine, and Lloyd George told Churchill that 'we' must not allow such a thing as representative government to happen in Palestine. Lloyd George also advised Weizmann to set aside some money for the purpose of bribing the Arabs.[68]

The League's ratification of the mandate did not close the debate on Palestine. In fact challenges to the government's position intensified. With a new prime minister who was not sympathetic to the Zionists, it appeared to the Arabs and their English supporters, headed by Lord Sydenham and Lord Islington, that new prospects had been opened for a change in government policy in favour of the Arabs.[69] After the frustration of their efforts to address the Lausanne Conference and to persuade Turkish delegates to support their cause, a second Arab Delegation, acting upon advice from its English supporters, proceeded to London, arriving there on 24 December 1922. In the same month, Herbert Samuel, increasingly desperate to find a way to resolve the policy impasse and ease political tensions in Palestine, revived his old proposal for a confederation of Arab states, first mooted in a report on the political situation submitted to Curzon in March 1920, before he became high commissioner in Palestine. He hoped that when the second Arab Delegation returned from Lausanne, 'presumably' as he put it, 'empty-handed', the revival of this idea would be of much assistance and the general situation might show a great improvement before the question of Palestine was debated in the new parliament.[70] He informed the new colonial secretary, the Duke of Devonshire, that while the Statement of June 1922 (the White Paper), had done much to clear the air, a settlement had not been obtained. And even on the Jewish side, the Jews felt 'insecure' about their future. Samuel felt that he could not go much further, 'if at all, along that road, without depriving the Balfour Declaration of its substance and the policy of aiding the Jews of all its value'.[71]

He argued that the idea of the confederation was a modified form of the plan of Sir Mark Sykes—then adviser to the Foreign Office on Near Eastern affairs—for dealing with the Arab question. He therefore wrote:

If there is a possibility that the present non-cooperation movement may be abandoned, there is no assurance that it will be abandoned. If there is little indication of any serious disturbance in the near future, the inflammable material is still there and the danger always exists.[72]

The nucleus of the proposed confederation would consist of the Hijaz, Palestine and Transjordan. The French would be consulted *ab initio* and invited to effect the 'adhesion of Syria'. The constitutional organs of the confederation would be a council with a president, the council to consist of delegates appointed by the adhering governments, and the president to be the King of the Hijaz. Among the functions of the confederation would be the control of communication lines, the Hijaz railway, customs, extradition, and matters relating to Arab culture and the Muslim religion.[73] Samuel advocated this line of policy because he knew that the Palestine Arabs complained that it was as a result of Zionism that Palestine was separated from Syria and the other surrounding states; the drawing of new boundaries by the colonial powers had created many economic hardships for the inhabitants of this area to which they had been unaccustomed under the Ottomans.[74]

But how seriously did Samuel take this confederation of Arab states? Obviously not too seriously, for it is clear that a nominal body was all that he had in mind. He wrote to Devonshire:

> More important, however, than any specific functions of the Council would be the fact of its existence. That in itself would be a satisfaction to Arab national aspirations ... The Confederation would be a visible embodiment of Arab unity, and a centre round which the movement for an Arab revival—which is a very real thing— could rally; it would give leadership and direction to that movement, especially on its cultural side.[75]

More significantly, how did the Jewish national home fit into Samuel's plan for a confederation of Arab states? He explained that an 'essential' part of the plan was that the policy in relation to Jews in Palestine 'should stand', and that the Arabs of Palestine 'should co-operate in the local legislature and in the federal Council on that understanding'. Given that condition, Samuel was confident that the Zionist movement would 'cordially' welcome the plan. As to the attitude of the Arabs of Palestine, Samuel expressed the belief that they would likely welcome the whole plan, 'except the continuance of Zionist developments' but that 'under pressure, and in the absence of any alternative ... also they, or the majority among them, might acquiesce'.[76]

Although he agreed that a change of policy was needed, Shuckburgh at the Middle East Department expressed the opinion that the Balfour Declaration 'cannot be further whittled down without risk of its final disappearance'. He did not approve Samuel's proposed plan for a confederation of Arab states and raised once again the subject of the McMahon promises to Sharif Hussein in 1915, emphasizing that it was never intended to promote 'a single Arab kingdom or federation in the whole area to be liberated from the Turks'. The other objection to the plan, according to Shuckburgh, had to do with Ibn Sa'ud, who would 'definitely' refuse to join any federation with his hated rivals, the Sherifians. Moreover, so far as Palestine itself was concerned, the plan would not go to the root of the difficulties. Shuckburgh observed that:

> What the Palestinian Arabs object to is our Zionist policy. As against Zionism they are prepared to accept allies from any quarter. But they have no real sympathy with their fellow Arabs to the East and to the South. The majority of them, at any rate in the large towns and on the Mediterranean coast, are not Arabs at all … Sir Herbert Samuel proposes to offer them, not what they want, viz. the elimination of Zionism, but merely an opportunity of periodical consultation with people whose manner and outlook differ almost entirely from their own. They could scarcely refuse an offer made in the name of Arab unity; but they would not thank us for it, and would merely make use of the new machinery (whatever undertakings we might extract from them) as a medium for further agitation against our Zionist policy.[77]

QUESTIONING THE BALFOUR DECLARATION

Britain's policy on Palestine had therefore never seemed less firm than during the first half of 1923, when the government appeared preoccupied with delving into its very foundations. In a debate in the House of Lords on 27 March 1923, Lord Islington remarked that 'Zionist policy in Palestine contributed its share, and no small share, I think, to the downfall of the late Administration. It assisted correspondingly in the accession to power of the present Administration.' Noting that there are 'many gentlemen today occupying quite prominent positions in His Majesty's Government who were last year and the year before among the most active and vehement assailants of Zionist policy in Palestine', he concluded that this 'would constitute a strong ground for early consideration of the whole policy … .'[78]

Indeed, such consideration was already under way, and something of the climate that followed the formation of the new government is conveyed in a lengthy secret memorandum entitled 'Policy in Palestine' submitted to the Cabinet on 17 February 1923, which declared:

> If there is to be a change of policy, the sooner it is announced the better. The present state of suspense is fair to nobody. It is not fair to allow the Jews to go on collecting money for their projects in Palestine if there is any question of non-fulfilment of the pledge on which these projects are based. It is not fair to the Arabs, if we mean to maintain our policy, to allow them to continue an agitation which may develop into action for which they will suffer in the long run … .[79]

From the first days of the new government, however, the Middle East Department, and particularly Shuckburgh, directed a steady stream of memoranda at the new colonial secretary, the Duke of Devonshire, who, unlike his predecessor Churchill, lacked firm convictions on the subject of Palestine. Two messages in particular were driven home repeatedly: that if Britain failed to honour its pledge 'We certainly should stand convicted of an act of perfidy from which it is hardly too much to say that our good name would never recover', and that the 'real alternative' facing the government was between 'complete evacuation or continuing to honour the Zionist pledge'.[80] The influence of such memoranda on Devonshire was considerable.[81]

In December 1922, for example, a memorandum by Shuckburgh argued that since the Balfour Declaration had already been integrated in the draft mandate, the British government was 'in fact committed to the policy in the clearest and most unequivocal fashion'. The head of the Middle East Department also pointed out that under the terms of the draft mandate, the Zionist Organization was in fact accorded a special position, and was recognized as a public body for the purpose of advising and cooperating with the administration in such economic, social and other matters as might affect the establishment of the Jewish national home. The Zionist Organization was an international Jewish body, 'with Dr. Weizmann as its presiding genius', and it was 'the best representative of the Jewish national movement as a whole'. The policy of the Balfour Declaration had been accepted by the principal Allied Powers at the San Remo Conference in 1920, it was embodied 'verbatim' in the Treaty of Sèvres in August 1920, and in the draft Mandate for Palestine submitted to the League of Nations in December 1920, and approved 'with some modification' by the League in July 1922.[82]

Shuckburgh insisted that if Britain were to abandon her pro-Zionist policy, it would mean abandoning the mandate itself. Such a step, in his view, would result in the Turks returning to Palestine following Mustafa Kemal's victories in the autumn of 1922. It was, moreover, a question of 'honour'.[83] Yet, if this memorandum reveals anything, it is the weakness of the argument provided by the Middle East Department. As Porath points out, 'had Britain actually decided to change its policy on Zionism and therefore made changes in the writ of the Mandate, it is highly doubtful if the League would in the end have opposed this'. Furthermore, with Britain's ally, France, in physical occupation of Syria, it was difficult to see how the Turks could have returned to Palestine.[84]

In the face of increasing hostility within the British government towards a pro-Zionist policy, Shuckburgh had felt compelled to come up with some 'new' interpretations of the Balfour Declaration and the McMahon pledges. Not long after the new government took office, anticipating fresh inquiries, he took it upon himself to look into the origins of the Balfour Declaration. The inquiry was remarkable for its revelation of the dearth of official documents on the subject. In

December 1922, five years after the publication of the Balfour Declaration, Shuckburgh maintained that the official documents on the origins of the declaration could not be found. Although he combed the records, he found nothing that shed light on the earlier history of the negotiations leading up to the Balfour Declaration. Balfour himself, pressed by Shuckburgh, pleaded a bad memory and regretted the death of Sir Mark Sykes, who 'had the whole thing at his finger ends'.[85]

Shuckburgh discovered that the correspondence prior to the declaration was not available in the Colonial Office, 'although Foreign Office papers were understood to have been lengthy and to have covered a considerable period'.[86] The 'most comprehensive explanation' of the origin of the Balfour Declaration the Foreign Office was able to provide was contained in a small 'unofficial' note affirming that

> little is known of how the policy represented by the Declaration was first given form. Four, or perhaps five men were chiefly concerned in the labour—the Earl of Balfour, the late Sir Mark Sykes, and Messrs. Weizmann and Sokolow, with perhaps Lord Rothschild as a figure in the background. Negotiations seem to have been mainly oral and by means of private notes and memoranda of which only the scantiest records are available, even if more exists.[87]

Shuckburgh then turned for help to William Ormsby-Gore, under-secretary of state for the colonies, who was closely involved with the discussions leading up to the declaration.[88] He wrote his own recollection of the events, which he had witnessed, in a one-page memorandum quoted here in full:

> The matter was first broached by the late Sir Mark Sykes early in 1916, and he interviewed Dr. Gaster and Sir Herbert Samuel on his own initiative as a student of Jewish politics in the Near East. Dr. Weizmann was then unknown. Sykes was furthered by General MacDunagh [sic], DMI [Director of Military Intelligence] as all the most useful and helpful intelligence from Palestine (then still occupied by the Turks) was got through and given with zeal by Zionist Jews who were from the first pro-British. Sir Ronald Graham took the matter up keenly from the Russian and East European point of view and early in 1917 important representations came from America. The form of the Declaration and the policy was debated more than once by the War Cabinet, and confidential correspondence (printed by Sir Maurice Hankey[89] as a Cabinet paper) was entered into with leading Jews of different schools of thought. After the Declaration, the utmost use was made of it by Lord Northcliffe's propaganda department, and the value of the declaration received remarkable tribute from General Ludendorf. On the strength of it we recruited special battalions of foreign Jews in New York for the British army with the leave of the American government. The Balfour Declaration in its final form was actually drafted by Col. Amery and myself. I wrote an article on the question in XIXth Century about 2 years ago which has some interesting data.[90]

Shuckburgh expressed surprise at the revelation made by Ormsby-Gore, added in the last paragraph of his memo in his own hand, that it was he (Ormsby-Gore) who, together with Colonel L. S. Amery,[91] had actually drafted the Balfour Declaration in its final form.

Given the paucity of documentation, Shuckburgh was able to develop his own interpretation (certainly influenced by Ormsby-Gore) in his 10 January 1923 memorandum 'History of the Negotiations leading up to the Balfour Declaration'. This emphasized the dire military straits in which Britain found itself at the time the declaration was drafted and its debt to the Zionists for their help in this time of need.[92] He conceded in a minute to Ormsby-Gore, written on the same day, that this memorandum was 'very inadequate', because the 'material available has not been sufficient to enable me to compile a complete and connected narrative'. He described it as 'a humble experiment in the art of making bricks without straw'.[93] The colonial secretary, Lord Devonshire, had Shuckburgh's 10 January memorandum printed as a Cabinet paper and distributed to the Cabinet along with a handwritten note declaring that the time had come when the attention of the Cabinet 'should be directed to this aspect of the Palestine question.'[94]

In February 1923, Devonshire presented to the Cabinet a memorandum embodying a review conducted by the Middle East Department of the previous government's Palestine policy. It concluded that the government was 'in fact, committed to the Zionist policy before the whole world in the clearest and most unequivocal fashion'. The memorandum rejected the charge that the McMahon pledge had been violated, or that an injustice had been imposed on the great majority of the people in Palestine. It argued that a Jewish state had been 'definitely ruled out', and that the Zionists had 'implicitly acquiesced in its elimination', concluding that Palestinian fears, while genuine, were largely the result of a 'misunderstanding of the real aims and intentions of the Government'.[95]

Devonshire's note accompanying the Middle East Department's report on policy urged that 'a definite statement' on Britain's policy be made with 'as little delay as possible'. The colonial secretary asked three questions:

> 1. Is there anything in the British Government's pledges to the Arabs that precludes effect being given to the Balfour Declaration in favour of setting up a National Home for the Jews in Palestine? 2. If the answer is in the negative, are we to continue the policy of the late Government in giving effect to the Balfour Declaration on the lines laid down in the White Paper of June 1922? 3. If not, what alternative policy are we to adopt?[96]

The answers to these questions involved further delving into questions on which the Middle East Department would have preferred to keep silent: the McMahon pledge to Sharif Hussein in 1915, and the Allenby Proclamation of 1918 (known also as the Anglo-French Declaration of November 1918).

By the beginning of 1923, the long-simmering controversy over the McMahon pledges had become a matter of public debate. Apart from the argument that Palestine was a burden on the taxpayer, British journalists and members of parliament expressed reservations about Britain's involvement in Palestine from a moral point of view, arguing that the Balfour Declaration was in flagrant violation of previous promises and pledges given to the Arabs in 1915.

The arrival in London in December 1922 of a second Arab Delegation from Palestine bought the issue of Britain's wartime pledges to the Arabs back to centre stage. The delegates met representatives of the *Morning Post*, the *Daily Mail*, and the *Times* and gave them copies of the Hussein-McMahon correspondence. In January 1923, J. M. N. Jeffries, the *Daily Mail* correspondent, published a series of articles under the heading 'The Palestine Deception', quoting parts of the Hussein–McMahon correspondence, which called for a British withdrawal from Palestine and the abrogation of the Balfour Declaration.[97]

The Middle East Department wrestled with this issue from 1921 until mid-1924. The crux of the controversy over the correspondence was whether or not Palestine was to be included in the areas which Britain had promised the Arabs would become independent after the war. McMahon's letter of 24 October 1915 had explicitly excluded 'portions of Syria, lying to the west of Damascus, Homs, Hama and Aleppo'. The Arabs and their supporters argued that Palestine lies well south of these areas, which according to them, had been excluded because of French interests there.

In October 1921, Eric Forbes-Adam, a diplomat who had been a member of the British delegation to the 1919 Paris Peace Conference and the 1920 San Remo Conference, had written privately to Shuckburgh that there were two principal interpretations of the McMahon letter's wording. Arnold Toynbee, in a Paris Peace Conference memorandum, had included Palestine 'in the area of Arab independence'. On the other hand, Hubert Young's 1920 memorandum on 'Negotiations with the Hedjaz', took the opposite view, 'which has been hitherto adopted by the Middle East Department'. Forbes-Adam continued:

> On the wording of the letter alone, I think either interpretation is possible, but I personally think the context of that particular McMahon letter shows that McMahon (a) was not thinking in terms of vilayet boundaries etc., and (b) meant, as Hogarth says merely to refer to the Syrian area where French interests were likely to be predominant and this did not come south of the Lebanon. ... Toynbee, who went into the papers, was quite sure his interpretation of the letter was right and I think his view was more or less accepted until Young wrote his memorandum.[98]

Shuckburgh also wrote privately to David Hogarth, formerly director of the

Arab Bureau (1916–18), orientalist and keeper of the Ashmolean Museum. In January 1918, Hogarth had visited the Hijaz and personally delivered a message to Hussein in which the policy of the British government on the Palestinian Holy Places and Zionist colonization was stated in the following terms:

> That so far as Palestine is concerned, we are determined that no people shall be subjected to another, but in view of the fact ... That since the Jewish opinion of the world is in favour of a return of Jews to Palestine, and inasmuch as this opinion must remain a constant factor, and further, as His Majesty's Government view with favour the realisation of this aspiration, His Majesty's Government are determined that in so far as is compatible with the freedom of the existing population, both economic and political, no obstacle should be put in the way of the realisation of this ideal.[99]

This became known as the Hogarth message of 1918, and is notable for its reference to the need to take account of the 'political and economic freedoms' of the existing population of Palestine, a formulation which was not included either in the Balfour Declaration or the mandate, which refer only to the 'civil and religious' rights of non-Jewish communities.

Commander Hogarth reported Hussein's response:

> The King would not accept an independent Jewish State in Palestine, nor was I instructed to warn him that such a state was contemplated by Great Britain. He probably knows nothing of the actual or possible economy of Palestine, and his ready assent to Jewish settlement there is not worth very much. But I think he appreciates the financial advantage of Arab co-operation with the Jews.[100]

The 1919 War Cabinet memorandum, in which this exchange was printed, also asserted that

> a general pledge was given to Husein [sic] in October, 1915, that Great Britain was prepared (with certain exceptions) to recognise and support the independence of the Arabs with the territories included in the limits and boundaries proposed by the Sherif of Mecca; and Palestine was within those territories.[101]

Shuckburgh, however, queried Hogarth's suggestion in a talk delivered in 1921, 'that Palestine was part of the area in respect to which we undertook to recognise the independence of the Arabs'.[102] In Shuckburgh's view, 'we made many rash promises in the agony of the war', but Palestine was definitely excluded from McMahon's pledge, and Hussein 'perfectly well understood at the time' that Palestine was excluded.[103] Hogarth replied on 17 October 1921 that the 'independence of the Arabs' as applied to the Palestinians 'is not really consistent with a Jewish National Home, as the Zionists understand this! But I suppose it is consistent with "Palestinian citizenship" in independence of the Turks'. He also believed that the pledge was not intended to apply to 'anything south of Lebanon'. In 1915, Palestine was a thorny question which, in his understanding, was 'slurred over *silentio*'. However, he pointed out that the Palestinians were presently basing their claims against the terms of the Balfour Declaration on their status as a majority in Palestine, not on the McMahon pledges.[104]

Unsuccessful in its efforts to demonstrate definitively that Palestine was *not* covered by the McMahon pledge, the Middle East Department concentrated on trying to keep the issue from public scrutiny. Thus, five days after a 6 January 1922 minute by S. M. Campbell, assistant principal of the Colonial Office, stating categorically (citing a Foreign Office memorandum) that 'geographically Palestine is included in the area within which Britain was to acknowledge Arab independence',[105] Shuckburgh minuted that though 'the view taken in this Office has been that Palestine was so excluded ... there is sufficient doubt in the matter to make it desirable not to drag the controversy out into the daylight'.[106]

Shuckburgh responded similarly when Samuel, having heard that he had sought and obtained an explanation of the matter from Sir Henry McMahon himself,[107] pressed the Middle East Department in a letter of 6 August 1922 to publish the explanation so that the Arabs would accept once and for all the *fait accompli* that Palestine was excluded from the pledge. Samuel's request, coming two months after the White Paper had addressed the McMahon pledges at some length shows how inadequate the latter's explanation had been. The White Paper had launched its own new interpretation of the McMahon correspondence, asserting that:

> it is not the case, as has been represented by the Arab Delegation, that during the war His Majesty's Government gave an undertaking that an independent national government should be at once established in Palestine. This representation mainly rests upon a letter dated 24th October, 1915, from Sir Henry McMahon, then His Majesty's high commissioner in Egypt, to the Sherif of Mecca, now King Hussein of the Kingdom of the Hejaz. That letter is quoted as conveying the promise to the Sherif of Mecca to recognise and support the independence of the Arabs within the territories proposed by him. But this promise was given subject to a reservation made in the same letter, which excluded from its scope, among other territories, the portions of Syria lying to the west of the District of Damascus. This reservation has always been regarded by His Majesty's Government as covering the vilayet of Beirut and the independent Sanjak of Jerusalem. The whole of Palestine west of the Jordan was thus excluded from Sir H. McMahon's pledge.[108]

It had been hoped that this statement, while firmly reasserting the government's adherence to the Balfour Declaration, would, by its definition of the national home, remove strong Arab opposition to it. However, the Arab response suggested that this interpretation had not been accepted. For example, on 7 July 1922, the Muslim-Christian Association of Nablus submitted a long memorandum to the high commissioner containing its observations on the White Paper in which it clearly rejected the British government's view of the McMahon pledges. It opened its arguments by rejecting the Balfour Declaration as

> illegal and based on no right whatever as it contradicts both the promises given in 1915 by the British Government to His Majesty the King of Hijaz and the desires of the Arabs who form the great majority of the population. These desires have since the Armistice been submitted to the British Government, to other Governments and to the official International bodies.

The Muslim-Christian Association also pointed out that although the British government had stated that it did not aim at making Palestine Jewish, nor at the disappearance of Arab population and culture, this would be the inevitable result of the 'void' policy of the Jewish national home.[109] (See Appendix C)

In his belated reply to Samuel dated 7 November 1922, Shuckburgh, who in the meantime had received critical comments on McMahon's explanation,[110] stated that he was 'rather against making any further public announcements on this troublesome question', which he had always felt to be 'one of the weakest joints in our armour'. Shuckburgh therefore advised against publishing the letter, explaining that the Middle East Department used the argument that Damascus in the pledge of 1915 meant the 'Turkish Vilayet of Damascus'.[111] He referred to Churchill's reply to Ormsby-Gore's question in parliament on 11 July 1922, noting that:

> The wording of that reply was drawn up with the most meticulous care and represents, I think, the best that can be said on the subject. I doubt whether anything is to be gained by further publication, and indeed it seems to me that our best policy is to let sleeping dogs lie as much as possible.[112]

Samuel was convinced. In answering Shuckburgh's letter, he agreed that it would be 'undesirable at the present stage to reopen the controversy about the McMahon pledge by publishing Sir Henry's letter'.[113]

The publication in the British press in early 1923 of parts of the Hussein-McMahon correspondence, provided by the second Arab Delegation, revived precisely the kind of public scrutiny the Middle East Department had tried so assiduously to avoid. Soon afterwards, Lord Sydenham proposed a parliamentary question in the House of Lords asking the government to lay on the table the entire correspondence on which the previous government had based its contention that Palestine was geographically excluded from the pledges, prompting a flurry of memoranda in the Middle East Department. R. C. Lindsay, under-secretary of the Foreign Office, replied to Shuckburgh on 19 February 1923 that 'we should not be likely to strengthen our case by publishing the McMahon letters'.[114] On 21 February, Sydney Moody, a senior Colonial Office official, minuted that the reasons for not publishing the correspondence 'remain good'.[115] On 28 February,

Shuckburgh received a letter quoting Lord Curzon's view that 'if you quote from a document in a statement in the House, you may be called upon to lay on the table of the House the papers from which the quotation is taken. In those circumstances, you will probably wish to revise the draft [illegible] in such a way as to avoid this danger.'[116]

The debate in the House of Lords took place on 1 March 1923. Lord Sydenham requested publication of the correspondence on the grounds that the public had the right to know 'exactly how our national obligations stand' with regard to the Arabs. In an exceptionally cogent summation of the topic, he rehearsed in detail—and with long verbatim quotes from the version of the correspondence that had been made available—the entire history of the McMahon pledges and those that followed. He gave a meticulous and scathing deconstruction of the theory 'invented' in the White Paper to explain Palestine's alleged exclusion from McMahon's pledge.

Lord Devonshire, who as colonial secretary was present at the debate, was too shrewd to address directly the arguments raised but confined himself to reaffirming in broad terms his acceptance of the White Paper's explanation. Following the advice of the Middle East Department, he deftly avoided making available ('much as I regret it') any of the correspondence on the grounds that passages not relating to the controversy could be 'detrimental to the public interest'. When asked whether only those passages relating to the correspondence could be published, he cited parliamentary custom against partial publications.[117] As to Lord Sydenham's request that Devonshire at least comment on the authenticity of the numerous passages cited in the course of the debate, Lord Devonshire quite simply ignored it.

In April 1923, a private conversation suggested that Shuckburgh did have his doubts about British policy on Palestine. He told Sydney Moody in confidence that he could see 'no end, no solution to the problem', and 'no hope of solving it or improving the situation':

> We had made promises to the Arabs in the McMahon Correspondence and these conflicted or appeared to conflict with the Balfour Declaration. But this was a technical point. The Balfour Declaration did in fact conflict with our whole attitude towards the Arabs and anyhow with what ought to be the attitude of a great modern European Power towards a conquered country like Palestine ... could we, ought we, to force on the Arab population of Palestine a mass of alien immigrants mostly Russian and Polish?'[118]

Shuckburgh went on to say that the McMahon promises were made during Asquith's government in 'the stress and strain' of war, and nobody in the Cabinet thought 'we should have to meet these promises'. They could not foresee all those developments, and when the Balfour promise was made, 'we had not set foot in Palestine'. He quoted a suggestion made by Dr Eder of the Zionist Commission, who had said: 'why don't you bang our heads together and make us agree?' Shuckburgh told Moody:

> We should say to the Arabs and the Jews, 'look here, we have made certain promises to both of you. We have promised the Jews a National Home in Palestine. We have promised the Arabs national independence. Now you must agree together. We will give you independence provided you agree on a basis of settlement about the National Home.[119]

In fact, no further serious debate on the McMahon pledges took place. When a Labour government came to power in early 1924, the colonial secretary, J. H. Thomas, acting on the Middle East Department's advice, circulated a secret Cabinet memorandum entitled 'Palestine' in which he noted that it had 'frequently been alleged that the Balfour Declaration was inconsistent with previous pledges given to the Arabs during the war'. However, he added that Sir Henry McMahon was 'personally' consulted in March 1922 and 'stated definitely' that his intention had been 'to exclude Palestine' from the area of Arab independence. He continued:

> Whether the actual language to the pledge, if interpreted as a court of law would interpret it, can be held to have given effect to this intention, is more doubtful. The natural meaning of the phrase 'west of the district of Damascus', has to be strained in order to cover an area lying considerably to the south as well as to the west of Damascus city ... I think it is important that we should come to a decision on the question of policy at the earliest possible date. The situation in Palestine is now calm, but uncertainty is always dangerous, and if the announcement of our policy is delayed there may be a revival of agitation. My own view is that we have no alternative but to adhere to the policy carrying out the terms of the Balfour Declaration as interpreted by our predecessors. I do not underrate the difficulties, but I am satisfied that the difficulties of any alternative course could be even greater.[120]

THE MCMAHON PLEDGES AND THE ANGLO-HIJAZ TREATY

The question of Britain's wartime pledges took on a wider significance in the Arab world when negotiations were initiated in 1923 for a treaty of friendship between Britain and King Hussein, whose correspondence with McMahon in 1915 was the subject of the controversy and who had been recognized by the British since 1916 as the independent ruler of the Hijaz. Hubert Young minuted on 21 February 1923 that 'the best counterblast to arguments based on the McMahon correspondence would be the signature and publication of a Treaty with King Hussein in which he accepts our position in Palestine'.[121]

However, difficulties arose over Article 2 of the draft treaty which required Hussein to recognize Britain's special position in Palestine, including, by implication, the Balfour Declaration and hence Zionist claims in Palestine.[122] Shuckburgh minuted on 23 March 1923 that the insertion of this article in the proposed Anglo-Hijaz treaty would oblige Hussein 'specifically to recognise our "National Home" policy in Palestine'. He reported that his discussion with Naji Asil, Hussein's representative, had resulted in an amended formula, which omitted specific mention of Zionism and contained a reference to 'eventual confederation' of the Arabs (with Transjordan and Iraq). The whole question had been 'very carefully considered' by the Middle East Department and the Foreign Office, though he was 'fully aware that, in hinting at 'eventual confederation' we are treading on very doubtful grounds'. He went on:

> On the other hand, it seems clearly to our advantage that a treaty of friendship should be concluded with Hussein; and if such a treaty is to be concluded, there are obvious objections to omitting all reference to our war-time pledges and our position in the mandated areas. The omission would certainly arouse comment and we should be told that we were afraid to face the issue with the man to whom our pledges were made.[123]

A draft of the treaty had been initialled in London in April 1923, but by January 1924, when King Hussein was to visit Palestine and Transjordan, the difficulties over Article 2 had not been resolved. The king reportedly told pilgrims in Mecca of his proposed amendments to the treaty:

> … amendments by means of which the Palestinians would have complete independence and the right to choose their own form of Government. King Husain would require His Excellency the High Commissioner for Palestine to make a declaration to this effect, and assured the Arab people that their leaders would be consulted as to the form of Government in case of acceptance of his proposals and as to the action to be taken in the case of rejection.[124]

In Amman, Hussein told a Palestinian delegation of his 'firm wish to continue his endeavours for the complete independence of the Arab countries amongst which is Palestine'. Negotiations with the British had not ended, and 'he would not conclude any treaty contrary to those pledges or to the nation's aspirations for independence.'[125]

The Middle East Department noted that King Hussein's assent to a formula which implied acceptance of the policy pursued by the British government in the mandated territories would have been an effective answer to those critics who asserted that the 'Zionist' policy in Palestine was a contravention of the promise given to Hussein in 1915. However, it had become clear that this object was unlikely to be achieved. Sir Herbert Samuel requested authorization to resolve the impasse by concluding a treaty with the king which omitted Article 2 but the Middle East Department objected to negotiations being conducted in Amman through the high commissioner for Palestine.[126] Acting on the Middle East Department's advice, the colonial secretary circulated a secret Cabinet memorandum entitled 'Palestine' on 19 February 1924 advising that Samuel should be told that His Majesty's Government did not think it desirable that negotiations should continue in Amman, but that they were willing to consider any further proposals which Hussein might make regarding Article 2 of the draft treaty and were prepared to transfer negotiations to Jeddah. The memorandum continued:

> They see clear objection, however, to conclusion through High Commissioner, Palestine, and under conditions which Hussein himself has engineered, of a Treaty in which if Article 2 is to go, Mandated territories will have little direct concern. Its conclusion in such circumstances could not but be construed as signal defeat of policy of Balfour Declaration and direct encouragement to Palestine Arabs to renew their agitation now happily quiescent.[127]

It is therefore apparent that the Palestine issue was the main stumbling block over which the Anglo-Hijaz treaty of friendship with King Hussein foundered. When Palestinian pressure on Hussein intensified, the British negotiators stressed even more strongly that Hussein's recognition of British policy in Palestine was, for them, the raison d'être of the treaty itself. Thus, on the eve of his downfall, when in 1924 Hussein was attacked by Ibn Sa'ud, he found himself virtually without friends.[128]

Ibn Sa'ud had coveted the Hijaz for many years, but his attempts to conquer it were on many occasions only stopped by the British who forbade him to enter Hijaz, even going so far as to bomb the Ikhwan raiders using planes and armoured cars. However, when the summer capital of Ta'if was captured by the Wahhabis on 9 September 1924, no such help was forthcoming to Hussein.[129] On 5 October, King Hussein abdicated in favour of his eldest son, 'Ali, in the hope of saving the situation.[130] However, the war continued, and Jeddah itself was shelled in February 1925. 'Ali had refused a demand for unconditional surrender, still hoping that the British would assist. In London, opinion strongly shifted towards Ibn Sa'ud. Finally, on 22 December, 'Ali surrendered, and sailed to Basra on a British warship. Three weeks later, Ibn Sa'ud, Sultan of Najd, proclaimed himself King of Hijaz.[131]

THE 1923 CABINET COMMITTEE ON PALESTINE

The future of Britain's involvement in Palestine was finally decided by a high-powered Cabinet Committee appointed on 27 June 1923 by the new prime minister, Stanley Baldwin. Chaired by the colonial secretary, Lord Devonshire, the committee included, among others, Lord Curzon of the Foreign Office, the secretaries of state for War, India, and Air, the First Lord of the Admiralty, the president of the Board of Trade, and the secretary of the Treasury.[132] It was charged with advising the government to enable it to make a 'prompt and final decision' on Palestine.

The committee deliberated for one month. During that time, opponents of the policy in the House of Lords continued to agitate. Even in the Commons, a group of 110 Conservative MPs, 'feeling that the matter is one of first class Imperial importance with far-reaching future results', sent a petition to the 'Middle East Cabinet Committee now sitting' urging that the 'definite PLEDGES' given to the Palestine Arabs be fulfilled and that the 'whole population of Palestine with its 93% Arabs, should be consulted, and a form of government agreed upon in harmony with their wishes'. According to the petitioners, 'to impose on an unwilling people ... the Dominating Influence of another race is a violation of natural rights' condemned in the covenant of the League of Nations.[133]

It was during that same period that the third Arab Delegation, encouraged by the appointment of the committee, arrived in London. Even before they made an official request to be heard by the committee, Ormsby-Gore, under-secretary at the Colonial Office and an ardent Zionist, wrote to the colonial secretary on 19 July that 'I deplore most emphatically the idea that the Cabinet Committee should see those people or make any concessions'.[134] Shuckburgh also advised against receiving them, noting that the delegation was 'in no sense an official body and to allow them to appear before a cabinet committee would be giving them too much importance', especially as they represented 'the extremist section of the Palestine Arabs, who constitute a majority perhaps, but certainly not the whole of the Arab population'.[135]

However, Shuckburgh warned that since the Middle East Department was constantly represented in the press as being 'wholly under Zionist influence' and 'accused of all kinds of Machiavellian designs to prevent any but the Zionist view on Palestinian questions reaching the Secretary of State or the Cabinet', care must be taken in refusing to allow the Arabs to see the committee.[136] When Musa Kazim al-Husseini, president of the Arab Delegation, wrote from the Hotel Cecil on 24 July 1923 to the chairman of the Cabinet Committee that the people of Palestine regarded the formation of the committee 'as a step, on the part of the British Government, towards a fair and equitable solution of the Palestine problem', Shuckburgh informed the delegation 'that the committee were not hearing oral evidence and accordingly could not receive them'.[137] In the end, Sir Herbert Samuel, who had arrived from Palestine in late June especially for the proceedings, was the sole outside witness.

The question of Palestine's strategic value to Britain was also revisited during this period. In January 1923, the General Staff of the British Army had given its view that Palestine was of no strategic value in defending the Suez Canal. Doubtless with the aim of countering this view, Shuckburgh had requested the Middle East Department's military adviser, Richard Meinertzhagen, to write a report on Palestine's strategic importance. Not surprisingly, being a staunch Zionist, his report in May 1923 presented detailed arguments as to why its importance was likely to increase.[138] Shuckburgh suggested that this report be submitted to the Committee of Imperial Defence, which should be invited to fix a day for the discussion of the whole question and to determine to what extent, 'quite apart from pledges and commitments of every kind', Palestine was of strategic value to the British Empire. It was decided that the subject should be discussed with Sir Herbert Samuel when he arrived in London.[139] In the event, the Committee of Imperial Defence concluded that Palestine was not as important strategically as once thought. However, the Middle East Department resisted the implications of this conclusion:

> Although the strategical value of Palestine is rated by the Imperial General Staff less highly than it has been placed by some authorities, yet none of us can contemplate with equanimity the installation in Palestine of another power ... we see no way of reversing the policy without throwing up the Mandate.[140]

Meanwhile, the full details of the Cabinet Committee's deliberations were being leaked by Meinertzhagen to Leonard Stein, the secretary of the Zionist Organization, who in turn urged Weizmann, who was in Europe at the time, to return immediately.[141] Weizmann immediately grasped the fact that the government's wavering on the Zionist question could deal a death blow to Zionist aspirations. As soon as he arrived in London, on 24 July 1923, he consulted influential British politicians, including Herbert Samuel.

The following day, he went to see Shuckburgh, who reported in a secret minute to the colonial secretary that the Zionist leader had been 'in a great state of agitation' over what he believed was the Cabinet Committee's intention to propose 'fresh concessions to the Arabs' which in his opinion would 'further whittle down the Balfour Declaration and the privileges of Jews in Palestine'. He told Shuckburgh that 'if this apprehension was fulfilled, it would have the effect of breaking up the Zionist Organization and killing Zionist activity in Palestine'. Shuckburgh remarked that Weizmann 'would feel bound to resign his position and there would be no one who could adequately fill his place'.[142]

On 26 July 1923, Weizmann sent a lengthy letter to the colonial secretary concerning 'certain aspects' of the situation in Palestine, in which he concluded: 'A fresh re-adjustment, and a re-adjustment involving the abandonment of vital principles, would be a shattering blow which might well prove fatal' to Zionism.[143] He further wrote to Balfour on 28 July 1923, referring to an anti-Zionist petition which had been submitted by a number of MPs to the Cabinet, which was 'more serious' than he had thought:

> It is signed by a very great number of MPs (not Peers), and it may certainly make an impression on the Prime Minister. The document is full of the usual Arab propaganda ... I feel that we have reached now a very serious crisis, and once more I can

only turn to you with the hearty request that you may possibly say something to the Prime Minister.

It seems that Samuel finally tipped the scale in favour of the Zionists. Despite the view of the Committee of Imperial Defence that Palestine was of little strategic value to the British Empire, the high commissioner argued that indecision was inadvisable, and insisted that from the point of view of internal security in Palestine, a final decision should be taken. His main line of argument was that a decision to abandon the Jewish national home at a time when the Zionists were at their weakest point, both in Palestine as well as in British politics, might well abort the whole Zionist enterprise.[144]

The Cabinet Committee's final report, entitled 'The Future of Palestine', was submitted on 27 July 1923. It is difficult to guess what impact the interventions of Weizmann, conveyed by Devonshire, may have had on the committee in buttressing the arguments presented by Samuel. At all events, the committee did not opt for a change of policy:

> There are some of our number who think that the Declaration was both unnecessary and unwise, and who hold that our subsequent troubles have sprung in the main from its adoption. But that was nearly six years ago … Further, it has been the basis upon which Zionist co-operation in the development of Palestine has been freely given. Those of us who approved the policy throughout would, of course, speak in much less equivocal terms … Nevertheless, the alternative of a complete reversal of the policy hitherto pursued is one that, whatever the price that might have to be paid for it, we have not dogmatically refused to consider.[145]

Even while noting that 'it is difficult to blame those who argue … that the entire Mandate is built on the fallacy of attempting to reconcile the irreconcilable' (i.e., securing the establishment of a Jewish national home while safeguarding the rights of the country's inhabitants), it concluded along the lines of countless Middle East Department memoranda: that whether the policy had been 'wise or unwise, it is well-nigh impossible for any Government to extricate itself without a substantial sacrifice of consistency and self respect, if not honour'.[146]

Four days later, the committee's recommendations were approved by the Cabinet, effectively ending, if not opposition to the policy based on the Balfour Declaration, at least the prospects of changing it. When the mandate came into force a few months later, in September 1923, the matter was 'settled'.[147] When the Balfour Declaration was issued in 1917, it was not exactly clear what was meant by it, and hence, the 1922–3 official British interpretation of it, emanating from the Middle East Department, was all the more influential in giving a legal status to what had initially been a political document, not a legal one, which could have been revoked by any successive government.

ZIONIST INFLUENCE ON THE BRITISH GOVERNMENT

It will never be known whether the Balfour policy could in fact have been reversed that summer of 1923. The Zionists apparently believed this to be the case. If they were correct, they owed a debt of thanks to the Middle East Department as well as to Dr Weizmann's considerable diplomatic skills. As politicians in Britain had become increasingly cool towards Zionist aspirations during the winter of 1922–3, after the fall of Lloyd George's government, Weizmann had managed to convince British statesmen and politicians that the Balfour Declaration, which many had come to regard as a political mistake, meant much more than was originally intended, and that abandoning the Palestine mandate and the Zionist policy would lead to a severe loss of prestige and ethical stature for the British Empire. Weizmann was able to do this despite the fact that the Committee of Imperial Defence had decided that Palestine was of no strategic importance to the British Empire. Moreover, from the point of view of British interests, it was becoming evident that adopting a pro-Zionist policy would serve no purpose other than overloading the British taxpayer with expenses, at the cost of funds needed at home.

Weizmann's 'moral argument' was vigorously defended by the Middle East Department during the crises of 1922–3. The relationship of confidence that Weizmann had patiently cultivated with John Shuckburgh bore fruit; the head of the Middle East Department secretly informed Weizmann of the reactions of the Arab Delegation in London, and sought the Zionist leader's views on how the Colonial Office should respond to their demands.[148] In January 1924, when the Labour government came to power, the attitude of the Middle East Department towards the Zionists appeared to cool slightly. The chairman of the Zionist Organization, Nahum Sokolow, fearing that a change of policy might follow, wrote to the new colonial secretary, J. H. Thomas, requesting an interview. Shuckburgh's advice to Thomas suggests that he had begun to question the intimate relations between the Zionists and the Middle East Department. Shuckburgh informed Thomas that His Majesty's Government had 'been in close relations with the Zionist Organisation for a good many years past', that the Department was 'in pretty frequent communication with the Organisation, both orally and in writing', and that the 'Zionists (thanks in the main to Dr. Weizmann) have played up well' in the past three years. 'Their failing', he maintained, was that they were 'too apt to overstate their case' and were not always 'too scrupulous in the methods they adopt'. He cautioned that if the secretary of state saw the Zionist delegation, they 'may attempt to rush him into some pronouncement in their favour which they can produce among their adherents', advising that the colonial secretary reply only in general terms. The Zionists, however, assured Shuckburgh that they did not expect any government pronouncement and were merely contemplating a courtesy visit.[149] In Weizmann's absence, and suspecting that the Zionists might have other motives in mind,

Shuckburgh minuted that in the circumstances it would be preferable that no communication be made to the press on the meeting, adding: 'The Zionists are nothing if not pushful, and we have to be constantly on our guard against being pushed too far.'[150]

It is not clear why Shuckburgh began to express more reserved views, but one possible answer, often expressed in his minutes, is that he found it difficult to deal with those who represented Zionism 'in its most violent and impracticable form'.[151] He considered Weizmann a 'moderate', who could be reasoned with, and was therefore preferable to extreme Zionists. He feared that if Weizmann were to resign, he would be obliged to deal with extremist Zionist groups.[152]

Whatever Shuckburgh's reservations, the perception of officials in the Palestine administration who did not favour the Zionists was that the Middle East Department had chosen to ally itself to the Zionist cause. E. T. Richmond, the political secretary to chief secretaries Deedes and Clayton (1920–24), resigned from his post in Palestine in February 1924. In a letter of resignation to Samuel on 13 March 1924 he wrote that he had been led

> gradually and most reluctantly, but definitely to a conviction that the Zionist Commission, the Middle East Department of the Colonial Office and this Administration are dominated and inspired by a spirit which I can only regard as evil, and that this spirit is, through the agencies I have mentioned, acting in a manner that is not merely unwise and impolitic but evil ... .[153]

Sir Gilbert Clayton, chief secretary in Palestine from 1923–5, also had strong reservations about the Middle East Department, which, he wrote to one of his close friends, with its 'mixture of Colonial Office bureaucracy and so-called expert local knowledge ... should never have been allowed to leave the F.O. which alone knows how to use it'. He concluded, 'There is an intangible "something" behind everything, an unseen influence—something [?un] healthy, and certainly not British, which has to be felt to be realized.'[154]

Despite their continuing influence on the Middle East Department, as well as in the Palestine administration, the Zionists continued to demand a still greater say in the affairs of Palestine. On 29 April 1924, the acting chairman of the London political committee of Po'ali Zion wrote to Lord Arnold, the under-secretary of state for the colonies, complaining that the Jewish position in Palestine had been prejudiced by the 'largely anti-Jewish and anti-Zionist attitude of a number of influential British officials in Palestine', and by the 'concessions' made by the British government 'to the ruling Arab classes'.[155] Shuckburgh commented in 1924 that the Middle East Department had always been against becoming involved with Jewish bodies other than the Zionist Organization, and suggested that it was advisable to adhere to this policy: 'We find the Z.O. quite troublesome enough', he wrote, but that there was at any rate 'great advantage in having a single body to deal with. Jewish organisations are numerous and persistent; if we open the door to all of them, I am afraid that the position will rapidly become intolerable'.[156]

Weizmann continued to press for still closer ties with the Middle East Department. In a lengthy letter to the colonial secretary dated 18 July 1924, he wrote that, throughout the past few years, he had been treated with the 'utmost consideration on the part of the Colonial Office and of all the gentlemen' with whom he had dealt, but that nevertheless he would like 'to devise means of ensuring a more intimate co-operation and of placing it on a more regular footing'.[157] Shuckburgh's response indicated that he felt the limits of cooperation had already been reached:

> Dr. Weizmann speaks ... of 'ensuring a more intimate co-operation' with the Colonial Office, and of placing their relations with us 'on a more regular footing'. His language on this point is rather vague, but the suggestion makes me uneasy. I think that our relations with the Zionist Organisation are quite intimate enough, as it is. I constantly see Dr. Weizmann when he is in England, and his Lieutenant, Mr. Stein, is in close touch with the Department. The Middle East Department has been attacked more than once in the Press for its supposed subservience to Zionist influences. ... Apart, however from Press attacks, which perhaps do not matter much, I do feel most strongly than [sic] it is essential for the Colonial Office, and through it the British Government, to maintain an atmosphere of complete impartiality and detachment. We are, of course, bound to carry out the policy approved by three successive Cabinets ... Once we place our relations with the Zionists on what Dr. Weizmann calls 'a regular footing', we shall, to some extent, have prejudiced our position of impartiality, at any rate in the eyes of the world. I hope that the Secretary of State will agree that this question should be left alone.[158]

The Middle East Department was an influential force in policy making on Palestine in the critical period from 1920 to 1923 when successive governments were trying to decide the extent to which the Balfour Declaration had committed Britain to supporting Zionism, and what its implications were for the Arab population of Palestine. The Arab point of view, whether presented through the various Palestinian delegations visiting London, or through British officials in Palestine who were sympathetic to the Arab cause, was often obstructed, and sometimes effectively prevented from reaching high government circles. In contrast, the Zionists, represented by Chaim Weizmann, received a largely sympathetic hearing through their easy access to the Middle East Department. Although the department, and particularly Sir John Shuckburgh, insisted that its position was one of impartiality, the scales were in fact largely tipped in favour of the Zionists to the detriment of the Arabs.

Herbert Samuel's Vision of Zionism

Herbert Samuel proved to be one of the key figures in shaping the future of Palestine from the beginning of the First World War until 1925.[1] As already shown, in the early 1920s he played a crucial role in convincing the wavering British establishment that the Zionist experiment should not be abandoned. This chapter examines the background to his beliefs and his role in developing the Balfour Declaration. How Samuel, as high commissioner in Palestine, translated his understanding of the Balfour Declaration into practice, as well as his understanding of the 'double pledge' contained in that declaration, will be the theme of Part II.

EARLY INTEREST IN ZIONISM

Samuel relates in his memoirs that prior to 1914 he had no special interest in the Zionist movement, attributing his indifference to the fact that the prospects of any 'practical outcome' had then seemed so remote that he had not been willing to take part in it.[2] Between 1905 and 1914, while serving in government, Samuel made little mention of Jewish affairs. He read Disraeli's novel *Tancred*, with its main theme of Zionism and Near Eastern politics, many times. But in 1903, when the Uganda project for Jewish settlement was mooted, he had no part in it, although in a newspaper interview he discussed the possibility of Jewish settlement there in purely practical terms.[3] The position was, however, 'entirely' changed with Turkey's entry into the war. Samuel saw that if the war ended in the defeat of the Turks, the question of the future of the non-Turkish provinces of the Ottoman Empire would be raised. He wrote in his memoirs:

> The break-up of the Turkish Empire, long overdue, was now almost inevitable. The future of Palestine would raise a question of the greatest interest. It became plain at once that Zionism had acquired a new actuality—vivid, urgent ... Events that were unexpected gave me a share in the writing of this chapter.[4]

Samuel quickly realized that the war had put Zionism on the political map and he seized the opportunity.[5] His latest biographer, Bernard Wasserstein, points out that, on a personal level, Zionism 'struck a deep chord' in him, representing a 'perfect synthesis of his Englishness and his Jewishness, his Liberalism and his imperialism, his political practicality and his religious sensibility'.[6] Be that as it may, Samuel's motive for adopting the cause of Zionism seems to have been a deeply felt concern for his Jewish brethren during the wave of anti-Semitism which was spreading in Eastern Europe. Palestine, with its emotional appeal to the Jews, seemed to be the place to solve that problem.[7]

Born in Liverpool in 1870 to a family of middle class Jews of German origin, Samuel belonged to one of the leading English Jewish families, known as the cousinhood,[8] which formed part of the Victorian Jewish elite. His upbringing was a religious one, typical of other Jewish families of a similar background. While in Oxford, Samuel's religious and philosophical convictions underwent a profound change; he went to the extreme length of renouncing his religious beliefs altogether, announcing that he was no longer prepared to adhere to the outward practice of religion.

In 1892, Samuel wrote to his mother[9] that although he would probably never give up the 'comparatively unimportant details' of the observance of kosher and of the Sabbath (for hygienic considerations as he put it), he would nevertheless never be able to attend synagogue. He continued:

> When one has become as thoroughly convinced as I have of the non-interference of God with the working of his own laws and of the absurdity of prayer and the insincerity of a ritual worship it would be the grossest hypocrisy for him to conform to the observances of a religion such as the Jewish and to allow others to think that he is a believer.

Consequently, not being an 'unprincipled' person, or one who would not live up to his convictions, he declared that it was impossible for him 'to continue to profess the Jewish religion'. Alarmed to hear all this, his mother pleaded with him to relent, eventually persuading him to accept a compromise whereby he would not be required to attend synagogue, but would nevertheless remain a member of the Jewish community.[10]

Samuel's philosophical and religious views crystallized over the years, and he eventually wrote nine books and many articles on different philosophical and political subjects. His most popular book, *Belief and Action*, published in 1937, and reprinted in two paperback editions, sold approximately 100,000 copies. In this philosophical work, Samuel tackled the problem of morality from a broadly 'deist' point of view and, although still maintaining a nominal adherence to religion, he advocated the need for some 'unifying universalist religion'.[11]

With this background in mind, it would seem unlikely that Samuel would easily 'revert' to religion, even on a superficial level. Paradoxically, the same Samuel was to emphasize, on religious grounds, the return of the Jews to their Promised Land, focusing on the spiritual and mystical aspect of Jewry. In 1935, in a lecture delivered at the Jewish Historical Society of England he declared that 'the prayers of a scattered people for a return to Zion, repeated for two thousand years every morning and every evening on every Sabbath and on every Holy day, were taking a new significance'.[12]

Although it was at Oxford that Samuel's political and social beliefs took more definite shape, his future political outlook was determined by an earlier experience in the interim between school and university. During his brother's[13] election campaign as Progressive candidate in Whitechapel, Samuel came in touch for the first time with extreme poverty, especially that of the Jewish immigrants living in the East End. Consequently, while in Oxford, he took part in Liberal politics, and continued to be a Liberal until the end of his political career.[14]

From 1894, Herbert Samuel considered himself an imperialist, and he became a member of the British Empire League in 1897. In 1902, he became a Liberal MP, and between 1905 and 1913 his progress up the political ladder was steady, though not too impressive. In June 1909, Samuel entered the Cabinet when Prime Minister Asquith offered him a job as the Chancellor of the Duchy of Lancaster. When the war broke out in November 1914, he had been a Cabinet member for five years, and held the office of president of the Local Government Board (minister of health), one of the departments least concerned with questions relating to the war. This did not, however, prevent him from taking initiatives on the matter of Palestine. Samuel pointed out that the question of Palestine had, for him, an 'additional and special' interest, in addition to strategic considerations and the importance of maintaining a friendly power in the vicinity of the Suez Canal. Being the 'first member of the Jewish community ever to sit in a British Cabinet (Disraeli had left the community in boyhood and never rejoined)', Samuel later said that he 'felt that, in the conditions that had arisen, there lay upon [him] a special obligation'.[15] He also stated that it was 'incumbent' upon him to at least learn about the Zionist movement and what it was doing.[16]

He therefore set about making a study of Zionist aims and achievements up to that point, and learnt everything he could about Palestine.[17] He arrived at the definite conclusion that if the war ended in victory for the Allies, Palestine should be separated from Turkey and that every opportunity should be taken to facilitate the establishment of an autonomous Jewish community there.[18] His new-found convictions led Samuel to contact the Zionist leader, Chaim Weizmann, in December 1914, obtaining the publications of the Zionist Organization and reading them carefully. 'The more I read,' he emphasized, 'the more I was impressed by the spiritual influences that evidently animated the movement.'[19] When Samuel met Weizmann for the first time in December 1914, the Zionist leader preached the acute distress of East European Jewry, explaining the political and moral dilemma of Jewry and the role of Zionism. Weizmann later commented that he was so impressed by Samuel that he could hardly tell him anything new.[20]

A decade later, when Samuel concluded his five-year term in office in the administration of Palestine, he wrote in his concluding report to the colonial secretary, Leopold Amery:

> Among the eight million Jews in Eastern Europe there are numbers of young men and women whose most eager desire is to get to Palestine; their ambition, once in Palestine, is to become producers on the soil ... They are well aware of the history of the Jewish people, of their present position in the world, of the difficulties and dangers that surround them. They do not want to live in ghettos.[21]

SAMUEL'S 1915 CABINET MEMORANDUM

Samuel further developed the Zionist position in a talk with the secretary of state for foreign affairs, Sir Edward Grey, on 9 November 1914, suggesting that 'perhaps there might be an opportunity for the fulfilment of the ancient aspiration of the Jewish people and the restoration there of a Jewish State'.[22] Although, according to Samuel, Grey was quite favourable to the proposal, it seems that he did not envisage the creation of a single political entity in Palestine, considering rather the possibility of establishing a Jewish 'cultural centre'.[23] Asked whether Syria should necessarily go with Palestine, Samuel answered that this had better be avoided because places like Beirut and Damascus, which contained a large non-Jewish population, could not be assimilated.[24] Samuel also advocated Syria's annexation by France, arguing that it would be far better for the 'Jewish State' to have a European power as a neighbour rather than the Turks.

In January 1915, a few weeks after this conversation, Samuel formulated his ideas in a draft memorandum for the Cabinet, advocating the establishment of a Jewish commonwealth under British auspices.[25] He had realized that the proposal for 'an autonomous Jewish State was impracticable', conscious that 'in the conditions that prevailed, five-sixths of the population of Palestine being Arabs, such a solution could not be adopted'. Nevertheless, foremost in his mind were the oppressed Jews of Russia and Eastern Europe. He wrote that the 'hard-pressed' Jews of Russia would have a chance of 'large-scale relief'. Samuel concluded that annexation to the British Empire, together with 'active encouragement of Jewish colonization and cultural development would be the best solution'. This he decided on the grounds of strategic and economic interests for the British Empire, and the moral advantages that Britain could be expected to derive from the support of Jewish sentiments, in addition to the 'ultimate interests, spiritual and material, of the Jewish people themselves'.[26]

Prime Minister Asquith was still not impressed and gave no encouragement to Samuel's proposals. On 28 January 1915, he wrote:

I have just received from Herbert Samuel a memorandum headed 'The Future of Palestine' ... He thinks we might plant in this not very promising territory about three or four million European Jews, and that this would have a good effect on those left behind. It reads almost like a new edition of *Tancred* brought up to date ... it is a curious illustration of Dizzy's [Disraeli's] favourite maxim that 'race is everything' to find this almost lyrical outburst proceeding from the well ordered and methodical brain of H. S.[27]

As Samuel was in the process of formulating his memorandum for the Cabinet, it is evident that he was troubled by the rising wave of anti-Semitism which was sweeping Poland in 1914–15; a fact which could have strengthened his Zionist argument for Palestine. Although he acknowledged that Palestine alone could not solve the Jewish problem, he suggested that Palestine 'could probably hold in time 3,000,000 or 4,000,000'.[28]

In March 1915, Samuel circulated a revised memorandum to the Cabinet, from which the word 'annexation' and the emotional language were dropped. It stressed the strategic value of Palestine, and gave a range of solutions to the future of Palestine if the war resulted in the break-up of the Turkish Empire in Asia: annexation by France; continued Turkish rule; internationalization; the establishment in Palestine of an autonomous Jewish state, or a British protectorate.[29] Samuel dismissed the idea of the immediate establishment of an autonomous Jewish state, and maintained that it would be doomed to failure at that point in history:

> ... the dream of a Jewish State, prosperous, progressive, and the home of a brilliant civilization might vanish in a series of squalid conflicts with the Arab population ... to attempt to realize the aspiration of a Jewish State one century too soon might throw back its actual realization for many centuries more.

He claimed that these considerations were fully recognized by the leaders of the Zionist movement. He concluded that the only feasible solution would be a British protectorate, under which 'facilities would be given to Jewish organizations to purchase land, to found colonies, to establish educational and religious institutions, and to cooperate in the economic development of the country', giving preference to Jewish immigration, 'so that in the course of time the Jewish inhabitants, grown into a majority and settled in the land, may be conceded such degree of self-government as the conditions of that day might justify'.[30]

Samuel declared that 'the course which is advocated would win for England the gratitude of the Jews throughout the world', perhaps the first time in any official record that enlisting Jewish support as a war measure was suggested. Two years later, the Balfour Declaration was based on this premise. Indeed, Samuel was the 'proto-Zionist', as his son Edwin described him in a television interview many years later. He was a Zionist long before other people[31] even realized the problem, surpassing, in his son's opinion, even Weizmann with his wit and imagination.[32]

Asquith, however, still could not comprehend the motives behind Samuel's advocacy of a British protectorate in Palestine, calling his memorandum 'dithyrambic'. Lord Kitchener, secretary of state for war (1914–16), also firmly rejected Samuel's proposal. He told the Cabinet that Palestine was of little value to the British Empire, strategically or otherwise, adding that it did not even have one 'decent' harbour. Samuel's memorandum was therefore, not adopted. Lloyd George continued to disagree with Kitchener on the strategic value of Palestine, and argued that it would be an outrage to let the Christian Holy Places fall into the hands of 'agnostic atheistic France'.[33] The memorandum also impressed Alfred Milner,[34] who, as a member of the War Cabinet in 1917, became, with Lloyd George, the most powerful advocate of a pro-Zionist declaration.[35]

Although Samuel's March memorandum produced no tangible result, it had succeeded in placing the Zionist question on the agenda for serious political discussion at the highest level. However, Samuel refrained from pushing the Cabinet towards a speedy decision lest it should have negative consequences.[36] In May 1915, Asquith formed a coalition government, and Samuel was dropped from the Cabinet. The prime minister offered him his old position as postmaster general, but Samuel was disappointed at being forced to leave the Cabinet, and found so little to occupy him in his new post that he asked Asquith if he could exchange offices with his cousin, Edwin Montagu, then financial secretary to the Treasury. However, Samuel returned to the Cabinet in December 1915 as postmaster general and Chancellor of the Duchy of Lancaster and became home secretary in 1916.[37]

When, after the fall of the Asquith government in December 1916, Lloyd George became prime minister, he invited Samuel to join his administration; but Samuel declined the offer, and over the next two years, while out of office, he was an opposition leader with Asquith. While out of office, Samuel continued to educate himself about Zionism, and quietly encouraged and advised the Zionist leader, Chaim Weizmann. He gave Weizmann information that the Zionists needed to advance their cause in influential circles, to be ready for the day of decision whenever that day came.[38]

The Zionists made utmost use of Samuel's influence in government circles. Between February and November 1917, and during the final stages of discussion leading to the Balfour Declaration, he was consulted by the Cabinet and was Zionism's most powerful ally. When a number of leaders of Anglo-Jewry, both Zionist and anti-Zionist, were consulted by the War Cabinet, during the same month, Samuel's pro-Zionist views counterweighted the views of those who argued against the Balfour Declaration, and especially his cousin, Edwin Montagu.[39]

ON THE ROAD TO PALESTINE

Although Samuel never became a member of the Zionist Organization, he did, by his own admission, cooperate closely with its leaders in 1918–19 and with Weizmann in particular.[40] Samuel's connection with the Zionists was further strengthened when in 1918 his son, Edwin, was appointed as a liaison officer to the Zionist Commission in Palestine. In October 1918, Samuel agreed to serve as chairman of a committee to prepare Zionist proposals to be submitted to the Peace Conference in 1919.[41]

In November 1918, during a dinner at which Weizmann and other members of the Zionist Commission were present, Samuel touched upon two fundamental matters which the Peace Conference would have to decide in relation to Palestine: the question of sovereignty and the question of boundaries. According to the London-based Zionist weekly *Palestine*, Samuel said the things 'which should be said, which must be said', namely that partition or joint administration by several powers would spell disaster, and that the 'ancient', 'historic' and 'natural boundaries' should be preserved.[42] In December, Samuel wrote to his son Edwin that there was a remote possibility that he would take up a governmental post in Palestine. 'The more I reflect over Palestinian affairs,' he told his son, 'the bolder seems to me the task of helping to lay the foundations of the future Commonwealth.'[43]

In January 1919, Samuel, along with Israel Sieff[44] and Chaim Weizmann, represented the Zionists at the Paris Peace Conference. The ambitious Zionist programme, which included demands for a Jewish governor and a Jewish majority in the Executive and Legislative Councils, alarmed the Foreign Office. Samuel therefore revised the proposals, eliminating these demands.[45] Throughout this period, Samuel's chief aim was to 'cement the Anglo-Zionist' alliance, preventing a deterioration of relations between Zionists and the British government, and to ensure that the Mandate for Palestine would be the responsibility of Britain alone.[46]

When the Peace Conference shortly afterwards decided to send a commission of inquiry to Syria and Palestine to ascertain the wishes of the inhabitants (the King-Crane Commission), Samuel felt uneasy. He wrote to Balfour, the foreign secretary, that delay in deciding the future of Palestine was causing great anxiety among Zionists and in Palestine. Balfour promised him that he would try to exclude Palestine from the scope of the commission of inquiry. However, he drew Samuel's attention to the reports that were reaching him, from unbiased sources, that 'the Zionists are behaving in a way which is alienating the sympathies of all other elements of the population', and asked him to convey the message to the Zionists. Samuel did so, but reported that the Zionists were very disappointed with the military authorities who acted as if the Balfour Declaration did not exist.[47]

In mid-1919, Sir William Tyrell, permanent under-secretary to the Foreign Office, informed Samuel of a report from the chief political officer, Egyptian

Expeditionary Force, Sir Gilbert Clayton, that if Great Britain held that the Zionist programme was a 'necessary adjunct' to the Mandate for Palestine, then the people of that country would select the USA or even France as mandatory power. The Palestinians 'desire their country to themselves and will resist any general immigration of Jews, however gradual, by every means in their power, not excluding armed resistance'. Clayton had also informed the Foreign Office that the Palestinians considered that Britain was 'more systematically' committed to the Zionist programme than either the USA or France. Balfour suggested that Samuel should be consulted, in his capacity as chairman of the Advisory Committee on the Economic Development of Palestine,[48] on how 'the present hostility to Zionism in Palestine can best be allayed by the administrative authorities on the spot'.[49]

Allenby, consulted by Samuel, made clear his firm position against any Jewish immigration and pointed out that the situation, especially in western Syria, was extremely delicate. Samuel nonetheless still pressed for more favourable conditions for the Zionists. In order to protect the Jewish colonies, Samuel tried to convince Allenby to keep his troops in a position to 'better protect the northern boundaries of Palestine', but Allenby bluntly replied that he had moved his troops to a strategic line, and that he had no intention of keeping his troops all winter in the snows of Mount Hermon.[50] This seems to have convinced Samuel at an early date that Allenby could not be won over to the Zionist side.

Thus, before Samuel embarked on his trip to Palestine in February and March 1920, he had a preconceived view that the tension in Palestine was caused by the military administration itself: 'The attitude of the administrative authorities,' he wrote to the Foreign Office on 5 June 1919, 'does not appear to be fully in harmony with that of His Majesty's Government.' He criticized the military authorities' reluctance to publish the Balfour Declaration, adding that

> from reports reaching us ... it would seem that the British Administrators in Palestine do not always conduct their relations with the Arabs on the basis that the Declaration of November 2nd 1917 embodies the settled lines of policy.[51]

Samuel suggested that the military authorities be informed first, that the Mandate for Palestine would embody the Balfour Declaration, and that the Arabs need not fear expulsion from their land; second, that there would be no rule of the minority over the majority; third, that religious liberty would be preserved; fourth, that the French and American governments were pledged to Zionism, and finally, that the population should be told that Zionism was a *chose jugée*, and that no good was to be expected from standing against it, and that opposing Zionism 'would certainly be without result'. On August 1919, the Foreign Office sent a telegram to Palestine on 4 August 1919 along the lines which Samuel had suggested.[52]

Towards the end of 1919, Samuel was asked by the Foreign Office to visit Palestine to report on financial and administrative conditions there, and 'to advise concerning the lines of policy to be followed in future in these respects, should a mandate fall upon Great Britain'.[53] In its issue of 17 January 1920, the Zionist weekly, *Palestine,* wrote that the Foreign Office was to be congratulated on the selection of Mr Herbert Samuel. Samuel enjoyed the 'fullest confidence of the Zionist Organization'. He had been, according to the Zionist periodical, an 'ardent supporter' of the cause while a member of the War Cabinet, and it was

> an open secret that for the last twelve months he has given close attention to the various phases of Zionist work and has acted in an advisory capacity to the Central Office in regard to the preparation of plans for the colonization, immigration and economic reconstruction of the country ... Samuel's mission may well come to be regarded as a most important step in the laying of the foundation of a Jewish Palestine.[54]

Samuel left London on 11 January 1920, arriving in Palestine at the end of January to spend two months in the country. Half of that time he spent assessing the administrative and financial situation at the headquarters of the administration in Jerusalem, and the other half visiting almost all parts of Palestine. He concluded his visit with two reports, one to Allenby,[55] and the other to Curzon.[56] Both reports echoed the Zionist view that the hostility of the military administration to the Zionist cause was an obstacle to the establishment of the Jewish national home. He stressed the necessity of bringing into the administration a 'number of new officers',[57] observing that the military authorities had 'regarded rather more seriously than they deserved the anti-Zionist manifestations' which had taken place, and that they were 'unduly alarmist'. He complained that the military administration had accepted the Zionist policy only because it was adopted by His Majesty's Government, whose servants they were, and 'not with any conviction of the wisdom of that policy'.[58] But until peace was made with Turkey, Samuel accepted that the administration 'necessarily remains in form military'. The administration was, he reported, over-staffed, and General Bols, the last chief administrator, was taking steps to reduce personnel. Samuel advised that any further changes, consequent upon the granting of the Mandate, should be gradual, and that it would be advisable to retain in the new administration those who had acquired invaluable experience and entered into 'personal relations with the principal inhabitants'.[59] Samuel noted that, as a result of the prolonged delay in determining the future status of the country, nothing had yet been done to promote its development, 'giving rise to disappointment'. Since land purchase had been suspended, private enterprises of urgent importance could not be started because the 'necessary land cannot legally be acquired'. The Zionist Organization, he wrote, would 'no doubt' be prepared to take part in many public works. To Allenby, he reported that the population 'over the greater part of the country', was, in his opinion 'scanty'.[60] Irrigation was hardly attempted, malaria prevailed,[61] the great amount of water power that existed was left unused, and there were hardly any manufacturing industries. There was no harbour, and in the absence of any cadastral survey, ownership of land was, in Samuel's opinion, often uncertain.

Despite the underdeveloped state of the economy, the financial situation of the country was satisfactory, but he advocated an immediate loan of £2,500,000 for the first two years. This loan was needed for railway rolling stock, for roads, telegraphs, telephones and certain government buildings, and it was, 'of the first importance politically that these works should be begun without delay'. He drew attention to the construction of a hydro-electric power station, for which 'the Zionists may be expected to provide funds'.[62] He also addressed, in detail, problems regarding the railways, Haifa harbour, Palestinian nationality, Palestinian currency, taxation, the flag of Palestine, the settlement of the northern boundaries, and the position of chief administrator.

He urged that, as soon as a civil administration was established, a small Advisory Council should be constituted, to be nominated by the governor, with an official majority, and three non-official representatives of each of the three religious sections. The Land Registers should be opened and the prohibition upon the buying and selling of land removed. He also suggested the enactment of legislation to enable land banks to be established, and to encourage the formation of financial institutions which would grant long-term credits to agriculturalists and urban businesses. Finally, he advocated the 'opening of the ports to immigration' on condition that the Zionists prepare schedules for employment to be offered to immigrants.[63]

Samuel reported that he had visited eleven Jewish agricultural colonies, which were 'full of promise for the future', and constituted 'the most energetic and most significant factor in Palestine today'. Samuel evidently believed that only through Jewish colonization did the country have any hope of improvement:

> With a progressive Government, with the introduction of an additional population characterized by industry and intelligence, and with the provision from outside sources of the capital that is necessary, Palestine could offer, in a comparatively short period, a comfortable livelihood to several times its present population, and could become a thriving country.

Towards the end of his report to Allenby, Samuel stated that the formation of mortgage banks was hindered by the absence of a cadastral survey, but that the Zionists were contemplating establishing a bank for this purpose, primarily for the assistance of Jewish colonization. He had discussed this question in Cairo with Harari Pasha of the Mortgage Company in Egypt, which was considering extending its operations to Palestine after the mandate was granted. Samuel's final conclusions about land colonization and the establishment of the Jewish national home were that, economically, the Zionist policy was quite practicable, and that, politically, 'if too much is not attempted at once, the difficulties that undoubtedly exist, are by no means insuperable'.[64]

He observed 'no antipathy, and remarkably little friction' between the Jewish agricultural colonies which had been founded in the last thirty or forty years, and their Arab neighbours. Samuel informed Curzon that only in the towns did anti-Zionist feeling prevail, and that 'a number of sheikhs', whom he did not identify, from the villages of Northern Galilee, had 'personally' informed him that they lived on the 'best of terms' with the Jewish population, dissociating themselves from the anti-Zionist meetings.[65] To pacify the local inhabitants, Samuel tried to explain the motives of the Zionist movement, urging Zionists not to be 'over-eager in the execution of their policy', and to offer the Muslims and Christians 'opportunities in participating in their enterprises'.

In Nablus, Samuel met an Arab delegation which told him that if the Zionists were going to immigrate to the country, 'a terrible revolution will break out'. He replied that 'If the Jews come to your country they will colonize the spare lands that are not cultivated ... They have historic rights in this country ... Their claims are religious and not commercial ones ... I am not a Zionist.[66] Samuel did not feel anxious at such manifestations of hostility because it was certain that 'a movement that rests upon errors cannot endure'. He anticipated that when those who opposed Zionism discovered that none of the expected evils had taken place, they would eventually change their attitude.

Samuel did find it expedient to clarify Zionist objectives in a press statement of 25 March 1920, before he left Palestine. Opposition to Zionism, he maintained, was not 'seriously disturbing': it was based on a 'false' idea of what Zionism was. The inhabitants had made a number of 'assumptions', which were 'untrue' in his opinion, and which made them adopt a hostile attitude towards Zionism. They assumed that the Muslim and Christian population were to be placed under the government of a Jewish minority and that the present owners and cultivators of the soil might be dispossessed of their property. There were fears that the ownership of the Muslim and Christian Holy Places would be affected and that the administrative offices would be filled by Jews to the prejudice of others. To allay their fears, Samuel went on to say: 'Although not a member of the Zionist Organization, I am fully acquainted with its policy, and I know that none of these ideas are entertained by it. I know also that, even if they were, the British Government would never permit the adoption of such policies.'[67]

The future high commissioner concluded his press conference by emphatically stating: 'I am strongly of the opinion, and I know it is shared by the leaders of the Zionist movement, that that movement will fail in its purpose if it is not able to show that it has been of real benefit to the existing Mahommedan and Christian population of the country'.

By presenting such optimistic views about the nature of the relations between the Arabs and the Zionists, did Samuel deliberately seek to mislead the British government? Wasserstein's explanation of this issue is particularly revealing. He wrote that Samuel 'was conscious that the foreign secretary was an opponent of Zionism who might turn such a report, if incautiously worded, against the Zionist cause',[68] and that Samuel therefore carefully phrased his report in the interest of the Zionists. In fact, the months of February and March 1920, when Samuel toured Palestine, witnessed a series of anti-Zionist demonstrations. He had also criticized the policy of the Zionist Commission towards the Arabs during his tour, saying that it had not recognized 'the force and value of the Arab nationalist movement',[69] and that this movement was 'very real and no bluff'.

SAMUEL'S VIEWS ON ARAB NATIONALISM

One week after the Balfour Declaration was issued, amid Jewish jubilation, the Zionists organized a 'great' thanksgiving meeting at the London Opera House on 9 November 1917. Samuel, second only to Weizmann in the 'paternity' of the Balfour Declaration, delivered a fiery speech, in which he stressed three conditions for the success of the Zionist programme in Palestine: firstly, there had to be full and just recognition of the rights of the Arabs who constituted the majority of that country; secondly, the Christian and Muslim Holy Places had to be respected, and should always remain 'in the control and charge of representatives of those faiths'; and thirdly, there should be 'no attempt to establish any political control over Jews in the Diaspora'.[70]

In March 1918, in a message to the Glasgow Zionists, Samuel welcomed their support for the ideal of a Jewish Palestine and of their determination to bring it into reality:

> Without injury to other inhabitants of the land and with scrupulous respect for the interests of other faiths in its holy places, there is room in Palestine, and there is now at last the opportunity, for the re-establishment of the ancient civilisation which gave to mankind many of its choicest possessions.[71]

Samuel gave his views on the Arab question two years later in a speech delivered on the occasion of the second anniversary of the Balfour Declaration:[72]

> The immediate establishment of a complete and purely Jewish State in Palestine ... would mean placing a majority under the rule of a minority; it would therefore be contrary to the first principles of democracy, and would undoubtedly be disapproved by the public opinion of the whole world.[73]

In his memoirs Samuel made an enlightening remark which touched upon the Arab question without mentioning the Arabs by name:

> All my life a convinced Liberal ... I was the last man to take a hand in any policy of oppression. And as a Jew I would have counted it a shame to the Jewish people if the renewal of their life in the ancient Land of Israel were to be marked by hardship, expropriation, injustice of any kind, for the people now in the land, whose forebears had tilled the soil and dwelt in the towns for a thousand years. Nothing could be worse than if it were to appear that the one thing the Jewish people had learnt from the centuries of their own oppression was to oppress others.[74]

However, in spite of all these public statements, there is evidence that the question of transferring the inhabitants of Palestine was openly discussed in official circles. At a meeting of the Palestine Advisory Committee in May 1919, attended by Foreign and War Office officials, as well as by Weizmann and other Zionists, Samuel objected to recent public statements by Zionists which suggested that Palestine Arabs should be removed to Syria to make room for the Jews. He nevertheless concurred that 'possibly with some kind of financial inducement', and 'with complete agreement and goodwill', a certain proportion of the population might be induced to leave, and if so 'all the better', but it would be 'an unspeakable disgrace', if 'we were to go to Palestine to oppress other people'.[75]

Samuel's advice to Curzon, as a result of his tour from January to March 1920, was that there was 'no evidence of anything in the nature of a widespread and formidable national movement against Zionism'. He went to great lengths to play down the resolutions of the Syrian Congress, and asserted that its declarations 'disturbed the Christian elements [who] did not at all welcome the prospect of being the subjects of an independent Moslem King'.[76] In his report to Curzon, he emphasized the Arab question, particularly with reference to the declarations made by the Syrian Congress at Damascus held on 8 March in favour of an independent and united Syria to include Palestine, under the kingship of Faisal. Samuel argued that the following motives combined to foster the pan-Arab movement:

1. There was a 'natural patriotic sentiment' among the small class of politically oriented Arabs for an independent Arabia, 'as extensive' and 'as important' as possible.
2. There was a general feeling that to insert economic divisions between neighbouring countries which had so far been under one single government would be a 'retrograde' step. Since boundaries and frontiers had never existed between Syria and Palestine, the Arabs feared that political separation would cause economic inconvenience, and that commerce and travel would suffer.
3. A united and independent Syria was regarded 'as the only means of combating Zionism'. The anti-Zionist movement widely held that large-scale Jewish

A Broken Trust

immigration 'would lead to the reduction of the rest of the population to a lower status'.

4. There was, according to Samuel, the personal interest of the effendi class, as they expected to fill higher governmental posts under an Arab government in comparison to a British one, especially if the latter were combined with a Zionist policy.

5. Finally, there was in Samuel's opinion the social question in Palestine, with the fallahin and the effendi classes being in antagonism to one another. Samuel held that the effendi class feared that any government which they did not control might 'exact social legislation'. However, he added that the movement was 'not deep-seated'. He said that the mass of the population was not concerned 'with any question of general politics'; and as a matter of fact, relations between the Arabs and the Zionists 'as a rule, were excellent'.[77]

Samuel's trip to Palestine coincided with a major event that took place in neighbouring Syria on 6 March 1920 when Faisal was proclaimed by the Syrian Congress as King of Syria, including Palestine.[78] On his way back from Palestine, Samuel met Allenby and Milner in Cairo. The future of Palestine was still uncertain; the mandate had not even been provisionally assigned to Britain. In this precarious situation, Faisal's move was a definite threat to Zionist aspirations in Palestine, and Samuel was alarmed. On 24 March he telegraphed to Lord Curzon: 'I see no sufficient reason for recognizing Faisal as King of Palestine ... This would tend to take life out of Zionist movement'.[79] He wrote to Weizmann in March 1920 that the Arab situation had been greatly underestimated, and that the Zionist Commission had the effect of an 'alien body in living flesh'. Samuel noted that he did not expect to convert the Palestine Arabs.[80]

Anti-Zionist demonstrations had taken place expressing popular support for Faisal's coronation as the king of a united Syria, but Samuel took no notice of them. There were slogans and speeches in favour of Faisal, demanding independence and rejecting Zionism.[81] And, at the same time that Samuel sent his 'pacifying' report, telegrams were reaching London from General Headquarters in Cairo, announcing that on 27 February, demonstrations had been organized in Jerusalem and other centres by the Muslim-Christian League. Their object was to protest against Zionism and to demand unity with Syria. Although Colonel Meinertzhagen, the chief political officer in Palestine (1919–20), tried to impress upon the Foreign Office that these demonstrations 'though taking advantage of presence of Mr. Samuel in Palestine', were not attributable to genuine nationalist sentiment, but merely to French propaganda, another Foreign Office official, sensing the difficulties that lay ahead, reported in a telegram of 4 March 1920 that 'I wish we could hand over Zionism and the prospective mandate to the French but I fear we can't'.[82]

Samuel himself believed that it was 'neither just nor politic to ignore the claims of the Arabs and to oppose a mere negative to their demands'. In his report to Lord Curzon, he acknowledged that there was 'substance in part' of the arguments that were advanced for a united Syria, explaining that: (i) it could not be denied that the establishment of customs and other barriers between the various parts of Syria would cause inconvenience to the inhabitants and be detrimental to its prosperity; (ii) to create an Arab state without access to sea was wrong, and (iii) Arab patriotic sentiment, 'to such extent' as it existed, ought to be respected, and as far as possible satisfied.

But, having made the case for Arab nationalism, Samuel warned that 'to meet these contentions by the recognition of Faisal as king of Palestine appears to me both objectionable and unnecessary'. He argued that the Arab kingdom would be used, if not immediately, certainly in a few years, 'as a means of introducing, in larger and larger degree, Arab administrators into the higher offices of the Government, and of ensuring the adoption of a policy hostile to all non-Arab aspirations'. This would be, in his opinion, 'a very powerful lever for those ends'. Samuel furthermore observed that 'the moral effect upon Zionism, if not fatal, would be most grave'. If Faisal was recognized as king of Palestine, Jews throughout the world, according to Samuel, would no longer be willing to devote their energy, their money, and their lives to a country which might prove to be nothing more than 'one province among others of an unprogressive Moslem State'. Anticipating a British withdrawal at some point in the future, Samuel expressed his fear that in such an eventuality, the Arab element would reign supreme: 'This would take the heart out of Zionism. The movement would feel that it had been betrayed.' At this point, Samuel posed the following question: 'Is it possible to find a method which would be likely to satisfy what is legitimate in the Arab demands, while avoiding the dangers and disasters which their full acceptance would entail?'

The solution, in his opinion, lay in the formation of a loose confederation of Arabic-speaking states, each of which should have its own government, while all of them should be combined together for common economic purposes. The seat of the confederation would be Damascus, and Faisal might be recognized as honorary head of the confederation, in addition to being sovereign in his own state.[83] Samuel's proposal for the loose confederation included five states:

1. Arab Syria, with its capital in Damascus, and with 'Emir'[84] Faisal as sovereign. The emir, as Samuel called him, would have the right to select European advisers, but if France and Britain saw otherwise, they might undertake not to allow their nationals to accept such posts.
2. Western Syria, to be administered by France under the supervision of the League of Nations. If the French would consent, the sovereignty of Faisal might be recognized in this area. 'If not, not.'
3. Palestine, to be administered by Great Britain, subject to a mandate under League

of Nations supervision. Its boundaries should be defined by the War Office. The mandate should embody 'provisions relating to the Jewish National Home, which should be satisfactory to the Zionists'. Samuel added that the sovereignty of Faisal 'would not be recognized in this area'.

4. The Hijaz, to be independent under King Hussein, who would be free to choose his European advisers. It would be desirable that the other Southern Arabian principalities should unite with this kingdom, but if not, they 'might constitute separate units in the confederation or they might be left outside'.

5. Mesopotamia, to be under British administration, and if desired, under an Arab sovereign. If it was decided that Basra and its neighbourhood should constitute a 'more purely British State' then such a state might form a sixth unit.[85]

A memorandum by Samuel along the same lines, entitled 'Syria, Palestine, Mesopotamia and the Arabian States', was submitted to the San Remo Conference on 18 April 1920.[86] In the face of French resistance, as well as opposition from Lord Curzon, Samuel's plans never materialized. [87]

THE FIRST HIGH COMMISSIONER

In his despatches to London during this crucial phase, Samuel rarely expressed his true feelings about Zionism. It is only from his personal letters to his family, and particularly to his son Edwin, that we get a glimpse of his thoughts at a more profound level. In February 1920, at about the time that he was preparing his report to Curzon, in which he emphatically affirmed that the anti-Zionist feeling in Palestine was not serious, and that the relations between the Arabs and Jews were on many occasions 'excellent', he wrote to his son: 'The more I see of conditions here the more I am confirmed in my original opinion that it would be inadvisable for any Jew to be the first Governor… Arab Nationalist and Anti-Zionist feeling is a very real thing.' He therefore reconsidered the wisdom of accepting an appointment in Palestine: 'It would render more difficult … and not more easy, the fulfilment of the Zionist programme.'[88]

On 17 April, while at San Remo to present the Zionist view at the conference, Samuel discussed with Lord Curzon, Sir Maurice Hankey, and Lloyd George, the question of Faisal, who had been proclaimed King of Syria and Palestine in March, and was assured that there was no question of Faisal becoming king of a united Syria. A few days later, Samuel, along with Weizmann and Sokolow, consulted Balfour. On 24 April, Lloyd George took the decision that the military administration could not carry out the mandate and had to be replaced by a civil administration and asked Samuel to become the first high commissioner.[89]

Samuel was at first reluctant to take up the offer, but Weizmann, who was keen to see a quick end to the Occupied Enemy Territory Administration (OETA South), urged Samuel to accept the post without delay. Upon further reflection, Samuel decided to take Weizmann's advice, concluding that the objections to a Jewish governor 'were not insuperable' as long as the measures taken were reasonable. On 25 April 1920, Samuel wrote to Lloyd George accepting the offer of the office of high commissioner. Three days later, London announced that a civil administration was to replace the military one in Palestine. [90]

Samuel was aware of the hostility of the generals of the military administration towards his appointment. Moreover, he was fully aware of the resolutions of the Syrian Congress meeting in Damascus in February 1920, proclaiming that Palestine could not be separated from Syria and firmly opposing Zionist immigration to Palestine. However, he was not made aware of the extent of Arab hostility to his appointment and the rumours that were spreading that there would be an attempt to assassinate him as soon as he arrived in Palestine. On 18 June 1920, a secret cable from General Headquarters to the War Office claimed that the chief administrator OETA South had reliable information of a conspiracy by seven individuals to assassinate Samuel, and that these individuals would be arrested and interned. [91] On 21 June, Young reported: 'I do not think that this should be repeated to Sir H. Samuel.' [92]

Further cables from General Bols in Jerusalem informed the Foreign Office that there were very strong rumours that the Balqa and Bani Sakhr Arabs intended to attack with 2,000 to 5,000 men with the intention of impressing Herbert Samuel at the time of his arrival, and that the military had been fully informed. [93] Ronald Storrs remembered those 'uncertain and exciting days'; Herbert Samuel had telegraphed inviting him to continue in the civil service as governor of Jerusalem, and to act as chief secretary until the arrival of Colonel Wyndham Deedes. Thus, the senior 'surviving' officer from the military administration, Ronald Storrs, was sent down to greet the new high commissioner on his arrival in Jaffa. Storrs writes that the man beside the driver was heavily armed and that he concealed from Sir Herbert that he carried in his left hand a 'loaded and cocked' Browning pistol, a precaution of which he kept Samuel ignorant for over fifteen years. On 30 June 1920, Sir Herbert Samuel arrived in Jaffa aboard HMS *Centaur*. His trip from Jaffa to Jerusalem was a safe one, with the governor of Jerusalem recording in his diary that 'neither before, during nor after the journey was there the slightest attempt at outrage or even incivility.' [94]

So how was Samuel to translate his views about the obligation of the Balfour Declaration and the mandate towards the Arabs? This study will show that he honoured this pledge on the verbal level, and was quite articulate in that sense. He was sensitive to Arab criticism of his policy, and made pacifying statements about Zionist and British intentions in Palestine; nevertheless, on the practical level, he went ahead and firmly laid down the foundations of a full-fledged Jewish state. He was a gradualist who believed in the gradual evolution of the Jewish state, and whose many reassuring announcements to the effect that he was bound by the 'dual obligation' had a definite role, merely serving as 'palliatives' as some Palestine Arabs saw it. Samuel himself declared that he would never have gone to Palestine had there been no Zionist question and no Balfour Declaration.[95] At the same time, he asserted in his memoirs that the Balfour Declaration 'gave two injunctions—first, to foster the establishment of a Jewish National Home; second, to do it without prejudice to the civil and religious rights of the rest of the population,' adding:

> some thought that the two were irreconcilable; that a National Home for the Jews must mean subordination, possibly spoliation, for the Arabs. I did not share that view. If I had it would have been impossible for me to accept the office of High Commissioner.[96]

Thus the key to understanding Samuel's policy was that as long as the Arabs were the great majority in the country, 'it was out of the question' to think in terms of a Jewish state, but that did not mean that he did not envisage such a state 'at some future time'.[97] He never conceived of that state 'being born overnight', for he recognized the strength of Arab opposition which Zionism must reckon with if the Zionist experiment was ever to succeed.[98] Had it not been for his gradualism, the more extreme elements in the Zionist movement might have well brought an early end to this experiment.[99]

As Samuel was getting ready to sail to Palestine in June 1920, he wrote to his niece that: 'For the time being there will be no Jewish state', and that immigration would be restricted. However, he predicted that after five years the pace would probably be 'accelerated and will grow after that progressively in speed'. He added:

> In fifty years there may be a Jewish majority in the population. Then the Government will be predominantly Jewish, and in the generation after that there may be that which might properly be called a Jewish country with a Jewish State. It is that prospect which rightly evokes such fine enthusiasm, and it is the hope of realising that future which makes me ready to sacrifice much in the present.[100]

In his memoirs, Samuel recalled that the most moving ceremony he had ever attended was at the synagogue in the Jewish quarter of Jerusalem immediately after his arrival in Palestine in 1920 as the first high commissioner. He saw himself as the saviour of the Jewish people, noting that:

> on that day, for the first time since the destruction of the Temple, they [i.e. the settlers] could see one of their own people governor in the Land of Israel. To them, it seemed that the fulfilment of ancient prophecy might at last be at hand.[101]

When he assumed office, however, Samuel, understanding the situation in Palestine clearly, suppressed his Zionist inclinations in public.[102] Although he continually emphasized that the 'clear duty' of the mandatory power was to 'promote the well-being' of the Arab population, and that 'the Zionism that is practicable is the Zionism that fulfils this essential condition', he firmly believed that the Zionists had a 'legitimate' right to found their home in Palestine.[103]

Samuel arrived in Palestine to face widely differing expectations—deep suspicion among the Arab population but very high hopes on the part of the Zionists. For the major part of his term of office in Palestine, he unsuccessfully tried to persuade the Arabs to accept the Balfour Declaration and the mandate, but by refusing the constitution, known as the Palestine Order-in-Council, which was based on the Balfour Declaration, the Palestine Arabs hoped to make the point that they were utterly devoted to the cause of achieving complete independence. They furthermore pointed out the intrinsic contradiction in the Balfour Declaration: 'how could the foreign Jews enjoy political rights in Palestine without prejudicing the rights of the Arabs?'[104] On the other hand, Norman Bentwich, the staunch Zionist appointed by Samuel in 1920 as legal adviser in the civil administration of Palestine, saw him as the 'saviour', and wrote: 'Samuel came with the sense of a messianic mission, and the Jews welcomed him as a messianic ruler'. He wrote that Samuel arrived with the conviction that, as the prophet Isaiah taught: 'On his throne no stranger shall sit, and no alien shall inherit his glory.'[105]

PART TWO

Implementing the Palestine Mandate

5

Samuel in Palestine: The First Steps, July 1920–May 1921

Herbert Samuel's conviction that the Zionists had 'historic' and 'religious' rights in Palestine, and that Zionism was a movement of historic importance, spurred him to facilitate Zionist objectives towards the establishment of a Jewish national home in Palestine, though his liberalism led him to pay lip service to the notion that Arab rights could and should be respected. However, it will be argued that actions speak louder than words, and that the actions he took as first high commissioner to meet Zionist objectives far outweighed his efforts to safeguard Arab rights.

Article 2 of the Palestine mandate stated that the mandatory should be responsible for placing the country under such political, administrative and economic conditions 'as will secure the establishment of the Jewish national home ... and the development of self-governing institutions', while at the same time, 'safeguarding the civil and religious rights of all inhabitants'. This provision was reinforced by the assurance given in a message from 'His Majesty the King to the People of Palestine', issued on 19 June 1920, when Samuel's appointment as high commissioner was confirmed. Assuring the population of the government's 'absolute impartiality', it continued:

> You are well aware that the Allied and Associated Powers have decided that measures shall be adopted to secure the gradual establishment in Palestine of a national home for the Jewish people. These measures will not in any way affect the civil or religious rights or diminish the prosperity of the general population of Palestine.[1]

From the moment he assumed office, Samuel stressed his commitment to this 'equality of obligation', and insisted that he was intent on adopting active measures to promote the well-being of the Arabs.[2] In his Interim Report on the first year of the civil administration, Samuel wrote:

The policy of His Majesty's Government contemplates the satisfaction of the legitimate aspirations of the Jewish race throughout the world in relation to Palestine,
combined with a full protection of the rights of the existing population. For my own
part, I am convinced that the means can be found to effect this combination. The
Zionism that is practicable is the Zionism that fulfils this essential condition. It is
the clear duty of the Mandatory Power to promote the well-being of the Arab population, in the same way as a British Administration would regard it as its duty to
promote the welfare of the local population in any part of our Empire. The measures to foster the well-being of the Arabs should be precisely those which we should
adopt in Palestine as if there were no Zionist question and if there had been no
Balfour Declaration. There is in this policy nothing incompatible with reasonable
Zionist aspirations. On the contrary, if the growth of Jewish influence were accompanied by Arab degradation, or even by a neglect to promote Arab advancement, it
would fail in one of its essential purposes. The grievance of the Arab would be a
discredit to the Jew, and in the result the moral influence of Zionism would be gravely
impaired.

He went on:

To install the Jews in Palestine might mean the expulsion of the Arabs. If there were
an unlimited Jewish immigration and finally a Jewish majority in the population,
how could the safeguards embodied in the second half of the Declaration be en-
forced? The ownership of the Arabs in their lands and homes would be imperilled.
The Moslem Holy Places, and particularly the Haram-esh-Sherif on Mount Moriah,
might be taken from them ... .[3]

Samuel added that there were some among the Zionists who, 'inspired by the
greatness of their ideal', sometimes 'ignore' the present inhabitants of Palestine,
forgetting that there were half a million people in Palestine.[4] Others, at the least,
did not present their goal as one of co-existence. For example, the *Jewish Chronicle*
wrote on 30 September 1921:

There are two courses open ... to let the two cultures exist in the same country
entirely separated, or to superimpose [Jewish] [sic] culture upon the Arab. The second course would certainly produce the best results, but the civilisation of the Jews
is so much higher than that of the Arabs that the two cultures may be too far apart
to be brought into touch at all; just as a British Colony in Australia has for its effect
upon the native Australians, not their transformation, but their gradual
disappearance.[5]

How seriously Samuel took the pledge to implement the 'dual obligation', and
how he interpreted it on the political level, is the main theme of this section. Was
the intention to prevent a Palestinian Arab national government from developing?

And was 'the development of self-governing institutions' intended for the Jews only? Although Samuel often asserted that Arab rights should not, and would not, be encroached upon, and frequently expressed the opinion that 'the degree to which Jewish national aspirations can be fulfilled in Palestine is conditioned by the rights of the present inhabitants', and that this had been the principle which had guided the policy of the administration,[6] the evidence tends to suggest that such statements were mainly intended as pacifying measures directed at two separate audiences. The first was the local Arab community in Palestine, and the second was the British parliament and sections of the British public who were becoming increasingly aware and concerned that Britain was involved in enforcing a policy against the wishes of more than 93 per cent of the population, a policy which would inevitably result, as they saw it, in the oppression of the vast majority of the population of Palestine.

During the period of Samuel's tenure as high commissioner, there were several major landmarks in the development of British policy towards Palestine. The first two years of his period in office were to prove the most eventful and will be dealt with in greater detail. The publication of Churchill's White Paper on Palestine, on 3 June 1922, was the first official and written interpretation of the Balfour Declaration. It stressed the 'historic right' of the Jews in Palestine, although stating at the same time that the British government did not contemplate the 'disappearance or subordination' of the Arab population. It remained the central document guiding British policy in Palestine until 1929[7] and paved the way for the ratification of the British mandate by the League of Nations on 24 July 1922, after it had received approval in the British parliament on 6 July 1922.[8]

The publication of the White Paper triggered widespread Palestinian Arab opposition to the British mandate and this period was characterized by a bitter confrontation between the Palestine Arabs and the Zionists; an Arab boycott of the measures taken by the administration in the field of 'political representation'; and a growing pro-Arab and anti-Zionist lobby among British politicians, which in its turn convinced the Palestinian Arab politicians that they could achieve their ends by diplomatic means.

In September 1923, however, when the mandate came into force, the Balfour Declaration was cemented in British policy, and Palestine technically ceased to be a military administered area. The following period, until August 1925, when Samuel's term in office came to an end, saw a weakening of the Arab nationalist movement, and a schism within its ranks, which was paralleled by the steady growth of Jewish institutions.

ESTABLISHING THE ADMINISTRATION: ZIONISTS AND ANTI-ZIONISTS

The civil administration which Samuel created was shaped by his policies and pre-occupations. Before analysing in detail these policies and their outcome, it may be instructive to examine the key figures whom Samuel appointed, and their influence on the conduct of policy throughout his term of office—a subject that will take us somewhat beyond the period that is the main concern of this chapter.

Four months before a civil administration was set up, at a time when the country was still under military rule, Chaim Weizmann wrote to Lord Curzon, then secretary of state for foreign affairs, complaining of the 'danger' of having Arab personnel in the administration, whom he called 'English-speaking Syrians', who 'may not be able fully to understand or intelligently to co-operate in the policy of the Jewish national home'. The 'infiltration' of numbers of British Jews in the administration would be 'highly desirable'. In the same despatch, Weizmann revealed that the Zionist Organization had already prepared lists of available candidates—for all levels of the administration, including the junior grade civil servants level and technical posts, as well as for high level administrative posts—and that these lists had been submitted to the Foreign Office.[9]

Upon assuming office, Samuel entrusted the two most important posts in the administration, those of the civil secretary (later chief secretary) and legal secretary (later converted to attorney-general) respectively to Wyndham Deedes and Norman Bentwich, the first a strong Zionist sympathiser, and the second a Jew who was a staunch Zionist. A small Executive Council of officials was established when Samuel took office in 1920,[10] with Bentwich, Deedes and the financial secretary, H. G. Smallwood as members. Bentwich subsequently maintained that real power rested in this council which met at least once a week under the presidency of the high commissioner, and advised on policy as well as on current affairs.[11]

Once control of the affairs of Palestine was transferred from the Foreign Office to the Colonial Office in early 1921, Samuel reported to the secretary of state for the colonies, who was responsible to parliament. In this way, Palestine was subject to the ultimate sanction of parliamentary control. Under the terms of the 1922 Palestine Order-in-Council, the high commissioner held all executive, legislative and judicial powers in his hands but his powers were, at least theoretically, limited by this overriding authority. Although the high commissioner's title included that of commander-in-chief, he did not actually command armed forces in the field. He was assisted by the executive council, which was formally established by the 1922 Order-in-Council, and corresponded to a Cabinet of senior officials.[12]

According to Edward Keith-Roach, who was appointed by Samuel as senior assistant to the chief secretary, the fact that Bentwich as legal secretary 'mixed himself up in political matters by ardently espousing the Jewish cause' caused complications for the administration.[13] Throughout the 1920s, Bentwich kept the Zionist

Executive informed of new ordinances while they were being drafted. His appointment as attorney-general greatly assisted the Zionists on the vital issue of land legislation and purchase.[14] Internal minutes indicate that the Colonial Office was well aware of Bentwich's Zionist bias. Commenting on his handling of the case when Article 46 of the Order-in-Council,[15] dealing with the jurisdiction of the civil courts, was being discussed, Young minuted: 'There is more in this than meets the eye—Mr. Bentwich's views are coloured by his vision of the Palestine to be (an independent nation, predominantly Jewish), and he cannot be expected to alter them.'[16]

The other key post in the administration was that of civil secretary. Although Wyndham Deedes was not a Jew, he was devoted Zionist.[17] He was acquainted with the Middle East and had been one of the heads of the Intelligence Section of Allenby's General Staff. Attesting to Deedes' achievements in Palestine, Yitzhak Ben Zvi, one of the founding leaders of the Histadrut, asserted that the three years of Sir Wyndham Deedes' tenure of office as chief secretary were among the 'most decisive' in the life of the country in the mandatory period. In his view, Samuel and Deedes had devoted much of their energies to laying solid foundations for the Jewish national home.[18]

A number of other appointees were Jewish, and some with strong Zionist connections. They included Colonel Harold Solomon, who became controller of stores, and Albert Hyamson,[19] who was associated with the Zionist Organization, and became deputy director of the newly established Department of Immigration under a non-Jewish director. Captain Harari, of a leading Jewish family in Egypt (Storrs' assistant in Jerusalem, during OETA) became director of the Department of Commerce and Industry, and Max Nurock, previously acting chairman of the Zionist Commission, was one of Samuel's private secretaries.[20] Later, in 1922, Nurock was promoted to the post of assistant secretary, where he became the link between the government and the Zionists.[21]

Samuel's ambition to fill government posts with Jews went far beyond what the Colonial Office found acceptable, or even justified. In July 1921, he wrote to Churchill that there were several American Jews in the service of the government, who had no intention of adopting Palestinian nationality, and who were unwilling to renounce their American citizenship even after the ratification of the Treaty of Sèvres. He advocated their retention in the service, explaining that it was the 'fair' thing to do. Although in principle he felt they should opt for Palestinian nationality he was concerned that American Jews might accuse the administration of 'unfair discrimination', since British Jews could retain their British citizenship.[22] O. A. Scott, a Foreign Office official, minuted on 8 August:

> Sir Herbert Samuel is particularly anxious not to offend American susceptibilities and perhaps he feels that the streams of gold from America may flow more freely to

Palestine if she has the appearance of having some influence and representation in the management of Palestine.

The Foreign Office, however, was reluctant to accept Samuel's proposal commenting that there was 'no place in the Jewish National Home for a Jew who is not prepared to become a local citizen'.[23] The Colonial Office subsequently decided that as a general rule, appointments in the civil service in Palestine would be confined to people who were either of British or Palestinian nationality.[24]

Having secured Zionist supporters on the Executive Council, Samuel sought to appoint people of different views to other sensitive posts. He retained Ronald Storrs as governor of Jerusalem for his 'wide culture' and his knowledge of the East, but above all, for his 'tactful handling of difficult problems—sectional, ecclesiastical and personal'. Samuel asserted that Storrs was of the greatest value in preventing the continually arising clashes in Jerusalem from developing into open conflicts.[25] With a fair knowledge of Arabic and Hebrew, Storrs maintained good relations with both communities. Although he described himself as a 'sioniste convaincu', he was often described as a pro-Arab and anti-Zionist. However, the best assessment of his views can be derived from his own memoirs. He wrote:

> Being neither a Jew (British or foreign) nor Arab, but English, I am not wholly for either, but for both. Two hours of Arab grievances drive me into the Synagogue, while after an intensive course of Zionist propaganda I am prepared to embrace Islam.[26]

In the final analysis, however, Storrs believed that Zionism was a 'world movement' and that 'Arabism' did not exist.[27]

Samuel's choice of two pro-Arab figures for high posts—E. T. Richmond for the post of assistant political secretary, and Sir Gilbert Clayton to succeed Deedes from April 1923—was calculated to pacify the Arab population. Richmond was an architect who had worked in Palestine in 1918, examining the structural condition of the Muslim shrines in Haram al-Sharif. His knowledge of Arabic and friendly connections with Arab families, Muslim and Christian, presumably explains Samuel's invitation to join the administration in November 1920, in the hope that he could provide a useful link between his administration and the Arab population.[28]

Richmond's son recalled that it never occurred to his father, and to many who thought like him, that the authors of the Balfour Declaration: 'really intended to change the demographic composition of Palestine so that its 90% Arab majority would gradually dwindle into minority status'. Nor could they believe that 'it could be the intention of the British Government to use its administration in Palestine to secure Arab acquiescence in that programme by force if need be'. They believed that the declaration 'must be intended to mean at least as much as it said about safeguarding the rights of the non-Jewish majority'.[29] However, it took three years for his father to become completely emancipated from these 'illusions'. In the process, Richmond discovered that Wyndham Deedes, his immediate superior, was

> a committed believer in Zionism as the fulfilment of the Old Testament prophesies; that Norman Bentwich, the legal secretary, was both Jewish and Zionist; that both men believed in the closest possible cooperation with the Zionist Commission, and that both distrusted the Arab population and regarded its nationalist leadership as the Administration's enemy.[30]

Richmond was described during those days as the 'sheet anchor of Zionism in Palestine' because it was he who 'gave the Arabs confidence in an administration, that for them would otherwise be wholly Zionist'.[31] Edward Keith-Roach, who was appointed by Samuel as senior assistant to the chief secretary Deedes, affirms in his memoirs that Deedes' work and his own was complicated because of the political secretary Ernest Richmond, who was 'an out-and-out champion of the Arab cause'.[32]

In this atmosphere, Richmond's time in Palestine became a continuous battle with his colleagues, and by the middle of 1921 his views on the way the national home policy was being carried out were already formed. He recorded these views frankly in a letter to his brother: [33]

> Our record in this country is not a bright one ... we were welcomed by an exceptionally friendly people ... But we adopted a Zionist policy, and allowed immigration of Jews on a scale for which labour conditions offered no justification ... We put many Jews and Zionists into high places. The Immigration Department is a Jewish department. The Legal Secretary is a Jew and a Zionist. The high commissioner is both. The people begin to regard the Government as Jewish camouflaged as English. They will not accept Jewish rule. We denied them all the representative institutions which they enjoyed under the Turks ... Hence we turned friendliness into distrust ... The country is in a state of ferment ... By giving representative government to Palestine and by returning as far as possible to the very reasonable form of it that the country had under the Turks we could satisfy Arabs and moderate Jews. Such a policy leaves no place for a Zionist Commission.[34]

Throughout his career, Richmond persisted in pointing out to the high commissioner the possible dangers of his policy.[35] During 1922, he recorded his activities as political officer in the reports submitted to the high commissioner, dealing with political, economic and other questions, and, in particular, correspondence and interviews concerning the Arab Executive Committee and the Supreme Muslim Council. Among the subjects discussed were the inconsistency between the White Paper and the mandate, and the under-representation of the Muslims in the Legislative Council. Richmond saw these as departures from normal British administration, and an unfortunate expression of the policy of the Palestine administration. In a report which he submitted to the high commissioner, he made a full statement of the 'numerous follies' against which he had fought:[36]

1. That the Executive Committee of the Palestine Arab Congress should be treated without enquiry as an illegal body and that the Administration should force a rupture with this Executive;

2. that the Administration should countenance and support an attempt to undermine the Supreme Muslim Council with a view to replacing its President and members with others, 'loyal' to the British policy in Palestine;

3. that Arab Nationalism is not as legitimate a political creed as Jewish Nationalism and that adherents of the former should be treated by the Police and by the Administration as potential criminals while adherents of the latter should be regarded as law-abiding citizens;

4. that the Arab people of this ancient country should have meted out to them the treatment of violence and unreason supposed by some to be proper for a 'backward' race;

5. that firing upon Arab demonstrating crowds is only a necessary incident (rather than a symptom of failure) in the process of ruling the country;

6. that the 'National Muslim Society', composed of paid agents of the Zionists, should receive countenance and encouragement from the Government on the grounds that it was loyal to the policy of the Government;

7. that Jews who possess fire-arms illegally should be negotiated with while Arabs should be arrested and prosecuted for the same offence;

8. that the press should be subsidised with a view to manufacturing a sham statement of public opinion;

9. that officers of the Administration should take part in politics and play the part of Zionist propaganda agents;

10. that the representative of any group of individuals who allege that their rights are infringed should be arbitrarily ignored on no other grounds than that his intervention is embarrassing to the Administration.

Richmond described the effect of this report in a letter to his brother: 'a silence, so thick that it could be felt, descended and lasted for more than ten days. Then Samuel spoke to me, rather hesitatingly.' Samuel told him that this was not what was wanted and that the Colonial Office would be surprised when they read it. What they needed was a 'colourless statement', not of his work, but of the political events of the year.[37]

Ironically, Richmond was seen as of value to the administration, despite his violent opposition to its policies. It was he who gave the Arabs confidence in an administration, which they would otherwise consider to be 'wholly Zionist'.[38] As Deedes wrote to Shuckburgh, in December 1921, no one was better acquainted with the views of the Muslim population in Palestine than Richmond who enabled the high commissioner and himself to keep their finger 'on the pulse of Moslem Public Opinion'. Deedes asked Shuckburgh if he could find time to talk to Richmond, then in London, adding that it might have been reported to him that Richmond was anti-Zionist, but that this was 'wholly untrue'.[39]

By early 1923, however, Richmond knew that his days in the Palestine administration were numbered, and that he had lost the battle to change the government's Zionist policy.[40] Apparently, both the Middle East Department and Samuel wanted Richmond to go, the only reason why Samuel had hitherto wanted him to stay being that he regarded him as a kind of 'safety valve' who had succeeded in keeping the sentiments of the Muslim Arabs from violently erupting. Richmond wrote that it was Ronald Storrs who had informed him that the Colonial Office wanted to get rid of him: 'They call me an *'imperium in imperio'*. They don't like such *'imperia'*, though as Ronald Storrs pointed out to them, they already have one in the Zionist Commission.'

In September 1923, Richmond wrote to his mother that he had informed Samuel of his intention to leave Palestine by April 1924. He explained that Samuel was uneasy and had pleaded with him to reconsider his resignation, or at least stay another year or six more months. Ronald Storrs also wished Richmond's departure to take place after the Nabi Musa festivities were over, for there was a belief that Richmond helped keep the Arab population less militant than it would be without him.[41] Clayton too thought Richmond's presence was of great value, and described Richmond as 'to some extent the counterpart of the Zionist Organisation'.[42] Nevertheless, Richmond's decision was final. As he explained to his mother:

> I have pondered long and deeply before deciding this ... I move in a Jewish Administration which regards me with disfavour, and only keeps me because it is afraid to get rid of me—the Colonial Office is confessedly hostile to me—no proposal ever made by me of a positive constructive character has been accepted—by staying on I am betraying the people of the country ... In a word Palestine is gaining nothing and I am losing much.[43]

Richmond's bitter resentment at the administration's pro-Zionist policy ended in a stormy resignation letter which he wrote to Samuel on 13 March 1924. Ronald Storrs reported that the departure of Richmond was greatly regretted in Muslim circles, especially that of the Supreme Muslim Council.[44]

The appointment of Sir Gilbert Clayton in April 1923 to succeed Wyndham Deedes as chief secretary was another measure calculated by the high commissioner to appease the Arab population to some extent. Clayton belonged to a group of officers who had run the Arab Bureau in Cairo during the First World War, and who tried to find a common denominator for British imperial interests and Arab nationalist aspirations.[45] It was he who had written to Mark Sykes, one month after the issuing of the Balfour Declaration in 1917, suggesting that it might have been a mistake: 'I am not fully aware of the weight which Zionists carry, especially in America and Russia, and of the consequent necessity of giving them everything for which they may ask.'[46]

When Deedes informed Samuel of his intention to resign in May 1922, Samuel persuaded him to stay another year until he was able to find a successor. Samuel then invited Clayton to take up the post of chief secretary, but Clayton, objecting to British policy in Palestine, politely rejected the offer. However, immediately after the publication of Churchill's White Paper in June 1922, Clayton wrote to Samuel that in view of the fresh statement of policy, he was ready to accept the offer. He believed that the White Paper was a whittling down of Zionist policy in Palestine, and clarified, in his opinion, the formerly vague policy of the British government.[47] By accepting the offer, Clayton hoped that he would again be at the centre of Britain's imperial strategy in the Middle East. In any event, Clayton eventually found himself installed as a 'genial figurehead', used by Samuel to assure the Arabs of British reliability, while Samuel went ahead and steadily laid down the foundations of the Jewish national home.[48]

When news of Deedes' resignation and Clayton's appointment became known in Palestine, *al-Karmel* wrote on 9 May 1923 that the Arabs were waiting to see what his policy would be. He was believed to be a wise man with enough experience to enable him to draw the policy to follow.[49] The Bethlehem paper, *Sawt al-Sha'b*, wrote on 5 July 1923 that Clayton would be 'of more impartiality and inclination towards the Arabs than his predecessor Sir Wyndham Deedes', but that he would not be 'less interested in the policy of colonisation and the assurances of the British policy than the latter'.[50] This was not an inaccurate prognosis of Clayton's career in Palestine, for he did, at various points, adapt himself to the policy set at higher levels in London, while he knew, and pointed out, that Britain was getting herself into unnecessary trouble by backing the Zionists.[51]

Clayton seems to have remained convinced of the administration's impartiality until 1924, when he became completely disillusioned with the government's policy. At the same time as Richmond submitted his resignation, Clayton was also indicating his own deep disenchantment and discouragement. He wrote to one of his close friends that he too disliked the Middle East Department of the Colonial Office, and after the first year in Palestine, he concluded with a rare premonition:

> In general, a year in Palestine has made me regard this whole adventure with apprehension. We are pushing an alien and detested element into the very core of Islam, and the day may come when we shall be faced with the alternative of holding it there by the sword or abandoning it to its fate![52]

But unlike Richmond, Gilbert Clayton believed that there was no use fighting this policy publicly and that it would serve no purpose except perhaps to bring an early end to his career.

Another powerful opponent of the government's policy, and one of the 'dissidents' in the Palestine administration, was Lieutenant-Colonel Percy Bramley, the director of public security who was appointed in 1921 and dismissed from his post by the high commissioner in 1923.[53] He believed that he was serving 'under Partisan and idealist superiors (both British and Jew) in the Secretariat at Government Headquarters', and made his opinions known to the Colonial Office as well as to top officials in Palestine.[54] Bramley wrote to the Colonial Office that he was led to the conclusion that the real reason why it had become 'imperatively necessary' to remove him from office was that he consistently 'but ineffectually' opposed: (i) the illegal importation of Jews in Palestine in direct contrast to the Immigration Ordinance; (ii) the illegal arming of the Jews and of any compromise with Jewish extremists in this regard; (iii) the introduction of Bolshevism into Palestine by Jewish immigrants under cover of Zionist operations; (iv) the leaking of secret political intelligence to 'partisan' Jewish officials. The full facts had been brought to the attention of Wyndham Deedes by the Criminal Investigation Department, but the civil secretary had failed to check all irregularities brought to his attention both by the CID and by his political assistant (E. T. Richmond). He further accused Deedes of completely crippling 'efficient control by responsible Heads of Departments outside the official cliques thus created'. His formal warnings and protests were on record, but had been completely unheeded, and responsibility for administrative defects, if any, in relation to public security in Palestine during Deedes' tenure in office 'rested entirely with him'. He fully realized the difficult position in which an administrator of Sir Herbert Samuel's religion, temperament, and inexperience of administration in the East was placed in Palestine under prevailing political conditions, and he had done his very best to avoid dragging the controversy into public cognizance.[55]

Bramley added that 'unless and until the present Zionist-controlled Government in Palestine is completely replaced by one which is exclusively and wholly British in character and composition', and until the whole of the area (Palestine, Egypt, Hijaz and Mesopotamia) came under one unbroken political and administrative control, there was no chance of eradicating Bolshevik 'centres of mischief' which had been firmly established in Palestine and Egypt. He wrote that in his humble opinion, the Foreign Office was the correct authority to exercise such control.[56] Bramley continued to lobby along these lines until his death in 1925.

Lieutenant-Colonel W. F. Stirling, governor of Jaffa from 1920 to 1923,[57] is an example of the doubts felt among those at the second level in the administration, that of district governors.[58] Stirling, who could not be considered an enemy of the policy of the Jewish national home in its early days, wrote many years later that it was 'fascinating' to watch the first beginnings of the colonization schemes of the Jews who got down to work with a courage and determination which were 'beyond all praise'.[59] However, he was gradually led to alter those views as he saw that policy implemented. He wrote that at the start of the mandate, the power and administration of the Holy Land lay in the hands of three men, the high commissioner, the chief secretary, and the attorney-general, and that although Samuel was essentially a fair-minded man, Stirling believed that he had insufficient experience to deal with the most difficult post in the whole of the British Empire. According to Stirling, Samuel knew nothing of the 'oriental mind', adding that he 'could only feel sorry for him, since everything he said or did, however well-intentioned, was suspect to the Arab mind'.[60]

Stirling saw Deedes as a religious fanatic who once told him that he hoped that by as much as he could bring more Jews to the Holy Land, he would 'hasten the second coming of the Lord'. Norman Bentwich, 'the most open exponent of the Zionist faith', was a clever lawyer in whose hands lay the making of laws and adjudication of concessions. Stirling remarked: 'His faith being what it was, how could he possibly be considered impartial by any Arab in Palestine?' Stirling added:

> These three men were good men in themselves, but that they should have been chosen by our Government for the posts they held blackened the good name of England in the Middle East, and led to the final downfall of our reputation for fair play.[61]

Towards the end of 1922, Stirling wrote a memorandum to the high commissioner pointing out that unless the British government came out in the open and declared what they really meant by the Balfour Declaration, there would be increasing trouble between Arabs and Jews. He argued that if the government 'did in fact, mean to create a Jewish Sovereign State, now was the time openly to declare such a policy', and if, on the other hand, it was the intention 'to abide by the wording of the declaration', then a statement of such a policy was also required to allay the apprehensions of the Arabs. Stirling alleged that his memorandum was so unpopular that an immediate plan was devised to get rid of him, and that it was eventually decided to 'reorganize' the administration and reduce the number of governorates from five to three. This decision naturally entailed the dismissal of two governors, and needless to say, he was one of them. Petitions from all over the country to reconsider the decision did not succeed in reversing this decision, and with the 'shedding of crocodile tears' by the government, and expressions of profound goodwill from the high commissioner, Stirling took leave in May 1923.[62] After a great deal of thought about the Jewish national home, and after three years of practical experience 'of the workings of the scheme', Stirling had come to the conclusion that the policy was clearly wrong, and that he felt no need to modify his opinions either with the passing of years, or in view of the recent events.[63]

Intelligence reports also give a glimpse of the views of more junior officials in the administration of Palestine. One such report stated in July 1921 that the Arabs felt that they were the 'victims of Zionist coercion of the Government, which they most thoroughly distrust', and that the feeling among some of the junior officials in the administration was 'a rather nervous one', adding:

> They do not like the policy but naturally wish to keep their appointments. They will therefore hang on rather than resign, hoping against hope that the policy may be changed or modified. They are fully aware of the gravity of the situation, but in some cases are afraid to report in a pessimistic sense, for fear of being considered alarmists ... These men are naturally anxious as to their future.[64]

Samuel consistently denied charges that the administration in Palestine was run by Zionists. He wrote in December 1922, that the administration in its highest ranks was 'frankly British', and that although Palestinians were being introduced as they showed their capacity, the heads of all the departments and all governorates were British.[65] In July 1923, Samuel commented on a letter sent by Clayton to the colonial secretary Devonshire, in which Clayton wrote that the Arabs had been put off by the fact that the 'administrative policy of the country is heavily weighed by Zionist influence'. Samuel conceded that the Arabs indeed made this complaint, 'but no concrete instance which can be substantiated is ever given'. He added: 'Every impartial observer who has visited the country ... has noted this.'[66] However, Devonshire wrote in October 1923:

> It may be contended, on the other hand, that, even though formally excluded from all share in the administration, the Jewish agency does, in fact, by reason of its official recognition and right of access to the High Commissioner, enjoy, and thereby confer upon the Palestine Jews as a whole, a preferential position as compared with the other inhabitants of the country. To that extent it is possible to argue that existing arrangements fall short of securing complete equality between the different communities.

This view was also shared by many British officials. At the Imperial Conference in 1923, five months earlier, it was asserted that:

> Our High Commissioner Sir Herbert Samuel, has displayed not only administrative abilities of the highest order, but also the strictest impartiality in dealing with the conflicting interests of the inhabitants of Palestine. A Jew himself, he has never been accused of showing undue favour to the Jews. On the contrary, his high sense of justice is recognised and applauded in every quarter.[67]

However, Arab leaders could clearly see that:

> the executive power is in the hands of a staunch Zionist Jew. The constitutional power is in the hands of an extreme Zionist, Mr Bentwich, another of the 'Jewish Palestine' [sic]. Another headed the Department of Commerce and Industry. Whatever be the status of the other officials they are bound to obey the heads ...[68]

On the other hand, the Middle East Department continued to deny that the Zionists had anything to do with the administration in Palestine. In a memorandum entitled 'Palestine' which was circulated to the Cabinet in February 1924, it declared that the 'charge' that the present administration was a 'Jewish Government' would not 'bear examination'. It went on to say that, although the high commissioner was a Jew, this had not prevented him from being a British Cabinet minister for many years. The memorandum asserted that 'the higher ranks of the administration contain only one other Jew, viz., Mr. Bentwich, the Attorney-General', who had been appointed, not by Herbert Samuel, but by the previous military administration,[69] adding:

> The administration is a British administration, controlled by a British High Commissioner, under directions of a British Secretary of State. In accordance with the terms of the Mandate, the Jews are accorded special facilities for settlement, enterprise &c., but they do not enjoy (as is sometimes asserted) a position of privilege of monopoly.[70]

SAMUEL AND THE PALESTINIAN ARABS: INITIAL IMPRESSIONS

When he arrived in Palestine, Samuel had been made aware of the deep-seated feelings of Arab hostility towards his person as a Jew and a devoted Zionist. From the outset, he therefore made an effort to meet Palestinian notables, 'showing himself courteous and considerate'. He sought to convince them that his aim, and that of the British government, was to build a 'bi-racial' Palestine in which they would participate with the Jews in the building of Palestine without losing their identity.[71] At first, he achieved some success, at least with a section of the population, and the Arabs decided that 'though he sometimes acted as though he were a second Moses, [he] was at least an honourable man'.[72]

Initially, Muslim leaders refused to attend the assemblies to which he had invited them on 7 and 8 July 1920, immediately following his arrival in Palestine as a protest against the pro-Zionist policy of the British government, 'and particularly against my own appointment'.[73] However, since most of those who were invited did eventually attend the assemblies, Samuel concluded that: '... it was right not to have been deterred by the somewhat alarmist accounts of the state of opinion in Palestine, which had been transmitted from time to time, but to have put the situation to the test at once.'[74] Yet, in a personal letter to Curzon on 12 July 1920, Samuel did not hide his surprise that the situation was satisfactory. How long this would last 'no-one can foretell ... The absence of any difficulties so far is as agreeable as it is unexpected.'[75]

At his inaugural assembly on 7 July 1920, Samuel read out the king's message, which contained two important points; first, an assurance of the high commissioner's 'absolute impartiality' and of the determination of the government to respect every race and creed, and second, the establishment of the 'Jewish National Home', without affecting the 'civil and religious rights' or diminishing 'the prosperity of the general population of Palestine'.[76] Samuel's own speech set the tone of his policy for the next five years: the boundaries of the country to the north and the east had not yet been determined;[77] he intended to nominate a small advisory council, consisting in the majority of officials of the government, but also containing ten unofficial members to be chosen from the various sections of the population; and the time had come when the economic situation of the country could be actively taken in hand.

The measures that were designed to promote the establishment of 'the Jewish National Home'[78] were, he stated:

1. Land sales and land transactions were to be resumed at the earliest date. A land ordinance was to be enacted immediately.
2. A land commission was to be appointed to ascertain what lands were available for closer settlement.
3. A cadastral survey was to be speedily begun. In connection with it, a land settlement court was to be established in order to settle the boundaries of properties to avoid constant disputes.
4. Banks were to be established at the earliest date for the grant of long-term credits for agriculturists as well as urban businessmen.
5. Railways were to be turned over to the civil administration. The Jaffa-Lydda connection was to be widened. Other railway developments were contemplated in the future.
6. Under consideration was a large programme of public works, including the construction and improvement of roads, telegraph and telephone communications, afforestation, the construction of Haifa harbour, the drainage of swamps, and the provision of electric power throughout the country.
7. As soon as the status of the country was finally decided, a loan was to be arranged.
8. The Department of Public Health would strive to improve the health of the population, and would pay special attention to the eradication of malaria.
9. The Department of Education would improve the educational standards of the population as soon as the revenues of the country expanded.
10. Archaeological research would be promoted and the historic buildings of Jerusalem would be preserved. Tourism would be promoted to encourage the visits of pilgrims to the Holy Land.
11. Steps would be taken to ensure the proper town planning of the new quarters that were expected to arise in Palestine.
12. On the question of Jewish immigration, Samuel said that the development of the country would not only promote the well-being of its present population,

'but will furnish a livelihood to a large additional number', adding that 'indeed, it cannot be carried out without the introduction of additional man-power'. Thus, the ports and frontiers would 'shortly be opened to a limited immigration', and an ordinance would soon be issued to regulate the question of immigration.

13. Finally, as a act of clemency, Samuel declared amnesty to those in confinement as a result of the Easter disturbances in April 1920, and to all political prisoners in Palestine.[79]

Samuel later claimed that this speech had a positive effect on the Jewish population, while the Muslims, who had expected the declaration of a 'much more drastic policy', were relieved and reassured. According to Samuel's account, the grand mufti told him in the course of a conversation that for the first time in several weeks, 'he was able to smile'.[80]

THE PALESTINIAN NATIONAL MOVEMENT: LOSING THE PAN-ARAB DIMENSION

The establishment in July 1920 of a civil administration entrusted with carrying out the Balfour Declaration significantly influenced the political development of the Palestinian national movement.[81] In the first half of 1920, campaigning against Zionism was closely bound up with events in the wider Arab world, especially in Syria. Since early 1920, Arab leaders had linked their protests against Zionism with their opposition to the separation of Palestine from Syria. In February 1920, the Muslim-Christian Association sent a petition to the representatives of Great Britain at the Peace Conference protesting that they were

> greatly astonished to learn from various sources that Palestine shall be separated from Syria, and to understand from the statements of the Chief Administrator in Nablus on 7.1.20, that the Peace Conference will give its decisions contrary to our wishes by allowing Jewish immigration.[82]

On 12 March, after an 'orderly' and 'solemn' demonstration, Arab leaders had submitted to the military governor of Jerusalem and to the representatives of France, Italy and the USA a protest which read:

> Again we demonstrate the intensity of our feelings and our continued insistence on the following demands: (1) An independent Syria with natural boundaries. (2) Non-separation of Palestine. (3) No Zionism and no Jewish immigration. Above [demands] we consider our inherited rights and we refuse to accept an arbitrary settlement detrimental to those rights. We mean to oppose any action at variance with our wishes and are ready to defend our position to the very end.[83]

When the news of Samuel's appointment as high commissioner in Palestine became known in June 1920, some Arab nationalists in Palestine and Damascus decided to take military action in protest. The executive council of al-'Arabiyya al-Fata (The Young Arab Society),[84] according to the account of one of its members, Muhammad 'Izzat Darwazeh, planned a military operation on the borders near Samakh. Darwazeh's brother, Muhammad 'Ali, took charge of it, and according to Darwazeh this was the first military operation against 'foreign occupation and Zionism'. The plan was that action of this sort would continue, but due to Faisal's short reign and his eventual expulsion from Syria by the French, military activity came to an end.[85]

The initiation of the civil administration in Palestine coincided with momentous political events in surrounding Arab countries, with important consequences for the areas of the former Ottoman Empire which fell under the mandate system, and implications for the future course of Palestinian nationalism. On 30 June 1920, a revolt in Iraq seriously undermined Britain's claim to the mandates assigned to her in Iraq and Palestine, as these, theoretically at least, rested on the consent of the governed. This rebellion was put down by force, consolidating British rule in the area, and creating a second serious shock in Palestine. Until then, the Palestine Arab nationalist movement functioned within the framework of the broader Arab nationalist movement. On 24 July, the French occupied Damascus and forced Faisal to flee the country.[86] This caused deep shock and widespread disappointment in Palestine, and brought an end to the first stage of the Palestinian nationalist movement, known as the Southern Syria stage.[87]

In September 1920, Samuel wrote to Curzon that the occupation of Damascus by the French might have been expected to lead in Palestine either to a feeling of 'active' antagonism towards Great Britain for not preventing the occupation, or to a feeling of pessimism with regard to Arab nationalism, as well as a feeling of 'deprivation of any political centre to which their cause might be attached'. Samuel saw Arab nationalism in Palestine as an 'offshoot' of Arab nationalism in Damascus, its goal being to form, with the Hijaz, a single great Arab state. But now that the nationalist centre in Damascus had disappeared, Samuel concluded—rather to his satisfaction—that the union of Palestine and Syria was the last thing that the Palestinians desired.[88]

With Syria and Iraq out of the picture, the Palestine national movement, facing the threat of Zionism and the British mandate, found itself in an unenviable position. The draft mandate, submitted to the Peace Conference in December 1920, gave the Balfour Declaration an entirely new significance.[89] Thus, according to the Palestinian leader Muhammad 'Izzat Darwazeh, the Third Palestine Arab Congress was convened in December 1920 in the shadow of the collapse of Faisal's short-lived kingdom in Damascus, in an atmosphere of 'dismay and bewilderment'. The Palestine Arabs found themselves under direct British rule with a 'Jewish and a Zionist high commissioner'.[90]

In view of the changing situation, the name Southern Syria (in reference to

Palestine) ceased to be used at this congress, and membership was now totally Palestinian: a total of thirty-six delegates drawn from all administrative districts took part.[91] The congress, held in Haifa between 13–19 December 1920, elected a nine-member body to implement its resolutions. This body, which was first known as the Central Committee but became known as the 'Executive Committee of the Palestinian Arab Congress' (henceforward the Arab Executive Committee), was headed by two Jerusalem notables, Musa Kazim Pasha al-Husseini as president, and 'Aref al-Dajani as vice-president.[92] From that point onwards, the Palestinian nationalist movement during the mandate period continued to be headed by the class of urban notables, and to be guided by the principles of the Third Congress.[93]

A new programme was adopted to meet the changed political situation created by Faisal's downfall and at this congress, too, the Muslim-Christian Associations became the main organizational framework of the Palestinian-Arab national movement.[94] The congress again rejected the Balfour Declaration and its incorporation in the League of Nations mandate, Jewish immigration, and land sales to Jews. It demanded the immediate granting of representative institutions as well as a national constitution. Darwazeh and other analysts maintain that these basic demands remained the main guidelines of the Palestinian national movement in its long struggle against Zionism.[95]

It was dissident members of the notable class in the Ottoman Empire who had articulated the ideas of Arabism and who joined the ranks of Faisal's Arab government in Damascus.[96] However, with the fall of Faisal, Arabism receded and Palestinian nationalism, with its total rejection of Zionism and opposition to Britain's policy on Zionism, was the only framework within which these notables could operate. It was they who constituted the main political leadership of the Palestinian Arabs during the mandate period and their leaders continued to be the office-holding elite among the Arab population.

After the fall of the Ottoman Empire, the Palestinian notable class, facing the reality of British authority in Palestine, found it necessary to moderate their position in order to convince the British that they were the traditional spokesmen of their society. To do this, they dropped their previous Ottoman perspective in favour of 'local nationalism', a process which, as Muslih asserts, took two years of painful confusion from 1918–20 and culminated in a 'geographically-defined ideology of Palestinian nationalism'. Through this adjustment, they hoped to continue to play the role of intermediaries between government and people. Thus they accepted administrative posts, and discretely opposed the policies of the occupied without provoking its wrath.[97]

However, the pressures created by the incoming Zionists and the nature of the relationship between the British and Zionists immensely complicated and undermined the position of the notables in their traditional role as leaders of their community. To further undermine their power, Herbert Samuel followed a policy of divide and rule.

In his inaugural speech, delivered in Jerusalem on 7 July 1920, Samuel announced that an advisory council which he was about to nominate would meet under his presidency. All drafts of ordinances dealing with matters of importance, and the annual financial budget of the Palestine administration, would be submitted to this council for its advice.[98] In addition to the high commissioner, the eleven official members of the Advisory Council were the legal secretary, the civil secretary, and the ten heads of the principal departments[99] (with the exception of the director of immigration, because Samuel wanted control of immigration under his own direct supervision). The ten unofficial members comprised four Muslims, three Christians and three Jews.[100] The unofficial members, who represented the communities, would not be elected, but nominated by the high commissioner.[101]

Samuel's choice of the Jewish members of the Advisory Council is interesting. David Yellin was described by Samuel in a confidential despatch to Curzon as an educationalist and president of the Va'ad Leumi, the National Council of Jews, in Jerusalem, and as Samuel pointed out, he was also 'one of two vice-presidents of that city'.[102] The second Jewish member, Haim Kalvarisky,[103] according to Samuel, was one of the principal representatives of the Jewish Colonization Association in Palestine which managed Baron Edmond de Rothschild's colonies. And the third, Yitzhak Ben Zvi, was described by Samuel as one of the leaders of the 'moderate' sections of the Jewish labour organizations.[104] However, Ben Zvi, leader of the Po'ali Zion party in Palestine was also responsible for organizing the illegal Jewish paramilitary force, the Haganah.[105] But Samuel did not mention any of this in his despatch to Lord Curzon, nor did he mention that David Yellin was chairman of the Zionist Commission.

The Arab members included three Christians and four Muslims from different parts of Palestine. These were Isma'il Bey Husseini (Jerusalem, Muslim), Michel Effendi Bayruti (Jaffa, Christian), Sulayman Bey Nasif (Haifa, Christian), Dr Habib Salim (Christian), Sulayman 'Abd al-Razzaq Bey Tawqan (Nablus, Muslim), Shaykh Frayh Abu Midyan MBE (Beersheba, Muslim), Shaykh 'Abd al-Hayy al-Khatib (Hebron, Muslim).[106]

The composition and status of the council raised questions in Britain. In September 1920, the *Morning Post* wrote that what the Arabs asked for was 'some form of self-government now which would allow them the voice they are entitled to in the affairs of their country, including the power of averting or controlling this threatened immigration'.[107] All they got from Sir Herbert Samuel, however, was an Advisory Council 'who meet when summoned to hear communications and who may ask questions'. The unofficial members were 'appointed by the leader of political Zionists', and 'this is what the much heralded self-determination for little nations amounts to'.[108]

Edwin Montagu,[109] the secretary of state for India, sent a private letter to Curzon, on 26 November 1920, in which he strongly protested against the 'inadequate representation' of Muslims in the Advisory Council. He said that he was 'shocked' to find out that the ten unofficial members consisted of four Muslims, three Christians and three Jews. He went on to say:

> I believe I am right in saying that at least 70% of the population is Mohammedan. I, therefore, with great respect wish to bring to your notice my opinion that this composition of the Council, which places Mohammedans in a Minority, is monstrous and a flagrant violation of the principles to which I understood His Majesty's Government were committed, that the Government of Palestine should be composed of the various races therein living in proportion to their numbers.[110]

Hubert Young, at the Foreign Office, commented that Montagu's protest was based on a 'misconception', because the Advisory Council was not an executive body and 'forms no part of the Government of Palestine'.[111] The unofficial half was 'symbolic' of the interests of Palestinians: 'No understanding has ever been given that the "Government of Palestine" should be based on proportional representation.' As Young made clear in this minute: 'The only specific commitment of H.M.G. in respect of Palestine is the Balfour Declaration constituting it a National Home for the Jewish People.'[112] Moreover, the high commissioner was responsible to the Colonial Office and to the Permanent Mandates Commission, but not, according to the legal secretary, Norman Bentwich, to any Palestinian representative body.[113] Bentwich, indeed, firmly believed that in order to carry out the pro-Zionist policy, it was necessary to restrict the representative institutions of the country.[114]

Although the Advisory Council did not have any legislative powers or executive responsibilities, it did serve, according to Norman Bentwich, 'usefully' for nearly two years to provide a channel of criticism and advice, and was the only 'central semi-representative' body which Palestine was to have for twenty years.[115] It was dissolved in 1922 to make way for a Legislative Council.[116] The Council's first meeting was held on 6 October 1920, and the drafts of measures to be considered were circulated in advance in English, Arabic and Hebrew.[117] The council's advice was not binding; and official members could always out-vote unofficial members. To this extent, the appearance of some form of self-government was illusory. The minutes of the meetings of the Advisory Council, in particular of its first sessions, show that the topics of discussion were varied and the discussion itself frank. Samuel reported that during the first meeting, on 6 October 1920, which lasted seven hours, criticism was not absent, and that this was a 'healthy sign', as there was the danger that the members of the council, being nominated, 'might regard themselves as being summoned not to advise the Administration, but merely to endorse its decisions'.[118] At this meeting, one Arab member of the Advisory Council stated that he was glad to hear that England desired self-government for Palestine, and pointed out that 'a positive definition of the meaning of the word 'mandate' had not been given, and it would be necessary to wait and see what was actually implied and what the results would be'.[119]

This 'cooperative' attitude towards the government on the part of Arab members can be attributed to the fact that, before the mandate was ratified by the League of Nations in July 1922, there still appeared to be some hope of reversing its pro-Zionist terms. The Third Palestine Arab Congress in December 1921 did not decide to reject the Advisory Council, partly because the council's members had been careful to avoid claiming that they represented the general public, but more importantly, because the council was seen as a temporary measure, useful as long as the status of Palestine had not yet been defined.[120] However, as time passed and it became evident that the government intended to carry out its Zionist policy, the minutes of the Advisory Council show that its meetings became brief and mechanical, and little of importance was discussed.

Meanwhile, efforts by the Arab Congress to obtain government recognition of its status as representative of the Palestinian Arab population were unsuccessful. Samuel argued that the Muslim-Christian Associations were few and not to be taken seriously, and that the members of the Arab Executive Committee, elected by small groups, were 'by no means representative of the population'.[121] The legal adviser, Norman Bentwich, took the view that the Palestine Arab Congress 'claims to represent the vast majority of the Arab population of Palestine', but there was 'no means of testing the validity of that claim'.[122]

In contrast to the restrictions placed on the development of Arab self-governing institutions, Samuel fostered those of the Jews. After being banned by General Bols the previous May from convening, Samuel allowed the Va'ad Leumi to hold the first meeting of the elected Jewish Constituent Assembly in October 1920, and he held regular meetings with members of its executive body.[123] This elected assembly guided the lay affairs of the Jewish community; in effect it was the same as the present Israeli parliament, the Knesset Yisrael. Any Jew, of either sex, above twenty-five years of age, who was resident in Palestine for not less than one year, and who could read, write and speak Hebrew, was eligible for election as a member. The members of the elected assembly elected a General Council of forty members. This General Council appointed from its members an Executive Committee.[124] The president of the Va'ad Leumi from 1920–28 was David Yellin and from 1931–1948, Yitzhak Ben Zvi, who became the second Israeli president, succeeding Chaim Weizmann.

FIRST STEPS TOWARDS 'THE JEWISH NATIONAL HOME'

During the first nine months of Samuel's term of office, from July 1920 to March 1921, Palestine was still under Foreign Office control, with Lord Curzon as foreign secretary. With Curzon's well-known anti-Zionist sympathies, it is tempting to ask whether the Zionist programme could have been greatly reduced had Palestine remained under Foreign Office control. There is reason to speculate that this may have been the case. One episode from this period may suffice to demonstrate this point.

Three months after Samuel took office, letters were received by the Foreign Office warning of an increasing 'Jewish ascendancy in Palestine'. On 2 November 1920, Cecil Harmsworth, an official at the Foreign Office, received a letter from a Mr Pike Pease, who had first-hand knowledge of Palestine, raising questions, which seemed to him 'of some considerable importance'. Pease informed the Foreign Office that he had received a letter from a friend on the spot indicating that the non-Jewish community were much agitated about Jewish claims and deplored the influx of Jewish immigrants. The letter went on to say that on 1 October 1920, the government of Palestine had issued new stamps to replace former Egyptian Expeditionary Force stamps. The stamps were surcharged with the word Palestine: at the top in Arabic, in the centre in English, and at the bottom in Hebrew, 'with the addition of two initial letters "Aliph and Yod" to signify the words "Eretz Israel"— "The Land of Israel"'. It noted that this was 'the first official use of this title as applied to Palestine; and is deeply resented by the Moslems and Christians'. Apparently not having been consulted by Samuel, Foreign Office officials were perplexed. In a minute on 5 November, Forbes Adam suggested that the letters 'should be dropped'. On the same day Hubert Young wrote:

> I think it would be better to say that we should be glad to know the reasons which prompted him to make this addition to the Hebrew version of the word Palestine in the case of the surcharges, and no corresponding addition to the English or Arabic, and to be informed whether he contemplates a similar addition in all Hebrew references to Palestine in official documents—If this is so, we should prefer to be consulted before a final decision is taken, since there appears to us to be no adequate reason for the name to figure differently in Hebrew characters—Such a distinction might give rise to the erroneous impression that H.M.G. have one policy for the Jew and another for the Gentile.[125]

On 8 November, Sir John Tilley wrote to Samuel asking for an explanation, adding that he 'should prefer to be consulted before a final decision is taken in the matter'.[126] However, when the affairs of Palestine were transferred to the newly-created Middle East Department of the Colonial Office in March 1921 a totally different picture emerged. This department had a close relationship with Chaim

Weizmann which tipped the scale on many occasions in favour of the Zionists, and to the detriment of the Arabs.

In spite of Arab protests against the national home policy, as early as September 1920, Samuel was able to send Curzon a detailed account of the steps which he had already taken 'in the execution of the policy of constituting in Palestine the Jewish National Home'.[127] Among the measures which he reported were:

1. An Immigration Ordinance had been enacted, and an Immigration Department set up.
2. The Hebrew language had been recognized as an official language.[128]
3. The Jewish Sabbath was recognized as a day of rest.
4. The representatives of the Zionist Commission had direct access to the high commissioner and had a weekly interview with him.
5. A standing Land Commission had been appointed to ascertain the area of land available for close settlement.
6. In order to assist industry, the activity of which was essential if immigration was to be promoted, Samuel had reduced the customs duty on building materials for a period of two years from 11 per cent *ad valorem* to 3 per cent.
7. A Jewish company, with a large capital, proposed to erect a factory and to employ several hundred people [i.e. Jewish immigrants], but was unwilling to begin its operations unless freed from custom duties, and Samuel reported that, although he regretted the possibility of removing all import duties, he was considering this option.
8. In the economic sphere, a Department of Commerce and Industry had been set up, and the establishment of one or more banks for granting long-term loans for agriculture and industry was under study.[129]

If those were the first steps taken in the execution of the policy of constituting a Jewish national home in Palestine, what indeed, as the *Morning Post* article put it, was 'being done as regards the civil rights of the people which are guaranteed by the Balfour Declaration and the San Remo Conference',[130] rights which Samuel himself promised in his inaugural speeches upon arriving in Palestine, and whenever the occasion arose?

During his first months in office, and up until the May disturbances in 1921, Samuel continued to play down the anti-Zionist feelings of the Arabs in his official reports to London. In September 1920, he wrote that tranquillity had 'continued unbroken' since his arrival in Palestine. In a private letter to Sir John Tilley, head of the Palestine Committee of the Foreign Office (dated 27 September 1920), the civil secretary, Wyndham Deedes, confirmed Samuel's impressions and pointed out that on the Arab side, the reaction of the Muslims and Christians had changed from 'great fear and apprehension' to one of 'reassurance and confidence'. In his opinion, this was due to the fact that the immediate inauguration of the new regime with Sir Herbert Samuel as high commissioner 'was not followed by a wholesale expropriation of rights and interests of one section of the population for the sake of another', and that Samuel's statements had shown that it was 'not the intention that there should be'. However, Deedes saw this as a temporary state of 'allayed apprehension'. 'The Zionist programme and all that it means today and tomorrow remains ... the governing factor in the internal political situation and the test will come when that programme begins to operate'.[131]

Samuel discounted the influence of pan-Islamism and Arab nationalism, reported to be spreading within a 'small section' of the population, suggesting that their adherents represented no one but themselves. The bulk of the population, he maintained, were not interested in politics.[132] Hubert Young stated on 8 January 1921 that 'there is little or nothing in this report [from Samuel] to justify the W.O. contention that we are enforcing an unpopular policy in Palestine'.[133]

However, in February 1921, the tone began to change. The text of the draft mandate was prematurely published in the *Jewish Chronicle*, and was reproduced by some local papers which voiced apprehension at its terms. Samuel still insisted that the situation was 'little affected',[134] attributing this to three factors. First, there were some who hesitated to regard the published text as a final version of the 'instrument destined to control the fate of Palestine in the immediate future'. Secondly, there were some who hoped that British policy in Palestine might still undergo a change, and thirdly, there were still others who anticipated that the League of Nations would introduce important modifications.[135] In February 1921, Deedes wrote that the approaching international conference to reconsider the conditions imposed by the Treaty of Sèvres (in August 1920) had attracted the attention of those who were opposed to the division of the territories situated between the Taurus Mountains and the Sinai Peninsula. Signatures were being collected in opposition to the separation of Palestine from the rest of the region, to which, it was contended, 'that country belongs geographically as well as ethnographically and historically'. Arab discontent was reportedly growing in all parts of Palestine. In the neighbourhood of Beisan, for instance, the rising feelings of anxiety and apprehension were attributed, according to Deedes, to the 'unfounded impression having gained ground that the Government intends to further the settlement of Jews in a manner detrimental to the interests of the Arab population'.[136]

CHURCHILL'S VISIT TO PALESTINE

Winston Churchill's visit to the Middle East in March 1921 took place immediately after the affairs of British mandated areas were transferred from the Foreign Office to the Colonial Office and entrusted to the newly established Middle East Department. The colonial secretary's visit was the chief event in Palestine in March 1921 and can also be regarded as the real starting point of Arab opposition to the

British administration. This opposition was a direct consequence of the disastrous meeting which took place in Jerusalem on 28 March 1921 between Arab representative leaders and Churchill. Prior to the meeting, a delegation of Palestinian leaders comprising Musa Kazim Pasha al-Husseini, Tawfiq Hammad, Ibrahim Shammas, Dr Burtkush, Mu'in al-Madi and 'Aref Pasha al-Dajani met Churchill briefly on 22 March in Cairo, but were told that he would not discuss anything political with them, and would meet them again in Jerusalem.[137]

Upon his arrival in Palestine, Churchill was met by Arab demonstrations all the way from Gaza to Jerusalem. From Samuel's Political Report, it is not clear whether the train carrying Churchill and himself was scheduled to stop at Gaza, or whether it was forced to do so a by a huge demonstration at the railway station. However, the official report admits that Churchill left the train and went to the town centre, where he was met by the mayor and the notables and dignitaries, and after the usual hospitality, was presented with the Palestine Arab national demands as formulated in the Third Palestine Arab Congress in Haifa.[138] Samuel's official despatch reports that among the slogans that were heard were: 'Down with Balfour', and 'We won't have the Jews' and claims that there was another 'Long live the high commissioner and Mr Churchill'.[139]

Before leaving Palestine, Churchill was given a lengthy memorandum by the president of the Palestine Arab Executive Committee on the situation in Palestine, with a résumé of Arab demands.[140] The committee stated that during the war, the Arabs had allied themselves with the British in order to get rid of the Turks and achieve their independence. What actually happened was the opposite, and Palestine found herself 'separated from her surrounding Arab sisters by vast distances which she had covered by running after an imaginary friend'; 'she found no friend, she found an enemy rather'. On the question of representation, they held that the Third Palestine Arab Congress was the 'true representative of Palestine, her mouthpiece'. They regretted the passing of Ottoman days when they had governed themselves through a representative parliament, adding that the only Turkish official in their midst had been the *wali* or *mutasarrif* who had his advisory native elected council to help him. Comparing this with their current state of affairs, they continued:

> Now all that has changed. We have no voice or say in the government of the country, no representative parliament. The Legal Secretary with a few under him are the source of our laws and legal system, in spite of the fact that the treaty with Turkey has not been signed and the Mandate not ratified.[141]

The committee also noted that although the mandate was 'replete' with assurances that their 'civil and religious rights would be observed', which, in their opinion, 'grants nothing new'. The Turks, they added, never interfered with the religious exercises of other communities, and even went to great lengths to safeguard the exercise of these religions. As for 'civil rights', the Arabs understood the term to mean nothing more than equality and justice before the law, and noted that 'obviously' there was no privilege contained in this. On the other hand:

> the Jews have been granted a true advantage, namely that of becoming our rulers. We are to have equal rights of justice with them before the Law, but they are to have in addition to this the preference in politics and in the economic life of the country, of which the Mandate has seen fit to deprive us.[142]

Moreover, under the Turks, all the judges in the courts as well as members of the bench were natives, and any local could work up to the highest legal position.

The Arabs saw Churchill's response as 'disappointing, if not downright insulting'. He bluntly informed the Arab leaders that British policy would not change, and that it was not in his power to change it, and even if it were, it was not his wish to do so.[143] In its issue of 23 March 1921, the Arabic newspaper *Filastin* had written in its leading article that Churchill was 'known for his sympathies towards the Arabs'.[144] However, Churchill's attitude towards the Arabs did not live up to their expectations, for in Cairo as well as in Jerusalem, he insisted that his conference with the Arab leaders was not a 'formal' one and that he met them in his 'personal' and not in his 'official' capacity.[145] Darwazeh described his attitude as 'impolite and crude', and asserted that it later became evident that Churchill was extremely pro-Zionist in his attitude, strongly favouring Jewish demands. According to his account, it was immediately after the meeting with Churchill that the Arabs became more apprehensive.[146]

Darwazeh reported after Churchill's departure that the Arab Executive Committee was invited by Samuel to discuss the Palestine Order-in-Council, the proposed constitution for Palestine, but the Arab leaders made it a condition that the constitution should not be based on the Balfour Declaration, as this would render all discussion useless. When the high commissioner refused this condition, the Arab Executive Committee declined to meet with him and rejected the constitution in principle.[147]

Deedes noted that the visit of the secretary of state 'gave satisfaction to the Jews and brought disappointment to the Arabs'. He also reported an increasing discontent with the administration among all sections of the Arab population as well as an increasing opposition to Zionist immigration. Feelings between Arabs and Jews were becoming 'extremely bitter'.[148]

6

Responding to Crisis:
The Jaffa Riots and their Aftermath

Until May 1921, Samuel maintained his view that the Arabs would eventually be ready to accept Zionism in return for the 'efficient' government which the British administration had brought, ending many centuries of corrupt Turkish rule. However, the May Day riots in Jaffa revealed the flaws in these assumptions, and a more realistic, if not pessimistic outlook emerged.[1] From then on, Samuel acknowledged increasing Arab discontent with the administration and more opposition to Jewish immigration.[2]

A secret report by Captain Brunton of General Staff Intelligence, dated 13 May 1921, described how the violence broke out. On the morning of 1 May, the authorities permitted a moderate Jewish socialist May Day demonstration to take place in Tel Aviv, but another unauthorized demonstration of about fifty communists carrying red flags clashed with the moderates. The police attempted to disperse the Bolsheviks and a conflict ensued. Muslims and Christians rushed to help the police against the Jews and a general disturbance ensued which, within an hour, spread to the southern end of the town. The 'wildest' rumours of Jewish attacks excited the rage of Arabs. The reception house for Jewish immigrants in Jaffa was then attacked and a number of Jews were killed. After the fifth day, 40 Jews and 18 Arabs (Muslims and Christians) had been killed, and 180 Jews and 50 Arabs wounded. According to the intelligence report, 'the state of the dead and wounded has proved that the Arabs were mainly armed with sticks while the Jews had revolvers'.[3]

The following day, the vice-consuls of France, Italy and Spain had been forced by a 'large and clamorous' crowd (who intended to grab the French flag and hold it in the demonstration but were with difficulty prevented from doing so by the French vice-consul), to visit the governor of Jaffa. They were asked by a large section of the population to submit the following demands: (i) Indian soldiers only to be used in Ajami [a suburb in Jaffa], because the people were unable to distinguish between British and Jewish soldiers, who it was believed were operating in British uniform; (ii) arms should be given to Arabs to defend themselves from Jews 'who were shooting them like birds'. A boycott of Jewish goods followed, and the institution of a commission of inquiry.[4]

In Haifa, an outbreak of violence seems to have been narrowly averted. According to the 'Political Report' for May, feelings between Arab and Jew there were 'extremely bitter'. A 'Bolshevik meeting' in Haifa had been met by the Arabs with 'disgust', which later turned into anger as soon as the reports of the disturbances reached them. Elsewhere in Palestine, news of the Jaffa riots produced great agitation. For instance in Beersheba, where the sheikhs had, according to the report, hitherto detached themselves from the nationalist movement, and had previously opposed the Palestine Arab Congress, they now supported all the resolutions of that congress. In Gaza, when the news from Jaffa reached the people, their feelings rose to an 'extraordinary degree' and it became necessary to put all Jews in a place of safety with guards to protect them. The whole of the local council went to the governor and was only pacified when the mayor himself was allowed to find out by telephone how things were, after which the deputation withdrew and the crowd was dispersed. In Nablus, too, a representative committee interviewed the governor and asked to know the truth. They wanted to know what had happened in Jaffa, and maintained that they did not believe government communiqués, had no confidence in the government which was 'controlled by Zionists', and that their 'cup was overflowing'. The governor reported that they were highly excited and in no mood to discuss matters calmly. They were only pacified by being given every facility for communicating with Jaffa.[5] It was in these circumstances, during the Jaffa disturbances, that Samuel declared martial law, and requested the commander-in-chief of the Mediterranean fleet to send warships to Jaffa and Haifa. However, by the time the ships arrived, order had been restored and the attacks on Jewish settlements had been driven off by cavalry, armoured cars and air attacks.[6]

Captain Brunton summed up the situation in May 1921 as

> nothing short of bitter and widespread hostility and the Arab population has come to regard the Zionists with hatred and the British with resentment. Mr Churchill's visit put the final touch to the picture. He upheld the Zionist cause and treated the Arab demands like those of negligible opposition to be put off by a few political phrases and treated like children.[7]

His report concluded that the troubles in Jaffa and other parts of the country were 'only the expressions of a deep-seated and widely spread popular resentment at the present British policy', adding that if that policy was not modified 'the outbreaks of today may become a revolution tomorrow'.[8] The causes of Arab opposition to British policy were, he said, the following:

1. The special privileges accorded to Jews.
2. The influence of the Zionist Commission and the openly declared political aims of the Zionists.
3. The use of *Hebrew* as an official language.
4. The immigration of great numbers of low class Jews.
5. The behaviour and immorality of the immigrants.
6. The fall in price of land, trade depression, and the prohibition of export of cereals affecting the peasantry.
7. Arrogance of Jews towards Muslims and Christians.
8. No representation in the Government of the country or control of expenditure being accorded to the *Arabs*, who realise that the money taken from them in taxes is spent on employing foreign Jewish labour instead of native, keeping up Jewish immigration offices and such like matters.
9. Loss of confidence in the Palestine Administration and in the British Government.
10. The realization of the injustice of self government being given to nomadic savages in Trans-Jordania and refused to Palestine.
11. Muslim and Christian religious feeling aroused by conduct and aims of the Jews.
12. The Government attitudes towards Muslim and Christian petitions, protests and complaints which are frequently not answered or disregarded while Jews appear to have at all times the ear of the administration.
13. The use of the Zionist flag.

Samuel later admitted that he was not surprised to learn that it was in the port of Jaffa that violence had broken out, for he knew that this feeling 'must, of course, be most acute in places where the irritant which causes it is most in evidence', i.e. where the new immigrants landed.[9] Although tranquillity was restored on the surface, 'beneath there is intense feeling on both sides'. The Arabs complained of Jewish boycotting of Arab traders, while Arab boatmen had refused to land Jewish immigrants.[10] On 8 May 1921, the Executive Committee of the Arab (Muslim and Christian) Palestine Congress had written to the secretary for foreign affairs that the Arabs 'have repeatedly notified the Governments of the Allies that Jewish immigrants are introducing the spirit and principles of Bolshevism', but that those notifications were, 'unfortunately' not given due consideration. They urged that Jewish immigration should be stopped, so that 'bloodshed and devastation in the country should come to an end'. Copies of this letter were also sent to the king, the House of Lords, the House of Commons, the Pope, and the secretaries for foreign affairs of France, the USA, Italy and Spain.[11]

At this point Samuel reflected on his Zionist policy and concluded that if Zionist activity was to be carried out 'at the point of the bayonet', it would make far less progress than if it were expressed by more moderate means. He knew that his 'new' policy would alienate his Zionist friends, but was convinced that it was the 'only policy' to be pursued, and that the Zionists themselves would later realize that it was 'in the best interests of the Zionist cause'. He was convinced that if the government of Palestine was placed on Weizmann's shoulders, he would come to exactly the same conclusions.[12]

On 24 May, Samuel telegraphed to Churchill that Article 4 of the draft mandate had met with strong opposition 'as it is regarded as constituting partnership between the Zionists and the Government of Palestine to the exclusion of the rest of the population', adding that the establishment of a representative assembly was closely connected with this question. Samuel suggested that the secretary of state should consider the insertion of a 'counterpoise in the Mandate'.[13] Deedes agreed that the Arab fear was a product of Article 4 of the mandate which recognized the Zionist Organization as an official agency whose task was to advise the government on everything concerning the national home policy.[14]

SAMUEL'S SPEECH OF 3 JUNE 1921

In the immediate aftermath of the Jaffa riots, Samuel suggested some measures to ease tension. They included the deportation of all 'Bolshevist' immigrants and the temporary suspension of immigration. Immigration would be resumed on condition, first, that the enterprises on which the men were to be engaged should be ready before the immigrants arrived, and second, that a stricter control should be exercised over the selection of immigrants individually. He also asked for reconsideration of the establishment of a local force and the very early establishment of representative institutions.[15]

His speech of 3 June, delivered on the occasion of the king's birthday, reflected his response to the violence and was the first attempt to interpret the Balfour Declaration. He began by speaking about his plan to improve education during the next four years, and about the question of *awqaf*, the dispute in the Orthodox Patriarchate, and the religious affairs of the Jewish community. He spoke of the economic development of the country, and of the improvement of transport, telegraphs and telephones, of improving the breeds of 'horses, cattle and donkeys'. He said a word about the prohibition on the export of cereals which had been strongly attacked by the Arabs.[16] He pointed to the need for mortgage and agricultural banks, and stated that it had been intended to raise a new branch of the police force, to consist of 500 men of a good standard drawn from all sections of the population. He also said that 'it was necessary to postpone for the time being the creation of the Military Defence Force which was recently contemplated'.[17] On the question of immigration, Samuel announced that it had been suspended 'pending a review of the situation', and that its extent must be strictly proportioned to the employment available in the country. Rules were laid down specifying that persons belonging to the following classes might be admitted into Palestine: (i) travellers who did not intend to settle in Palestine and whose stay did not exceed three months; (ii) persons of independent means; (iii) members of professions 'who intended to follow their calling' in Palestine; (iv) wives, children and other persons wholly dependent on residents of Palestine, and (v) persons who had a definite prospect of employment with specified employers or enterprises. A 'limited' number of immigrants, who had already disposed of their possessions, and had arrived at European ports, would be exempted from the suspension of immigration.

On the question of implementing the mandate, Samuel stated that the British government would make provision for the government of Palestine in an instrument which would be registered with the Council of the League of Nations, and that 'the interests of the non-Jewish population will not only be fully safeguarded by the Mandate itself, but will certainly be provided for also in that instrument'. He very briefly announced the establishment of a system of elections in municipalities, without entering into details.

Finally, Samuel turned to the political situation. There was an 'unhappy misunderstanding' with reference to the phrase in the Balfour Declaration, 'the establishment in Palestine of a National Home for the Jewish people',[18] and elaborated:

> I hear it said in many quarters that the Arab population of Palestine will never agree to their country, their Holy Places and lands being taken from them, and given to strangers ... I answer that the British Government, which does indeed care for justice above all things, has never consented and will never consent to such a policy. That is not the meaning of the Balfour Declaration. It may be that the translation of the English words into Arabic does not convey their real sense. They mean that the Jews, a people who are scattered throughout the world but whose hearts are always turned to Palestine, should be enabled to found here their home, and that some among them, within the limits that are fixed by the numbers and interests of the present population should come to Palestine in order to help by their resources and efforts to develop the country, to the advantage of all its inhabitants. If any measures are needed to convince the Moslem and Christian population that those principles will be observed in practice and that their rights are really safe, such measures will be taken. For the British Government, the trustee under the Mandate for the happiness of the people of Palestine, would never impose upon them a policy which that people had reason to think was contrary to their religious, their political, and their economic interests.[19]

A minute by Eric Mills at the Colonial Office, about a year later, on 24 May 1922, noted: 'Lord Balfour expressed unqualified approval of Sir Herbert Samuel's definition of the Jewish National Home in the Birthday Speech'.[20]

On 8 June 1921, *Filastin* published an Arabic translation of Samuel's speech.[21] In a commentary three days later, the paper noted that the people had been expecting to hear a statement of policy which would have removed their fears regarding Zionist ambitions, but that the high commissioner's speech contained nothing of the kind. Instead, they heard about improving the roads, telephones and telegraphs, and even about improving the breed of donkeys. In the aftermath of the Jaffa disturbances, *Filastin* continued, people were not too keen to hear about internal religious disputes, or economic improvements, which in their opinion were to the benefit of the Jews, nor even of improvements in education, however small they were, and however much they had asked for them. What they wanted to hear about was the political situation, which had deteriorated because of the policy of the Balfour Declaration. *Filastin* ridiculed Samuel's comment that the Arabic translation might not have conveyed the true meaning of the declaration, and commented: perhaps the Arabs had misunderstood the real meaning, but had Lord Sydenham, and all the anti-Zionist British politicians who strongly condemned the Balfour Declaration also misunderstood the meaning?

On the question of immigration, *Filastin* criticized Samuel's five categories, commenting that this was no restriction on immigration, but on the contrary, opened the gates of Palestine widely to new immigrants, for there was hardly any person who did not fit under one or other of the five categories. Moreover, who were the people of independent means? Were they those who owned £30? And how many were those who were stranded in Europe and who had sold their belongings? In the opinion of *Filastin*, these measures were extremely liberal, and in no way amounted to a restriction on immigration.[22]

Concerning the proposed municipal elections, *Filastin* held that at first, upon hearing this, the Palestine Arabs had been happy to learn that elections would be held, and that this was a reform long awaited. However, they had been greatly disappointed when they found out the conditions for such elections: anyone who paid a yearly rent of £20 had the right to vote, and anyone who paid £40 could be elected. What was the meaning of this? *Filastin* argued that this measure was calculated to deprive most Palestine Arabs of the right to vote, because most of them lived in houses or held shops that were offered to them by religious endowments, both Muslim and Christian, free of charge. Hence, in Jerusalem for example, rarely could there be found anyone who paid £20 in yearly rental.[23]

The Zionists were also unhappy at Samuel's response to the riots. After his speech on 3 June 1921, Weizmann went so far as to suggest replacing him as high commissioner for Palestine with George MacDonogh, director of military intelligence (1916–18) and a pro-Zionist sympathizer. Weizmann's latest biographer, finding this suggestion quite curious, notes that it is not clear, however, 'why he [Weizmann] felt he had enough clout to do so'.[24]

A War Office report on the situation in Palestine argued that the high commissioner's statement of policy on 3 June 1921 had satisfied neither party, and that the Arabs were demanding the removal of the high commissioner himself, together with Mr Bentwich, the legal adviser. The Arabs felt that they were 'the victims of Zionist coercion of the Government, which they most thoroughly distrust', and that 'nothing short of a modification of the Jewish policy and the establishment of some form of proportional representation will ease the situation'. According to the same report, a measure of confidence could be slowly restored only if the administration was able to prove that they were 'not bound hand and foot to the Zionists, as is popularly supposed to be the case'.[25]

On 10 June 1921, the *Morning Post* reported that Samuel could not travel without an escort of armed cars, and that during a recent visit to the northern districts of Palestine, 'His Majesty the High Commissioner, was greeted by the people with old shoes on sticks, an insulting symbol, and with cries of "Down with the Jews". His life was also threatened, and he was compelled to promise a national Government.'[26]

THE HAYCRAFT COMMISSION

Another propitiatory measure taken by Samuel in this period was to publish the Haycraft Commission of Inquiry Report into the Jaffa riots of May 1921. The inquiry, which submitted its report on 10 August 1921 was chaired by Sir Thomas Haycraft, chief justice of Palestine, with H. C. Luke, assistant governor of Jerusalem and Mr Stubbs of the Legal Department as members. The inquiry commission reported that the immediate causes of the disturbances, i.e. the MPS (Miflagah Po'alim Sotzialistim) demonstration which clashed with the authorized Jewish Labour Party (Ahdut Ha-Avodah), 'could not have been sufficient to give rise to more than a street riot of the ordinary kind'. The Bolshevik demonstration was simply the spark which led to the Arab-Jewish feud. The commission noted the argument made by some Jews that the cause of all the trouble was the propaganda spread by a small class of Arabs who regretted the departure of the old regime, because the British 'had put an end to privileges and opportunities of profit formerly enjoyed by them'. They were merely making use of the anti-Zionist cry in order to wreck the British mandate. The Haycraft Report was 'satisfied' that this was 'not the case' and that the feeling against the Jews was 'too genuine, too widespread, and too intense to be accounted for in the above superficial level'.[27]

According to the report, discontent with the government was partly due to its policy on the Jewish national home, partly to Arab misunderstandings of that policy, and partly to the manner in which that policy was interpreted 'by some of its advocates outside the Government'. This culminated in a suspicion that the government was 'under Zionist influence', and that it was therefore led to 'favour a minority to the prejudice of the vast majority of the population'. The commission added that:

> We have been assured, and we believe, that had there been no Jewish question, the Government would have had no political difficulty of any importance to deal with so far as its domestic affairs were concerned. We consider that any anti-British feeling on the part of the Arabs that may have arisen in the country originates in their association of the Government with the furtherance of the policy of Zionism.[28]

Moreover, there was a universal belief among the Arabs that the aims of the Zionists and Jewish immigration were a danger to their 'national and material interests'. There was 'no evidence worth considering' that the Jaffa riots were planned; 'had that been the case, we hesitate to conjecture what the consequences would have been'. As long as the Jews remained an 'unobtrusive minority' as they did under the Turks, they were not 'molested or disliked'; it was only when the Arabs came to believe that they were exercising a 'preponderating influence over the Government' that a state of feeling emerged which required 'but a minor provocation on the part of a small number of undesirable Jews to ignite an explosion of popular anger against Jews in general'. The report noted that:

> Moslems, Orthodox Christians, Catholics, Maronites and other Uniates, Anglicans have been represented by witnesses, who included priests of the above Christian bodies: and it has been impossible to avoid the conclusions that practically the whole of the non-Jewish population was united in hostility to Jews.[29]

The Commission of Inquiry ended its report by stating the grievances of the Arabs which led to their state of exasperation:

1. When Great Britain took over the administration of Palestine, she was led by the Zionists 'to adopt a policy mainly directed towards the establishment of a National Home for the Jews, and not to the equal benefit of all Palestinians'.
2. In pursuance of this policy, the government of Palestine had an official advisory body, the Zionist Commission, an *imperium in imperio*, which placed the interests of the Jews above all others.
3. There was an undue proportion of Jews in the government.
4. Part of the Zionist programme was to flood the country with people who possessed 'greater commercial and organising ability' which would eventually lead to their gaining the upper hand over the rest of the population.
5. The immigrants were an 'economic danger' to the country because of their competition, and because they were favoured in this competition.
6. Immigrants offended the Arabs 'by their arrogance and by their contempt of Arab social prejudices'.

7. Owing to insufficient precautions, Bolshevik immigrants were allowed into the country leading to social and economic unrest in Palestine.[30]

On Zionist activities and intentions, the commission also reported that, for instance, Dr David Eder, head of the Zionist Commission, had stated that only Jews should be allowed to bear arms, and that 'there can only be one National Home in Palestine, and that a Jewish one, and no equality in the partnership between Jews and Arabs, but a Jewish preponderance as soon as the numbers of the race are sufficiently increased.'[31]

Moreover, the Arabs regarded Jewish immigration not only as an 'ultimate' means to subject the Arabs politically and economically, but also as an 'immediate' cause of Arab unemployment. The Haycraft Commission noted that the Arabs were aware that Jewish predominance was envisaged 'not only by extremists but also by the responsible representatives of Zionism'.[32]

Samuel reported in October 1921 that the publication of the report on the whole had a useful effect, the Arabs regarding it as favourable, although the Zionists regarded it as 'a powerful weapon for anti-Zionist propaganda'.[33] The Haycraft findings were largely identical to the Palin Report of 1920, the major difference being an emphasis in the former on Arab fear that through extensive Jewish immigration Palestine would become a Jewish dominion. But once again, no action to remedy the situation was taken in the Middle East Department of the Colonial Office, and the Haycraft Report went unheeded. Only Clauson in the Colonial Office took alarm at the views which Eder expressed to the Commission of Inquiry, but no one took any notice of him.[34] He minuted in September 1921:

> The question of the Zionist Commission is a more serious one and I am afraid that we must intervene in this matter ourselves. Dr Eder in his evidence, which must by now be common knowledge in Pal. apart from this report, disclosed views which are so entirely incompatible with the policy of H.M.G. and with the professed policy of Dr Weizmann that, if we are to make our policy a success, it is urgently necessary that both we and the Z.O. should publicly disavow them. The only disavowal which would be regarded as sincere by the people of Palestine would be the removal of Dr Eder from his present position, a step which I think we are fully entitled to invite the Z.O., in its official position as the Jewish Agency, to take.[35]

In October, Clauson warned: 'I am afraid the Palestine Government are a trifle inclined to whistle to keep their courage up.' He added that Stirling (the governor of Jaffa) had received a letter from his second in command saying: 'I spend all my time stamping on sparks, before they have time to spread—and wondering when I shall miss one'.[36] In his secret despatch dated 8 October, Samuel wrote that for political reasons it was urgent that Muslim opinion be satisfied 'as soon as possible'.[37]

The urgency of the situation was now acutely felt. Another outburst of violence on 2 November 1921, the fourth anniversary of the Balfour Declaration, convinced the high commissioner and his civil secretary, Wyndham Deedes, that the functions of the Zionist Commission had to be restricted to 'purely economic and cultural matters', leaving politics to the Zionist Organization in London. In a private and secret letter on 22 November, Deedes wrote to Shuckburgh that 'an exception has been made in this country for which, I think, there is no precedence elsewhere, of associating with us in the administration of the country another body, the Zionist Commission'.[38] Deedes also pointed out that if the Zionists had adhered to the same policy as the government, this association might have been understandable by the Arabs, but since the Zionists did not comply with the policy of the government, the Arabs could only conclude that: 'H.M.G. was bound hand and foot to the Zionists, that the statement of the 3rd June was mere dust thrown in their eyes, and all Legislation here was, and would continue to be inspired by Zionist interest.'[39]

Even Deedes, a passionate supporter of Zionism, believed that Article 4 of the mandate, which recognized the 'anomalous position assigned to the Zionist Organization', should be abolished and suggested that the country should be governed with the help of a body which would adequately represent all sections of the community.[40]

In December 1921, desperate to provide the Arabs with a reason to find something positive in his administration, Samuel wrote to the colonial secretary that it was 'essential, in order to win the confidence and goodwill of the population of Palestine, that the Administration should be able to point to definite benefits that have followed from its establishment'.[41]

He was referring to a 'comprehensive' programme of primary education for a period of four years, after which 'the whole of the country' would be covered with elementary schools.[42] Since the question of education had always been referred to as a grievance by the Muslim population, Samuel attached great importance to a more positive policy in the field as a means of appeasing the Arabs. He conceded in his despatch that the Arabs complained, and rightly so, that higher education was very inadequate, and that under the Turks much better opportunities had existed. The Jewish organizations provided secondary education for their own population, and the various missionary schools maintained the same for the Christians, but the needs of the Muslim population, were 'met hardly at all'. In an agricultural country like Palestine, the Muslims maintained that opportunities for agricultural education were essential.[43]

However, in spite of the government's avowal of the need to introduce a comprehensive programme of primary education, it did not enact a compulsory education law, even for the elementary grades, as this would have involved a greatly increased educational expenditure, and the Arab leaders constantly complained about the inadequacy of funds for education. Thus, a dual system of education developed in Palestine, a Hebrew one under the auspices of the Zionist Organization, and an Arab public school system conducted and paid for by the government.[44] With all his good intentions, Samuel's ambitious plan amounted to very little in the end. His son, Edwin, who was a government official in Palestine during his father's administration, said in a television interview in 1978 that Samuel's idea was to build 300 schools in Arab villages in a period of five years, but that after the first year the money 'ran out', and after 50 schools were opened, 'the whole scheme was abandoned'.[45]

To sum up, after the Jaffa disturbances in May 1921, Samuel undertook a number of steps to pacify the Arabs. He immediately suspended immigration, albeit temporarily, and in the first official interpretation of the Balfour Declaration on 3 June 1921, he assured the Arabs that immigration should be controlled according to the 'economic absorptive capacity' of the country. Together with his civil secretary, Wyndham Deedes, he suggested the abolition of Article 4 of the draft mandate, published the Haycraft Report in October, and hastened the establishment of the Supreme Muslim Council. In the field of education, which was a major Arab grievance, Samuel made some improvements, and in December 1921 he claimed that he had 'successfully' solved the problem of the Beisan land in favour of its Arab tenants. On the other hand, the administration in practice allowed the Zionists to consolidate their position, including developing the armed strength of the Haganah, the clandestine Jewish defence force formed in 1920.

SAMUEL AND THE RISE OF JEWISH PARAMILITARY FORCES

Samuel's role in arming the Jewish population in Palestine went far beyond what the mandate itself stipulated, or what many British officials found acceptable or tolerable. Although the development of the Haganah itself lies outside the scope of this book, Samuel's contribution to the rise of Jewish armed forces in Palestine, and the birth of an ambiguous relationship between the underground forces and the administration, cannot be overlooked. The material available on the subject in the British archives is mainly found in Military Intelligence reports[46] and in Samuel's own 'top secret' reports to the Colonial Office. In many instances, these reports were accompanied by clear instructions that they be 'kept in a safe place under lock and key',[47] which indicates Samuel's acute awareness of the objectionable nature of this undertaking.

Arms smuggling became so serious a problem that throughout 1922 and 1923 intelligence reports as well as reports from British officials in Palestine constantly warned of the grave danger of such illicit activities.[48] Arab leaders set out to expose the Palestine administration's policy with regard to arming Jewish settlers, in the reports they filed to the British government, in their delegations to the Muslim world as well as in the press.[49] Samuel, seeking to disprove their accusations, drafted a letter to no less than sixteen representatives in Muslim countries 'to counter any false stories' that the government had 'armed the Jews against the Moslem community of the country'.[50]

Without the government's implicit approval, it is hard to imagine how Jewish 'self-defence' could have grown in Palestine in the way it did. Had the Palestine administration been willing to put an end to this illicit arms trafficking at its inception, it could easily have done so. Indeed, in 1929, H. C. Luke (assistant governor of Jerusalem in 1921 and a member of the Haycraft Commission of Inquiry), in his capacity as chief secretary under High Commissioner Sir John Chancellor, did in fact refuse Zionist requests to arm 500 Jews to defend outlying colonies.[51]

Immediately following the May 1921 riots, Samuel initiated a scheme for the defence of Jewish colonies. In order to 'provide for the possible contingency of attacks upon Jewish Colonies' the high commissioner deemed it necessary to 'draw up a general defence scheme' as well as special schemes for different districts, 'in conjunction with the Military Authorities'. The main features of the scheme, as Samuel put it, were:

> (1) The registration of colonists of suitable type and experience as special constables; (2) the allotment of brassards and rifles, with proportionate quantity of ammunition, for each colony, each rifle being secured by a bond not less than ten pounds and all to be kept under lock and seal in an approved Village Armoury, the Governor having the power to impose severe penalties for unauthorised breaking of the Armoury seal or abuse of rifles; and (3) the formulation, under military advice of a special Defence Scheme for each colony or group of colonies, by Districts.[52]

In his 'Political Report' for June 1921, Samuel reported the details of this scheme to the colonial secretary Winston Churchill. He wrote that, since his speech of 3 June, the Jewish population had been 'very nervous and apprehensive' and considered the speech a 'severe set-back' to their aspirations. He maintained, however, that this feeling had been 'a good deal modified' since Jewish colonies had been 'provided with Arms (under conditions strictly limiting their use to self-defence)'.[53] On 22 June, Samuel despatched a 'top secret' telegram clarifying his proposals: 'a small number of Jewish special constables, provided with police uniforms and rifles, have already been enrolled'; additional rifles and ammunition 'have been or are being placed in sealed armouries in Colonies'; 'bonds' were being taken against misuse. District governors would 'in the event of disturbances authorise opening of armouries and arming reliable colonists named in lists previously prepared', but that the head of a colony could also give 'necessary authority' in case a sudden attack took place. The high commissioner also noted that 'a definite scheme has been worked out for each colony under advice of military authorities'.

Samuel made it clear that these special constables were not full-time police, and, being well aware that 'violent controversy would probably result from their being embodied for training', he wrote: 'reserve armouries will undoubtedly act as a deterrent against attack', and that if attacks occurred, 'they would nevertheless enable defence to be maintained until arrival of gendarmerie or troops'. In case of a general rising, the commander-in-chief had prepared plans for concentrating inhabitants of outlying farms in centres where their safety could be guaranteed by the troops. Samuel also reported that a gendarmerie section of civil police numbering 500 men was being organized, drawn from all sections of the population. This force was 'in all respects' part of the police but 'it was to be in camp with British units while receiving its first six months training under its own instructors'. The task of this force was 'to take offensive against bands of disturbers of peace from within Palestine or from Trans-Jordania'.[54]

On 11 July 1921, Wyndham Deedes wrote confidentially to Hubert Young at the Colonial Office that he was content with the measures to protect Jewish colonies. He said that the 'Armoury Scheme' was now complete and in working order, adding that the Arabs had been informed that the scheme existed, 'and that it will be their fault if it were put into execution'. As to the gendarmerie, Deedes informed Young that recruits were forthcoming, but that it was difficult to persuade the Jews to refrain from boycotting the scheme:

They object to it in principle, and demand a 50% proportion of Jews. I meet the case by saying that I hope to give them a 50% 'Reliables' in this way:– 30% Jews, 10% Circassians, 10% Cypriots. We cannot accept 50% Jews today. I would willingly accept 100%! but we only excite extreme hostility and introduce all the evils of 'Politics' into a Force that I want to keep clear of that disease.[55]

According to Deedes, it had been necessary 'to postpone for the time being the creation of the Military Defence Force which was recently contemplated', consisting of two battalions, one Arab and the other Jewish. The Jews had agreed to the scheme, while the Arabs were totally opposed to it on two grounds: its organization into separate units, and that it would be equally divided between Arabs and Jews. After the Jaffa riots, feelings ran high, and it was decided that the force would be composed of one-third Jews, one-third Palestinian Arabs and one third non-Palestinian elements, if they could be found.[56] On 17 July 1921, *Filastin* reported that a large number of Jewish youths had joined the newly established gendarmerie, and that very few Palestine Arabs had been admitted. The Jaffa paper asked that the conditions for acceptance in the gendarmerie be made public, pointing out that information had not been published in Arabic papers, only in Jewish ones.[57]

The disturbances of May 1921 had aroused 'popular Jewish concern' for the organization of the Haganah.[58] Jewish recruits to the new Palestine gendarmerie did what the Zionists expected of them: they stole arms and ammunition from the government and gave them to the Haganah.[59] Commenting on the 'Political Report' for May 1922, an official at the Middle East Department noted that 'Mr. Ben

Zwi's activities are not calculated to assist the causes of peace and order', and that the need for an arms ordinance was 'a matter of urgency'.[60]

On the Arab side, there were protests that the government was turning a blind eye to the existence of this Jewish paramilitary force.[61] The British response was summed up by the Zionist historian Arthur Koestler, who said that the mandatory government had two courses of action open to it:

> ... either to put permanent garrisons into every Jewish settlement and outpost, or to legalize some form of Jewish defence organization. The first alternative would have put a heavy burden on the British Forces and the British taxpayer. The second course would probably have led to Arab claims for some form of armed organization of their own. So the Administration, by way of compromise, while refusing to give Haganah its official sanction, tolerated its existence.[62]

Koestler maintains that, in theory, the Jews were not allowed to possess any arms, except a few 'old-fashioned shotguns', which were issued after the 1921 disturbances to isolated settlements, to be kept in sealed boxes and only used 'in a serious emergency'. However, the authorities knew quite well that isolated settlements could only be defended by 'machine guns'. Therefore the Jews smuggled arms into the settlements, and the administration, 'well aware of this ... not only tolerated this practice, but at times even issued 'illegal' arms to Haganah.' [63]

The 'legal' position of the Haganah was therefore extremely ambiguous. Officially, its existence was 'overlooked' by the administration. The colonial secretary, Lord Devonshire, instructed the high commissioner to allow the Zionists what arms they needed, so as to avoid 'the greater evil of a clandestine Jewish military force'. The secret army was therefore formed, and while it was officially condemned, 'the right to Jewish self-defence was recognized'.[64] After Samuel's speech on 3 June 1921, Weizmann spoke to Lloyd George, Balfour and Churchill of the 'lack of security' of the Jewish population, informing them that the Jews were 'gun running', shipping guns and ammunition illegally to Palestine. Although the three sanctioned this activity, Churchill asked Weizmann not to speak of it publicly.[65]

In the autumn and winter of 1921, the Zionists were occupied with strengthening their position.[66] By September 1921, the high commissioner reported that there was some evidence 'that there has been an influx of arms into the country'. In Jaffa, the governor was of the opinion that since the May riots, 'every individual has secretly armed himself', but that the most rigorous search 'rarely produces any finds'.[67] According to Zionist sources, November 1921 was considered as the real 'coming of age' of the Haganah. During the 2 November disturbances, marking the fourth anniversary of the Balfour Declaration, the Jews were well prepared: there were many Arab casualties and deaths but no Jewish casualties.[68]

By the end of 1921 arms smuggling was becoming an acute problem in Palestine. That the government was fully aware, and decidedly unmindful of this, is suggested by the following reports. In December 1921, the 'Political Report' stated that an event which had caused a 'considerable amount of adverse comment' in the press was the seizure of 300 revolvers and a quantity of ammunition at Haifa consigned to Isaac Rosenberg from an Austrian individual named G. Fleikheer. The revolvers were concealed in beehives and steel cylinders, and one of the consignees, according to the report, had been arrested while the other absconded.[69]

In January 1922, Edward Keith-Roach, deputy to civil secretary Deedes, wrote from Jerusalem that 'considerable apprehension continues to be felt by the Arab population at the attempt on the part of the Jews to arm themselves', and that in addition to the most recent attempt at Haifa to smuggle arms there was enough reason to believe that 'further attempts on a smaller scale, have been made by Jews in the country, to procure arms and ammunition for their protection'.[70] In the same despatch the civil secretary Wyndham Deedes wrote that on 27 February he had received an Arab delegation from the Muslim-Christian Associations who protested in writing about Jewish arms smuggling. They expressed their opinion that the Palestine administration 'secretly favoured it', and that the administration had furthermore not carried out the policy and promises regarding immigration as laid down in the high commissioner's declaration of 3 June 1921. The delegation 'placed on record their fear of their inability much longer to restrain their own people should the importation of arms and the immigration of Jews continue'.[71]

Deedes repeated to the Colonial Office verbatim what the Arab delegation had told him: that the government 'should expect bitter consequences from the responsibilities' of which they now washed their hands. They demanded that (i) immigration should be suspended until the future of the country had been decided; (ii) that the administration should take back the arms distributed to Jewish colonies; and (iii) that the administration should appoint a representative commission to collect all arms from the people, 'irrespective of race or nationality'. In reply, the civil secretary pointed out that there was 'no point' in disguising the fact that 'the cause of the importation of arms by Jews was the belief that the Administration was not able adequately to protect them', and that the last events in May had provided ample proof that they 'needed protection against the hostility of the Arabs'. Deedes went on to say that:

> … when a greater measure of efficiency had been achieved by the Civil Forces of the Administration and further when the hostility shown from some sections of the Arab population to Jewish immigration had disappeared, the need for extraordinary measures such as those taken to give arms to Jewish Colonies, would disappear also.

The civil secretary did not hide the fact that the delegation was 'far from satisfied' with his reply.[72]

The armed forces, however, had diametrically opposed views. One month earlier, on 27 January 1922, the under-secretary of state at the Colonial Office received a letter from the War Office, forwarding copies of a report received from General Congreve, the general officer commanding the Egyptian Expeditionary Force, on the subject of arms smuggling into Palestine. The War Office stated that the Army Council 'view with concern the facts disclosed in this report', and expressed the opinion that they felt sure 'Mr. Secretary Churchill will agree with them that this traffic must be stopped'. The Army Council expressed their fear that otherwise, 'the Palestine garrison may not prove adequate to its task'. The report in question insisted that it was important that 'the organisations in Europe or elsewhere apparently responsible for this importation should be traced', and that 'action should be taken to prevent these occurrences'. Congreve added that the high commissioner was 'in agreement' with him on this subject.

Arms smuggling continued in earnest throughout 1922. And although this issue was reported in detail to the Colonial Office, there is no indication that any drastic measures had been taken by the Palestine administration to put an end to it. What is even more intriguing is the fact that the administration's reports demonstrate that it did not disapprove of the arms smuggling as such; what it found objectionable was that this 'illegal' importation of arms had taken place without the necessary formalities.[73]

The administration considered it unwise and 'useless' to search for arms as this was only bound 'to cause alarm and excitement'. The report concluded by stating that since March, there had been 'no trace' of a satisfactory reply from the Zionist Commission, that the Haganah continued to organize in Jerusalem and Jaffa, and that:

> By now it is thought that every town with any considerable Jewish population has its 'Hagonah' and that large numbers of arms have entered the country for the use of Jews. This last conjecture has considerable evidence to support it, since up to the 23rd January, 1922, it was an easy matter to bring in arms at Jaffa owing to lack of port control. It is also known that ships' firemen and others were purchasing arms for sale here.[74]

Among the 'prime movers' were Ben Zvi and David Yellin in Jerusalem.[75] Colonial Office minutes noted that early in 1922 the Haganah began to 'manifest itself more openly'. A report on its activities was sent in May 1922 to the Colonial Office by General Headquarters Expeditionary Force. Shuckburgh wrote that the Zionist Organization seemed to have a good deal of information and probably connection with 'Hagonah'. Eric Mills commented on 15 June 1922:

> I am not sure we have not encouraged 'Hagonah'. We have a Firearms Ordinance which ought to be applied firmly. I am not sure that it always is. Furthermore our establishment of armouries in Jewish Colonies has probably given Jews to understand that we look with favour on self-defence corps. To my mind the armouries

lead logically to self-defence corps: it's of no good to have arms at your disposal if you're not trained to use them effectively.[76]

By July 1922, the question of illicit arms trafficking was becoming so serious that E. T. Richmond in the Political Section of the Secretariat drew up a long memorandum which was forwarded (not without comments) by the civil secretary, Wyndham Deedes, to the colonial secretary.[77] After giving a history of the labour movement, it maintained that since the break-up of the Miflagah Po'alim Sotzialistim (the extreme Bolshevik party) following the May 1921 riots, it had been assumed that extreme organized Bolshevism had ceased to exist in Palestine. The memorandum noted that this was not the case, and that adherents of the former party had been absorbed into the Ahdut Ha-Avodah, the right wing of Po'ali Zion.[78]

Po'ali Zion, the memorandum noted, was an organization of some ten years standing in Palestine, with members numbering from 3,000 to 4,000. Its headquarters was believed to be in Vienna. The leader of Ahdut Ha-Avodah, Ben Zvi, who was up till April 1921 a member of the Advisory Council, first tendered his resignation, according to this memorandum, 'as a protest against the high commissioner's pronouncement on June 3rd regarding immigration'. The memorandum adds that it was also to be noted that while a member of the Advisory Council, Ben Zvi

> strenuously opposed Article 3 of the Crimes Prevention Ordinance, an Article which enables a Governor to require a bond for good behaviour from any person who disseminates seditious matter, or any matter likely to cause disturbance between sections of the people.

From that time onwards, Ahdut Ha-Avodah strove to 'drive a wedge between Arab peasants and Arab landowners to emphasize the need of force and in general to adopt the methods and aims of extremists in other countries as well as to call insistently for unrestricted immigration'.

Richmond reported that two days after the Rosenberg arms importation incident in Haifa, Ben Zvi had delivered a speech to Ahdut Ha-Avodah in Jaffa, 'urging the need of an armed Jewish Defence Force in Palestine', and at the same time it had been reported that the Zionist Organization in Vienna had urged immigrants to bring arms into Palestine. Richmond noted that when Ben Zvi was delivering his speech urging the need for a Jewish Defence Force, 'such a Force was already in existence', and that its existence was 'successfully' kept a secret from the government for a considerable time after its formation, when by law, all organizations had to declare themselves. When the existence of the Haganah became known, Dr Eder, the representative of the Zionist Commission, had been asked by Sir Wyndham Deedes 'to see that the Organisation declared itself and broke up'. Richmond noted: 'It has not done so.'

The report furnished more evidence about the connection between the Ahdut

Ha-Avodah and the Haganah, pointing out that Ben Zvi was the 'leader of both bodies'. In a meeting which took place on 3 June 1922, Ben Zvi delivered a speech on behalf of the Ahdut Ha-Avodah in which he 'urged the importance of a Haganah Force so as to effectively oppose the Arabs in case of necessity'. In the same meeting, a Mr Sloutz also emphasized 'the need of a strong military force behind which the National Home could be built up'. The report concluded: 'it seems clear that there is in Palestine a by no means negligible extremist movement; and that active in this movement are the Achduth Avoda and the Jewish Defence Force.'

The Arabs' chief fear, according to Richmond's report, was

> due to their knowledge that the Jews are armed and organised. This fear is increased and made an important factor in the situation by their belief that the inaction of the Government in regard to this armed organisation is a proof of Government sympathy with the organisation.[79]

The memorandum asserted that although it could not be known with precision to what extent the Zionist authorities were in sympathy with the doctrines of Ben Zvi, 'and with the establishment and maintenance of an illegal Jewish Armed Force', the Zionist Commission had 'done nothing effective towards the dissolution of the Haganah Force'. Moreover, the government 'received no assistance from them in the matter of tracing extremists after the Jaffa Riots and … Dr. Eder stated before the Haycraft Commission that Jews only should be armed'.

The civil secretary, wholeheartedly sympathetic with the Zionist cause, wrote to Churchill that the views expressed in the memorandum towards the Jewish labour movement were 'exaggerated', and that since its extremist members had been deported in June 1921, 'a more moderate spirit has prevailed throughout the party'. He furthermore expressed his opinion that the Haganah

> is not an organisation or irregular defence force but rather represents the devotion to an idea animating the whole Jewish Community, viz., that the Jews must be prepared to defend themselves in case of attack, which in time of trouble would undoubtedly take some concrete form, varying according to time, place and circumstance … acting on this idea, Jews have smuggled arms into the country either through individuals or through organisations … The idea of Hagonah is cherished as much by the farmer colonists and by the bourgeoisie of Tel-Aviv and other Jewish town suburbs as it is by the co-operative groups and labour unions.[80]

Echoing Deedes in Jerusalem, Meinertzhagen, expressing veiled agreement with the idea that it was acceptable for Jews to arm themselves, wrote in July 1922 commenting on the report 'Written by Richmond! … In reading this report it should be remembered that if we had adequately defended Jewish lives and property in the past, there would have been no motive for the more recent desire and materialisation of the Jews to arm themselves in Palestine.'[81]

On the other hand, the civil secretary's agreement one year earlier, to allow 18 rifles to be used in Jaffa for the defence of Tel Aviv during the 1921 disturbances, had been made an excuse for 'a party of Jews in British Military Uniform to march through the streets of Jaffa under Captain Yaffe late of the 38th Royal Fusiliers, with fixed bayonets, another act which tended to increase the racial hatred'.[82]

With the benefit of hindsight, Samuel's contribution to the Zionist cause in the military sphere was vital: what he initiated in 1921, whether by coincidence or design, influenced future events.[83]

THE ISSUE OF REPRESENTATION REVISITED

Following the May disturbances in 1921, Samuel took some further steps on the vexed question of representation, attempting to enlarge the Advisory Council and to arrange for the unofficial members to be elected. This, however, was not approved by the Colonial Office. Although Samuel himself firmly believed that the time was not yet ripe for establishing a full representative government, an elected council, albeit advisory, would, in his opinion, have gone 'some way to satisfy public opinion as a further stage on the road to full self-government'.[84] It was Shuckburgh, however, who vetoed Samuel's suggestion, and reminded the colonial secretary on 20 May 1921, of what he had written to Samuel on 14 May in the aftermath of the Jaffa riots:

> I deprecate placing Advisory Council on elective basis ... The institution of an elected Council is in any case such an important matter that I cannot approve it off hand. To make such a concession under pressure is to rob it of half its value. We must firmly maintain law and order and make concessions on their merits and not under duress.[85]

In proposing an elected Advisory Council, Samuel was faced with a real dilemma, for it is doubtful that he contemplated preparing the ground for 'full self-government' for the Palestine Arabs. What he always had in mind was the 'gradual' development of the Jewish national home until the Jews became a majority. This is evident from what he wrote on 8 May 1921: 'A much more difficult question, under the conditions that prevail in Palestine [i.e. because of the Zionist policy] ... is the establishment of a central legislative on an electoral basis.'[86] On the one hand, Samuel believed that there was a 'serious objection' to dividing the electorate into separate religious communities, while on the other, he thought that there was also a serious objection to accepting the 'ordinary geographical basis, for that would result in the minorities [i.e. the Jewish minority] being swamped'.[87]

In June 1921, the *Morning Post* wrote that the high commissioner was known by his fellow Zionists not as Herbert Samuel but as Eliezer Ben Menachem, and the flatterers around him did not hesitate to address him as the 'Prince of Israel'. Under the Turks, the *wali* was assisted by an administrative council which was elected, and the various districts in Palestine sent their elected representatives to the Turkish parliament in Constantinople. Sir Herbert Samuel's council, however, was nominated by himself:

> It is obvious that if it were elected, its members would be not Jews, but Christians and Moslems, who form over 90% of the population. Self-determination does not rule in Zion, and it is no wonder that the people complain that they were better off under the Turks than under the British.[88]

Samuel also saw it as expedient to hasten the establishment of a body to handle Muslim affairs (to control *shari'a*, Islamic law and *awqaf*, sing. *waqf*, religious endowments). Soon after he assumed his responsibilities as high commissioner, Samuel had announced that he intended to give the Muslims complete control of their religious endowments.[89] But it was not until the summer of 1921 that Samuel felt the matter to be more urgent, especially in light of the fact that, in October 1920, he had recognized the assembly elected by the Yishuv, the Va'ad Leumi, as a representative Jewish body in Palestine,[90] with no equivalent for the Palestine Arabs. Meanwhile, the powerful Zionist Executive, formerly the Zionist Commission, was recognized as the Jewish Agency mentioned in Article 4 of the mandate.[91]

Apprehensive of a possible recurrence of the disturbances, Samuel now pressed the Colonial Office for a quick solution to this problem. Moreover, he was well aware of how the Arabs viewed his administration: the head of the administration—Samuel himself—was a Jew, his legal secretary who handled all legal affairs was also a Jew.[92] The last thing that the high commissioner needed in this potentially explosive situation was to arouse the religious sentiments of the Arabs. He thus saw that the appointment of Hajj Amin al-Husseini as head of a new Muslim Council would at least partly appease the Palestine Arabs, and prevent the outbreak of violence. By January 1921, he had sent to the secretary of state for Foreign Affairs a complete proposal for the formation of a council for the management of Muslim religious affairs, and, in particular, for the administration of *awqaf*.[93] However, Samuel's proposal took one year to implement, and it was not until January 1922 that the establishment of the Supreme Muslim Council was announced.

After the Jaffa riots, Samuel had repeatedly pressed the Colonial Office for some sort of formula that would pacify the Arabs, and in particular, he pointed to the fact that Article 4 of the mandate recognized a Jewish Agency, but gave no recognition to any equivalent non-Jewish body. He telegraphed to Churchill on 25 May 1921:

> Article 4 of the draft Mandate meets with strong opposition as it is regarded as constituting a partnership between Zionists and Government of Palestine to the exclusion of the rest of the population. The establishment of representative assembly is closely connected with this question. I should be glad if you would consider insertion of a counterpoise in the mandate.[94]

Samuel was now suggesting the recognition of an appropriate body, to be consulted by the administration 'on matters affecting interests of non-Jewish population pending establishment of a responsible government'.[95] Even Wyndham Deedes, one of Zionism's closest allies, proposed the removal of Article 4 of the mandate. As mentioned above, he wrote to Shuckburgh in November of the same year that the preferential position of the Zionist Organization written into the draft mandate would have to be abolished. But in London, Deedes' views were seen as too radical and were not accepted.[96]

Samuel's main motive for pressing for the speedy establishment of the Supreme Muslim Council was to prevent any further eruption of violence, and to make the Muslim community feel that the *shari'a* courts were presided over 'by persons of their own choice'.[97] Samuel made it unequivocally clear to the Colonial Office that he was 'most anxious to avoid at the present juncture any adverse criticism on the part of the Moslems, particularly in respect of the attitude taken by the Administration towards their religious affairs'.[98] He therefore wrote to the colonial secretary that for political reasons it was 'urgent' that Muslim opinion be satisfied as soon as possible. This satisfaction could best be secured by giving approval to the immediate establishment of the Supreme Muslim Council.[99] After describing in the same despatch how the system of *awqaf* had operated under the Ottoman government in its capacity not as a political government, but as a Muslim government which possessed the treasury of the Muslims and received the revenues of certain *awqaf*, he pointed out that these revenues had, since the British occupation, been received by the administration and the Muslim treasury had ceased to exist.[100]

According to Samuel's proposal, the Supreme Muslim Council would be composed of the *ra'is al-'ulama* (its head), and four members, two from Jerusalem and one each from Nablus and Acre. The *ra'is al-'ulama* would be the permanent chairman of this council and the members would be elected for four years, the Muslim community having the right to control the activities of the council through an 'electoral college'.[101] In addition to controlling *awqaf*, the duties of the council would consist of approving the annual budget submitted to them by a general *waqf* committee, and nominating for the approval of the government and, 'after signification of such approval', appointing inspectors and *qadis* of the *shari'a* court and the president and members of the *shari'a* court of appeal.[102] Samuel emphasized that negotiations with the Muslim leaders had been under way for the last nine months, and that any further delay would 'aggravate the extreme impatience which is being expressed by that Community'.[103] Samuel also told Churchill that 'much political advantage may be expected to accrue to the Administration as a result of the arrangement proposed'.[104] To his great relief, Samuel was able to record in December 1921 that the settlement of the *awqaf* and Muslim religious affairs (as well as the Beisan land question, which will be discussed in chapter 9) had created 'a very good impression' and convinced the Muslims of the 'good intentions' of the government towards their community in Palestine.[105]

A meeting was finally held at Government House on 9 January 1922 for the purpose of carrying out the elections to the Supreme Muslim Council. Of the fifty-six members, fifty-three were present, and the results of the elections were as follows: Hajj Amin Effendi al-Husseini, Mufti of Jerusalem, was elected *ra'is al-'ulama* (he received 40 out of 47 votes);[106] Muhammad Effendi Murad, Mufti of Haifa, member of council for the former Turkish *liwa* of Akka; 'Abd al-Latif Bey Salah, member of council for the former Turkish *liwa* of Nablus; Hajj Sa'id Effendi al-Shawa of Gaza and 'Abd al-Latif Effendi al-Dajani of Jaffa, members of council for the former Turkish *liwa* of Jerusalem. The choice of Hajj Amin al-Husseini as president confirmed his status as head of the Muslim community in Palestine, and went far to satisfy Muslim public opinion in an area which they considered of crucial importance,[107] and in which they were not prepared to compromise.[108]

This was the zenith of Arab approval of Samuel's policy in Palestine. The high commissioner was well satisfied with the composition of the council and anticipated cordial relations between it and the administration.[109] After its establishment until the final days of Samuel's term in office, the Supreme Muslim Council strove to prevent any disturbances that might have occurred during the potentially explosive Nabi Musa festivals each April.[110] According to the 'Political Report' for January 1922, the good effect of the settlement of the *awqaf* question continued to be felt and to find expression in the press.[111] Moreover, its creation stimulated the efforts of the Muslims in the religious and educational fields. A Muslim university was being founded and developed, the Boy Scout movement was encouraged by the council, and the Council School for Muslim Orphans, which was a 'very complete establishment', was contemplating the improvement of technical education by sending teachers to Europe for additional training.[112] The Muslim-Christian Association in Nablus thanked the government for recognizing the legitimate rights of the nation, and Jamal al-Husseini, secretary of the Arab Executive Committee, described the event as a victory for the nationalist movement.[113]

It may be argued that the establishment of the Supreme Muslim Council was a conscious attempt on Samuel's part to placate the Muslim Arabs by providing them with some form of representation, in order to compensate them, at least partially, for the autonomous representative institutions which he had granted to the Zionists. Although it was Samuel's creation, the Supreme Muslim Council was henceforward dominated by the Palestinian religious elite and notables. Faced with the British policy of supporting a Jewish national home and with the activities of the Zionist movement, and in the absence of a recognized secular alternative, the council assumed additional roles and eventually, from the late 1920s, became the vanguard of the Palestinian nationalist movement.[114]

7

The Palestine Arab Response: The Path of Diplomacy, June 1921– September 1923

The Palestine Arab leadership during this period emphasized peaceful and diplomatic means to resist the implementation of the Balfour Declaration and to present their case to the British government and public, in the hope that the British would change their policy once they 'understood' the reality of Arab grievances and demands. However, by officially denying the representative character of Arab Palestinian leadership, Samuel obstructed the development of self-representative institutions and prevented Arab views from receiving a serious hearing from the government in London. Without such an agreed structure, there were limits to what the Arab leaders could achieve by diplomacy and lobbying in Britain.

THE FIRST ARAB DELEGATION TO LONDON, 1921–22

The Arabs' first opportunity to put their case directly to the British government came in March 1921, when the Arab Executive Committee met Churchill in Jerusalem, and presented him with a memorandum explaining their case.[1] Shocked by Churchill's blunt response, detailed in the last chapter, the Arab leaders resolved, as Egyptian leaders had advised them in Cairo in March 1921, to elect a delegation to go to London to counteract the pro-Zionist policy of Samuel's administration.[2] This diplomatic effort, decided at the Fourth Palestine Arab Congress, held in Jerusalem on 29 May 1921, was speeded up as a result of the Jaffa disturbances earlier that month. The delegation was instructed to stay in London for as long as was required to persuade the British government to change its pro-Zionist policy,[3] and was authorized to speak in the name of the Arab people in Palestine.[4]

On 23 June 1921, before proceeding to London, the Arab Delegation asked for a meeting with the high commissioner to request permission to depart. Samuel tried to persuade it to remain in the country and cooperate with him, but the Arabs were by now convinced that only in London was there any hope of convincing the British government to reverse its policy. When the delegation insisted on proceeding to London, Samuel made it quite clear that they would not be recognized as an 'official representative' body.[5] Nonetheless, the Palestine Arab Delegation, composed of nine members, both Muslim and Christian, and headed by Musa Kazim Pasha al-Husseini, the elected president of the Palestine Arab Congress, set out for Britain in June 1921, arriving there in August.[6]

Their main demands were twofold: first, the abandonment of the Balfour Declaration and the idea of establishing a national home for the Jews in Palestine, and secondly, the introduction of representative government.[7] The delegation strove to achieve its aims through diplomacy, political pressure and propaganda.[8] According to its secretary, Muhammad 'Izzat Darwazeh, Shibli Jamal sent regular reports on its activities to the Arab Executive Committee in Palestine. The latter met once every two weeks to discuss the reports and return its observations to the delegation in London.[9]

While the delegation was in London, Samuel was desperate to secure Arab approval of the proposed Palestine Order-in-Council (the Constitution for Palestine). In August 1921, he suggested the establishment of what he called a 'Consultative Committee' to be composed of Muslims and Christians, in order to meet the complaint that the administration was not in 'sufficiently close touch' with the leaders of the Arab community in Palestine. His real aim, however, was to secure this committee's approval for the proposed constitution. Those who had been invited to the meeting declined to discuss the constitution. They pointed out that it would 'hamper' the work of the delegation in Europe, who had already telegraphed that the government's invitation to the notables to discuss the proposed constitution was ill-advised. Since the Arab Executive Committee was the legally elected representative of the people, it was the body to deal with in such matters, and as such, it refused a constitution which was based on the Balfour Declaration.[10] When asked by the notables who attended the meeting why the leaders of the Jewish community were not represented in the proposed committee, Samuel replied that the Jews had for some time past had opportunities of meeting him, and that they already had an elected assembly. They also had the Zionist Commission, which from time to time sent representatives to discuss various issues with him.[11]

The Arab notables refused to discuss a constitution based on the Balfour Declaration, insisting that such a constitution could not be drawn up except by a council elected by the people of the country. They reminded the high commissioner that the Arab Delegation in London had requested that discussion of the constitution should be postponed until the future of the country was definitely known.[12] As a result, the 'Consultative Committee' met only twice, and at the second meeting on 29 September 1921, only six of the forty-six members attended; of these, two were sheikhs from Beersheba, who had received no notification of the intention of the majority to absent themselves. By letter, the members of the 'Consultative Committee' thanked the high commissioner and apologized for not attending the meeting in order not to complicate the efforts of the delegation in London.[13] Despite the failure of the 'Consultative Committee' and the clear Arab opposition to any constitution based on the Balfour Declaration, the legal adviser, Norman Bentwich, arrived in London to submit such a constitution.[14]

When the Arab Delegation met Churchill, shortly after its arrival in August 1921, its secretary, Shibli al-Jamal, asked him how the British government could reconcile its guarantees under the Balfour Declaration to safeguard the rights of the people of Palestine with its current pro-Zionist policy. Churchill responded that the government had made promises, and that it would 'endeavour to keep those promises'. Al-Jamal contended that the Arabs had been promised self-government, to which Churchill answered: 'No. When was that promised? Never. We promised you should not be turned off your land'.[15] The Palestine Arabs had 'never yet understood what the National Home of the Jews really means', al-Jamal said, adding that they believed that the Zionists had put 'a great deal more interpretation into it than perhaps the British Government ever intended'. They would like to hear officially what was meant by a national home.[16] Churchill's reply—that he could not improve upon Sir Herbert Samuel's words (in his speech on 3 June 1921)—did not, as far as the Arab Delegation was concerned, explain anything.[17]

During the course of the conversation, Churchill told the delegation that the 'easiest way' to understand the Zionist policy regarding the question of immigration would be to get in touch with Weizmann, and 'to have a discussion with the controlling authorities of the Zionist Organisation'. The delegation replied that they had come to negotiate with the British government and not with the Zionists, and that they did not recognize Weizmann.

The delegation also raised the question of the Legislative Council, but Churchill made it clear that the Council would not be allowed to control the government or check Jewish immigration. If the people of the country had any say in controlling immigration, 'it will immediately say no Jews are to come in, and bring the whole thing to a standstill. It is impossible to put claims like that. How can the British Government allow the policy to which it is publicly declared to be brought to naught in that way?' Churchill ended the meeting by saying, 'We want to take you into partnership in the management of the country, provided you can make us feel you will be partners in guaranteeing the policy to which we have committed ourselves.'[18]

This left very little room for the Arab Delegation to negotiate; their views were entirely opposed to those of the colonial secretary. By October, the delegation had been in London for nearly three months and it had become clear that talks between them and the Colonial Office had reached a deadlock. At the Middle East Department, where the Arab delegates presented a series of complaints against particular acts by the Palestine administration, Shuckburgh replied that 'the place to make complaints of this kind was in Palestine, not in London' and that Sir Herbert Samuel had established the Consultative Committee in Jerusalem for this specific purpose.[19] Although the delegation insisted that this body was 'useless', and that the Arabs refused to attend its meetings, Shuckburgh merely complained that the delegation was trying to force the hands of the government 'by demonstrating the futility of the government's machinery in Palestine'. Of the delegation, he remarked:

> Their attitude is: 'We are the representatives of the people and you must deal with us or not at all.' But seeing that they were plainly warned that they would not be treated as an official delegation, I submit that this is not a position that we can accept.[20]

Samuel meanwhile stressed the 'absolute necessity' of securing a settlement of the question of the mandate to end this period of political uncertainty. The enactment of a constitution (the Palestine Order-in-Council), he wrote, was no substitute for recognition of the British administration by the League of Nations.[21] He also urged Weizmann to consider the conflict from the Arab perspective, pointing out that the Arabs viewed Zionism as a real and immediate danger to their political and economic welfare.[22] On 14 October 1921, Samuel wrote to Churchill that 'the view is held that the Zionists have other and more extensive objects, and that, if not in the present, yet in a not distant future, it may be the policy of the Zionist Organization and not that of H.M.G. which may prevail'. He added that many Arabs still pressed for the complete abrogation of the Balfour Declaration. In Samuel's view, the establishment of a Jewish national home 'in the presence of ... strong opposition on the part of a very large section of the population, must be unduly slow, difficult and costly'. He went as far as suggesting a new and revised edition of the Balfour Declaration, proposing that the form of announcement 'which would carry most weight, would probably be a letter from H.M.G. to the Zionist Organization, or to Lord Rothschild, embodying a declaration on the suggested lines', to which by previous arrangement, an 'assenting reply would be returned'.

In his view, the Arabs should cease to demand the cancellation of the Balfour Declaration or the halting of Jewish immigration, and the Zionists should agree to announce the following:

1. That their purpose was not the establishment of a state in which Jews would enjoy a position of political privilege, but a commonwealth built upon a democratic foundation.
2. That the statement as to Palestine becoming 'as Jewish as England is English' should be qualified in such a way as to bring it into conformity with the resolution relating to 'the common home'.
3. That Jewish immigration of the labouring class should be in proportion to the numbers who could find employment in new enterprises.

4. That the rights of the present population to their holy places and the security of their property 'should be absolutely guaranteed'.[23]

Towards the end of October, 1921 the Palestine Arab Delegation in London submitted a memorandum to Churchill, in which they asserted that the people of Palestine would 'never admit the right of any outside organisation to dispossess them of their country, and to threaten their very existence as a people economically and politically'. They also requested that the memorandum be put before the Cabinet, and that they be informed of its views.[24] (See Appendix E)

Samuel, concerned that the Delegation's return 'empty-handed' would coincide with a potentially explosive occasion in Palestine (the fourth anniversary of the Balfour Declaration), had pressed the Colonial Office to keep it in London until some solution was reached.[25] The secretary of state concurred, 'and was even willing' to give them another personal interview,[26] in order to win more time. But although the delegation remained in London, riots broke out in Jerusalem on 2 November 1921. The delegation accused the legal adviser, Norman Bentwich, of being 'unjust' in his condemnation of the Arabs following these riots. They wrote to Samuel saying that: 'The Government should know that this favouritism of Jews is harmful to the Jews themselves in the first place, and in the second place it destroys the dignity and prestige of the Administration, while it drives the Arabs to despair.' They pointed out that the 'dislike which Arabs cherish towards the Zionists is the fruit of such preferential treatment'.[27]

In response to the November disturbances, Samuel was anxious that the colonial secretary should reach some form of understanding with the Arab Delegation, as any détente in London would immediately be followed by a 'great improvement' in the situation in Palestine.[28] In the meantime, the nationalist leaders in Palestine had received no encouraging news from their delegation in England. Deedes wrote in December that it was understood that no news of any importance had been received by the local political leaders from the delegation, but that efforts continued to be made to collect money for the delegation, and, although 'the assistance of Ladies has been called', the results had not been satisfactory.[29]

The internal minutes of the Colonial Office reveal, however, that the Middle East Department did not contemplate making any significant concessions. Shuckburgh concluded that there was 'little advantage in further round table discussions with the Arab Delegation, or in further attempts to induce them by methods of persuasion to leave high politics alone and to co-operate with us in the details of Constitution making in Palestine'.[30]

In any case, Shuckburgh pointed out, the delegation had been 'clearly informed' by Samuel before starting 'that they could not be regarded as having any official character, and that they would not be "formally received" by the Secretary of State'.[31] On the question of representation, Shuckburgh emphatically asserted that 'it has been clearly explained to them that the immediate grant of full self-government to Palestine is an impossibility'.[32] Furthermore, the colonial secretary himself had told the delegation that they should place themselves in direct communication with the Zionist Organization in London to sort their problems out.[33] Shuckburgh stressed once more that the British government was 'deeply pledged to the Zionists', and had always made it clear to the Arabs that there was 'no prospect of wavering on this point', adding that 'to waver now, in the face of renewed Arab violence, would be absolutely fatal'.[34] At this point, it seems that both Shuckburgh and Weizmann took the view that the Arabs would 'acquiesce' in the mandate if it were a *chose jugée*, and therefore sought to hasten its ratification by the League of Nations, while at the same time keeping the delegation in London in the hope that it would run out of funds.

The Middle East Department had meanwhile tried hard to bring the Arabs and Zionists together, as Churchill had suggested. However, it only achieved the Delegation's agreement to 'attend' a meeting at which Weizmann would be present and at which the colonial secretary would deliver a statement of policy. This gathering, scheduled for 26 November, was cancelled at the last minute, and was replaced by a discussion on the 29 November, chaired by Shuckburgh. Here Weizmann made it clear that the draft mandate was not open to change, to which Musa Kazim, the president of the delegation, replied that the draft mandate was 'unacceptable' to the Arabs because of the special rights it granted to the Jews. He asserted that a clear interpretation of the Balfour Declaration was required before any further discussions could be held.[35]

The delegation, for its part, tried to improve its position by cultivating sympathetic British politicians.[36] Lord Sydenham, an anti-Zionist spokesman in the House of Lords,[37] presiding at a luncheon given at the Hotel Cecil by the Palestine Arab delegation in November 1921, warned that the Balfour Declaration was 'loaded with dynamite', that it had already cost many lives and was now a threat to the peace in the Near East. If the British people understood what was going on, 'they would insist on justice to Palestinians … If we did not give justice and peace to Palestine assuredly we should light a fire in the Near East which would strain all our resources to extinguish.' He described the injustice under which the Palestine Arabs were labouring as 'unprecedented in history'.[38]

In February 1922, Shuckburgh again tried to get the delegation in London sent back home, but Samuel again warned that their return would coincide with the Nabi Musa and Easter festivities. The fact that they had achieved nothing would foster unrest. Once more he urged the Colonial Office to retain the delegation in London. Deedes received a letter which clearly shows the prevalent British attitude to the delegation:

I send you a copy of the last letter received from the Arab Delegation. You see how hopeless it all is! Anyway it is our intention to send once more an argumentative reply in order to detain them in the country until the 'nervy' season in Palestine is over. After that we shall have nothing to do with them in all probability and may send them away.[39]

Shuckburgh attempted to renew contact with the delegation in April, but to no practical effect, and no further attempts were made until the arrival of Samuel himself in London in May 1922.[40]

THE PALESTINE ORDER-IN-COUNCIL

In February 1922, Churchill informed the Arab Delegation of the proposed constitution for Palestine, which was to be embodied in an Order-in-Council (the Palestine Order-in-Council 1922) based on the Balfour Declaration. His Majesty's Government intended to carry out elections for a Legislative Council immediately after the enactment of the Palestine Order-in-Council. According to its terms, elections for the Legislative Council were to be held within six months of its publication in the *Palestine Gazette*;[41] it was to consist of 22 members, in addition to the high commissioner, of whom 10 would be official and 12 unofficial, elected members.[42]

The Arab Delegation rejected the proposed constitution.[43] Their reasons can be summarized as follows: (i) the Balfour Declaration was incorporated in the constitution; (ii) the high commissioner was not responsible to the legislature; (iii) The high commissioner controlled a majority of votes in the council. (iv) the high commissioner had veto powers over all laws; (v) ten members constituted a quorum allowing official members to meet alone; (vi) Hebrew was recognized as an official language; (vii) the constitution could be changed or annulled at any time by the high commissioner or the colonial secretary.[44] Moreover, the high commissioner had the power to dissolve the Legislative Council at any time.[45]

A number of articles in the proposed Order-in-Council appeared specifically designed to promote the Jewish national home. Article 12 stated that all rights relating to public lands would be vested in the high commissioner. He also had power over: 'all mines and minerals of every kind and description whatsoever being in, under or on any land or water, whether the latter be inland rivers or seas or territorial waters.' Article 13 gave the high commissioner the means to grant or lease 'any such public lands or mines or minerals ... as he may think fit'. Article 18, providing for the powers of the Legislative Council, stated: 'No Ordinance shall be passed which shall be in any way repugnant to or inconsistent with the provisions of the Mandate.' Article 85 provided that 'any religious community' who felt that the terms of the mandate were not being fulfilled could protest by presenting a petition to the League of Nations through the high commissioner.[46] This last article seemed to have been especially tailored to enable the tiny, but rapidly growing, Jewish community to complain about any future administration which proved unenthusiastic about the Jewish national home policy.

On 21 February 1922, the Arab Delegation wrote to Churchill, who had shown them a draft copy of the proposed Order-in-Council, submitting their detailed observations and giving reasons why they thought no useful purpose would be served by the document.[47] (See Appendix F) They objected to the official and nominated majority in the Legislative Council, the excessive centralization of power in the hands of the high commissioner, and the exclusion of the people of the country and their representatives from any real power, either administrative or legislative, in matters which profoundly affected the destiny of Palestine and its people.[48] The delegation maintained that if the Legislative Council was not authorized to control vital affairs of the community, such as immigration, it would be ineffective and impotent. They repeated their demand that a government should be set up which would be responsible to a parliament elected proportionately by the Muslim, Christian and Jewish inhabitants of the country who had lived there before World War I.[49]

Wyndham Deedes reported from Palestine in February 1922 that the proposed constitution had been 'very unfavourably' received by the Muslims and Christians who had presented him, instead, with the following demands: first, that immigration should be suspended until the future of the country was decided; second, that the administration should take back the arms distributed to Jewish colonies; and third, that it should appoint a representative commission to collect all arms from the people, irrespective of race or nationality. They had placed on record their 'fear of their inability much longer to restrain their own people should the importation of arms and the immigration of Jews continue', and had warned that the government 'should expect bitter consequences'.[50] On 15 February 1922, in a private and confidential letter to Young, Deedes wrote that: 'The country as far as one can tell is quiet. We are making every possible arrangement to guard against trouble this spring ... However, if an agreement over the constitution can be arrived at at home between the two parties that would be very helpful indeed.'[51]

THE ORIGINS OF CHURCHILL'S 1922 WHITE PAPER

During the first half of 1922, the uncertainties about Palestine's future further increased tensions within the country.[52] Wyndham Deedes reported a considerable growth in political consciousness among the Arabs, even in hitherto 'inarticulate' districts such as Gaza and Beersheba, adding that this growth was one of many symptoms of a general tendency which was noticeable in all fields of activity, religious, educational and economic as well as political, 'towards the attainment of an increased measure of cohesion and solidarity' among the Muslims.[53]

Samuel continued to urge the Colonial Office to make a public pronouncement to allay Arab fears, and pressed the government for a clarification of its intentions. In March 1922, he sent a despatch to the colonial secretary, which he intended for publication 'both locally and in Britain', and which he hoped would serve as a statement of policy. At a time when his relations with the more extreme Zionists were subject to considerable stress, Samuel declared that the condition of 'unrest and tension which has long prevailed continues almost unchanged'. Although Samuel attributed the feeling of unrest in Palestine to the delay in granting the mandate, a large section of the population of Palestine, he added, had become persuaded that the present British government threatened their fundamental interests: 'Put in the simplest terms, and in the language used among the people themselves, they believe that it intends to take the country away from the Arabs in order to give it to the Jews.'[54]

Samuel informed Churchill that 'no measure of assurances' removed this conviction from Arab minds, and that Zionist pronouncements such as 'Palestine is to become as Jewish as England is English'[55] only made matters worse and confirmed their deepest fears. He noted that:

> ... a leading British Jewish newspaper with strong Zionist tendencies has selected this very expression as summarizing the true meaning of Zionist policy, and week by week has reiterated the declaration that, to conceal from the Arabs that this is its real intention would be mere dishonest hypocrisy ... With an Arab population in Palestine out-numbering many times the Jewish, that Arab population itself virile and growing, it is wholly impracticable to make Palestine as Jewish as England is English.[56]

He also cited the uncompromising attitude of the Zionists displayed in the evidence which the acting chairman of the Zionist Commission, Dr David Eder, had given to the Haycraft Commission following the May riots in 1921. Eder had stated that the aim of the Jews was to secure predominance, and had given it as his opinion that the Jewish population of Palestine should be armed, and the non-Jewish disarmed. In Samuel's view:

> When the history of Moslem rule in Palestine during the last seven centuries is remembered, it may readily be conceived with what feelings has been received by the majority of the people this suggestion, that the population of Palestine should now be divided into two sections, a Jewish minority largely armed and a totally disarmed Arab majority.[57]

Urging better understanding and better relations with the Palestine Arabs, Samuel recalled the resolutions of the Twelfth Zionist Congress, held at Carlsbad in 1921, to live with the Arab people 'on terms of unity and mutual respect, and together to make the common home into a flourishing community'. He noted that the Zionists had paid very little attention to these important resolutions. On the other hand, the high commissioner described the Arabs on the whole as: 'a kindly and well disposed people, and by no means turbulent or blood-thirsty. It may be confidently anticipated that these out-breaks are temporary consequences of the present political situation.' Samuel attempted to explain what was meant by the term 'Jewish National Home'. During the last two or three generations the Jews had 'reconstituted' in Palestine a community of over 70,000 persons. In his opinion, this Palestine Jewish community,

> with its town and country populations, its political, religious, and social organizations, its own language, its own customs, its own life, has in fact National Characteristics. When it is asked what is meant by the development of the Jewish National Home, it may be answered that the development of this Community is the development of the Jewish National Home.[58]

Some of Samuel's ideas in this despatch were later embodied in the 1922 White Paper:

> ... in order that this Community should have the best prospect of a free development and a full opportunity of displaying whether the Jewish spirit in modern times is capable of repeating the achievements of its early prime, it is essential that it should feel itself wholly independent and free; that it should know that it is in Palestine as of right and not on sufferance, as an owner, within the limits of its own properties, and without prejudice to the claims of other owners, but not as a tenant; not in a lodging, but in a Home.

He also stressed the 'ancient historic connection' of the Jews with Palestine, and insisted that the existence of the Jewish national home should be internationally guaranteed.[59]

Shuckburgh wrote in response that publication of this document 'would serve no useful object at this stage, or indeed at any stage', and that 'it adds nothing of consequence to the statements already published on behalf of the government'. Shuckburgh continued:

> There are passages in it which would certainly cause an outcry among the Jews as 'whittling away' the Balfour Declaration. On the other hand there is little in it that would be likely to conciliate our Arab critics. In fact it seems to me just the kind of 'trimming' document that never satisfies anybody or achieves any definite results. The earlier paragraphs strike me as particularly inappropriate. We do not want to revive the old tags about 'making Palestine as Jewish as England is English', etc. The sooner they are forgotten the better.[60]

Following Shuckburgh's suggestion, Churchill finally disapproved of publication, and asked Samuel to take no further action.[61]

Upon his arrival in London in May 1922, Samuel held meetings with the Arab

Delegation, as well as with the Zionists. He informed Shuckburgh that from his interview with the delegation he 'derived the impression that they would not press their three main demands' (abrogation of the Balfour Declaration, representative government, and control over immigration),

> if they could be given some clear assurance that the policy of the British Government was not directed towards the accomplishments of the ends desired by the more extreme Zionist elements or towards the extinction of Arab culture and political rights in Palestine.[62]

Samuel conveyed to Shuckburgh his fear that, although the local situation in Palestine was 'outwardly calm, the undercurrent of political unrest' was 'unabated', and until a political settlement that would 'satisfy the reasonable claims' of all parties could be reached, there could be no immunity from disturbance. He was particularly apprehensive of what he thought would ensue if the Arab Delegation returned to Palestine 'empty-handed ... with the conviction that they have nothing more to expect from His Majesty's Government'.[63] The high commissioner argued that the time had come to make a public pronouncement which would 'definitely put both parties in their proper place and make it clear to both' what British intentions were.

On 24 May, the *Morning Post* reported that a large gathering of members of all parties had been convened by Lord Eustace Percy to hear an address by Sir Herbert Samuel on his work in Palestine. Lord Robert Cecil chaired the meeting, and although the proceedings were not open to the press, it appeared from conversations with members who were present that Samuel 'made a good impression on a great majority of his audience'. 'He insisted several times that his aim was to secure a fair British Administration.' He said that the Jews 'were bound to increase and ultimately become the majority'. Under another title, 'Crushing out the Arabs', the *Morning Post* claimed that when Samuel was asked, 'how, in the name of self-determination, he could justify the immigration of Jews to the extent that they would ultimately become a majority, thus dispossessing the native Arab population', he had said: 'if the self-determination argument were pushed to the extreme it would have prevented the colonisation of America and Australia', and contended that the Jewish settlement, by increasing the riches and economic resources of the country, would not be to the ultimate disadvantage of the Arab community.[64]

In collaboration with Shuckburgh, Samuel drew up a fresh statement of policy which reaffirmed the government's commitment to the Balfour Declaration and the Jewish national home. As already mentioned, it was formally published on 3 June 1922 and became known as Churchill's White Paper. Its importance lies in the fact that it was the first official and written interpretation of the Balfour Declaration since its publication in 1917. In consultation with the Middle East Department, Samuel proposed to show the statement informally to both Zionists and the Arab

Delegation in order to get both parties to accept it in advance. Shuckburgh wrote, on 24 May 1922, that if Samuel succeeded

> the statement will then be sent to them officially for formal acceptance. If he does not succeed the statement will in any case be published and the Arabs will be given to understand that this is our last word, and that if they cannot accept it off-hand they had better go back to Palestine and take counsel with their supporters on the spot.[65]

The Arabs 'doubtless will not be satisfied', according to Shuckburgh, but they might be glad of the opportunity to return to Palestine 'not entirely empty-handed'. Shuckburgh also doubted whether the Zionists would accept the statement, for it contained passages, as he wrote, 'not at all to their liking'. However, they were beginning to realize that: 'they must modify their ambitions; that the patience of His Majesty's Government is not inexhaustible; and that by claiming too much they may seriously risk losing everything.'[66]

The main points of the White Paper can be summarized as follows:

1. The British government re-affirmed the Balfour Declaration.
2. A 'Jewish National Home' would be founded in Palestine. The Jewish people would be in Palestine 'as of right and not on sufferance', but the British government had no intention that Palestine should become 'as Jewish as England is English'.
3. The British government did not contemplate the disappearance or subordination of the Arab population, language or culture.
4. The status of all citizens of Palestine would be Palestinian. No section of the population would have any other status in the eyes of the law.
5. The British government intended to foster the establishment of a full measure of self-government in Palestine, and as the next step a Legislative Council with a majority of elected members would be set up immediately.
6. The special position of the Zionist Executive did not entitle it to share in any degree in the government of the country.
7. Immigration would not exceed the economic capacity of the country at the time to absorb new arrivals.
8. A committee of the elected members of the Legislative Council would confer with the administration upon matters relating to the regulation of immigration. Any difference of opinion would be referred to His Majesty's Government.
9. Any religious community or considerable section of the population claiming that the terms of the mandate were not being fulfilled would have the right of appeal to the League of Nations.[67]

The White Paper did not meet Arab demands by reversing its pro-Zionist policy. To allay Zionist fears, it 're-affirmed' the Balfour Declaration, thus confirming all the previous ambiguities inherent in it, which was the main Arab objection to it. However, it did place severe limits on what the national home meant and what its outcome would be. A totally Jewish Palestine was thus overruled.

Although the White Paper gave the Zionists much of what they asked for, it was in many respects as unwelcome to them as it was to the Arabs,[68] but the Zionist Organization formally accepted the policy set forth in it for fear that rejection might endanger the promulgation of the mandate by the League of Nations, a step which was of vital importance to the development of a Jewish national home.[69] The Palestine Arab Delegation in London, on the other hand, refused to accept it.[70]

RATIFICATION OF THE PALESTINE MANDATE

The controversy caused by the White Paper among British politicians did have one important effect: on 21 June 1922, the House of Lords passed a motion by a large majority rejecting the Mandate for Palestine 'in its present form' on the grounds that it directly violated the pledges made to the Arabs by the British government in 1915 and 1918, and was opposed to the wishes of the majority of the people in Palestine. They also said that its acceptance by the Council of the League of Nations should be postponed until modifications complying with previous pledges were made.[71]

On 23 June 1922, Hubert Young minuted that, in this situation, the best solution was to bring the new constitution into force at the earliest possible date since, encouraged by the House of Lords motion, the Arab Delegation might persist in its 'obstinate attitude' and foment trouble upon its return to Palestine.

> What exact form this will take is difficult to foresee ... If it had not been for the Lords debate, we might have had a good chance of suggesting to the Delegation through some non-official that they should make capital out of the Zionist resolution[72] and should use it to cover their retreat. This may still be possible if the House of Commons definitely turns down the decision of the House of Lords.[73]

However, on 4 July, Churchill succeeded, through a vote of confidence in the House of Commons, in reversing the Lords' motion. Churchill immediately informed Samuel of the Commons vote, adding that the policy could now be pursued vigorously, as it was now 'clear that the country supports His Majesty's Government in their Palestine policy'.[74]

On 24 July 1922, the British mandate over Palestine was confirmed by the Council of the League of Nations. The fact that Chaim Weizmann and Herbert Samuel set such store by the League's ratification of the mandate demonstrates its psychological importance to the Zionist cause at the time. Weizmann rightly saw ratification as 'the end of the first chapter of the Zionist political struggle'.[75] Indeed, Samuel had admitted more than a year earlier (in February 1921) that although the text of the draft mandate had been 'prematurely' published in the *Jewish Chronicle*, and reproduced in local papers in Palestine, the situation remained calm because many Palestine Arabs still hesitated to regard the published text as a 'final version of the instrument destined to control the fate of Palestine in the immediate future', hoping that the policy of the British government might still undergo a change.[76]

In London, the announcement of the White Paper caused the activities of the first Arab Delegation to come to an immediate end. After the Arab leaders rejected the White Paper, discussions with the Middle East Department of the Colonial Office became pointless. The delegation had been greatly encouraged by the House of Lords motion of 21 June 1922 rejecting the mandate as incompatible with British pledges to the Arabs, and contrary to the wishes of the majority of the population of Palestine, which reinforced the belief that they could pursue their aims by political means.[77] However, when the House of Commons supported Churchill's declaration, having reversed the Lords' motion, the delegation was immediately summoned back home by the Arab Executive Committee, and left London in July 1922.[78]

The Arab Delegation was unable to bring about a significant change in British government policy on the incorporation of the Balfour Declaration into the Palestine mandate. However, in its goal of explaining the Arab point of view to British statesmen and the British public, it was successful. Wyndham Deedes had already noted in August 1921 that 'one of the main objects of the Delegation was to win the sympathy of the British public and this sympathy is, it is believed, being won'.[79] Apparently encouraged by the growing support for their cause in parliament, the Arab leaders made it clear that they intended to stick to constitutional and legal methods and ruled out any revolutionary course of action.[80] However, despite the influence they had had on public opinion, delegation members grew disillusioned with the response from both the government and the Palestine administration, confirming fears they had voiced since the end of 1921 when the delegation was already asking: 'How can the British Public, how can any reasonable man or woman after this expect Arabs to have faith in pledges? How can Arabs believe that the High Commissioner for Palestine is a British official, sent out to work for their good and well-being, and not to accomplish Zionist ambitions?'[81]

Before the delegation returned home there were already indications that, in Palestine, other avenues of advocacy were being sought. The governor of Jerusalem had warned that, while hitherto Arab opposition had been confined to the national home policy, if the mandate was ratified, there was a tendency to believe that the only way to oppose the 'obnoxious' clauses was to oppose the British mandate itself, 'and to move for the total independence of a united Syria and Palestine'.[82] At the Assembly of the Executive Committee of the Fourth Palestine Arab Congress in June 1922, convened primarily to decide upon the policy to be adopted if the mandate was ratified by the League of Nations, plans were made for a peaceful demonstration, with measures to be taken to preserve public peace, to close shops on 13 and 14 July,[83] and to urge all societies to communicate their protest to the League of Nations by 1 July. In case the mandate was approved in its present form, the delegation was to be recalled from London for work in Palestine and among Eastern nations. It was agreed to despatch a Muslim delegation to Mecca and a Christian one to Rome as the capital of the Catholic world.[84]

However, at this point there was still no attempt by Arab leaders to revert to violent means, and their methods remained legal and peaceful. Samuel himself had previously reported that there was no evidence that the leaders of the Arab community had 'either organised or participated' in the November 1921 disturbances, and that

> it can with truth be said of them that while they are in political opposition on matters of principle to the Policy of His Majesty's Government in this country, they have not themselves in the past advocated the employment of direct action in order to attain their aims.[85]

The Palestinian national movement was also increasingly seeking the support of the millions of Muslims around the world, appealing to Muslim sympathies and arguing that Haram al-Sharif (the area including the Dome of the Rock and the al-Aqsa mosque, the second holiest shrine in Islam), was threatened by the Zionists. Following the declaration of the White Paper in June 1922, and during the Hajj (pilgrimage) season of 1922, a delegation was sent to Mecca, where a pan-Arab Congress was held and anti-Zionist literature was distributed among the pilgrims.[86] The delegation, consisting of Shaykh 'Abd al-Qadir al-Muzaffar, Rafiq al-Tamimi, and Amin Nur Allah, with Adib Abu Dabbagh as secretary, took with them some 500 copies of Jewish new year greetings, which were ornamented with representations of the Dome of the Rock and Haram al-Sharif as an illustration of the intentions of the Jews in regard to these places.[87] Samuel wrote to Churchill in August 1922 that he understood the specific allegations made by the delegation to the Hijaz against the administration were the following: (i) that the Mosque of al-Aqsa was to be handed over to Jews so that they could re-establish a Jewish temple;[88] (ii) that the administration had interfered with Muslim *awqaf* and religious affairs; (iii) that the administration had seized the lands of Arab cultivators and handed them over to Jewish immigrants; (iv) that Muslims were given no opportunity of participating in the administration of the country, and that the administration was favourable to the Jews; (v) that the government had armed the Jews against the Muslim community in the country.[89]

To counteract the activities of the delegation, Samuel asked for his circular to be seen as widely as possible. He thus asked the colonial secretary to forward his despatch to the high commissioner of Egypt, to the governor-general of Sudan, the high commissioner of Iraq, the viceroy of India, the British high commissioner in Constantinople, the British resident in Aden, the British agent in Jeddah, the British minister in Teheran, the British consul in Damascus, the British consul general in Beirut, the chief British representative in Amman, the governor, Straits Settlement, the British consul in Aleppo, the governor in Kenya Colony and the high commissioner in Cyprus.[90]

Already on 17 July 1922, the same day that the Mandate for Palestine was being discussed at a special meeting of the Council of the League of Nations, Samuel had summoned the members of the Advisory Council and noted that the ratification of the mandate had given rise to a 'remarkable series of false rumours', and that it had been asserted that possession of Haram al-Sharif was threatened. Samuel assured the Palestine Arabs that they need not go to so much trouble to repel an attack which 'no-one has made or will make', and so far from threatening them, the mandate was 'an additional protection … of the existing rights of each community to its Holy places'.[91] He added that it was also rumoured that on the passage of the mandate British flags over the governorates would be replaced by Zionist flags; the government of the country would be transferred to the Zionist Organization, and 30,000 Jews would immediately enter the country to occupy it.

Samuel assured the Arab members of the Advisory Council that the approval of the mandate would 'make no difference whatever in the present administration of the country, nor in the laws relating to immigration'. Beyond the establishment of an assembly with an elected majority, he went on to say, 'no other appreciable change of any importance will follow the enactment of the Mandate, except that it will then become possible to issue a Government loan'.[92] But Samuel's assurances went unnoticed.

The ratification of the mandate thus brought bitter disappointment. To the Arabs, it seemed clear by August 1922 that the British government was unquestionably committed to its pro-Zionist policy. This policy led the Palestine Arabs to boycott the 'institutions of self-rule' which the administration tried to set up. They made it unequivocally clear once again that they had not made peace with the pro-Zionist policy of the British government, even on an indirect level.[93] Non-payment of taxes and civil disobedience were among the responses that were contemplated.[94] The governor of Haifa, Colonel Symes, reported in July 1922 that 'opinion was drifting to the idea of developing a passive resistance movement', which would comprise the non-payment of taxes, 'as opposed to the project (which is also frequently discussed) of enlisting Bedouin assistance to promote guerrilla warfare'. Colonel Symes noted that advocates of loyal cooperation with the government were few.[95]

A general proclamation signed by Omar al-Bitar, president of the Executive Committee at the Fourth Palestine Arab Congress, stated: 'The purpose we are after in our National Movement is to reach our legal right—in every legal means

[sic]'. Therefore the Executive Committee requested 'every native to do his utmost and all in his power to keep peace and order during the two days of cease-work 13th and 14th instant in sign of protest against the British Mandate based upon the Balfour Declaration'.[96] (See Appendix G)

A general strike did in fact take place in Palestine to protest against the mandate, and according to Muhammad 'Izzat Darwazeh, the people expressed their feelings of outrage and anger and some disturbances occurred.[97]

BOYCOTTING THE ELECTIONS FOR THE LEGISLATIVE COUNCIL

The Palestine Order-in-Council provided for a Legislative Council to be composed of eleven official and twelve elected members, the latter to consist of eight Muslims, two Jews and two Christians. The Fifth Palestine Arab Congress, meeting in Nablus on 20 August 1922, immediately after the arrival of the Arab Delegation from London, called for the abolition of the Balfour Declaration rejecting both the mandate and the White Paper. It also rejected the Palestine Order-in-Council, announced in Palestine on 10 August 1922.[98]

By thus refusing in principle to accept the Balfour Declaration, Darwazeh asserts that the Palestine Arabs recognized neither the mandate nor the Palestine Order-in-Council and hence boycotted the elections for the Legislative Council.[99] A policy of non-co-operation with the administration was adopted in this congress. Musa Kazim informed the delegates that the pro-Arab British politicians in both houses of parliament, as well as the British press, had urged the Palestinian Delegation to persevere, and had supported them in boycotting the elections, which, they said, would eventually convince the British government of the futility of its policy, leading it in the end to abandon its pro-Zionist policy in favour of the Arabs.[100]

The Arab Executive Committee declared in a proclamation at the Fifth Palestine Arab Congress, on 1 September 1922, that the policy of the national home for the Jews would have nothing but disastrous national and economic consequences for the Palestine Arabs. 'After very careful consideration', the Arab Executive Committee stated, it had been found that accepting the Legislative Council would mean acquiescence in the Zionist policy and the mandate and an implicit acceptance of the Balfour Declaration; hence it was decided to boycott the elections.[101]

The real dilemma which faced the Palestine Arabs was that if they accepted a Legislative Council that could only advise the government and had no power to control immigration, they would find that such an institution would help the Jewish community to legitimize its position and eventually become the majority, threatening the status of the Palestinians in their own country.[102] According to Darwazeh, since of the ten elected members of the Legislative Council, two were to be Jewish and two others were to be Christians, the Arabs would find themselves in a minority, because the two Jewish members, together with the ten official British members, would form the majority.[103] Darwazeh records that the boycott of the elections in the summer of 1922 was universal. Only three Arabs nominated themselves.[104] However, after facing the 'wrath' of a population who saw them as 'traitors' they were persuaded to withdraw.[105] The Muslim-Christian Association of Nablus was instrumental in bringing about this widespread boycott.[106] Darwazeh points out that it was a complete success and that it was widely reported with admiration in the local papers in Egypt, Syria, Lebanon and Britain.[107]

The Muslim-Christian Association published a statement on 13 November 1922 explaining the reasons why it was found 'useless' to cooperate with the government in the Legislative Council. First and foremost was the fact that Article 18 of the constitution stated that the Legislative Council had no right whatever 'to go into any question of principle relating to the Mandate'. Since, according to the mandate, the government was responsible for placing the country under such political, economic and administrative conditions as would guarantee the establishment of the Jewish national home and facilitate Zionist immigration, provision also being made for the 'donation of lands to Jewish people', and since this was 'utterly in contradiction to the interests of the country and its inhabitants', and since the Council was not allowed to enquire into such principles, the cooperation of its Arab members would be entirely pointless. As to immigration, the constitution provided that this question would be vested in a mixed committee in which the 'preponderant' opinion would be vested in the government as Article 84 of the Palestine Order-in-Council provided. The president of the Muslim-Christian Association went on:

> The Constitution and the Mandate have deprived us of any right to put our proposals and to communicate on such important questions which are so vital to the interests of the nation. Consequently, participation of the Arabs in such a Council is valueless.[108]

On the question of safeguarding Arab rights, the Muslim-Christian Association pointed out that the government had claimed that it was anxious to protect the interests of the Arabs as provided by the Balfour Declaration, and, at the same time, it was anxious to establish the Jewish national home. The Arabs considered this an impossibility. The government had applied the above conditions regarding the Jewish national home, 'without paying any regard to the interests of the Arabs. This proves that the second paragraph dealing with the rights of the Arabs has only been laid down as a decoration and as a political pose which has no operative value whatever.'[109]

The administration finally admitted its failure and cancelled the elections for the Legislative Council. Darwazeh pointed out that although the high commissioner was desperate to carry out elections and enter into a more regularized and legal phase based on a constitution, he did not take any drastic steps to force these elections. By convincing the Arabs to take part in the Legislative Council, Samuel intended to secure the approval of the Arabs for a constitution which was based on the mandate, and hence on the Balfour Declaration. In this manner, Darwazeh argues that 'the Jewish high commissioner', hoped to achieve the Arabs' official recognition of the Balfour Declaration, which they consistently refused to do. He furthermore hoped to weaken the nationalist movement by diverting its attention away from the more vital issues by keeping the Arabs busy with the Legislative Council and its 'trivial' issues. Moreover, by securing a constitution for the country and electing a Legislative Council to replace the existing Advisory Council, Samuel hoped to encourage world Jewry to invest in Palestine, which he hoped would lead to an increase in immigration and land sales, and this is why the Jews, in the opinion of the Arabs, immediately agreed to take part in the elections, knowing too well that their two votes would always form a majority with the other ten of the official British members, causing the obstruction of any Arab demand.[110]

Following the failure to elect a Legislative Council, Samuel made an attempt in February 1923 to revive the old Advisory Council in a revised form. It was henceforth to consist of twelve appointed members: ten Arabs chosen from the notable families, and two Jews, in addition to the ten official members.[111] But once again, the Arab Executive Committee rejected the new proposal, and urged the nominated members to resign.[112] Some of the members insisted on keeping their governmental positions, but according to Darwazeh, their decision to side with the government only caused them 'disgrace' amongst their own people. The refusal of the Arabs to cooperate was so complete that Samuel himself decided to carry on with the administration without even this nominal representation and with the help of official members only.[113]

The Sixth Palestine Arab Congress, held in June 1923 in Jaffa, confirmed the rejection of the new Advisory Council and proposed further steps of non-co-operation with the government.[114] The purpose of the congress was to follow up on the successful boycott of the elections and the rejection of the Palestine Order-in-Council. The other major issue was the question of the non-payment of taxes. This issue was raised by Jamal al-Husseini, the secretary of the Arab Executive Committee, who maintained that the government obtained taxes and distributed them among the Zionist societies and Jewish immigrants, and urged the non-payment of taxes on the basis of 'no taxation without representation'.[115]

LINGERING HOPES OF CHANGE

Samuel wrote in December 1922 that the Arabs paid close attention to British politics.[116] With every change in the British government, there were hopes in Palestine that British Zionist policy might witness a change. In October 1922, after the fall of Lloyd George's government, a strong rumour circulated that the Balfour Declaration was about to be repudiated by the British government.[117] There were rumours in London that Samuel might resign, and in Jerusalem that 'Abdallah might be declared amir over Palestine and Transjordan.[118] Nonetheless, the new government kept repeating after assuming office in November 1922 that no change of policy regarding Palestine would take place, and that the new colonial secretary, the Duke of Devonshire, would adhere to the policy of his predecessors.[119]

Moreover, the Arabs hoped that the new Peace Conference in Lausanne between Turkey and the Entente Powers would reassess the mandatory system. Their hope was based on the fact that Mustafa Kemal had forced the European powers to renegotiate the Treaty of Sèvres of 1920 which laid down the 'legal' basis for the mandatory system in the Middle East. The Arab Executive Committee thus decided in November 1922 to despatch a three-man delegation to Istanbul to try and convince the Turks to uphold their cause. One delegate, Shaykh 'Abd al-Qadir al-Muzaffar, stayed in Istanbul until the end of December 1922, while the other two, Musa Kazim and Amin al-Tamimi proceeded to Lausanne. There they tried, albeit unsuccessfully, to appear before the conference for the purpose of influencing the Turks. But the Turks were mainly preoccupied with securing their own needs, and therefore the question of mandated territories was dropped.[120]

Also during this period, following the Kemalist victories in September 1922, there was a tendency among the ranks of the Palestinian nationalist movement to contact the Turks and obtain their support against Zionism. The strongest advocate of this movement was Shaykh 'Abd al-Qadir al-Muzaffar. After his return from Turkey, he reported that Turkish leaders had promised to support Arab aspirations for independence. It was then that some Palestinians pleaded for independence under a Turkish mandate.[121] Having received a disappointing reply from the secretary-general of the League of Nations as to a rumour that had circulated to the effect that the Balfour Declaration was to be repudiated by the British government, the delegation proceeded to London to clarify the situation.[122] The new colonial secretary, the Duke of Devonshire, stressed to the delegation that the Balfour Declaration would not be repudiated, and again, no results were achieved in the Colonial Office, but the Arabs scored another success in parliament and in the press. The *Daily Mail* published for the first time excerpts from the Hussein-McMahon correspondence, which strengthened the Arab case and prompted the House of Lords to pass a second motion criticizing the draft mandate.[123]

THE THIRD ARAB DELEGATION, JUNE 1923

In June 1923, the Cabinet sub-committee on Palestine, which was chaired by Lord Curzon, met to review British policy, which prompted the Sixth Palestine Arab Congress, held on 16 June 1923, to send a third delegation to negotiate with the

British government in the hope of reversing the Balfour Declaration. The Third Arab Delegation placed very high hopes on the committee, and held the view that its establishment was 'a step towards a just and fitting solution of the question of Palestine on the part of the British Government'.[124] The delegation consisted of Musa Kazim and Amin al-Tamimi, later joined by a Maronite lawyer of Lebanese origin, Wadi' al-Boustany; they arrived in London on 22 June 1923. Samuel felt that this delegation was more unyielding than the previous ones, and advised the Colonial Office to avoid them.[125] The Middle East Department concurred.

Shuckburgh rehearsed the arguments against receiving the delegation: they were 'in no sense an official body and to allow them to appear before a Cabinet Committee would be giving them too much importance', for they were 'decidedly weaker' than the delegation of the previous year, and represented 'the extremist section of the Palestine Arabs, who constitute a majority perhaps, but certainly not the whole of the Arab population'. Shuckburgh added that 'we are at present trying to rally the moderates to our side' and that Samuel hoped that the moderates would be induced to serve on his Advisory Council. They were the people 'least in sympathy with Musa Kazim and his friends'.[126] Shuckburgh furthermore claimed that the 'moderates' would surely be 'alienated if they see the rival faction accorded the honour of appearing before a Cabinet Committee and treated as though they were the recognised spokesmen of the whole country', and since the moderates on the whole 'behaved well' during the last year, Shuckburgh noted that anything 'tending to discourage them' was to be avoided. He also argued that it would be 'contrary to general practice for a Cabinet Committee to invite witnesses and hear evidence like a Royal Commission'. The Iraq Commission had heard Sir Percy Cox and 'no one else', and this would seem a 'good precedent for the Palestine Committee hearing no one but Sir H. Samuel.' He pointed out that 'if the Arabs are heard, the Zionists are certain to claim to be heard as well. Such a claim could hardly be refused.'[127] As a result, the Cabinet Committee refused to hear the representatives of the delegation; the formal reason that was given was that the committee did not listen to witnesses other than government officials, but the real reason was that Samuel objected to it being heard.[128] Samuel himself proceeded to London in June to discuss Palestine policy with the new Conservative government. (See Chapter 3)

In conclusion, three important points must be made. Firstly, Shuckburgh's insistence that the Palestine Arabs had no recognized spokesmen meant that 93 per cent of the people of the country could not even claim to have officially recognized representatives to speak in their name, while 7 per cent of the population were officially represented by the Zionist Organization which spoke not only in the name of local Jews, but of world Jewry as a whole. This policy was advocated by Samuel and he had indeed warned the first Palestine Arab Delegation in 1921 that it would not be recognized as an official body. This was arguably the first step

towards ensuring political ascendancy for the Jewish community once they became a majority. Moreover, it was only the Zionists who were heard by the Cabinet
Committee because their case was actually made through Samuel.

Second, official policy, both in Jerusalem and London, was clearly to divide the
Arab front by encouraging a small faction to split the nationalist front in such a
way as to enable Samuel and the Middle East Department to claim that the Arab
Executive Committee did not represent the whole population. This schism was to
cripple the nationalist movement throughout the rest of the mandate period.

Third, it was upon Shuckburgh's insistence, and not that of the British government in general, that the pro-Zionist policy was portrayed as a policy not in any
way susceptible to change. Shuckburgh asserted that he could say 'with the full
authority' of the government, that 'there is no question whatever of reversing the
policy to which His Majesty's Government have over and over again expressed
their adherence of the Balfour Declaration', and that there was 'no question of
reopening the general question of policy'. What the Cabinet Committee was considering was 'not a reversal of policy but merely the best means of giving practical
effect to a policy already settled'.[129]

The Cabinet Committee concluded on 27 July 1923 that it was impossible now
to go back on the pledges to the Jewish people and that the government could not
withdraw its support for Zionism because there was 'no way of reversing the policy
without throwing up the mandate', which would result in Palestine being occupied
by France, Italy or Turkey.[130] Nevertheless, the committee recommended that steps
should be taken to appease the Arabs, and therefore, advocated the establishment
of an 'Arab Agency' to correspond to the Jewish Agency, and to advise the government on all questions affecting the 'non-Jewish' population in Palestine. The
functions of the Immigration Committee which was to be set up under Article 84
of the 1922 Palestine Order-in-Council, would be transferred to the proposed 'Arab
Agency'.[131] In October 1923, Samuel officially announced in Palestine the proposal to set up an Arab Agency, discussed in the next chapter. For the rest of the
1920s, Arab diplomatic efforts to alter British policy towards Palestine almost came
to a complete standstill. Having thus failed to bring about such a change, the Palestine Arab politicians were divided over the methods that should be adopted to achieve
their national objectives.[132]

8

An Uneasy Truce: Samuel's Last Years, September 1923–July 1925

By the time the Mandate for Palestine came into full operation by the resolution of the Council of the League of Nations on 29 September 1923, the attitude of the three parties in the Palestinian 'triangle' had taken a more definite shape. The British government made it clear that it stood firmly by the Balfour Declaration and by its pro-Zionist policy. The Zionists, who systematically opposed representative institutions and self-determination in Palestine, were content that the articles in the mandate would allow them to achieve their ultimate aim of becoming a majority through immigration and land settlement, and thus eventually achieving political supremacy. The Arabs strongly contested the policy of the administration. Samuel himself summed up the Arab position in January 1924 with the following words:

> The large majority of the population of Palestine are Moslem Arabs, and among them, a majority possibly equally large, favour the general views of what may be termed the local opposition to the Palestine policy of His Majesty's Government as applied by this Administration.[1]

Sydney Moody, an official in the Middle East Department, assessing the situation in Palestine in a minute on 24 January 1924, commented that, 'since we put an end to constitutional expedients as a means of placating the implacable' there was no doubt that

> we must in the near future concentrate on saving the economic soul of Palestine. Economic renaissance will bring its own troubles. When things are at their worst serious political disturbances do not usually occur: it is only when they begin to improve. That generalisation ought to give us ten years' peace but I don't suppose it will.[2]

RIFTS IN PALESTINIAN ARAB POLITICS

The period from the end of 1923 till 1925 and beyond, until 1929 when Palestine witnessed the second major outbreak of violence, was characterized by the steady development of the Jewish national home,[3] and an interlude in the Palestinian Arab struggle against Zionism.[4] One important reason for the reduction of Arab pressure on Samuel's administration was the rifts which developed within the nationalist movement.

The district governor of Samaria, C. H. F. Cox, wrote that by the end of 1923 the political atmosphere in Palestine was becoming less electric. At the same time, the people had lost confidence in their leaders, whose policy was 'in no way calculated to raise the country from the state of economic depression in which it finds itself'. Consequently, the leaders, finding that their power had decreased, were inclined to be 'much more friendly' with the government.[5] This crisis of confidence, and the strains on nationalist unity were in part the result of the dilemmas posed by British policy and its emphasis on giving priority to the undertakings in the Balfour Declaration. However, internal personality clashes and power struggles within the Arab elite, and efforts by the Zionist movement to promote dissent, also played their part in the divisions which from 1924 onwards, were to characterize the Palestinian nationalist movement into the 1930s.

Zionist efforts to divide and weaken the Arab nationalist movement from within began in 1921. The most important motive behind this new Zionist strategy, besides establishing and funding what were known as the 'National Parties', was to call into question the representative character of the Arab Delegation in London and undermine its activities in Britain. Members of the Zionist Executive, particularly Haim Kalvarisky, who headed its Arab Department,[6] had already identified some elements among the Arab political elite who, for reasons of personal family feuds, opposed the Arab Executive Committee. The Zionist Executive immediately set out to encourage those men both morally and 'materially' to work against the leaders of the Arab Executive Committee.[7]

This was not the first Zionist attempt to manipulate Arab political activity. As early as 1920, Muhammad 'Izzat Darwazeh recalled that Kalvarisky, who had established an organization called the Society for Jewish-Arab Peace in Palestine in March 1920, had travelled to Damascus during the same month to promote his society and to meet Palestinian leaders. Darwazeh writes in his memoirs that he was among those whom Kalvarisky had met in Damascus, and that he had taken a very firm stand against him, telling him that his 'tricks' would not deceive any enlightened Arab, and that his attempts were like 'poison'. He also told him he understood that such manoeuvres were only calculated to pacify the Palestine Arabs until the Zionist movement got stronger and was able to establish its Jewish state on the ruins of the Arab. He furthermore made clear to Kalvarisky that the

Palestine Arabs were aware of his 'wicked designs', and that there would be no peace between the Palestine Arabs and the Jews. Darwazeh went on to say that a secret society (Jam'iyya Fata Filastin) in Damascus had attempted to assassinate Kalvarisky: an ambush had been prepared for him on his way back to Palestine, but the attempt failed because the Zionist leader travelled via the Beirut road instead of Qunaytra, where the ambush had been set. Darwazeh explains that the attempt on Kalvarisky's life was calculated to send a message to the Zionists, and to prevent Kalvarisky from gaining such adherents as he might be able to deceive.[8]

It was during the summer of 1921, that the Zionists attempted to organize all the opponents of the Arab Executive Committee under one political framework with a programme favourable to Zionism. When the first Palestinian Arab Delegation departed for England in July 1921, various Zionist elements, including the Zionist Organization, argued that the delegation was not representative of the entire Arab population of Palestine. The Zionist-inspired and funded National Muslim Association (al-Jam'iyya al-Islamiyya al-Wataniyya) was set up in 1921[9] enabling Zionist spokesmen in London to argue that the existence of rival organizations was 'proof' that the Arab Delegation was not representative of the Palestine Arabs as a whole.[10]

Samuel had reported in October 1921 that the object of the National Muslim Association was to cooperate closely with the government, and that its branches were 'opposed to the policy of the delegation, of whose composition and methods they disapprove'. However, Samuel warned that 'their origin' had to be borne in mind, and that the 'danger of an attempt to cause a split in the Moslem Community from outside is manifest'.[11] In January 1922, the Zionists attempted to form a National Christian Society on the same lines as that of the National Muslim Association. Edward Keith-Roach, assistant to the civil secretary Deedes, wrote in the monthly Political Report to Churchill that the formation of this society was also due to the influence of Kalvarisky.[12] British officials regarded these parties as a 'highly artificial product'; the only reason that they had not been dissolved was that, in the eyes of a few of their members, the financial advantages of membership offered by the Zionists still seemed to outweigh 'press abuse' and 'public contempt'. But, by April 1922, there were reportedly resignations from the National Muslim Association.[13]

The success of the Arab Executive Committee in boycotting the elections for the Legislative Council in the spring of 1923 brought disaster to the National Muslim Association. Because of its ties with the Zionists, it was abandoned and disappeared from the scene. But a new grouping soon emerged to oppose the leadership of the Arab Executive Committee, at a critical moment when the Mandate for Palestine had been ratified by the League of Nations.[14] This group was at first referred to as the 'Moderate' party, and took formal shape as the National Party (al-Hizb al-Watani al-'Arabi al-Filastini) in November 1923.

Towards the end of 1922, Samuel himself began to advocate the formation of a 'moderate party'.[15] In December 1922, he wrote to the Duke of Devonshire that there was a section of the population which took a different view to that of the Arab Executive. Although their numbers were small, they included, according to Samuel, some of the leading men in the country. The high commissioner described them as Arab nationalists who recognized that Palestine could not, at present, govern itself, and who welcomed the British mandate and believed in the 'sincerity of our declarations that we will help the country to ultimate self-government'. They realized, according to Samuel, that the accusations that the land of the Arabs was to be taken from them and given to the Jews, and that a Zionist government was to be established to dominate the majority, were false.[16] Their motives were varied. Some were 'largely animated' by personal antagonisms to persons in the other camp, some were under the impression that they might obtain some advantages by standing with the government, and yet others

> were influenced by favours received from one of the Jewish organisers, who has set out to form a pro-Zionist Arab party. Many regard the question of the Balfour Declaration as a *chose jugée*, and do not propose to waste time, energy and physical comfort, on beating their heads against a brick wall. All these make up what has come to be called the Moderate Party.[17]

Samuel alleged that they had 'considerable support' in the press, although they had not yet a definite organization and he questioned whether they would have the 'moral courage' to stand up for their views. Pan-Islamism held little appeal for them, and they were anxious for a quiet life. They wished to get richer, and believed that the government's policy 'was best calculated to make the country more prosperous, and themselves with it.' At the same time, the government derived 'a good deal of support from groups and individuals for no other apparent reason than that leading opponents of the Government are opponents of those groups or individuals'.[18]

In February 1923, Samuel informed the Duke of Devonshire that he had received an 'overture' from important sections of the Arabs, stating that they would be prepared to abandon opposition to the Balfour Declaration and cooperate with the government in the elections on condition that: (i) annual immigration should be limited numerically; (ii) the election to the Legislative Council of Arab members by the high commissioner should be from lists submitted by local bodies in such number as to constitute a majority with elected members; (iii) British officials should retain their positions in the administration but the number of Palestinians in important positions should be largely increased; and (iv) an Arab amir should be appointed in Palestine, the high commissioner remaining in his position. While Samuel objected to the last condition, and had reservations about

ELECTED KING OF SYRIA: THE EMIR FEISUL—ENTERING HIS CARRIAGE AFTER ATTENDING THE FRIDAY SERVICE AT THE MOSQUE IN DAMASCUS.

PLATE 1

British Rule in Palestine: The New High Commissioner Arrives.

1. HIS EXCELLENCY'S DISEMBARKATION AT THE HISTORIC PORT OF JAFFA : SIR HERBERT SAMUEL'S BOAT ALONGSIDE THE LANDING-PLACE.
3. THE MAYOR OF JERUSALEM'S ADDRESS : (L. TO R.) : SIR H. SAMUEL, COL. STORRS (GOVERNOR OF JERUSALEM), COL. POPHAM (ASSISTANT GOVERNOR).

2. BUILT FOR THE EX-KAISER ON THE MOUNT OF OLIVES, WHEN HE VISITED JERUSALEM : THE HIGH COMMISSIONER'S RESIDENCE FLYING THE UNION JACK
4. AT THE MAIN GATEWAY ENTRANCE TO THE GROUNDS OF THE HIGH COMMISSIONER'S RESIDENCE : THE GUARD OF THE YORKSHIRE REGIMENT.

Sir Herbert Samuel, the new High Commissioner for Palestine, arrived at Jaffa on June 30. He was received by a guard of honour with a band and a salute of 17 guns, as he landed in a boat from H.M.S. "Centaur," accompanied by the Governor of Jerusalem, Sir Ronald Storrs. Travelling by special train to Jerusalem, a deputation, headed by the Mayor, met him at the railway station, and read an address of welcome, after replying to which the High Commissioner proceeded to his official residence, the palace built on the Mount of Olives for the ex-Kaiser when he visited Palestine. The Union Jack was hoisted above the palace buildings from the flagstaff over the church, on either side of which, in niches in the wall, are still to be seen statues of the ex-Kaiser and Kaiserin. (Photo. Sheepstone

PLATE 2

SIR HERBERT SAMUEL in Palestine : *The New High Commissioner at Work*

The Chief Rabbi of Jerusalem and the Head of the Bokhara Jews

Some of the important Jewish Rabbis who went to Jerusalem on Sir Herbert Samuel's arrival to hear the King's message and the Commissioner's statement of his policy

The Chief Rabbi of Jaffa in Jerusalem

Sir Herbert Samuel Reading the King's Message to the various dignitaries of the Government

The King's message was read to the various dignitaries of Jerusalem in Arabic, English, and Hebrew, on his arrival. The message was in English, Arabic, and Hebrew

The First High Commissioner of Palestine

Sir Herbert Samuel is one of the most distinguished of his appointment as first High Commissioner of Palestine. It is a very fitting that the first High Commissioner should be a distinguished Liberal scholar, a former Home Secretary.

Colonel Ronald Storrs

For a long time Military Governor of Jerusalem, and now the first British Civil Governor of Jerusalem. Colonel Storrs is a well-known authority on and a distinguished financial scholar

The Union Jack Over the ex-Kaiser's "Palace"

Sir Herbert Samuel, the new High Commissioner for Palestine, has his own headquarters is putting to work. He has taken over the ex-Kaiser's palatial hospice on the Mount of Olives as his official residence. This was known as Government House. It is to George an official building, and was built by the German extremely finest and most costly edifice in Palestine, and was built by the German extremely magnificent rooms, and a sum of £300,000 is said to have been spent upon it. After has arrived Sir Herbert raised several invitations to the Arab Sheikhs, representatives of the

The Commissioner's Guests in the Quadrangle of Government House

different Christian and other sects, heads of communities and other officials, who gathered in the Assembly Hall, where the new Governor read a message from King George in English, Arabic, and Hebrew. He then read a lengthy statement of his policy, which was likewise translated into Arabic and Hebrew, a copy of which, together with the King's letter, was presented to everyone present. As the guests passed from the hall into the courtyard, where refreshments were served, they were presented to the new Governor.

PLATE 3

OPENING A JEWISH VINTAGE : THE HIGH COMMISSIONER IN PALESTINE.

Photographs by the American Colony at Jerusalem

WITH THE FOREMOST PAIR CARRYING A LARGE CLUSTER OF GRAPES HUNG ON A STAFF A PROCESSION OF CHILDREN PRECEDING SIR HERBERT SAMUEL ON HIS WAY TO THE WINE-PRESS AT RICHON EL ZION.

SIR HERBERT SAMUEL'S VISIT TO THE FIRST JEWISH COLONY FOUNDED IN PALESTINE BY LORD ROTHSCHILD : THE BRITISH HIGH COMMISSIONER LEAVING A BOWER ARCH AT RICHON EL ZION ON HIS WAY TO THE SYNAGOGUE.

Sir Herbert Samuel, the British High Commissioner in Palestine, restored decreed in white and draped with vines and fruit-bore, the foremost two from Jerusalem on July 23 to open the vintage season at Richon el Zion, the a large cluster of grapes hung on a staff. Next, he proceeded to this first Jewish Colony founded by Baron Rothschild in Palestine. He was met wine-presses, into which he emptied grapes from baskets handed to him by little outside the village, by Colonists on horse-back, and escorted along the avenue girls, while the press was simultaneously applied of Olives, surrounded between rows of youths on white and blue (the Zionist colours) he then inspected the coffers, which are among the largest in the world, having and escorted between rows of youths on white and blue (the Zionist colours) to a capacity of 1,500,000 gallons. In reply to an address, he said that the British the little Synagogue, where a short service was held. He next visited the edifice and Zionist flags in the decorations symbolised the future of Palestine, and he of the Richon wine-cellar. Before him went a procession of school children emphasised the importance of co-operation with the Christian and Moslem inhabitants.

PLATE 4

The FRENCH in SYRIA : In the Streets of Beirut.

GENERAL GOURAUD AND GENERAL GOYBET IN BEIRUT BEFORE THE FRENCH OCCUPATION OF DAMASCUS

PLATE 5

A Joint Moslem and Christian Delegation from Palestine

Four Moslem and two Christian delegates, elected to represent the 700,000 native inhabitants of Palestine, are now waiting at the Hotel Cecil to hear the Government's reply on the future of Palestine. The names of the members seen here are Hajj Tewfik Hammad (President), Mousa Kazin Pasha El-Husseini, Amin Bey El-Tamimi, and Mouin Bey El-Madi. Standing are : Mr. Shibly Jamal and Mr. Ibrahim Effendi Shammas

PLATE 6

INCLUDING SIR HERBERT SAMUEL (HIGH COMMISSIONER), LADY SAMUEL, AND FIELD-MARSHAL LORD ALLENBY: A GROUP TAKEN IN JERUSALEM ON THE OCCASION OF THE RECENT CEREMONY OF THE PROCLAMATION OF THE PALESTINE MANDATE.

PLATE 7

THE PROCLAMATION OF THE PALESTINE MANDATE AT JERUSALEM: READING THE KING'S COMMISSION BEFORE SIR HERBERT SAMUEL, LORD ALLENBY, AND THE EMIR ABDULLAH.

PLATE 8

33

THE RETURN OF THE ARAB
DELEGATION TO PALESTINE.

Arab Boy Scouts at Gaza

Bedouin Chief Awaiting the Arrival of the Arab Delegation

A Native Welcome from Arab Horsemen

A Native Band Sets Out to Meet the Delegates

The Palestine Arab Congress Held at Nablus

Prayers for the Return of the Delegation

PLATE 9

RIVAL ARABIAN KINGDOMS: MECCA IN PERIL; THE HEJAZ ABDICATION.

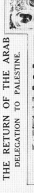

1. THE RULER OF THE HEJAZ WHO HAS ABDICATED: KING HUSSEIN—THE FIRST PORTRAIT OF HIM EVER DRAWN.

2. THE RULER OF THE WAHABIS WHO HAVE THREATENED MECCA: IBN SAUD (RIGHT), SULTAN OF NEJD.

3. RECENTLY THREATENED BY THE WAHABI FORCES OF SULTAN IBN SAUD: MECCA, THE HOLY CITY, THE PROCESSION OF THE MAHMAL OVERTAKING THE HOLY "CARPET," BROUGHT EVERY YEAR BY PILGRIMAGE FROM CAIRO.

4. THE HOLY CITY OF THE MUSLIM WORLD, LATELY PANIC-STRICKEN AT THE APPROACH OF THE WAHABIS: MECCA, FILGRIMS AROUND THE BLACK-DRAPED KA'ABA IN THE COURT OF THE GREAT MOSQUE.

It was announced on October 3 that King Hussein of the Hejaz had abdicated in favour of his eldest son, the Emir Ali. Sherif Hussein, brother of Feisal, of Iraq, and the Emir Abdullah of Transjordania. King Hussein declared the independence of the Hejaz in 1916, and took upon himself the title of King of Arabia, against the Turks. On June 21, 1917, he assumed the title of King of Arabia, but he was only recognised by Great Britain as King of the Hejaz. Last March he assumed the title of Caliph. Meanwhile the Wahabis, under the Sultan Ibn Saud, ruler of the Wahabis, who recently captured Taif, the interior capital of the Hejaz, advanced towards Mecca, and spread of religious bought the coast, but it was the Holy City into panic, and crowds of religious bought the coast, but it was

...reported on October 6 that it was uncertain whether the Wahabis had really occupied Mecca, and that their attack on the Holy was a religious one. Full details are still awaited. In any case, it is evident that the Holy City is in danger. [...] etc.

PLATE 10

Lord Balfour in Palestine: Scenes during His Visit to Open the Hebrew University.

LORD BALFOUR AT TEL-AVIV, NEAR JAFFA: LISTENING TO A SPEECH OF WELCOME BY DR. BOGARCHOW, PRINCIPAL OF THE TEL-AVIV SECONDARY SCHOOL.

AT THE FIRST MODERN JEWISH AGRICULTURAL SETTLEMENT IN PALESTINE: LORD BALFOUR (CENTRE) AT RISHON-LE-ZION, A CENTRE OF THE WINE-MAKING TRADE.

SIGNS OF ARAB OPPOSITION TO ZIONISM AND LORD BALFOUR'S VISIT: BLACK FLAGS HUNG FROM HOUSES IN JERUSALEM.

A GUARD OF HONOUR TO THE EARL OF BALFOUR AT THE OPENING OF THE HEBREW UNIVERSITY: THE PALESTINE POLICE BAND (ALL JEWS) WITH THEIR CONDUCTOR, CAPTAIN SILVER (FOREGROUND).

Lord Balfour's visit to Palestine, which caused rejoicings among the Jews and opposition among the Arabs, brought into prominence the racial discord in that country. In opening the Hebrew University at Jerusalem on April 1, Lord Balfour made an effort towards reconciliation: "I hope," he said, "the Arabs will remember that in the darkest days of the Dark Ages, when Western civilisation appeared almost extinct and smothered under barbaric influences, it was the Jews and Arabs together who gave the first sparks of light which illuminated that gloomy period. If in the tenth century, for example, Jews and Arabs could work together for the illumination of Europe, cannot Jews and Arabs work now in co-operation with Europe?"—[PHOTOGRAPHS BY C. N., "THE TIMES," AND TOPICAL.]

PLATE 11

"A NEW EPOCH HAS BEGUN": LORD BALFOUR INAUGURATING THE HEBREW UNIVERSITY AT JERUSALEM.

"FROM WHERE YOU ARE SITTING YOU CAN SEE THE VERY SPOT WHERE THE CHILDREN OF ISRAEL FIRST ENTERED THE PROMISED LAND": LORD BALFOUR (IN CENTRE) DELIVERING HIS INAUGURAL ADDRESS IN THE AMPHITHEATRE ON MOUNT SCOPUS BELOW THE NEW UNIVERSITY BUILDINGS.

Lord Balfour, whose subsequent visit to Damascus caused disturbances there, performed on April 1 the principal task of his visit to Palestine, the inauguration of the new Hebrew University at Jerusalem. The ceremony took place in an open-air amphitheatre of Greek design, on the side of Mount Scopus just below the University buildings. The principal guests, among whom were also Lord Allenby and Sir Herbert Samuel, were in a tribune constructed over the gully in front of the amphitheatre. Lord Balfour may be seen standing in academic robe, near the centre of the photograph, delivering his inaugural address. He has since left Palestine, and arrived at Alexandria on April 12. When he rose to speak on the occasion here illustrated, the whole assembly rose with him and gave him a great ovation. In his speech he said: "What is it that has brought together this vast concourse? . . . It is the consciousness that this marks a great epoch in the history of a people who made this little land of Palestine the centre of great religions, whose intellectual and moral destiny is from the national point of view envying, and who will look back to this day as an celebrating at one of the great milestones in their future career. . . . From where you are sitting you can see the very spot where the Children of Israel first entered the Promised Land, and it was from this very hill that the Roman destroyers of Jerusalem conducted their siege which brought to an end that great chapter of the Jewish people. . . . Well, a new epoch has begun. The great effort within Palestine which came to an end so many hundreds of years ago is going to be resumed in the ancient home of the people. . . . We are now engaged in adopting Western methods and a Western form of university to an Eastern site and education in an Eastern language."

PLATE 12

LORD BALFOUR AT JERUSALEM BEFORE HIS HURRIED DEPARTURE FROM DAMASCUS

Lord Balfour's long-planned visit to the Holy Land ended a few days ago in his flight from Damascus before bands of incensed Arabs, who have seen in the English statesman's visit the perpetuation of a system of government to which they are strongly antagonistic. The tour of Palestine itself went off with no very untoward incident, but when Lord Balfour arrived at Damascus the hostility of the Arabs at once became apparent, and he was compelled to take refuge on board the *Sphinx*, under police protection. The picture we reproduce here shows Lord Balfour in Jerusalem delivering the opening address at the inauguration of the great Hebrew University. Immediately on Lord Balfour's left is Dr. Weiszmann, and on his right Lord Allenby (in top hat)

PLATE 13

LORD BALFOUR'S HOSTILE RECEPTION IN DAMASCUS—THE POLICE IN EL MARGI SQUARE TURNING BACK THE MOB OF ARAB RIOTERS WHO DEMONSTRATED BEFORE THE HOTEL IN WHICH THE STATESMAN WAS STAYING

PLATE 14

THE HOSTILE ARAB DEMONSTRATION AGAINST THE PRESENCE OF LORD BALFOUR IN DAMASCUS: THE SCENE IN EL MARGI SQUARE DURING THE FIGHT BETWEEN LEBANESE GENDARMERIE AND THE MOB ATTEMPTING TO REACH LORD BALFOUR'S HOTEL.

PLATE15

The Resignation of the Zionist Leader who Converted Lord Balfour to Zionism

PLATE 16

others, it was the colonial secretary who eventually rejected the suggestions made by the Arabs.[19]

As the campaign to boycott the Legislative Council towards the end of 1922 and during the course of 1923 gained momentum, both Samuel and the pro-government 'moderate' elements found themselves in a corner. The pro-government party sought to extract some concessions to justify its inclination to work with the government. On 10 August 1923 a letter to the editor of *La Palestine* from a certain Ibrahim al-Muhib attributed the formation of the Moderate Party to the Zionist Executive. He himself had been called upon to form the party and amalgamate the National Muslim Association with it, which he refused to do. He earnestly warned the Palestinians to be on their guard, and to adhere to their congress and the Arab Executive Committee.[20]

According to the Political Report for September 1923, a party which called itself the 'Liberal Moderate Party', and subsequently the 'Arab National Party', was in the process of formation. Although 'nationalistic', it opposed the Muslim-Christian Association, and sought to achieve its ends through cooperation with the government rather than opposition. It had not yet been organized, and was largely due to individual effort, but had succeeded in gaining the support of the editor of the Jerusalem paper, *Mir'at al-Sharq*.[21] On 11 September 1923, *La Palestine* wrote that the new Moderate Party claimed that its aim was to rescue the country from its deplorable state, but the writer remarked that the country would only be saved through constant unity and not through the formation of new parties.[22]

On 22 September 1923, *Mir'at al-Sharq* asserted that this party would adopt entirely new methods, and answered allegations that it was estranged from the nationalist movement and was pro-English and pro-Zionist.[23] On 29 September, the same paper published an outline of the new party's programme. The editor explained that its aim was to obtain, by cooperation with the government in the political, economic and educational fields, 'that which the Arab nationalists [i.e. the Arab Executive Committee] have been hitherto unable to obtain through opposition'. The party believed that in this way, some improvement might be achieved. However, if the government was unwilling to reach an understanding with the nation, they would, according to the Jerusalem paper, be 'forced to relax their efforts and to leave the matter in the hands of destiny'.[24]

The Palestine Arab National Party (al-Hizb al-Watani al-'Arabi al-Filastini), founded in November 1923, split the nationalist movement and weakened it for the rest of the mandate years, for no other reason than to challenge the leadership of the Arab Executive Committee. Its members were basically the same as those of the National Muslim Association but having learnt from their previous failure, they adopted an anti-Zionist programme similar to that of the Arab Executive Committee.[25] Article 3 of the party's programme stated that it did not acknowledge the Balfour Declaration and the constitution passed by the government, the

Legislative and Advisory Councils, the Arab Executive Committee or any influence except that of the people of the country. Article 4 insisted on establishing a national democratic government, and Article 6 pledged to continue to enlighten the 'outer world' of the Palestine cause, by sending delegates on a regular basis, and by writing and lecturing and other diplomatic means.[26]

This caught the attention of one member of the Colonial Office, Sydney Moody, who wrote:

> It is amazing to read that the Jews were disappointed that the programme of the Nationalist Party does not include anything approaching an acceptance of the Balfour Declaration ... No Arab Party ever can or will openly accept or approach an acceptance of it. There is nothing, in my opinion, to be gained by pretending that it is possible. There would however be even less to be gained by abandoning it on that account.[27]

The Arab Executive Committee fought this new party from the outset, labelling it as 'treacherous'.[28] Meanwhile, on 3 October 1923, in a lengthy editorial, *al-Karmel* criticized both parties for their unfair attitude towards each other, and suggested that a conference be held in Nablus, which was centrally located and not involved in the dispute between them, to formulate plans to unite the contending forces.[29]

Reporting on the emerging party in December 1923, Ronald Storrs wrote that although the Arab Executive Committee was criticized, on the other hand severe criticism came from Nablus against the new party which 'indulged even more freely in the pursuit of personal questions'. Indeed, as Storrs observed, 'the similarity of the new programme has caused many to enquire why there should be two parties at all since they pursue the same object'. Storrs felt that another defect in the new party was the 'comparatively small calibre' of its directing forces. Sulayman Taji al-Faruqi was the only notable of any standing who openly supported it: Raghib Bey Nashashibi (as mayor and therefore to a certain extent non-political) 'remains behind the curtain, whilst Aref Pasha appears to be drawing once more near the opposite side'.[30] The district governor of Gaza also wrote in December 1923 that while the Arab Executive Committee under Musa Kazim Pasha appeared to have lost favour, the new party had not gained many active adherents. The more enlightened sections of the inhabitants realized that both parties were out for 'personal aggrandisement' and 'family influence' rather than for national service. The *fallahin* were too preoccupied with next year's harvest to pay attention to politics.[31]

The Zionists, although happy to have caused an open schism in the ranks of the Palestinian nationalist movement, were hardly satisfied with the anti-Zionist programme of the new party. They renewed their efforts to set up Arab organizations opposed to the Arab Executive Committee and openly supporting Zionism.[32] Early in 1924, Haim Kalvarisky and Colonel F. H. Kisch, chairman of the Political

Department of the Zionist Executive, set out to establish the Peasants' Party (Hizb al-Zara'a), which would form an association of village cooperatives, this time exploiting old antagonisms between the villages and urban centres.[33] The fate of these new enterprises, however, was no better than that of the National Muslim Association. The Political Report for January 1924 observed that the Arabs considered the recently formed party to be a frankly Zionist creation.[34]

By August 1924, the 'Political Reports' from Palestine showed that in Hebron, for instance, the Peasants' Party had very few followers, and that in Beisan, 'much to the chagrin' of Colonel Kisch and Mr Kalvarisky, a branch of the Muslim-Christian Association, their main rival, had opened. Eric Mills wrote that 'the personal activities of these two gentlemen, at Beisan would be amusing if they were not pitiable'.[35] Thus, by September 1924, it was becoming all too evident that the formation of agricultural parties in the villages had been unsuccessful, as it was widely accepted by the people that they had a 'Jewish paternity'.[36] In October 1924, Ronald Storrs reported that the national 'Agricultural Parties' were limiting their action to opposing the influence of the Arab Executive Committee.[37]

In June 1924, there had been reports of a reconciliation between Arab political parties and suggestions for forming one single party.[38] In August, Ronald Storrs reported that lack of funds and internal dissension continued to hamper Arab political activity. The Arab Executive Committee faced difficulties mainly as a result of the decline in public confidence in them, and members themselves made no attempt to hide the shortcomings of their colleagues. Jamal al-Husseini had renewed his activities to breathe new life into the movement, but in spite of all his efforts, it was impossible to find one single Christian member of the Jerusalem Muslim-Christian Association.[39] In October, an attempt was made by the rival parties to reconcile their differences, the first step being taken by the Arab Executive Committee. But the 'fierceness' of Jamal al-Husseini's attack on Shaykh As'ad Shuqayr, an opposition leader in Acre, made this possibility seem remote.[40]

By the end of the year, Storrs wrote that there was a marked trend in the two opposing Arab parties towards reconciliation, assisted by a press campaign on both sides. There was general agreement to keep personal rivalries under check, and delegates from the two parties had met, although no formal decisions were taken. The attempts at reconciliation were not affected by articles by Jamal al-Husseini, in *al-Karmel*, which had opened the Husseini-Nashashibi feud.[41] However, nothing seems to have come out of these initiatives. As Arab divisions reached their climax, an effort by 'Abd al-'Aziz Tha'alibi[42] to promote the unity of all Arab parties before the advent of the Seventh Palestine Arab Congress (which was eventually held only in June 1928) also failed.[43]

PROPOSALS FOR RADICAL ACTION

This stagnation did not prevent other Palestinian factions from calling for more revolutionary courses of action. At the time when Samuel was encouraging the emergence of a Moderate Party, revolution was again being discussed in other quarters. There were reports that at a special meeting in the offices of the Arab Executive Committee, convened by Shaykh 'Abd al-Qadir al-Muzaffar and Khalil Sakakini (a Palestinian leader and educationalist), the opinion had been expressed that revolution was the only alternative if systematic opposition to the elections failed, or if the pro-government forces succeeded in helping the government make the elections a success. It was also reported that one speaker had doubted that a nation 'incapable of organising successful propaganda' would succeed in revolution. But Shaykh al-Muzaffar had said that revolution in Palestine was inevitable, if not today, then tomorrow, and that it would take place 'suddenly as a result of continued oppression'. 'Awni 'Abd al-Hadi[44] had allegedly quoted a French saying: 'Revolution we ever bear in mind but its name we never utter'.[45] In February 1923, Shaykh al-Muzaffar continued to campaign against the elections to the Legislative Council, telling the people that the majority of the council would not be with the Arabs, that the high commissioner held all the power in his hands, and that he could pass any order or sentence. Samuel's authority was unbounded, 'greater than the kings and prophets, but not greater than the power of God'.[46]

In August 1923, there were reports of an abortive attempt to revive the Fida'iyya (self-sacrifice) movement in Nablus.[47] The call for a revolution was heard again after the Mandate for Palestine had come into force. In a widely attended meeting on 26 October, at which the Mufti of Jerusalem and Muhammad 'Ali Tahir,[48] secretary of the Palestine Committee in Cairo, were present, the latter declared that a revolt was the only means of attaining Arab demands. Musa Kazim Pasha was said to have advocated this 'to a modified extent', and to have claimed that one of the British supporters of the Arabs in England (probably referring to William Joynson-Hicks) also advised the same course. However, Musa Kazim 'deprecated any action at present', and was satisfied with the progress made so far.[49]

Others looked to Islamic revivalism in the wider Arab world as a way out of this impasse.[50] Its leaders sought to combat not only the mandate but all foreign influence and penetration in the country. This revival frightened the Christian element, who quietly withdrew from participation in Muslim nationalist movements. Although their sentiments were genuine and they still associated themselves with the anti-Zionist movement, the Christians refused to take part in the movement against the continuance of a European mandate.[51] It was during this period that the Supreme Muslim Council sent delegations to Muslim countries: to India late in 1923 (headed by the *muftis* of Haifa and Gaza, Shaykh Muhammad Murad and Shaykh Muhammad al-Husseini), and to Egypt, Iraq, Kuwait, Bahrain and southern Iran in 1924, to appeal to both Sunni and Shi'i Muslims against Zionist infiltration in Palestine.[52]

THE WAHHABI MOVEMENT IN PALESTINE (1922–1925)

During the latter part of Samuel's administration, some Palestinian leaders began to turn for help to the Wahhabi Ikhwan movement coming from Najd. Samuel frequently referred in his despatches to the 'Wahhabi threat'. At the beginning of 1922 the Wahhabis began to push outward from Najd in all directions,[53] a movement which alarmed Samuel because of its potential consequences for the future of the Jewish national home. The earliest mention of Wahhabism in Palestine came in the high commissioner's 'Political Report' for February 1922. Samuel wrote that the Muslim population were showing increasing interest in the affairs of Egypt, Transjordan, Mecca, Iraq and India, as well as the question of the caliphate. The rumours that Medina held a favourable attitude to Ibn Sa'ud 'did not escape their notice'. There was even 'reason to believe that a missionary movement of the peaceful penetration sort is going on in Palestine in favour of Ibn Saud', adding that any considerable success of his in Central Arabia or the Hijaz would naturally have a 'profound repercussion in Palestine'.[54]

By June 1922, the Wahhabi movement was more frequently discussed in Palestine, with approval in some quarters, and apprehension in others. The tone of the Arabic press was increasingly anti-British, and Samuel reported that after repeated warnings, the paper *Lisan al-'Arab*, which supported the movement, had been suspended for a month.[55] In July 1922, after a two-day visit to Amman, Samuel informed the secretary of state for colonies that Ibn Sa'ud had just despatched one hundred camels to Jawf, an area which was the subject of dispute between Ibn Sa'ud and Amir 'Abdallah of Transjordan. He added: 'Danger to Palestine if Wahibism [sic] spread to Trans Jordania needs no emphasis from me ... the movement is being closely watched.' Furthermore, he urged the colonial secretary to 'clearly' inform Ibn Sa'ud that his sphere of influence 'must not embrace Trans-Jordania'.[56] The governor of Jaffa also reported in July 1922 (following Churchill's White Paper) that Wahhabi tendencies were penetrating the country and that Ibn Sa'ud was 'regarded as one to whom the people can look for help in the future'.[57] Another secret cable from Samuel, on 15 August, informed the Colonial Office that Wahhabis had attacked two villages in Transjordan and that 'Abdallah had begged for immediate assistance. Samuel gave instructions to his generals to take immediate action any time on receipt of a request from Transjordan.[58] One month later, in a secret despatch on the political situation, he wrote to Churchill that the most important political event in Transjordan was the Wahhabi raid of 15 September.

In the same context, he reported that Kamil al-Budayri, ex-editor of the Palestinian paper *al-Sabah*, had been to Najd, passing through Amman, Kerak and Ma'an, and that he apparently considered himself, and was generally considered, as 'an emissary of the Palestine Arabs to Ibn Saud for the purpose of inducing the latter to support them in their efforts to bring about the breakdown of the Zionist policy in Palestine'. According to the same report, Budayri did not see Amir 'Abdallah or any of the top ranking officials, but he did succeed in persuading Awda Abu Tayih[59] to despatch a threatening letter to King Hussein of the Hijaz, to the effect that if the latter and Amir 'Abdallah 'could not help the Palestine Arabs, these would turn to the Wahabis for help'. Kamil al-Budayri was further reported to be in communication with the Arab Executive Committee. The high commissioner concluded that the matter had been 'wisely' settled by Amir 'Abdallah, who had arrested Abu Tayih and brought him to Amman on a charge of 'insubordination and disloyalty'. Samuel added: 'The action taken in this case by His Highness appears to afford good evidence of the correctness of attitude which His Highness has hitherto assumed towards questions directly or indirectly affecting the political situation in Palestine.'[60]

More reports on the Wahhabi question followed from other sources. A secret report prepared in September 1922 by W. F. Stirling, governor of Jaffa District, revealed that there had recently been much discussion going on among 'sincere' Muslims as to the political advantages that could be gained by 'preparing the minds of the people of Palestine to accept the Wahabite Creed'. Although it was accepted that the rigid principles of this creed would not be willingly accepted among the people of Palestine, Arab leaders, who were anxious to seek 'some way out', advocated Wahhabism in order to 'avoid European domination and the imposition of the hated Balfour Declaration'. Two solutions presented themselves to the Arab leaders: either to seek help from the victorious Turkish Army, or from Ibn Sa'ud, 'who with his fanatical followers may be considered the spearhead of Pan-Islamism'. According to the same report, a certain Adib Sarraj, a teacher, had been preaching in the Jaffa mosque a doctrine 'closely resembling that of Wahabism', and attracted a 'very large following' especially among the lower classes. Stirling had ordered him to return to his native Jerusalem.[61] At the end of 1922, Ibn Sa'ud, the traditional enemy of the Hashemites, threatened Faisal in Iraq, and 'Abdallah in Transjordan. Consequently, the British met at the port of al-'Uqayr and imposed upon Ibn Sa'ud a frontier agreement defining boundaries between Saudi Arabia and Iraq (and Kuwait).[62]

However, in 1923, Wahhabi attacks were resumed, threatening Amman at one point with a big force of camel mounted warriors.[63] Samuel thus strongly urged the colonial secretary to seek an immediate settlement of the disputed frontiers between Ibn Sa'ud and Amir 'Abdallah. He feared that Ibn Sa'ud, and the Wahhabi influence which he represented, was coming nearer and nearer to Palestine. The Wahhabis were now firmly established in Jawf, and were pushing gradually up the Wadi Sirhan to Kaf, posing a serious threat to Transjordan, and hence to Palestine.[64]

But the colonial secretary, the Duke of Devonshire, was reluctant to take any 'premature action' with regard to boundary questions, unless there was an immediate threat of armed invasion on the part of Ibn Sa'ud; it was furthermore preferable, in his opinion, to postpone discussion of the Najd-Transjordan frontier until the political situation in Arabia became more clear. Devonshire wrote to Samuel that the spread of Wahhabi influence was likely to proceed 'independently of political frontiers', and noted that no political settlement would be effective in controlling the religious opinions of the nomad tribes.[65]

Throughout 1923 and 1924, the Wahhabi menace continued to preoccupy the mandatory authorities. In May 1923, E. T. Richmond, the assistant political secretary, wrote a brief note to the chief secretary, Wyndham Deedes, entitled 'Wahabi Movement', in which he raised a number of questions, without giving any comments. Among other questions, he asked: 'Are the Wahabis successfully proselytizing? Has Auda abu Taiyeh turned Wahabi? Is his tribe going that way? Is there a large concentration of Wahabis north of Jawf? Is there any real probability of Wahabi hostilities?'[66]

More than a year later, it appears that the Wahhabi threat was still causing Samuel considerable anxiety. A secret despatch from the Air Ministry to the under secretary of state for the Colonial Office reported that the high commissioner for Palestine had telegraphed to the Air Ministry, commenting on the fact that 'H. M. Government have not rebuked the Sultan of Nejd for the attack upon Trans-Jordan in August last.' The Air Council concurred that a protest should be made to Ibn Sa'ud.[67] Ronald Storrs reported in October 1924 that it was 'rumoured' that a number of politically minded young Arabs had 'betaken' themselves to Ibn Sa'ud, and that they were well received by him.[68]

In October 1924, G. F. Clayton, chief political officer in Palestine, wrote from Jerusalem that Sultan Ibn Sa'ud 'has been warned that any unprovoked attack on Trans-Jordan will be repelled, as was the recent raid upon Amman'. The sultan was also informed that the British government regarded Transjordan territory as extending as far as Mudawwara in the south.[69] Throughout 1924–25 the movement seems to have been checked. From Samuel's despatches for the same period there is no evidence that the Wahhabi threat to Palestine continued much beyond 1924.[70] This was despite the continued advance of Ibn Sa'ud inside Arabia and his final conquest of the Hijaz in December 1925.

THE ARAB AGENCY

In the political reports for the period 1924–5, the district governors, in sharp contrast to earlier documents often remarked that there was little or nothing of political interest to report.[71] In his own annual report Samuel wrote in January 1924 that the Arabs were subsiding toward 'their usual attitude of placid acceptance' while the Jews forged ahead with enormous energy.[72] Between 1920 and 1925 the Jewish community in Palestine doubled its size, and the number of settlements rose from 44 in 1918 to 100 in 1925.[73]

On the British side, the Arab Agency advocated by the Cabinet Committee on Palestine in July 1923 was the last measure the British government was willing to take which would offer the Arabs a means to 'participate in the country's development', albeit subject to the control of the administration.[74] In October 1923, Devonshire wrote to Samuel that the numerous representations made on behalf of the Arab community showed that the special position accorded to the Jewish Agency, recognized under Article 4 of the mandate, was a general object of complaint. He added, to the extent that it was possible to argue, that 'the existing arrangements fall short of securing complete equality between the differing communities', and to remove this feeling, that the alternative was 'to accord similar privilege to an Arab agency'. Devonshire went on to say:

> His Majesty's Government are accordingly prepared to favour the establishment of an Arab agency in Palestine, which will occupy a position exactly analogous to that accorded to the Jewish agency under Article 4 of the Mandate, i.e., it will be recognised as a public body, for the purpose of advising and cooperating with the administration in such economic, social and other matters as may affect the interests of the non-Jewish population, and subject to the control of the administration, of assisting and taking part in the development of the country. As regards immigration (Article 6 of the Mandate), the Arab agency will have the right to be consulted as to the means of ensuring that the rights and position of other (i.e. non-Jewish) sections of the population are not prejudiced. With regard to public works, it will be entitled to be consulted by the Administration in the same way as the Jewish agency is to be consulted under the terms of Article 11 of the Mandate.

The question of immigration was of 'primary importance': on the one hand, a Jewish national home was to be established by making facilities for the admission of Jewish settlers, while, on the other, the proper regulation of immigration and 'its strict correlation to the economic capacity of the country to absorb new inhabitants', were matters of 'vital concern' to the people of Palestine as a whole. For this reason, he wrote, the previous government had recognized that the matter was one in which the views of the Arab community 'were entitled to special consideration', and accordingly he proposed that the high commissioner should be required to 'confer on all matters relating to immigration with a standing committee of elected members of the Legislative Council (the majority of whom would be Arabs)' and that in the event of any differences of opinion the question should be referred to the secretary of state. Provision to this effect was formally embodied in Article 84 of the constitution of Palestine (the Palestine Order-in-Council 1922). But since no legitimate council had been elected, and the committee never came into existence, it was proposed that the Arab Agency should 'take its place for the purposes of the functions indicated in article 84 of the order'. The composition of the Arab Agency, Devonshire added, was to be left to the discretion of the high commissioner. He would nominate suitable persons, both Muslim and Christian, in consultation with local leaders. The colonial secretary authorized Samuel to take such steps as were necessary to approach the representatives of the Arabs of Palestine and to invite their acceptance of the policy outlined above.[75]

When, on 11 October 1923, Samuel invited twenty-six notables to Government House and formally presented them with the proposal for the Arab Agency, Musa Kazim al-Husseini, after a brief interval for consideration, spoke on behalf of all present, and informed Samuel that they could not accept the proposal as it fell short of the demands of the Arab population.[76] Although the Arab Agency was to be nominated by the high commissioner (needless to say, the Jewish Agency was not nominated by him), and although it was made clear that the immigration policy would only be discussed subject to an 'agreed settlement to which both parties are prepared to adhere', in retrospect, the Palestine Arabs may have lost an opportunity of having at least some say in the policy of the Jewish national home. The Zionists themselves were suspicious of the proposal for the Arab Agency and gave no encouragement to it. Moreover, Samuel had already hinted that if his idea was accepted in principle, he was ready to discuss the possibility of electing the members rather than nominating them.[77] Nevertheless, the Palestine Arabs were by that time highly suspicious of Samuel and made the worst assumptions about his motives, and they were in no mood for compromise. The Colonial Office instructed Samuel, on 12 October 1923, to break off negotiations with the Arabs and to administer the country without their consent or 'assistance'.[78]

Darwazeh wrote that the Arab Agency was another attempt on Samuel's part to 'set a trap' for the Arabs. The idea of placing the Palestine Arabs on the same footing as the Jews by merely providing them with an Arab Agency was seen as a 'new trick' on the part of the administration. To them, accepting the Arab Agency would have meant, according to Darwazeh, that they, who formed the vast majority of the population, had accepted a minority status, and being treated as a minority group in their own country. It has often been alleged that the negative attitude of the Arabs towards the administration, and their rejection of the Legislative Council, the second Advisory Council and the Arab Agency caused them to lose many opportunities to obtain a say in their own affairs. Darwazeh writes that these allegations had been made as early as 1922 and had weakened the Arab movement by causing dissension in its ranks. He pointed out that British-Jewish propaganda played a significant part and thus contributed to the weakening of the movement. He explains:

The Arab nationalist movement was then very strong, while the Zionist movement was weak; barely able to pull itself together. The Legislative and the Advisory Councils were based on the Balfour Declaration and on the Mandate, and possessed no real powers in the spheres of legislation and administration. They had no right to discuss any subject that would even question the basis of their policy, and so it was impossible, under the circumstances, to accept such a setting. The Legislative Council was also a useless body in terms of subject and scope.[79]

Some recent scholars have agreed with this point of view. McTague, for instance, notes that it was often argued that the Palestinians were 'obstinate' and did not try to work within the administration, and that if they had agreed to the Palestine Order-in-Council they would have obtained a say in the government. He concludes that this is a 'silly' line of reasoning because it completely ignores the composition of the Order-in-Council: it was drawn up so as to exclude the possibility of the Arabs gaining control of the policy of the administration. Had they cooperated with the administration, the result would have been mass resignation and frustration, and, under the circumstances, the Arabs' course of action 'was the best one they could have chosen'.[80] Moreover, the Arab leaders feared that accepting the Arab Agency would be interpreted as a recognition of the status of the Jewish Agency in the mandate, the article in the mandate which recognized the Jewish Agency being one of the articles most hated by the Arabs.[81] The governor of Jerusalem reported in October 1923 that rejection of the Arab Agency was so widespread that the Arab Executive Committee had in fact 'derived very little credit or prestige from its rejection'. [82]

A REFLECTION ON SAMUEL'S 'IMPARTIALITY'

In October 1924, R. V. Vernon, of the Middle East Department of the Colonial Office, wrote in a minute:

> I think that Sir Herbert Samuel is feeling that in his last year of office he must do rather more than he has done in the past to promote the Zionist cause, and that his Jewish friends are also urging him to enable them to make 'hay while the sun shines', and before a possibly non-Zionist moon rises. I think that these influences have made Sir Herbert Samuel a little less impartial in dealing with Arab and Jewish interests than he used to be, and a little less inclined to see the danger of giving uncharitable critics an excuse for saying that Palestine is being definitely brought under the Jewish yoke.[83]

Two issues stand out in Samuel's last years as high commissioner and may be cited here with one question in mind: to what extent could Samuel claim that he was an impartial administrator? The first issue is Samuel's handling of the organization of the Jewish community (which led later to the Jewish Community

Ordinance) and the second, which is not by itself a political issue but had serious political implications at the time, was the question of the water at Artas.[84]

On 24 April 1924, Samuel wrote to the colonial secretary, J. H. Thomas, requesting the early settlement of the organization of the Jewish community in Palestine, asking for a lay authority with the power to levy taxes, a subject which the official documents reveal had caused a long controversy between Samuel and the Middle East Department.[85] On 20 May, Edward Keith-Roach noted that the high commissioner had been instructed in August 1923 by the secretary of state to submit a draft ordinance constituting a supreme Jewish body on the same lines as the Supreme Muslim Council. The secretary of state 'gave definite orders that no power to levy duties should be accorded'. Keith-Roach reported that the high commissioner had not replied to the secretary of state's despatch 'in the usual manner, viz., by framing his remarks to correspond' with the despatch of the secretary of state, and that 'to a large extent', those instructions were 'not adhered to'. The high commissioner held that

> the regulation constituting the Supreme Moslem Council did not afford an altogether suitable model for the regulation of the Jewish community. The community requires to be organised not simply for religious purposes and the control of religious endowments as was the case with the Moslems, but for a variety of lay purposes to which there is nothing to correspond in the other case.[86]

Keith-Roach went on to say that Samuel had written that the Jewish community attached 'extraordinary importance' to the solution of this question, and regarded 'the grant of a Statute as a fundamental part of the execution of the policy of the mandate'. He therefore looked at what were the mandatory power's obligations under the mandate, and after examining Articles 2, 4, 9, 15 and 16 he concluded that the main functions and obligations of the Palestine government were similar to the functions of any government, 'neither more nor less'. He continued:

> I cannot agree, therefore, that under the terms of the Mandate, the grant of a special Statute to the Jewish Community giving them legal authority among other things to impose taxation upon their own followers, is a fundamental part of our obligations, and I think this argument must be refuted. It is obvious the Jewish Community misinterpret the Mandate as meaning that His Majesty's Government are bound to assist the Jews to build up a National-Jewish-Self-contained Community in Palestine.[87]

. Keith-Roach maintained that the high commissioner had not adhered to the instructions of the Colonial Office, which were sent to him on 29 March and 27 August 1923, and in which (i) he was clearly instructed to draw up statutes constituting a supreme Jewish body on the same lines as the Supreme Muslim Council, and (ii) it was 'distinctly' stated that the principles outlined in the secretary of state's secret despatch of 29 March 1923 should be adhered to, and 'that no power should be given to the Va'ad Leumi to levy duties and that no status should be accorded to it which could not legitimately be accorded, or had not already been accorded to a similar representative body of the Moslem or Christian communities'. According to Keith-Roach, the draft reply to Samuel should state that 'considerable difficulty has been found in tracing the high commissioner's replies to our direct instructions, but that it is noticed with regret these instructions have been in the main disregarded', and also to state that the statutes enacted by the high commissioner were 'contrary to the instructions given' in the despatch of August 1923, adding that 'our direct instructions that no power should be given for duties to be levied has been ignored'.[88]

On 22 May, Young minuted that Keith-Roach's note was 'a very clear statement of the High Commissioner's divergences from our instructions', adding, 'The present despatch from the High Commissioner confirms the view taken in this Dept. that he is out for something altogether objectionable', and that there were now in Palestine two heads under which the Jews of Palestine regarded themselves as a community, religious and lay. Young noted that he had no objection to recognizing the religious organization: 'But to recognise the lay organisation is a very different matter. It definitely distinguishes the Jews from the Gentiles as a separate body. It is in conflict with the White Paper. And it is open to all objections which we have consistently held.'[89]

Vernon minuted six days later that it was clear that 'the High Commissioner's proposals involve just the kind of *"imperium in imperio"*, a Jewish authority with taxing powers conferred by statute, which we were bent on avoiding'.[90]

In a minute to the secretary of state on 23 June, Shuckburgh reported that this subject had caused 'a protracted controversy between Sir Herbert Samuel and ourselves', and that the minutes and correspondence on the subject were 'extremely voluminous'. Briefly, under the Turkish regime, the Jews of the Ottoman Empire, like other non-Muslims, were organized as a *millet*, literally a 'nation', as Shuckburgh explained, or separate community recognized by the law and exercising powers of taxation, for communal purposes, over its own members. This *millet* system was devised to protect minorities against misgovernment, and relieved the Turks of certain administrative tasks. The Jews were now 'pestering' Samuel to revive the *millet* system, which Shuckburgh noted was 'clearly quite inappropriate' to a country under British administration, and the Middle East Department had resisted this movement. Shuckburgh informed Thomas that the previous secretary of state 'took a decided view on this subject'. Although Samuel conveyed his proposals as a 'modest degree of recognition of the Jewish community', Shuckburgh averred that 'it has always seemed to us that very much more was involved', and that the question raised was one of principle. Shuckburgh added:

Are the Jews to be merged in the general body of Palestinian citizens, or are they to constitute a kind of State within the State with a separate organisation, conditions of life, etc? Our whole policy under the Mandate points to be [sic] former as the right alternative. The important statement of policy published by the Coalition Government in June 1922 (usually known as the 'White Paper policy') laid it down that 'the status of all citizens of Palestine in the eyes of the law shall be Palestinian and it has never been intended that they, or any section of them, should possess any other juridical status'. Or, to quote the language of the Duke of Devonshire's despatch of the 29th March, 1923, what we have always contemplated is 'the development of the Jewish community, not as a separate national entity, but as a body of Palestinian citizens.[91]

Shuckburgh went on to say that in 1921, the high commissioner had created the Supreme Muslim Council, and that the late government was prepared to do exactly the same for the Jewish community, i.e., to create a supreme Jewish body, with powers of control over Jewish religious affairs, and that Samuel had been 'instructed accordingly'. However, Samuel had asked in his letter of 24 April 1924 'not only for a Jewish religious authority but also for a lay authority with powers of taxation, etc., over the Jewish community'. Shuckburgh commented that Samuel proposed to re-establish the *millet* system in a modified form, and noted that this proposal 'cannot be regarded as acceptable', as it provided for powers of taxation. Shuckburgh realized Samuel's difficulties, that he was 'hard-pressed' by the Jews, who were urging their claim 'with their usual persistence' and 'tendency to exaggerated language', and who spoke of the 'complete ruin of our inner life' (quoting Va'ad Leumi's letter of 19 June 1923). Shuckburgh insisted that he was

decidedly of opinion that we should not give way. On grounds both of principle and of expediency it seems to me essential not to give powers or privileges to the Jewish community in Palestine which we are not prepared to give in equal measure to the other communities; whether Moslem or Christian.[92]

Shuckburgh's minute on 22 July indicates that the secretary of state had at first initialled his name in agreement with Shuckburgh, but that he had subsequently changed his mind and decided that no action should be taken until he had seen Weizmann.[93] On 18 July, Weizmann wrote to Thomas saying that the Jewish Community Ordinance represented 'the first step towards the formal establishment of the Jewish National Home in Palestine'.[94] Moreover, to convince the secretary of state of their point of view, both Samuel and Weizmann referred to an extract from the 1922 White Paper:

During the last two to three generations the Jews have recreated in Palestine a community, now numbering 80,000, of whom about one-fourth are farmers, or workers upon the land. This community has its own political organs; an elected assembly for the direction of its domestic concerns; elected councils in the towns; and an organisation for the control of its schools. It has its elected Chief Rabbinate and Rabbinical Council for the direction of its religious affairs. Its business is conducted in Hebrew as a vernacular language, and a Hebrew press serves its needs. It has its distinctive intellectual life and displays considerable economic activity. This community, then, with its town and country population, its political, religious and social organisations, its own language, its own customs, its own life, has in fact 'national' characteristics ... But in order that this community should have the best prospect of free development and provide a full opportunity for the Jewish people to display its capacities, it is essential that it should know that it is in Palestine as of right and not as [sic] sufferance.[95]

Shuckburgh reported that, since his last minute, he had discussed the matter fully with Samuel and Dr Yellin, the chairman of the Zionist Commission, and that his opinion remained 'unaltered'. He wrote that he was 'opposed as ever' to the question of Jews having the right to levy taxes. He had gathered from Samuel and Yellin that 'the Jews mean to fight this question high, and to try to make it a kind of test case of our sincerity in giving effect to the Balfour Declaration.' Shuckburgh suggested that the secretary of state should discuss this question directly with Sir Herbert Samuel.[96]

According to a subsequent and undated minute by Shuckburgh, after the secretary of state had discussed the subject with Samuel and himself, and 'after hearing the arguments on both sides' he had decided to accept 'the local Government's [i.e. Samuel's] proposals in their main outline'. Not convinced of the rightness of this decision, Shuckburgh wrote:

I will not reiterate the misgivings which I feel over this business, and which I have already explained to the Secretary of State. My apprehension is (and I sincerely hope that I may be quite wrong) that we shall be attacked for introducing a system quite alien to British institutions, and that the attack may lead to a revival of the general campaign against our policy in Palestine which raged with so much violence in 1922 and 1923. If this happens, we may find it necessary to publish the whole correspondence on the subject, and from this point of view we had better be careful about the precise wording of our instructions to the High Commissioner. I hope that the draft despatch will be carefully scrutinized from this standpoint.[97]

The draft Jewish Community Ordinance was at first rejected by the Colonial Office, but upon Samuel's persistence, it was approved in 1925 by the pro-Zionist secretary of state for the colonies, L. S. Amery, and his under-secretary, William Ormsby-Gore, another staunch Zionist sympathizer. However, the Ordinance was not officially promulgated until January 1928.[98]

Another contentious issue which arose in 1925 further illustrated the way in which Samuel prioritized the needs of the Jewish community. He sanctioned the diversion of water, by government ordinance, from an Arab village to Jerusalem for the benefit of the growing community of Jerusalem Jews. This ordinance was enacted 'to enable the authority undertaking the public supply of water to Jerusalem to acquire temporarily, water available from the spring at Urtas village for the purpose of relieving the water shortage of Jerusalem'.[99]

The Arab Executive Committee sent a memorandum on the subject to the colonial secretary[100] in May 1925, entitled 'Spoliation in Palestine', in which it was claimed that, owing to insufficient rainfall during the winter of that year, there was a scarcity of water in Jerusalem. The Arrub and Solomon Pools water supplies meant that this did not threaten a severe shortage of drinking water. However, the lack of water had imposed a 'complete lull' in the building activity carried out to a large extent by Jewish settlers. For this reason, the government had passed an ordinance to acquire the water of the Artas Spring in the Bethlehem sub-district. The sub-governor of Bethlehem had asked the inhabitants of Artas village to sell all or part of these waters to the municipality of Jerusalem for one year. They 'instantly and absolutely refused', pointing out that the water was barely enough for their own livelihood. Later, their representatives were brought to the governor of Jerusalem who informed them that the government had decided to take the waters of Artas Spring and ordered them not to use it for planting vegetables under penalty of a fine. When asked, the governor refused to give this order in writing.

The memorandum of the Arab Executive Committee held that this 'high handed' resolution had led the poor owners to bring an action against the governor of Jerusalem in the court of justice, adding that: 'The lawlessness of the Palestine Government manifested in the usurpation of the water of the inhabitants of Artass terrified all Arab inhabitants ... The more wicked it appears [sic] when such usurpation is effected by means of an ordinance enacted by the usurper himself.'[101]

In its issue of 10 June 1925, *al-Karmel* reported that the case of the Artas water had been taken to court and had been won by the Arabs. The Arabs had for centuries built cisterns to collect rain water, and Jewish ignorance of this procedure had caused this severe shortage of water.[102] On 1 July, *al-Karmel* wrote again that on 25 June the court of justice had ruled that the high commissioner's act was illegal, and annulled the Artas water ordinance, as it was in contravention to the mandate and the Palestine Order-in-Council of 1922. *Al-Karmel* commented that this was proof of the justice of English government.[103]

RESOLVING CONFLICTING OBLIGATIONS?

After the turmoil of the years leading up to the confirmation of the mandate, the period from 1924 to 1929 was one of apparent peace in Palestine. During this tranquil phase, Zionism enjoyed seven years of undisturbed growth, doubling the size of its population and enlarging its map of settlements.[104] An economic depression during 1924–25 resulted in a decrease in immigration, which in turn contributed to the tranquillity on the Arab side. Hence Arab 'quiescence' was attributed to the check on Jewish immigration caused by this depression. In 1925, only Balfour's visit to Jerusalem on the occasion of the opening of the Hebrew University caused Arab protests and general strikes.[105]

The last phase of Samuel's term in Palestine was characterized by economic growth in the Jewish sector. On the other hand, the Arab population, with its leaders hampered by political rivalries and divisions, saw few tangible economic benefits from British rule. In the White Paper of June 1922, as even Norman Bentwich noted, the British government publicly declared that the Jewish people were not to exercise political domination over the rest of the population. Samuel, in other words, had instructions that the administration should be conducted in accordance with this interpretation of the mandate.[106] Nevertheless, he did not run the administration according to the 'declared policy' of the British government. Ever since 1922, British officials had specifically ruled out a Jewish state in Palestine, but it would appear that Samuel chose to disregard his government's clear intent.[107]

In his book *England in Palestine*, Norman Bentwich wrote, under the heading 'The Conclusion of the Book of Samuel, January–June 1925', that the 'end crowns the work' (*finis coronat opus*). Events had combined to make Samuel's last six months a period of 'fulfilment and of promise', and to give him the reward for the past four years of patient work in which he had 'struggled successfully against adverse circumstance'. The 'greatest reward' was the inauguration of the Hebrew University on 1 April 1925, in the presence of Lord Balfour. The inauguration during the term of the 'Jewish High Commissioner' was, in Bentwich's words 'the harvest festival' of Balfour's Declaration. It was, moreover, the spiritual revival of the Hebrew people in their ancient land. To the Arabs, however, Bentwich noted that Balfour was the 'symbol of Palestinian woe'.[108]

Samuel's services to Zionism were deeply felt by the leaders of Zionism as his term neared its end. A few days before he left Palestine he received a letter from the Zionist Organization, as well as from Weizmann, its president, in which the Zionist leader wrote:

> Much has happened in this fateful decade [i.e. since Weizmann first met Herbert Samuel in 1915] and you were privileged—to my great joy—to play a fundamental part in laying the foundation of the Jewish National Home. You are leaving the country confident that the work you have done, and the wisdom with which you have guided the destinies of Palestine, have created stable conditions which will enable us to carry on further what you have begun so successfully. I feel that my own work has been bound up so much with what you did in Palestine that it would

not be quite right for me to express my compliments and congratulations on this subject.[109]

On 17 September 1925, he received another letter from the Zionist Organization in London, thanking him on behalf of its Executive, and informing him that a resolution had been unanimously adopted by the recent Zionist Congress in Vienna, stating that the congress bids a 'heartfelt farewell' to Sir Herbert Samuel, whose five-year term of office as the first high commissioner for Palestine had 'witnessed the completion of the first stage in the establishment of the Jewish National Home'.[110]

Despite Samuel's 'acute soul-searching' after the May 1921 disturbances, his view of Zionism in 1925 had changed little since he first wrote his Cabinet memorandum in 1915. He demonstrated the depth of his personal commitment to Zionism when he proposed to continue living in Palestine after his term ended in July 1925. He wished to remain because Zionism was for him 'a form of self-realization'. However, Lord Plumer, the high commissioner succeeding him, protested on the grounds that the continued presence of a former high commissioner would be 'a source of very grave embarrassment'. Samuel appealed to the colonial secretary, Amery, but to his great disappointment, Plumer's ruling was endorsed.[111]

Whatever his pronouncements in regard to the dual obligation, his practice suggested that Samuel viewed the two communities in a very different light. His understanding of the development of 'self-governing institutions' would be as expansive as possible for the Jews, and as restrictive as possible for the Palestine Arabs. For the Jewish national home to develop, the road to Palestinian self-determination had to be blocked from its very beginning. Equally, Samuel's efforts to develop the economic base of the Jewish national home, as the final chapter will show, did not contribute significantly to the economic well-being of the Palestinian population as a whole.

Samuel's pronouncements on the dual obligation also have to be set against the fact that it was during his tenure in office, and especially in the first two critical years before the mandate was ratified, that the foundations of the Jewish national home in Palestine were firmly laid down.[112] The Royal Commission of Inquiry in 1937 (the Peel Commission) acknowledged that all the major manifestations of the Jewish national home were firmly established by 1925, and that eleven years later, when they had conducted the inquiry, the situation was no different from that prevailing in 1925, that no new factors had emerged, and that it was only the 'old situation intensified'. Most of what had happened since then, had been, 'a repetition, on a steadily increasing scale of gravity, of what had happened before 1925.'[113] This leaves no room for doubt that, only a decade after Samuel had first envisioned a 'Jewish state' in Palestine in his 1915 Cabinet memorandum, the project was well under way by the time his five years in Palestine as first high commissioner ended.

9

Building the Jewish National Home:
Immigration, Economy and the Land

Soon after the Balfour Declaration was announced, and Palestine came under British occupation, the Zionist leader, Chaim Weizmann, devised specific plans for Jewish immigration. As head of the Zionist Commission, his two immediate concerns were to initiate an organized system of Jewish immigration, and to search for 'vacant' land for the anticipated influx of Jewish settlers. By 1919, Weizmann was advocating the eventual absorption in Palestine of four to five million Jews.[1] Such optimistic projections preceded the San Remo Conference, which convened in April 1920, at a time when there was still confusion in official circles in London as to its policy toward Zionism.[2] The appointment of Herbert Samuel, whom the Zionists saw as the 'first High Commissioner for Judea' encouraged them to embark on such a policy of large-scale immigration.[3]

SAMUEL'S IMMIGRATION POLICY

Samuel's term as high commissioner witnessed the latter period of the Third *Aliyah* (1919–23) and the beginning of the Fourth *Aliyah* (1924–31). *Aliyah*, in Hebrew meaning literally ascent, was used to describe the waves of Jewish immigration into Palestine. The Third *Aliyah* brought some 35,000 immigrants to Palestine, almost doubling the size of the Jewish community there. During the fourth wave (1924–31), the year 1924 alone brought 12,865 immigrants, increasing sharply in 1925 to 33,801.[4] By the end of Samuel's term in office, the Jewish population had doubled from 61,000 in 1920 to 120,559 in 1925. The Arab percentage of the total population fell from 89.9 per cent in 1920 to 83.2 per cent in 1925.[5]

Until 1924, the majority of immigrants were poor Russian or Polish Jews fleeing ill-treatment, with few independent financial resources.[6] In contrast, it is estimated that at least 80 per cent of the Fourth *Aliyah* were middle class urban families with capital resources to invest in industry and commerce, who settled in towns and cities such as Tel Aviv, Jerusalem and Haifa.[7] Many arrived after a tax on income was introduced in Poland in 1924, which weighed heavily on wealthy Jews. At the same time, the USA placed tighter restrictions on the entry of Jews to America, diverting more immigrants to Palestine.[8] The direct result of this wave of immigration was the sudden and rapid expansion of economic and industrial activities during the mid-1920s, creating a short-lived economic boom within the Yishuv economy and a proportionately large inflow of capital during 1924–26.[9]

There is no question that the ultimate aim of the Zionists was to change the demographic balance in Palestine, so that, as Samuel himself had written in 1915, 'in the course of time the Jewish inhabitants grown into a majority and settled in the land', might be given such degree of self-government as the conditions of that day might justify.[10] Before his arrival in Palestine, Samuel had already reached an agreement with the leaders of the Zionist Organization on the immigration policy to be adopted. Weizmann, Sokolow and Samuel had agreed on three main principles: that the entry of Jews to Palestine should be facilitated; that there should be no 'organised immigration' without the consent of the Zionist Organization; and that the Zionist Organization would be authorized to permit the entry of Jews if they had, in its opinion, independent means of subsistence. Samuel suggested establishing six-monthly schedules for labour immigration for those for whom the Zionist Organization could guarantee work for one year. He rejected a further Zionist demand to set up a joint immigration board with equal representation for the Palestine administration and the Zionist Organization, on the grounds that it was undesirable from the political point of view, since the Palestine Arabs would demand similar representation. He assured the Zionists, however, that their interests 'would be equally well served by informal consultation'. [11]

No sooner had Samuel assumed office in July 1920 than Weizmann telegraphed to him the 'agreed' Zionist schedule for immigration and employment for the first year.[12] Dr Arthur Ruppin, the economic adviser of the Zionist Commission, calculated that only 10,000 workers could be successfully absorbed into the economic life of Palestine during that first year. But for political reasons, the Zionist Commission raised the figure to 17,000. The administration finally accepted the figure of 16,500 Jewish workers to be admitted as immigrants on an annual basis. They were divided into four categories: immigrants whose maintenance was guaranteed by the Zionist Organization; persons of independent means or those who could produce evidence that they would become self-supporting; persons of religious occupations who had means of maintenance; and members of families of present residents in Palestine.[13] Samuel had presented a memorandum on immigration to the Foreign Office on this basis, stressing that it was 'essential to make a beginning as soon as possible with the establishment of the Jewish National Home'.[14]

One of Samuel's first priorities as high commissioner was to issue the Immigration Ordinance, drafted in the summer of 1920 by the head of the legal department, Norman Bentwich.[15] The drafting of the Immigration Ordinance involved frequent consultation with the Zionist Commission. The fact that the Commission's political secretary, Dr Eder, made only trivial suggestions indicates that the Zionists were quite satisfied with the draft, which was extremely liberal, permitting immigration to anyone who was in good physical and mental health, was not a danger to society, and could support himself in Palestine.[16]

The Ordinance, which was enacted on 26 August and came into force on 1 September 1920,[17] remained effective until 1925, but in practice it continued to evolve, especially when new measures were introduced following the May riots in Jaffa 1921. It was replaced by the Immigration Ordinance of September 1925, which organized immigration on a new basis. Although this ordinance came into force immediately after Samuel's term in office had ended, it was nevertheless formulated and enacted during his period. To carry out his policy, Samuel set up an Immigration and Travel Department, with Major Morris as temporary director. Three of the five senior officials of the department were British Jews sympathetic to Zionism: in Jaffa, the main port for immigration, N. I. Mindel was chosen as the Immigration Officer; Dennis Cohen was appointed in Jerusalem and Albert Hyamson became assistant director of the department. Hyamson had been a Zionist activist and a close associate of Chaim Weizmann during the war.[18]

The task of organizing Jewish immigration fell to the Zionist Organization, as the Jewish Agency recognized by the British government. Towards the end of 1920, the Colonial Office authorized it to introduce into the country a 'fixed' number of Jewish immigrants each month, on the understanding that it accepted the responsibility for their maintenance and employment for a limited period after their arrival. The immigrants were to be carefully selected by submitting a special form of 'recommendation', though the Colonial Office later complained that these recommendations were given to a number of 'quite unsuitable' immigrants.[19]

In October 1920, 4,000 immigrants were brought into Palestine, all of whom were approved by the Zionist Organization. Although this number was far smaller than that agreed in the schedule, it soon became evident that the Zionist Organization lacked the financial means to provide the immigrants with subsistence, let alone employment. Weizmann had anticipated a budget for the Zionist Organization of some £2 million a year, and such a sum could only come from American Jews. The Zionists were, however, disappointed to find that American Jews would not provide more than £100,000 per year. The Zionists therefore found themselves obliged to request a reduction in the immigration schedule to 1,000 from the previously agreed figure of 16,500 for the year 1920.[20] In August 1920, a report from Palestine to the Central Zionist Organization asserted:

The present mode of immigration means nothing less than an early collapse, an

early emigration and the destruction of every possibility to create in the near future the conditions for a more orderly and more extensive immigration.[21]

The high commissioner, however, 'refrained from harming the Zionists' image
at such an early stage', and did not act immediately to restrain immigration. He
was certain that the Zionists would eventually obtain the funds.[22] In fact, by the
spring of 1921, an additional 9,000 immigrants were given permission to enter
Palestine.[23]

Economic Absorptive Capacity

The Jaffa riots of early May 1921, indicating the Palestinian Arab population's
discontent with British policy towards the Zionists, and especially their anger over
immigration,[24] caused Samuel to introduce temporary restrictions.[25] His speech
of 3 June 1921 reviewed the administration's immigration policy and divided potential immigrants into seven categories: Category A meant travellers not intending
to settle in Palestine; B were persons of independent means; C were members of
professions who intended to 'follow their calling in Palestine'; D were wives and
children and other persons wholly dependent on residents in Palestine; E were
persons who had definite prospects of employment with specified employers or
enterprises; F were persons of religious occupations who could show that they
could maintain themselves; and G were residents returning from abroad. All categories, except E, could enter Palestine freely, but immigration would be restricted
by the capacity of the country to absorb more persons into its industrial life.[26]

The phrase 'economic absorptive capacity', which Samuel used in the speech as
'a useful political tool … to show H. M. G.'s concern for the protection of Arab
interests', in reality reflected a policy dictated by the economic performance of the
Jewish community rather than the state of the Palestinian economy as a whole.[27]
It was this principle which guided Samuel in his policy on immigration from 1921
until the next Immigration Ordinance was promulgated in September 1925.

To regulate immigration more efficiently, a high level meeting between Zionist
leaders and the Colonial Office was held on 25 November 1921.[28] Weizmann briefly
outlined his proposals for immigration in the immediate future, arguing that the
Rutenberg concessions and the purchase of land in the Esdraelon (Jezreel) Valley
(see below) would provide enough labour for the number of immigrants guaranteed by the Zionist Organization. His programme did not envisage the introduction
of more than 1,500 'bread winners' per month. It was generally agreed that the
figure did not seem excessive 'provided that the Rutenberg Concessions actually
did materialise in the form of labour'. Weizmann then insisted upon

> the recognition of the only true principle that should govern immigration i.e. that
> immigration cannot be ended or suspended for any reason save the operation of

economic factors of the country. No departure should be made from this principle; so long as that was clear it would always be possible to form agreements between Zionist Organisation, His Britannic Majesty's Government and High Commissioner.[29]

From June to December 1921, the number of Jews who entered Palestine under the new system was 4,784.[30] Major Morris, the director of immigration, complained that almost all (up to 95 per cent in this period) were refugees from Russia or Poland who had entered the country from which they were to be sent to Palestine from some other country, or Jews who have 'failed to make good and unsuccessful businessmen'. Few of those who entered Palestine as skilled or unskilled workers had 'any real knowledge' of the trade they professed.[31] The governors of Jaffa and Phoenicia districts complained that unemployed immigrants were much resented by the townspeople who generally regarded this as evidence that the government was not bringing in immigrants in proportion to the economic needs of the country, as promised in the 3 June speech. The governors pointed out that the mere presence of these people 'with no work to do' was 'a source of danger' and that a disturbance might easily arise between them and the local population.[32]

Throughout 1921, Jewish unemployment rose steadily, even though Jewish immigrants were employed by the government in public works and in road building. In 1922, the termination of military projects and cuts in road building caused further unemployment and in March, Samuel was again forced to suspend immigration temporarily. He had already written to Weizmann in January 1922:

> if I had not enforced fairly close restrictions on immigration during the last few months and incurred a good deal of censure from the Zionist world for doing so, the Zionist Organisation would have had to act in the same direction, and borne the odium itself. I hope you will appreciate my friendly service![33]

In December 1922 Samuel reported that a large number of Orthodox Jews were emigrating to America because of the bad economic conditions and lack of security. In May 1923, he reported that the *halutzim* (pioneers) of Tel Aviv had held a meeting at which they had asked that no more immigrants should be admitted into the country because of unemployment.[34] In July of that year, Zionist leaders, commenting on the question of the emigration of Jews, urged people not to emigrate, telling them that the situation was just as bad elsewhere, and that if the Jews left, they would never obtain a majority in Palestine.[35]

Despite differences of opinion which arose between Samuel on the one hand, and Major Morris, the director of immigration, together with Zionist leaders on the other, on how to control and implement the reorganization of immigration, there was general agreement that controls should be made stricter and more efficient.[36] In December 1922, Samuel wrote to the colonial secretary, the Duke of Devonshire, that the Jews, whatever their political or religious views, all realized that the success of the Zionist movement in Palestine was 'absolutely conditioned' by the increase in their numbers. He added that they were aware that the new immigrants might find it hard to find employment, but that they were convinced that 'by hook or by crook employment would in fact be found'.[37]

Nevertheless, the leaders of the Yishuv in Palestine seemed to have already devised their own plans, which were different from those envisaged by the British government, regarding the demographic 'future' of Palestine. The Hebrew paper *Do'ar Hayom* complained on 7 February 1923 that there was not a single district in which the Jews were in the majority. What the Jews must do, the paper maintained, was to endeavour to create a majority in the Haifa, Jerusalem and Jaffa districts and demand their rights on a Swiss system (i.e. a confederation of separate cantons); this would help them pave the way to the national home.[38]

During 1923, Weizmann fought against the restrictions on immigration. He particularly objected to a publicly stated annual maximum (in this case to 10,000) for Jewish immigration to Palestine. He informed Shuckburgh in the Middle East Department of the Colonial Office that he was ready to restrict immigration in any given year to such a number as the British government might suggest to him, but if this were formally announced, it would 'take the heart out of the whole movement'.[39]

But could Britain's immigration policy alone, restricted by a certain yearly quota, have ensured an eventual Jewish majority in Palestine? Shuckburgh, commenting some years later on a letter from Weizmann to the colonial secretary, J. H. Thomas, in which the Zionist leader referred to Palestine as a 'refuge for persecuted Jews' from Eastern Europe, wrote:

> It must always be remembered that Palestine is a very small country. The present population is about 760,000 of whom only 11% are Jews. It is estimated that the maximum population that the country is ever likely to support is not more than 3,000,000. Even that figure cannot, in the most favourable circumstances, be reached for many years to come; possibly not for a century. If and when it is reached, we must assume that the non-Jewish population of the country will have increased very greatly. The rate of increase among the Arabs has already been enhanced as a result of settled administration, sanitary measures, better medical facilities, and so forth. Out of the eventual figure of 3,000,000, it will not be safe to place the non-Jewish elements at less than half; probably they will be substantially more than half. In any case, the total number of Jews that can ever be absorbed in Palestine cannot be put higher than 1 1/2 [one-and-a-half] millions, which is not a large proportion out of Dr. Weizmann's 10 million outcasts ... .[40]

Another senior Colonial Office official, Eric Mills,[41] acting principal at the

Colonial Office (1920–25), devised a formula based on the approved numbers of immigrants to be admitted annually to Palestine. In a secret memorandum, 'Some Sociological Aspects of Jewish Immigration into Palestine', Mills worked on the following assumptions: (i) that the net natural increase per annum was between 10 per thousand and 19 per thousand of population; (ii) that this natural increase was the same for Christians and Muslims; (iii) that annual Jewish immigration was between 10,000 and 15,000; and, (iv) that the above figures would give him the maximum and minimum numbers. He arrived at the conclusion that the total population of Palestine after 30 years would be 1,631,188 out of which 523,119 would be Jews.[42] By this crude formula, Mills came very close to real figures which show that in 1946 the number of Jews was 608,225 and the total number of the population was 1,845,559.[43] After a number of calculations, Mills found that 'the Jews will always be in the minority since they obtain a majority only in the 85th year with a low net natural increase'. He concluded:

> In these circumstances it would seem impossible to contemplate as practical politics a definition of the Jewish National Home that implies a Jewish State as dominant in Palestine. Only a visitation many times more terrible than the Tenth Plague could render possible of fulfilment that extreme interpretation of the meaning of the Balfour Declaration … A Jewish State could only be established by the parallel operation of two factors: first an abnormally low birth rate and an abnormally high death rate among the Arabs; and, secondly, the maintenance of a large annual quota of immigrants. There is no ground for supposing that the former is probable; and the economic conditions of Palestine forbid the latter.[44]

Mills, like Shuckburgh, estimated that the maximum population Palestine could support was 3,000,000. His calculations indicated that, when this limit was reached, the Jews would only be in a 'slight majority'—approximately 51 per cent of the population to the Arab's 49 per cent. He concluded that 'No political ascendancy by one half of a population over the other half could be contemplated', adding:

> In these circumstances the Jews possess a small political domination at the polls, but not enough to justify political ascendancy of such a nature as is implied by a Jewish State … That being so no modern form of Government could establish Jewish political ascendancy in Palestine without infringing the civil rights of the Arabs in Palestine.[45]

More vital statistics from Jerusalem enabled Mills to work out 'a still more reliable forecast' as Hubert Young, at the Middle East Department, minuted on 14 June 1922. Young stated:

> The conclusion reached is that even with an immigration of 10,000 a year, which is admittedly a high figure, and even if Jewish increase remains abnormally high, there

can never be a Jewish majority in Palestine, though by the end of 72 years the Jews will practically equal the Arabs in number.[46]

Young suggested that Mills' memorandum should remain on record in the department and that no action was required. Shuckburgh commented on the memorandum on 29 June: 'The upshot is that when the maximum [expansion] (3,000,000) is reached 72 years hence, the Arabs will still be in a majority.'

The Issue of Citizenship

Closely connected with immigration policy was the question of providing Palestinian nationality to new immigrants in order to give them the right to vote. On 19 November 1924, Samuel wrote to the Colonial Office enquiring whether it would be possible to indicate when the Palestine Citizenship Order-in-Council would be promulgated and urging that no delay be allowed to occur. Keith-Roach explained in a minute that the draft Citizenship Order-in-Council was first framed in Palestine and submitted by the high commissioner on 9 February 1921, and that Mr Malkin[47] had stated in a minute that it appeared to him very important that Jews who settle in Palestine should quickly become citizens in order to take part in the political activities of the country. When, in August of that year, the Palestine Citizenship Order-in-Council was submitted, neither the Home Office nor the Colonial Office raised any objections. Keith-Roach went on to say that in September 1921 the Zionist Organization suggested that the period of residence for naturalization should be reduced from two years to one. He commented on 24 November 1924:

> It is often argued ... that the Palestine problem presents a set of circumstances unparalleled in the history not only of Great Britain, but of the world ... When the Mandate for Palestine was conferred by the League of Nations on Great Britain, and Article 7 of the Mandate was passed, it is obvious the League did not expect the Mandatory Power to give Jews greater facilities than any other country gives to persons who desire to become citizens of that country.[48]

This caused a member of the Colonial Office, John Risley, to remark on 5 December that: 'From a legal aspect two years is a very short period for this purpose, but the question is, in Palestine as elsewhere, mainly one of policy.'

Upon hearing that chief Rabbi Kook had requested an audience with the king to ask for Palestinian citizenship—and that Herbert Samuel had made the request on his behalf, describing him as 'Ex Chief Rabbi, Poltava and Jaffa. During the war was Rabbi in London. Scholar, philosopher; has considerable spiritual influence'— Keith-Roach commented: 'I am certain in Palestine the Arabs will get up a tremendous howl when they learn that a man from a ghetto in Poland can qualify in two years for citizenship in Palestine...'[49]

The Palestine Citizenship Order-in-Council, allowing Jews to hold Palestinian nationality, did not finally come into force until 1925, after the Treaty of Lausanne was ratified.[50] But in 1922, Samuel was already making arrangements for the immediate provisional assumption by Jews of Palestinian nationality. This was discussed by the representatives of the Arab Executive Committee with the high commissioner at a meeting on 30 October 1922. Musa Kazim pointed out that it appeared from the announcement that foreigners could now temporarily change their nationality for one year, the object being to give them the right to vote, although legally they were nationals of other countries. He argued that this was illegal because the Treaty of Sèvres had not yet been signed. When asked by 'Abd al-Qadir al-Muzaffar what would be the status of those who acquired temporary nationality between now and the promulgation of the Palestine Citizenship Order-in-Council, and whether they would have dual nationality, Samuel answered that this was a 'difficult legal question', and that a lawyer would probably say they had only one nationality. Al-Muzaffar commented that Palestine was a land 'of marvels', and this new regulation was one of them.[51]

Arab Reactions to Jewish Immigration

The Palestine Arabs consistently demanded the suspension of Jewish immigration throughout the five years of Samuel's term in office.[52] They spelled out their fears about being flooded by immigrants from Eastern Europe and pointed out that the problems of East European Jewry could not be solved in Palestine. The arrival of masses of Jewish immigrants was looked upon as nothing less than the 'coming of doom', and Arab leaders constantly made the simple but cardinal point which summed up the whole problem from their point of view: that the Jewish national home was being built up 'in somebody else's home'.[53]

In February 1920, before Samuel took up office, the Muslim-Christian Association had delivered a petition to the representatives of Great Britain at the Peace Conference in which they declared:

> We reject absolutely Jewish immigration, and we do not see the Peace Conference has any authority whatever to force us to accept it, nor even is it entitled to consider the question. We have already submitted several protests containing most reasonable objections to 'Zionist' claims, and we have also often raised our voices and made every man whose heart throbs in sympathy with the tortured humanity hear. We now repeat what we previously said, that the Arab inhabitants of Palestine, whatever their religion may be, are the only persons who have any legal and natural right in the country. And it is for them alone to decide the question of immigration. It is most annoying to us and to the absolute Right and Justice that a whole nation should be sacrificed for the sake of political promises demanded by the interests of strong nations. How does justice grant the Jews the right of immigration into Palestine against the desire of its owners and inhabitants, while other nations, large and

small, which are not even affected by immigration, pass laws prohibiting it in case it does not agree with their own interests.[54]

It was for this reason that the military administration refused entry permission for persons other than 'genuine Palestinian refugees', i.e. those who had been resident in Palestine before the war, and placed heavy restrictions on immigrants coming from Eastern Europe and Russia, and who constituted the bulk of Jewish immigrants after the war. This policy was loathed by Weizmann, who wrote to the Foreign Office complaining, and succeeded in getting the sympathy of a senior official there, O. A. Scott, who wrote in a minute that the situation was 'getting impossible', and had to be taken up with the War Office.[55]

At the first meeting of the Advisory Council, on 6 October 1920, an Arab member, Dr Habib Salim, pointed out that it was expected that 'intended immigrants should be rich', but those already here were poor and were 'a drain on the country'.[56] The Third Palestine Arab Congress, meeting in Haifa in December 1920, adopted strong anti-Zionist resolutions and made clear their absolute opposition to immigration. These demands were repeated in all their petitions to the British government. The Arab complaint that the new immigrants were 'Bolshevists who advanced socialist ideas', thus introducing a disturbing element into the political life of the country, was said to be 'fully borne out' by Major Morris, the director of Immigration.[57] As Deedes wrote to Young in May 1921, immigration was to the Arab 'the tangible, visible evidence of Zionism. It was a measure they could judge by.' He added that their verdict in this regard 'explains their attitude towards, and suspicion of, our Policy in general'.[58]

In November 1921, while the first Arab Delegation was in London, Shuckburgh minuted that a 'legitimate concern' which the Arabs had raised was that of Jewish immigration. He wrote that they always 'professed to think that the intention was to bring in Jews wholesale, and to swamp the Arab population', and that despite continued British denial they were still apprehensive of such an outcome. Shuckburgh added that the Arabs would be assured that the whole question was being 'closely investigated', and that measures would be framed for its future regulation.[59]

However, the Palestine Arabs still saw Samuel's immigration policy as one which 'prepares the way to create a Jewish majority'. In 1923, Jamal al-Husseini, secretary of the Arab Executive Committee, delivered a speech at the Sixth Palestine Arab Conference in which he stated that Jewish immigrants were admitted into the country without restraints, and were allowed all the rights which the people of the country enjoyed as soon as they stepped on the land. More than that, they were given Palestinian citizenship, and the government, in order to sustain them, strove to find work for them which the country did not need. He reminded his audience of what he claimed Samuel had said in 1919:

The Zionist policy to which adheres every Zionist with all his strength requires that the country be placed in a position which would fit Zionist immigration and imperialism. That public concessions be given to Jews, and that the country should enjoy self-government, to its extreme limits so that it will be possible at the end to form an independent Government under the control of a Jewish majority.[60]

The view that Jewish immigration could benefit the majority population by increasing the pace of economic activity did not materialize during Samuel's administration. However, it became very clear that Samuel and the Colonial Office set the precedent of treating economic absorptive capacity as relating only to the Jewish economy. Little attention was paid to the economic impact of Jewish immigration on the rest of society until very much later, although from early in the 1920s there was evidence of this impact. In March 1921, the Arab Executive Committee, in its petition to Churchill during his visit, stated that Palestine was an agricultural country, and depended largely on the export of cereals for a living. In order to keep prices down, in the interest of the Jewish consumer, the government had prohibited the export of certain cereals (Prohibition of Export of Cereals and Legumes Ordinance, 24 September 1920), with the result that the granaries of Palestine had become over-stocked with products, with the merchants unable to find an outlet for their trade. Consequently, a financial crisis set in, and hundreds of merchants had gone bankrupt. The Arab Executive Committee remarked: 'Now if this is the policy of Zionists while they still form a small minority what will it be when they become more numerous.'[61]

THE DEVELOPMENT OF THE YISHUV ECONOMY

After making the necessary provisions for immigration, as well as Palestinian citizenship, in order to give Jewish immigrants the right to vote in the Legislative Council elections as well as those for municipal councils, Samuel's next priority was to promote the economic development of Palestine 'through Jewish financiers'.[62] In September 1920, Weizmann had informed Samuel that an Anglo-Jewish conference was to be held with a view to promoting the economic development of Palestine, and suggested that Samuel send them his observations. Samuel replied, on 5 September 1920, that the largest demand for funds was for the establishment of agricultural colonies and for the building of houses. In order to encourage construction activity, he had reduced the customs duty on building materials from 11 to 3 per cent. Large financial resources would also be needed for land colonization. There was a demand, 'among leading men of all sections of opinion', for banks which would make long-term loans in order to assist industrial and agricultural progress. Another urgent matter for the development of the national home was the provision of hydro-electric power stations.[63]

At the first meeting of the Advisory Council in October 1920, Samuel openly affirmed the 'extreme importance' to the country of establishing banks for making long-term loans on the security of real property. A large programme for road construction and repair had been initiated and was in progress. Samuel maintained that the Jews who were arriving immediately found employment in the building of roads, and 'in the redemption of land previously derelict'. Echoing Theodor Herzl twenty years earlier, Samuel added: 'Their presence is thus not only no detriment to the interests of the existing population but of direct advantage to them, by increasing the resources and prosperity of the country.'[64] The growing numbers of Jewish unemployed for whom the Zionist Organization was unable to provide led Samuel to come to the rescue with a programme of public works. Indeed, Weizmann had already written to Curzon that the Zionists 'fully appreciate' the dangers of Jews coming to Palestine at a speed greater than they could be absorbed by its economic capacity, and that the presence of a large idle and unemployed body would hardly advance the Zionist cause.[65]

To finance development projects, Samuel proposed the floating of a public loan. He privately informed the Foreign Office in the summer of 1920 that £2.5 million would be needed, but his request was immediately rejected by the Treasury which raised the question of how the loan was to be guaranteed. Samuel was under the impression that the loan could be raised on the security of Palestine itself, particularly if it was levied from Jewish capital. However, this was not acceptable to the Treasury, which also regarded with suspicion any guarantee scheme devised by the Zionists. Samuel himself was disappointed when it became evident that even the Zionists were unwilling to commit their money without some form of guarantee.[66]

Samuel wrote to Curzon, in January 1921, that this loan was 'of great importance to Palestine'. While in ordinary circumstances, 'the natural course was to postpone all capital expenditure' until the mandate was conferred and the loan was issued, in the present conditions, such a policy was 'open to grave objection'. There was considerable Jewish immigration into Palestine, and to stop it would have 'serious political disadvantages'. This would result in a great 'discouragement' to Zionists throughout the world, and would be 'especially resented' by Zionists in Palestine. Samuel furthermore feared that a delay would give the impression that the policy of creating a Jewish national home 'was being minimised, if not abandoned'. Since land settlement took time, and since the growth of new industries was slow, the granting of a loan, to be used in public works to provide employment, was 'absolutely essential' as a 'suitable temporary resource', as hundreds of young immigrants were already employed in road-making and railway reconstruction. Samuel stressed that if capital expenditure were to stop during the next few months, or if it were not to be expanded, 'the effect with respect to immigration would be most serious'.[67]

Despite Samuel's lobbying, the British government did not finally issue the

Palestine loan until 1927, two years after he left office. In the meantime, the proposed loan raised strong feelings among the Arab leadership. Writing to Churchill in August 1922, Samuel informed the colonial secretary that the question of the loan had been discussed in the extraordinary meeting of the Advisory Council on 17 August 1922, and the Arab members asked that the ordinance to raise a loan should not be passed until they had had the opportunity of examining the estimates and pending the report of the Estimates Commission. However, Samuel reported that the ordinance was passed 'without their concurrence'.[68]

Even before the extraordinary meeting, the Arabic press had roundly condemned the proposed loan, whose purpose, according to *Filastin*, was not to further the 'economic improvement' of the country, but to create work for Jewish immigrants and to build railways and metalled roads between the Jewish colonies.[69] In similar vein, *al-Sabah* wrote:

> No doubt this loan will be covered by Jewish capitalists in Europe and spent on the Jewish immigrants here, while the Arab will be burdened with the greater part of this loan just as they are now burdened by the maximum part of the Administration's expenses—the Administration whose only aim is to drive them out of the country and to replace them by their enemies.[70]

In their petition to Churchill in 1921, the Arab Executive Committee, commenting on the provision of new roads [71] and other improvements 'not so keenly needed at this moment', noted: 'The poor tax-payer has been charged with costs. On the other hand, needs of more vital importance such as public education have been grudged their due budgets.' It would be wise for the treasury not to exceed its financial capacity, and put vital and essential projects before those which were a 'comparative luxury'. The committee argued that these works were undertaken more in order to give employment to the thousands of Jewish immigrants than because they were 'immediate necessities', and complained that the Jewish labourer on these works was paid double the amount given to the native, 'though he does less work'. They also complained that as soon as the high commissioner took office, he had proposed the floating of a loan for public works, or, as they put it, 'he wants to borrow money in the name of the native tax-payer in order to help out Jewish immigrants'.[72]

In the years from 1920 to 1923, Samuel engaged in a development-oriented policy of large public investments and deficit financing but, by 1924, pressures from the British government ushered in a period of fiscal conservatism which was to last well into the 1930s.[73] His conviction of the importance of infrastructural projects, particularly as a source of employment, made a significant contribution to the absorption of Third *Aliyah* immigrants.[74] By 1924, new sources of private capital allowed the Palestine Zionists to forge ahead with their economic projects and created a temporary economic boom in the Jewish economic sector.

Not only did Samuel contribute to the future of the Jewish national home by trying to promote economic conditions favourable to the Zionists, he also succeeded in laying the cornerstones for future projects vital to the Zionists before he left Palestine. Samuel himself wrote in 1925 in his 'Book of Chronicles' under the heading 'Future Work' that it was to be understood that what had been accomplished 'in so short a period could be no more than the beginning', and that there was work 'already in sight which will tax the energies of the Government for many years to come'. The principal requirement for commerce and industry to develop, he noted, was the construction of a harbour at Haifa. He added that 'they', without calling the Jews by name, 'were heavily handicapped by the inconvenience and the costliness of handling goods in the open roadsteads of Haifa and Jaffa'.[75]

Samuel wrote personally to the secretary of state for the colonies in September 1924, as his term in office was nearing its end, outlining proposals whereby a harbour at Haifa could be built with finances provided by the 'Economic Board'.[76] According to Colonial Office minutes of 4 October 1924:

> The Board is of course composed of Jews, and as it would obviously be impossible politically to allow a public work of this magnitude to be financed by the Jewish community only. The High Commissioner suggests that the activities of the Board in this direction should be, as it were camouflaged by the creation of a 'Haifa Improvements Board' ...

On 17 October, Vernon commented that it might not be possible to 'turn down' Sir Herbert Samuel's proposal at present, but that future requests for more details should be 'so carefully worded as not to give him the impression that the idea was accepted in principle'.[77] The Haifa harbour project was subsequently provided for by the Palestine loan of 1926, and was constructed for 'Imperial purposes'.[78]

The Rutenberg Concession

The largest and most politically controversial Zionist scheme during Samuel's period of office was the Rutenberg Concession. Its significance for the Zionists was to provide employment for the thousands of Jewish settlers, which would in turn 'justify' the influx of Jewish immigration. On the other hand, the Arabs saw it as a Jewish monopoly that would place the economic life of Palestine under the grip of the Zionists. The Rutenberg Concession involved two schemes. The 'Awja Concession, which was signed in September 1921, granted the Russian electrical engineer, Pinhas Rutenberg, the exclusive right to produce energy by means of water power within the district of Jaffa for a period of thirty-two years. The Jordan Concession was a much larger undertaking, to become operative within two years, with a capital of £1 million, of which at least £200,000 had to be paid up before the concession was granted. It conferred upon Rutenberg's company an exclusive right for the generation of electrical energy by means of water power throughout the whole of Palestine (except Jaffa where the 'Awja Concession was signed) for a period of seventy years.[79]

The Zionists' aim was to secure control over, or gain access to, the headwaters of the Jordan and Litani rivers. In the early 1920s, the northern boundaries of Palestine were being negotiated with the French, with close Zionist involvement, and Rutenberg himself was appointed to the Anglo-French Water Commission. However, the final agreement was disappointing to the Zionists, as only one of the major sources of the Jordan river fell within the territory of Palestine. Rutenberg's original plan for the hydro-electrification and irrigation of all of Palestine therefore proved impossible.

Nevertheless, the 'Awja Concession for irrigation and hydro-electrification, did materialize and the concessions, granted to an individual entrepreneur but clearly intended to benefit the Zionists, 'remained a symbol of the preferential treatment accorded to the Zionists by the terms of Article 11 of the Mandate'.[80] In both cases, the high commissioner could extend the concessions indefinitely, and preferential clauses were inserted in them. These included reduced taxes, deferred customs duties, the abolition of any conflicting and pre-existing concessions even if they were still valid, the right of expropriation and police protection.

The significance of the concessions for the Zionists lay in their national scale. The Arabs amply demonstrated that they understood these implications and raised the slogans: 'In Rutenberg's scheme our slavery' and 'Rutenberg's poles are nothing but guillotines'.[81] Shuckburgh remarked on 7 September 1921 that Rutenberg's schemes would, 'if successful', enable very considerable industrial development to take place, and would 'supply a large amount of employment which will go far to justify the increased immigration without which the Zionist policy can never be carried into effect'. He went on to say:

> This means the setting up of a monopoly, extensive in area and prolonged in time, but in view of the heavy risks of the undertaking and the large capital involved we consider this to be not only reasonable but necessary ... Mr. Rutenberg has been privately in communication with the members of the Moslem Christian Delegation in this country and has succeeded in interesting them in the scheme. This may minimise the danger, which nevertheless must be recognised to exist, of an attack on these concessions on the ground that we are giving to a Jewish organisation a grip over the whole economic life of Palestine.[82]

In view of this evident Arab hostility, and in order that Rutenberg's chances of raising funds should not be put at risk, Samuel and the Zionists decided that the negotiations for the concession should be conducted in secret. Once an agreement was reached, the benefits of the scheme to Palestine could be publicly explained. Samuel continued to hope that this would eventually secure Arab consent.[83] In

September 1921, Young wrote that Rutenberg had received a telegram from Weizmann 'predicting calamity unless the Zionist Congress can be informed within the
next few days that the Jordan concession is to be signed'. This delay had been due
to Samuel's reluctance to sign the agreement, for fear of strong Arab opposition:
indeed, Samuel had made it clear to Rutenberg that he would not sign the agreement until Rutenberg obtained Arab concurrence. Nevertheless, Young recorded
in the same minute that Samuel did not say that he 'would never agree'.[84]

As a way out of this difficulty, Shuckburgh suggested that perhaps Rutenberg
could be induced 'to state in writing' what he often admitted to him verbally, namely,
that 'in practice, it will be quite impossible for him to give effect to his project
unless he can carry local opinion with him'. Shuckburgh had, accordingly, sent for
Rutenberg and his solicitor, and they had agreed.[85] When the Rutenburg Concession was signed in September 1921, Shuckburgh wrote that it 'did something to
put the Zionists into a better humour, and to remove some of their dissatisfaction
at the slow rate of progress towards the establishment of a Jewish National Home'.[86]

Rutenberg's claim to have convinced the Palestine Arabs of the benefits of his
project was not actually met. Churchill, the secretary of state for the colonies, was
convinced that it was not possible to induce the (first) Arab Delegation, then in
London, to approve the project, and wrote to Samuel on 12 September 1921 that it
was 'very unlikely' that the Arabs would give 'general approval and it would bind
no one in Palestine if they did give it'.[87] *Filastin* wrote in October 1921 that Rutenberg had come back from England with a signed concession in his hand, in spite of
strong Arab protests.[88] Indeed, one of the resolutions of the Fifth Palestine Arab
Congress in August 1922 was to boycott the Rutenberg project. This was repeated
in the Sixth Congress in June 1923 when it was resolved to send a petition to the
Colonial Office in protest at work which had begun in the Rutenberg project, and
demanding that Rutenberg should be made to pay the expenses for the poles and
electrical cables in Jaffa.[89]

In addition to Arab objections, the Rutenberg Concession was attacked in the
British press and parliament on the grounds that a concession of such magnitude
had been given to a foreigner, and not to British companies—a foreigner, moreover, who had bought the machinery for his project in Germany. On the international
level as well, the Rutenberg Concession, through its connection with the Mavrommatis case, made such a bad impression that one member of the Permanent Mandates
Commission remarked that it was a 'European scandal'.[90]

Euripides Mavrommatis, a Greek subject and financier, had been given several
hydro-electric and irrigation concessions by the Turkish government. The Palestine administration refused to accept the validity of his concessions on the grounds
that he was an Ottoman subject, but when he proved that he was a Greek subject,
the administration still refused his claims as they conflicted sharply with
Rutenberg's scheme. When the Colonial Office realized in 1922 that some of his

concessions were probably valid, Mavrommatis was offered £10,000 to relinquish all his claim to the concession, half of which was to be paid by the Colonial Office, and the other half by Rutenberg. When he refused, the sum was doubled, but the offer was again turned down. In 1924, Mavrommatis convinced the Greek government to take up his case at The Hague. The Permanent Court of International Justice decreed on 26 March 1925 that not only was Mavrommatis' Jerusalem concession valid, but the clause in Rutenberg's concession regarding the expropriation of pre-existing concessions was illegal. The Colonial Office thereafter decided to let him proceed with his plans, but with every intention to block his way so as to make his task an impossible one.[91] Shuckburgh subsequently wrote:

> I have always felt that the Rutenberg Concession was the one point on which Sir H. Samuel did not emerge from his examination with 'flying colours'. The general attitude of the Permanent Mandates Commission on the subject was clearly very hostile.[92]

JEWISH SETTLEMENT AND THE QUEST FOR EMPTY LAND

Land and immigration were crucial to the Zionist project since the establishment of a Jewish state in Palestine required, first, that the incoming Jewish settlers should form a majority of the population, and, second, that Jews should expand their land base by gaining possession of the bulk of the cultivable land. The two issues were inextricably linked: given that Palestine was an overwhelmingly agricultural country, the Jewish colonization envisaged by the Zionists had necessarily to be in large part agricultural colonization. The achievement of a Jewish majority on the basis of the urban population was inconceivable. A particular feature of Jewish land acquisitions was that once land was bought by the Jewish National Fund or on its behalf by affiliated companies such as the Palestine Land Development Company, it was held in 'perpetuity' as an 'inalienable' trust for 'the nation'. This concept was established at the World Zionist Conference in 1920.[93]

The process of acquiring land for Zionist purposes proved to be slow and difficult: the percentage of land in Palestine owned by the Jews rose from 2.04 per cent in 1920 to only 3.8 per cent in 1925.[94] By 1937, when the Peel Commission advocated the partition of Palestine into two separate states, Jewish organizations still held no more than 5.5 per cent of the land. In 1948, when the Jewish state was established, after almost seventy years of Jewish agricultural colonization, Jews had still acquired no more than approximately 7 per cent of the total area of Palestine.[95] Contrary to Zionist claims, Palestine was not an 'empty' country; the bulk of the land was already owned or exploited by Arabs, whether as private landlords or as legally established tenant farmers.

The OETA and Zionist Views of the Land Question

From the beginning of Zionist colonization, in the final years of Ottoman rule, land ownership had been a sensitive issue between Arabs and Jews in Palestine. In 1912, the Arabic newspaper *Filastin* accused the Ottoman *mutasarrif* (governor) of Acre of selling state lands to the Jews in the face of widespread Arab opposition. In the following year, *Filastin* and another Arabic paper, *al-Karmel*, took up the cause of Arab villagers who were protesting against the sale to Jews of state lands in Beisan, in north-east Palestine. The Beisan issue led to demonstrations in Nablus and to the organization of the first Arab anti-Zionist society, based in Nablus, with branches in other Palestinian towns. When, in 1913, the First Palestine Arab Congress met in Paris, it received a telegram from the notables of Beisan and Jenin, urging it to declare its opposition to the sale of the Beisan lands, whose loss, they maintained, would threaten the whole Arab nation.[96]

By the end of the First World War Palestine's economic life had been severely disrupted. Some impoverished Arab landowners sought loans and mortgages from Jewish creditors, and the ensuing defaults and foreclosures led, on a small scale, to transfers of land to Jewish hands. Arabs viewed this as an attempt by the Zionists to buy up these mortgaged lands, the consequence of which, in their opinion, was to 'oust the owners and rule in their place'.[97] To check such tendencies, and in conformity with the military administration's obligation to preserve the status quo, the military administration closed all land registries in 1918, prohibited transactions in immovable property and restrained the courts from ordering the sale of land in execution of mortgages or judgements.[98]

The Zionist Commission, on its arrival in Palestine in April 1918, immediately began considering a scheme for bringing under cultivation large tracts of land which, according to William Ormsby-Gore, the British liaison officer to the commission, would give employment to Jews and Arabs. However, Gilbert Clayton, the chief political officer of the military administration, objected that the land in question had owners, that the Zionists would meet with strong Arab opposition, and that this would generally be regarded as 'the first step towards dispossessing the Arabs of their land'.[99] Nevertheless, Weizmann wrote from Palestine in a private letter to Balfour on 30 May 1918, that the implementation of the land scheme was 'essential for the successful carrying out of the policy enunciated in your declaration'. He claimed that the 'whole of southern Palestine ... was practically unoccupied land', and that the maintenance of the status quo was in direct contradiction of the Balfour Declaration.[100]

Weizmann, moreover, demanded that the military administration should 'at once' authorize the Zionist Commission to examine the land laws and identify state lands. But Clayton insisted that the land question must wait till the formation of a civil government.[101] However, Weizmann was able to influence land policy under the OETA by specifically opposing agricultural loans to Arab farmers,[102] and by instigating the closure of the Ottoman Agricultural Bank.[103] Under the Turks, loans had been provided to Arab cultivators through the bank, but during the war this system collapsed, and the military administration soon realized the urgency of the matter for Arab farmers. During the latter part of 1918, the administration advanced short-term loans in the most urgent cases.[104]

In 1919, a long-term arrangement was reached with the Anglo-Egyptian Bank to grant loans for up to five years, with very easy conditions: 6.5 per cent interest, representing 6 per cent for the bank, and 0.5 per cent for administrative charges.[105] However, after the military administration had obtained the money to advance from the Anglo-Egyptian Bank in 1919, and the arrangements 'were in working order and giving great satisfaction', the Zionists raised strong objections on the grounds that there was 'favouritism' to the Anglo-Egyptian Bank and that the Anglo-Palestine Bank—a Jewish bank—should have been given the opportunity of advancing money to the administration. The Zionists also objected on the grounds that the scheme interfered with the status quo by causing an appreciation in the value of land.[106] By order of the Foreign Office, the granting of further loans was suspended in September 1919.

According to the Palin Report of 1920, Weizmann's veto on agricultural loans further inflamed the growing irritation of the population against the Zionists, and convinced the Palestine Arabs of the power of the Zionist Commission:

> … the people at once came to the conclusion that the Zionists had interfered in order that they should be left in great straits and should ultimately have to sell their lands to the Zionists at any price. Although Dr. Weizmann subsequently agreed that there had been a mistake, the mischief was done.[107]

The interference of the Zionist Commission drew a vigorous protest from Major-General Money, who pointed out that: 'the action of the Commission was a bad augury for any future Administration of the country attempting to carry out the usual British practice of governing the country in the best interest of all sections of the community without giving undue preference to any particular section.'[108]

The Palestinian Arab organizations were equally apprehensive of Zionist plans to obtain land, and upon hearing that the Peace Conference, meeting in February 1920, aimed at establishing a Jewish national home in Palestine, the Muslim-Christian Association transmitted a petition to the representatives of Great Britain through the military governor of Nablus. They affirmed that all the lands of Palestine had been, and still were, owned by the people, and that there was 'nothing known as Government lands except the *mudawwara* lands which the late Sultan 'Abdul Hamid seized and made his own private farms'. They made it clear that these lands were all the property of their original owners, who mostly held documents proving their ownership, that they had built their villages in them and tried their best to improve them.

> Consequently, they are the first persons entitled to them on account of both long possessions and labour and original ownership … So if the Peace Conference gives its decisions in this manner the whole Arab Nation will be annoyed and will consider such an action as intended to scatter the Arabs and to take their lands by force.[109]

During the military administration, Foreign Office officials expressed great doubts whether any considerable amount of waste land was available in Palestine. A minute by O. A. Scott in the Foreign Office in April 1920 indicates that 'there was a curious divergence of opinion' as to how much cultivable land was lying waste, and that according to Dr Alois Musil, an expert on Syria and Palestine, there was 'hardly any land available for settlement'.[110]

The Palin Report noted that 'unfortunately, there was a very wide diversity between the various estimates', as to how much unoccupied land was available. Lieutenant-Colonel E. R. Sawer, the director of agriculture under OETA, would not put the quantity of arable land available at a figure higher than 6,000,000 dunums, and noted that of this figure, 4,209,000 dunums were already under cultivation in 1920, leaving only 1,796,000 dunums for development. Moreover, the greater part of this cultivable surplus was said to be in the Jordan Valley, the arid and semi-arid areas to the south of Gaza and Beersheba, the broken and hilly country between Acre and Safed and in the line of country between the Jordan and Beisan. Thus, in Colonel Sawer's opinion, 'the only possibility of there being a surplus land capable of supporting immigrants after allowing for the natural increase of the population' depended on intensive cultivation and improved schemes of irrigation, and on the possibility of colonizing the Jordan valley, which in his opinion, was not suitable for colonization by Europeans. On the other hand, Zionist sources quoted in the report put the total percentage of cultivable land in Western Palestine as high as 50 to 60 per cent. However, Colonel Sawer contrasted the Zionist claim that 60–70 per cent of the desert country of Beersheba was cultivable with his own estimate of 6.3 per cent for the same district. The Palin Report noted that 'in view of such a discrepancy one cannot but suspect a serious error on one side or the other', and that as the territory in question was largely desert, it was possible that Zionist figures were 'unduly optimistic'.[111]

Samuel's Land Policies

When the civil administration was set up, Samuel immediately authorized the resumption of land transactions by promulgating the first Land Transfer Ordinance in September 1920, reversing the 1918 ordinance prohibiting all transfers of immovable property. The land registries were to be opened, but the consent of the government was to be obtained for all dispositions of immovable property.[112] Under the Turks, land was held mainly under two distinct tenures known as *mulk* and *miri*, (with subdivisions). *Mulk* was confined to urban sites (mostly buildings) and was held in complete freehold, enabling the owner to freely dispose of his land. This type constituted a very small percentage of land in Palestine, which was mostly *miri*, usufruct tenure of land whose ultimate ownership rested with the state. In *miri* land, the right of possession, inheritance or sale was granted to private individuals, but if an owner of *miri* land died without heirs, the land reverted to the state. The Ottoman government did not interfere with *miri* land holders as long as the tithe was paid, and as long as land did not remain fallow for three consecutive years without a legal excuse. However, the owner of *miri* land could not sell or mortgage his land without the consent of the state, which was obtained, under the Ottomans, from the Land Office. There were two sub-categories of *miri* land, *mahlul* and *jiftlik*, over which the state had more direct control. Large quantities of *jiftlik*, also known as *mudawwara* land, existed in Palestine in the 1920s, most of which was cultivated by long-established tenant farmers.

Samuel's administration made numerous attempts to interpret these Ottoman laws, of which it had little understanding,[113] to suit Zionist purposes. In particular, it sought ways to make 'state lands' available for Jewish settlers, and to facilitate the sale of land from absentee landlords to Jewish companies. Between 1920 and 1925, Samuel's preoccupation with land legislation resulted in no less than ten ordinances on land-related questions.

It is generally accepted that a decisive factor in facilitating land acquisition by the Jews during the 1920s was land legislation drafted by the legal secretary, Norman Bentwich who 'enjoyed unparalleled influence over land matters' until 1929. Kenneth Stein asserts that, in the 1920s, Bentwich's Zionist sympathies advanced the Zionist cause, for while Bentwich was in office, the Palestine administration neither prohibited land transfers nor contemplated prohibitions.[114] As with questions relating to immigration, the British authorities worked closely with and consulted the Zionist Commission on land policy.[115] The most important of these measures were the first Land Transfer Ordinance of September 1920, amended on 4 April 1921; the Mahlul Land Ordinance of October 1920; the Mewat Land Ordinance of February 1921; and the Palestine Jewish Colonization Association (Edmond de Rothschild Foundation) Ordinance of 1924.[116]

Land policies during Samuel's administration have been studied in depth by other scholars.[117] This section will focus on their political aspect: in particular, their contribution to the achievement of the Zionist objective of gaining control over large tracts of state land; and the impact of land sales to Zionist organizations on Arab tenant farmers.

The Question of State Lands: The Land Commission

Article 6 of the Mandate for Palestine enjoined the administration to 'encourage, in cooperation with the Jewish Agency … close settlement by Jews on the land, including state lands and waste lands not required for public purposes.' However, it was also called upon to ensure 'that the rights and position of other sections of the population are not prejudiced'. The Zionist leadership viewed Article 6 as binding the government to place most state lands at the disposal of the Zionists for settlement and economic development as rapidly as possible.[118] The government moved more slowly than the Zionists would have liked, since it had little information on the real extent of state lands. Soon after he came to office Samuel appointed a Land Commission under the chairmanship of Albert Abramson,[119] with Haim Kalvarisky[120] and Faydi al-'Alami, a large landowner and former Mayor of Jerusalem (1906–9), as members, to examine and report on what lands, 'governmental or otherwise', could be made available for 'closer settlement'. Samuel reported at the same time that no decisions would be put into effect without consultation with the Zionist Commission.[121]

Samuel was clearly optimistic that extensive state lands would be found for Zionist settlement. In December 1920, before the Land Commission had a chance to submit its report identifying *mahlul* lands (*miri* land which, remaining uncultivated, reverted to state control) and *mawat* lands (hilly, scrub woodland and grazing grounds not held by title deed), he assured Weizmann that land would be available for colonization, that state lands in Palestine included a cultivable area of approximately 250,000 acres, but that the proportion of uncultivated land available for close settlement could not be known until the Land Commission had examined the question 'district by district'. He ended his letter by saying that he was confident, after careful enquiries, 'that of the three factors necessary for Jewish colonization on a large scale in Palestine—land, men and capital—it is not the first which will be lacking.'[122]

In its lengthy report, submitted in May 1921, the Land Commission concluded: 'At first sight, therefore, there would not appear to be any land available for fresh settlers.' However, there were factors to be considered as bearing on this point, namely the necessity of intensive cultivation, as well as the necessity of making use of *mawat* and *mahlul* lands (see below). The commission also pointed out that there were three classes of *waqf* lands (religious endowments) 'which could be affected by proposals for closer settlement', *awqaf masbuta*, *awqaf mundarisa* and *awqaf sabit*, and recommended the appointment of a special commission to examine their position.[123]

According to the report, 50 per cent of the country could 'be considered free for closer settlement but not agriculturally possible', and although there was no cadastral survey of the country, nor any figures available for the total cultivable area,

even the 'casual observer must realize that large areas are quite uncultivable because of the nature of the soil, the scanty rainfall, the absence of springs etc.'[124]
However, this early revelation did not prevent Samuel from subsequently writing
to Devonshire, in December 1922, that the country was 'lamentably empty and
undeveloped', and: 'There can be no doubt that, looking only to the immediate
future, it could maintain, without difficulty and without delay, double the existing
population, with no disturbance or loss to any of the present inhabitants.'[125]

Nevertheless, Samuel himself later conceded that so-called state lands were not
available for 'closer settlement'. He wrote in 1925 that 'it had not been found possible' to go far in giving effect to Article 6 of the mandate because on most of the
state lands Arab cultivators were settled. Possession could not have been 'transferred to others without injustice, and without infringing the clause in the article
itself inserted for their protection'. Samuel further stated that the total area of
Palestine was estimated at nearly 10,000 square miles, that the cultivable area was
about one-half of the total, and that large tracts were barren mountains or dunes,
or sandy desert in the south. He added that to attempt close settlement on this
waterless and rocky half would be 'to invite certain disaster', and that 'apart from
some areas of minor importance, the only instance in which it has been possible as
yet to apply this provision of Article VI of the mandate has been in the case of the
swamps of Kabbara'.[126]

So what were the real prospects for close land settlement? This was the question which Eric Mills at the Colonial Office had tried to answer in his memorandum
on the sociological aspects of Jewish immigration to Palestine already described.
Mills wrote that about 7 per cent of the cultivable land in Palestine appeared to be
available for Jewish settlement. It had been suggested that intensive cultivation
would gradually release more land, and that the restriction of grazing would assist
towards that end. Mills argued that it was inconceivable that intensive cultivation
could be taught to Arabs in less than three generations, and that this period of time
was greater than the time required to reach a population limit of 3,000,000 (the
accepted maximum that Palestine could ever support economically). Mills observed:

> In other words, it will be impossible to maintain that figure of 10,000 immigrants
> per annum since the land will not be proportionately available—the economic situ-
> ation will automatically constrain immigration to its proper limits. Hence, the time
> taken actually to reach the limit of 3,000,000 is automatically extended—the far-
> ther that limit recedes into the distant future the more impossible becomes the
> hope of Jewish dominance; for the Jewish population will be in these circumstances
> always behind the Arab population as the figures show.[127]

The real dilemma which faced both the administration and the new settlers was
that Palestine was already a populated country with limited natural resources.[128]

The Significance of the Mahlul and Mewat Land Ordinances

Since most of the land in Palestine was of *miri* class, the rights of the holder were preserved as long as he cultivated his land. According to Ottoman law, if the land was left uncultivated for three consecutive years, it reverted to the state as *mahlul*. It is significant that after the Paris Peace Conference in 1919, the Zionists had hoped that vacated *mahlul* land would come immediately into Jewish ownership.[129] In seeking lands which could be made available for Jewish settlement, the administration took steps to prevent further inroads into state land not currently under cultivation. In October 1920, the Mahlul Land Ordinance aimed at demarcating and regulating state land, and requiring notification of land which had been seized or worked on after it had reverted to the state under Ottoman law.[130]

Because the Palestine administration had little knowledge of which land belonged to the state, but wished to retain full control of state lands for Jewish settlement, it also passed the Mewat Land Ordinance in 1921 which required the registration of reclaimed waste land.[131] The Land Commission report had recommended that all uncultivated land for which no title deed was held and which was one and a half miles from the outside houses of villages should be considered *mawat*. These were estimated in 1920 to constitute 50–60 per cent of the total area of Palestine. In urban areas, lands which had never been cultivated or for which there was no title deed should also be considered *mawat*.[132] The Land Commission was moreover of the opinion that:

> Every encouragement should be given to landowners to sell their excess areas and that there should be no restriction on sales. With regard to the fear that the *fellah* will alienate all his land if the 300 dounom [sic] restriction in the Land Transfer Ordinance is removed, we are of opinion that as he is dependent on his cultivation as his means of livelihood having no other regular method of supporting himself and his family and as he is an intelligent person and a keen agriculturalist he is not likely to part with all his lands.[133]

Under Ottoman law, anyone could convert *mawat* or *mahlul* land into *miri* by cultivating it, registering it and paying its unimproved value, after which a title deed was issued.[134] This was no longer possible under mandatory law, and anyone who cultivated waste land was prosecuted on the charge of 'encroaching' on state land. Samuel was able to effect this by repealing, in December 1920, Article 103 of the Ottoman Land Code, which made provisions for converting *mawat* and *mahlul* land into *miri* land. Tibawi notes that at the Foreign Office, the newly appointed under-secretary, Ronald Lindsay, 'saw the injustice of the proposed ordinance' and expressed his misgivings at the abolition of the Ottoman Land Code in 'this brusque manner', which was likely to cause hardship. Samuel apparently 'exploited' the confusion during the transfer of responsibility for Palestine from the Foreign to the Colonial Office, and published the ordinance before it had been officially approved. When he was asked by the Foreign Office to cancel the publication and give an explanation of the need to repeal the Turkish law, he suggested the omission of the words 'close settlement' from the preamble, but urged that the paragraph repealing the Ottoman law should be kept. In the end Samuel received the approval he expected.[135]

Aware of the government's intentions, Arab villagers obstructed the work of a commission established for the demarcation of *mawat* lands. Samuel reported in June 1922 that *mukhtars* and peasants alike had refused to accompany the commissioners to their work, and had resisted giving them the necessary information. He added that 'their determination to give no help and their lack of confidence in the Administration and of the intentions of the commissioners' were marked.[136] The Mewat and Mahlul Land Ordinances were calculated to make available for Jewish settlers even the small percentage of land in cultivable areas which had been uncultivated for one reason or another.

Land Legislation and the Protection of Tenants

The administration's speedy introduction of the Land Transfer Ordinance in 1920 was guided by political considerations, namely to fulfil the pledge of securing the establishment of the Jewish national home. However, in removing some of the curbs on land sales, Samuel was also conscious of the need to give some protection to those who were tenants on land being sold off. In addition to ending the freeze on land sales imposed by the OETA, the 1920 Ordinance advanced Zionist interests in several ways. Although it imposed restrictions on the size and value of land transactions, Clause 8 strengthened Zionist land-purchasing powers by allowing corporations, under certain conditions, to own immovable property, and allowed the high commissioner, in certain circumstances, to 'consent to the transfer of larger areas of land than may be transferred with the assent of the district governor where he is satisfied that the transfer will be in the public interest or will serve some purpose of recognised public utility'.[137]

In theory, Arab landowners and tenant-cultivators were protected by Clause 6 of the ordinance, which stipulated that the purchaser must be resident in Palestine, limited the amount of land bought by a single buyer, and insisted on immediate cultivation or development of the purchased land. The Arabs, however, argued that Clause 6 was in fact aimed at facilitating the transfer of the large areas of land owned by absentee landlords to Jewish buyers, and that this was calculated to make use of these large estates which Bentwich had hoped would supply the bulk of intended Zionist purchases.[138] An open letter from the Muslim-Christian Association of Jaffa to Samuel indicated that the 1920 ordinance was widely viewed among the Arabs as an open attempt to aid Jewish land purchase.[139]

Since the restrictive provisions of the 1920 Land Transfer Ordinance were easily circumvented, it was replaced by the amended Land Transfer Ordinance of December 1921, which removed the limits on the area and value of land to be sold, and on purchases by persons living outside Palestine.[140] The revised ordinance placed the administration under the obligation to provide any tenant of land it wished to transfer with 'sufficient land elsewhere' for the maintenance of himself and his family.[141] Mandatory law, therefore, even though it provided for the 'protection' of tenants by providing land 'elsewhere', legally 'made the tenants vulnerable to eviction'.[142] Because of tenants' 'weak legal status', landlords were able to dispossess them in the courts.[143] Furthermore, although both ordinances, at least in theory, provided some protection for tenants in occupation, this did not extend to owner-cultivators or agricultural labourers.[144]

An important consequence of these ordinances was that, for the first time, the notion of 'land use' became distinct from that of 'land ownership'. Up to that point, there had been little difference, under Ottoman law, between the tenant who worked the land, and the small landowner. Existing property rights were still determined by Ottoman law. The first Land Transfer Ordinance also specified that the 'legal' form of land ownership required registration in the Land Registry Department. This meant that the tenants who worked on the land would be unable, because of the complicated Ottoman system of land tenure, to produce the legal documents, and thus became liable to eviction. Samuel was well aware of the policy followed by the Jewish National Fund which insisted that land purchased should be 'free of tenants'. Conscious of this Zionist doctrine, he had therefore made provision to 'protect' the tenants under the amended Land Transfer Ordinance of 1921.[145]

In the report presented to Churchill in March 1921, the Arab Executive Committee argued that it was inconceivable that the government believed it had the right to hand over to Jews Crown (state) lands which were not its own. It declared: 'These Crown Lands are the property of the nation, and belong to the tenants who from time immemorial have lived on them and cultivated them;' the government, therefore, could not 'give them over to Jews'. The committee also complained of the effect of Jewish colonies on the surrounding peasant population. The peasants had been obliged to sell their land and migrate, for the Jews would not employ them, and had depreciated the value of land and property and manipulated a financial crisis, 'in order that landlords, under the stress of need, should sell out at ruinous prices'.[146]

Although the largest Jewish land purchases during this period were from landowners resident outside Palestine, there were also economic pressures on landowners within Palestine which arguably aided Jewish land acquisitions. These were described by Musa al-'Alami, a large landowner[147] who was appointed in 1925 to the legal service under Norman Bentwich. According to his biographer, Geoffrey Furlonge, al-'Alami believed that these economic measures 'must have originated in the astute brains of the high commissioner and his brilliant lieutenant Norman Bentwich'. For the first time, urban property tax was imposed on unused land within municipal boundaries, and the *'ushur* (tithe) on unused land in the countryside. Another measure abolished the Ottoman Agricultural Bank, without providing an alternative. Al-'Alami commented that the first two measures were 'officially' described as 'progressive' and 'intended to encourage full land utilisation', and the second as an 'encouragement to private banking'. However, in his experience, their combined effect was to encourage Jews and damage Arabs. Since urban Arab proprietors lacked the capital to build on their land, and were often unable to meet their increased tax obligation, they found themselves forced to sell their unused land for any price it could fetch, and there was 'almost always a Jew waiting to snap it up.'

Similarly, in the rural areas, landowners found that additional taxation on land which they were unable to cultivate put them under financial pressure, forcing them to turn to village money lenders who charged interest as high as 60 per cent. In this way landowners, according to al-'Alami, fell into serious debt. Those whose land was foreclosed frequently discovered that the money lender had been financed by the Keren Kayemeth (Jewish National Fund) or some other Jewish land purchasing organization, which duly took possession of the land in question. These measures were, according to al-'Alami's account to Furlonge, 'responsible for the gradual impoverishment of many Arabs and for large tracts of land falling into Jewish hands'.[148] Some confirmation of these claims was given by the district governor of Samaria, C. H. F. Cox, who reported in December 1923 that the people of Tamra, Na'ura and Taiyiba had been 'compelled by their unhappy financial position' to sell some 15,000 dunums to the Jewish-owned Palestine Land Development Company, and that the importance of this land to the Zionists was that it provided for its connection to Jewish-owned lands in the north near Mount Tabor.[149]

In the course of the 1920s, the restrictive elements in the Land Transfer Ordinances of 1920 and 1921 were in practice removed. Monetary compensation of tenants, rather than ensuring that they had sufficient land to cultivate, became increasingly common, often at the behest of the tenants themselves.[150] In 1929, these Ordinances were replaced by the Protection of Cultivators Ordinance, which provided for compensation to tenants who 'received a valid notice to quit the holding of which they had been in occupation'. The 'previous requirement, that a cultivator must retain a subsistence area elsewhere, found no place in the new Ordinance'. The purchaser was no longer obliged to allot another piece of land to the tenant, and instead he could only pay material compensation.[151]

Not only did Samuel's administration actively seek to promote Zionist land purchases while providing only ineffective safeguards for resident cultivators, but throughout the 1920s the British ignored the need to support Arab agriculture and relieve the indebtedness of the peasant. The government took a piecemeal approach which 'neither initiated nor supported agrarian change'.[152] A particular complaint was the absence of long term agricultural credit. The agricultural loans issued by the Anglo-Egyptian Bank between 1919 and 1923 comprised the only large-scale ongoing agricultural credit scheme undertaken by British administrations. Later measures provided only seasonal credit or on-off responses to crises.[153] It was not until the 1930s, when the problem of Arab landlessness assumed political importance for the British, that a further effort was made, in the Cultivators (Protection) Ordinance of 1933, to provide more protection for tenants and sharecroppers. However, in 1937, the Peel Commission concluded that all these ordinances 'failed to achieve their purpose of safeguarding Arab tenants and cultivating owners. They proved in fact to be unworkable. Neither vendor nor purchaser applied for the consent of Government to the transaction.'[154]

However, the longer-term significance of land sales to Zionist organizations went beyond the fate of displaced Arab cultivators. Their political importance was to provide the Zionists with the opportunity to establish 'Jewish national territory upon which a state could function and in which a population could survive'.[155]

Following the establishment of the civil administration in 1920, various Zionist colonization and land purchasing companies set out to acquire state lands, and also lands owned by absentee landlords resident in Lebanon, Syria or Egypt. The most notable example of the first type was the Beisan state lands,[156] and of the second type, the Jezreel Valley lands, the so-called 'granary of Palestine'.[157] Between 1920 and 1927, 82 per cent of all land purchased and registered with the Jewish Agency was bought from landlords living outside Palestine at prices well below prevailing market rates.[158] It is notable that only a small proportion of land was sold to Zionist land purchasing companies by resident Palestinian Arabs. However, land owned by the state or by absentee landlords was not 'unoccupied'; it had well-established tenants with legal rights under Ottoman law. The impact on tenants of major land sales during Samuel's period was not felt immediately, but in the next decade thousands of Palestinian peasants were evicted as a result of decisions taken during this time. Many evictions occurred without the provision of other land for their occupation. In some cases, the dispossessed Arabs received cash compensation, and no criticism could be made against the Jewish land companies, because—as Wadi' Boustany, the lawyer who represented the Arab cultivators in the Ghor Mudawwara agreement with the Palestine administration, pointed out—those companies acted with the knowledge of the government.[159]

The Beisan Lands: The Ghor Mudawwara Tenants' Agreement

State lands comprised only a small proportion of Jewish land acquisition; their importance in the creation of the Jewish national home was political. Moreover, they were situated, like the large tracts of land bought from absentee landlords, in the most fertile plains of Palestine.[160] In February 1921, there was rising anxiety among Palestine Arabs in Beisan who had gained the impression, as the Political Report for that month stated, that the government intended to settle Jews in the Ghor Mudawwara 'in a manner detrimental to Arab interests', though the report noted that this impression was 'unfounded'.[161]

In the potentially explosive months before and after the May 1921 riots, Samuel had little choice but to settle the Beisan land question in a manner 'acceptable' to the Arabs. According to the Political Report for May 1921, the mayor of Beisan informed the government that in his opinion Jewish settlement in the Ghor was 'out of the question' for at least a year. Later, it might be possible for those who had more land than they could handle to sell to Jews, but Jewish settlement must, if it was to be attempted 'with any degree of safety, be very gradual'.[162] In July 1921, a military intelligence report reached Churchill stating that a 'rising could take place suddenly caused by any action of the Government, such as the allotment of Arab land to Jews'. At Beisan, the report predicted that 'any attempt on the part of the Government to evict Arabs from certain land in dispute, for the purpose of allotting it to Jews, will be the signal for local combined anti-Jewish action on the part of the Moslems'.[163]

The difficulty concerning the state domain of Beisan was 'settled' during the winter of 1921. Article 6 of the mandate called on the Palestine administration to make state lands available for close settlement by Jews, on condition that the rights of other sections were not prejudiced in transactions involving state lands. Therefore 'it was clear', according to Norman Bentwich, that the tenants' rights had to be respected. The government initially proposed to confer long leases in the areas which were cultivated by the tenants of Beisan but, according to Bentwich, the tenants protested on the grounds that they were entitled to ownership. After the government examined the claim, it finally negotiated the Beisan Agreement under whose terms the Arab cultivators were to become owners of the areas actually occupied and cultivated by them.[164] After the government had demarcated the area, it was expected that large areas of state lands would still be available for Jewish settlement. Bentwich maintains that part of the 'surplus' land ultimately found its way to Jewish hands.[165]

An additional significance of the Beisan area from the Zionist point of view was that it was to be the site of the Rutenberg Concession for irrigation and hydro-electrification. A minute by Clauson at the Middle East Department on 24 June 1921 states:

It is exactly in this district that Mr. Rutenberg proposes to build his power house, and it is his intention to buy 50,000 donums (16,666 acres) of 'crown land' and convert it into an enormous colony or series of colonies partly Arab and partly Jewish to act as a sort of permanent 'defence force' for the protection of the works: He regards this as an indispensable preliminary to any large expenditure of capital on the Jordan scheme.[166]

But the Colonial Office found the idea was politically unacceptable. In August 1921, Deedes reported to the Colonial Office that 'a good deal of attention was being paid to questions of land', that the Rutenberg scheme was strongly opposed by the Arabic press, and that the acquisition of land by the Jews was being watched with interest and 'some misgivings'.[167]

The Arabic newspaper *Filastin* wrote in October 1921 that the owners of the land where Rutenberg aimed to build his project were opposed to any Zionist project, even if there were benefits to be derived from it, because the Rutenberg project, as they saw it, was a means of destroying them. Rutenberg was a Zionist who was

> saturated with the ideals of Zionism and Jewish colonization and intent on killing the nationalist Arab movement in Palestine. He is animated by the spirit of Herzl and echoes Weizmann and Jabotinsky and Zangwill and other Zionist leaders who make no secret of the necessity of driving the Palestine Arabs out of their land, and who do not hesitate to revert to any means of deception available to them. We have no hope in him who sings the song of hope [i.e. *hatikvah*]. We do not accept Zionism and Rutenberg's name makes us tremble in fear, for he is intent on taking our land and aims at destroying us and getting hold of our resources and denying us everything that is rightfully ours ... If Rutenberg succeeds in getting this concession he will decide our destiny and do to us whatever he pleases.[168]

The Arabic newspaper *al-Sabah* conceded that the 'poor light of lamps with glory and freedom is better than electric light with oppression and degradation'.[169]

The Rutenberg Concession was signed in September 1921, and the Ghor Mudawwara, or Beisan Agreement, was signed in November, one month later. Samuel claimed that the settlement of the complicated Ghor land was a 'matter of great satisfaction', and that it was regarded 'as evidence of the Government's impartiality and desire to uphold the rights of the peasants'.[170] He emphasized to the Colonial Office that the settlement of 'two outstanding political events', the Beisan land question and the religious *awqaf*, had created a good impression and convinced the Muslims 'of the good intentions of the Government'.[171]

Samuel subsequently wrote to Churchill that the 'only State land disposed of by way of sale was a large area in the northern end of the Jordan valley [referring to Beisan], which has for many years been in the possession of Arabs who cultivated it. Owing to tribal disputes, Sultan 'Abdul Hamid had expropriated the land in 1881.' In 'recognizing these rights', the administration had agreed to sell to the cultivators their holdings at 150 piastres[172] per dunum for irrigable land and 125 piastres for non-irrigable land, spread over fifteen years.[173] Samuel wrote in August that the area in question, which amounted to 800,000 dunums, covered some of the most favoured land in Palestine, and was 'particularly suitable' for Jewish settlement, but that 'nevertheless, the Palestine Government had made it over to the cultivators', who, in his opinion 'had no legal right to this land whatsoever'.[174]

In April 1925, the Arabic newspaper *al-Karmel* drew attention to the fact that the government intended to alter or give a new explanation to Article 16 of the Beisan Agreement, in an attempt to facilitate the sale of land to Jews before a title deed (*tapu*) was registered. Article 16 stated:

> As from the date of this Agreement, all persons entitled under its provisions as transferees shall be deemed to be owners of Miri lands, and subject to the Laws relating to such lands, and free to exercise all the rights and privileges relative to the owners of Miri land, such as the planting of trees and the erection of buildings on the land transferred to them; provided that no disposition, except by way of mortgage to the Government or of succession shall be made until the whole transfer price (Badal Taweeb) has been paid.[175]

Al-Karmel commented that this was a step which would enable the Zionists to buy large tracts of land in easy instalments for fifteen years, adding: 'we took the Beisan Agreement in good faith but now we hope that the government will not go back on its word and facilitate Jewish acquisition of the Ghor after the Jews bought most of Marj Ibn Amer [Jezreel valley].'[176] In its issue of 26 August 1925, *al-Karmel* pointed out that the title deeds for Beisan lands had not been registered after the agreement was signed, and that the administration was demanding the *werko* tax (tax on immovable property) which was paid by owners of the land who held title deeds. If the peasants in Beisan still held no title deeds, how could they be expected to pay the *werko* tax?[177]

In the final analysis, the administration seems to have succeeded in helping Jewish land purchasing companies in acquiring land in Beisan. This was achieved by converting *miri* land into privately owned land. Jewish acquisitions of the Beisan lands would have virtually been impossible had this land remained in the *miri* category.[178] Samuel knew well that *miri* land could not be disposed of at will at all, but devolved according to the Ottoman Law of Succession of 27 February 1328, unlike *mulk* land, which could be disposed of at will.[179] Most agricultural (*miri*) land in Palestine was cultivated under a system known as *musha'*, in which land collectively owned by the village was periodically redistributed between cultivators. It was often said that the system discouraged investment and changes in farming methods because most farmers lacked the interest to improve land which might be taken from them. The system of *ifraz*, or the partitioning of *musha'* land into individually owned parcels, was not effectively implemented during the mandate, as the government was keen on avoiding the impression that the legal implementation of *ifraz* would be perceived by the Palestine Arabs as an 'intentional British effort to make blocks of land available to Jewish purchasers'.[180] *Ifraz* was nevertheless put into practice in Beisan, the vital area where the Rutenberg project was to be set up.

Although Samuel's policy regarding Beisan was not immediately felt, land in Beisan did in the end find its way to Jewish buyers. Kenneth Stein asserts that Jews started actively buying land in Beisan as early as 1922, and that the Beisan lands gradually came into Jewish possession in the 1930s.[181] Stein argues that 'some tenants received areas far in excess of the amount they could cultivate themselves', and that some hired additional agricultural labourers, while others 'preferred to sell their excess land to Jewish purchasers even though it was in direct contravention of Article 16 of the Beisan Agreement'.[182]

The Jezreel Valley Land Sales

The Jewish National Fund's land-buying policy in the 1920s concentrated on particular regions and on the acquisition of large and continuous blocks of land. According to Avraham Granovsky, who later became managing director of the JNF from 1934–45, post-war purchases were made 'almost exclusively in the Valley of Jezreel, a district of great geographic importance, whose soil is accounted the most fertile in Palestine'.[183]

For example, the largest transaction of 1921 was the purchase by the Jewish National Fund and the Palestine Land Development Company of seven villages in the Galilee, the area of which comprised 62,634 dunums.[184] These transactions, which took place between 1921 and 1925, represented approximately 240,000 dunums out of the total area held by absentee landlords, which has been estimated at about 500,000 dunums.[185]

The Jezreel Valley land sales had particular significance as the first which were made to official Jewish agencies during the mandate, setting a precedent for dealing with tenants' compensation under the British mandate. According to Kenneth Stein, they also proved how tenants' rights could be easily circumvented 'under the pliant eye of subdistrict officials'.[186] Immediately after the promulgation of the first Land Transfer Ordinance in September 1920, the Palestine Land Development Company resumed negotiating the purchase of lands in the Jezreel Valley, which had been under discussion with Jewish buyers since Ottoman times.[187] The land was bought from absentee landlords (primarily the Lebanese Sursock family), mostly by the Jewish National Fund and the American Zionist Commonwealth. The largest transaction in 1921 consisted of seven villages in the Galilee district, and during 1924 and 1925, many more villages in the same area found their way to Jewish hands. The land bought comprised twenty-two villages; all their inhabitants had to quit. Michael F. Abcarius, senior assistant treasurer in the administration, writing many years later, noted that the Land Transfer Ordinance (1921) prohibited land sales without the government's approval. However, the government's consent was granted 'in pursuance of the national home policy, regardless of the fate of the cultivators'.[188] John Ruedy,[189] argues that these evictions were 'technically illegal' under the terms of the Land Transfer Ordinance, and that the enormous Jewish National Fund purchases in the Jezreel Valley and elsewhere evicted thousands.[190]

In July 1924, Weizmann informed the colonial secretary, J. H. Thomas, that the Zionists were 'at present negotiating a considerable tract of land' in the Jezreel Valley, the importance of which lay in its close vicinity to the colonies established there two years previously.[191] However, in February 1925, a secret political report stated that these large purchases by Jews in the Galilee, amounting to 176,124 dunums,[192] were causing 'great dissatisfaction' among the Arabs.[193] The villages which changed hands in 1924 included five strategic villages with the lands attached to them: 'Afuleh, Shunem, Shatta, Khnayfis and Jabata, situated in the northern end of the Plain of Esdraelon (Jezreel Valley). Their combined population amounted to some 3,000 or 4,000 people. Since they paid tithes to the banking firm Sursock in Beirut, the government deemed them tenants. In a memorandum entitled 'Creating the Jewish National Home in Palestine: the five villages', Colonel Bramley, a former director of public security in Palestine (1921–23), gave an account of the transfer of these villages and the consequences for their tenants.[194] Bramley pointed out that, although the Land Transfer Ordinance decreed that no transfer of land should be registered until the government was 'satisfied that in the case of agricultural land, either the person transferring the property, if he is in possession, or the tenant in occupation if the property is leased, will retain sufficient land in the district or elsewhere, for the maintenance of himself and his family', this was 'no easy matter to be settled offhand for there was hardly to be found a score of consecutive acres in the country which were not already owned by somebody'.[195]

Although the absentee landlord might be free to sell the land, he was not free to sell the villages, for the houses were the absolute property of the peasants, 'who have built them and lived in them from generation to generation down through the centuries'. After the lands in question were sold, the population of the five villages could not remain in their homes without land to cultivate, and therefore the terms of the ordinance as to the provision of sufficient land for their maintenance became of great importance, especially as it was decreed, by the government, that this question must be settled before registration could be made. In the case of 'Afuleh, for instance, which was situated on a strategic position on the main railway line from Haifa to Damascus, and where the inhabitants numbered about 100 families, about a quarter seem to have accepted compensation, receiving between 5 and 20 Egyptian pounds according to family size. However, the majority refused to

accept cash compensation, saying 'these houses are ours in virtue of ancestral inheritance, our dead lie buried here, we do not wish to move'.

The government made repeated offers of land 'elsewhere', all of which were
refused by the peasants on the grounds that the land offered also belonged to
Sursock, and that what was his today might belong to the Jews tomorrow. Another
reason was that the land offered was already being cultivated by other peasants,
who would resent the influx of newcomers. In addition, on the land to be provided
'elsewhere', no houses were available for them to live in. When matters reached an
impasse, the question was taken up by the Supreme Muslim Council, who made
certain proposals to the government as a solution. Bramley reported that the Supreme Muslim Council and the government were in complete agreement on one
point: that to give cash compensation to individual peasants was 'fundamentally
unsound' and was no way out of the difficulty. The Supreme Muslim Council
pointed out that the peasant, 'never having known what it means to be without a
roof over his head' would take the money, spend it right away, only to awaken to
the fact that he had become homeless. Bramley noted: 'To pay compensation in
cash to such helpless people is simply to create vagabonds, and vagabondage in its
turn, creates criminals.' The proposals of the Supreme Muslim Council were directed at finding 'a remedy which should enable the uprooted peasants, if uprooted
they must be, to remain respectable and self-respecting citizens of Palestine'. Since,
as Bramley pointed out, 'the inevitable corollary of the sale of the land to Jews
involves the removal of the Arabs from the villages', and compensation must be
made in some form or the other, the Supreme Muslim Council suggested that it
should be paid to a trustee, or a board of trustees, to be used in securing for the
deportees houses to live in and land to cultivate.

In Shunem, one of the villages in question, the peasants had a certain amount of
land registered in their name, and this gave them the legal right of pre-emption
over the rest of the village land. Bramley noted that, under the circumstances, it
was morally as well as legally right to have paid compensation to the four villages
to be spent in the purchase of Shunem lands, and in this way the terms of the
ordinance to 'maintain' tenants would have been met without 'too great a disloca-
tion of the peasant life in Palestine'. Therefore, a resolution was put forward by the
Supreme Muslim Council, and its lawyer was authorized to present it to the government. However, Bramley reported that before it was possible for him to do so,
the transfer was 'rushed through and the transaction registered'. Registration had
thus taken place regardless of the fact that the needs of the majority of Arab peasants had not been met. The explanation of the government was that since the Arabs
refused the offer of land 'elsewhere', they had 'forfeited' all rights to any further
consideration at the hands of government officials.

Bramley cited the official communiqué on the events which followed, dated 30
November 1924:

Dispute arose early in the morning of the 28th of November between Arab cultivators and a party of Jews who were starting ploughing operations on the land recently acquired by them in the neighbourhood of 'Afuleh village. Stones were thrown and during the fight which ensued an Arab was hit at close quarters by a revolver shot and died almost immediately. About eight Jews and two Arabs were slightly wounded by stones. The police and a doctor from Nazareth arrived on the scene immediately after the incident and enquiries are being prosecuted vigorously as to the origin of the fight and to ascertain by whom the single revolver shot was fired.

A second official communiqué issued the same day stated:

As it has been established quite clearly that the land which the Jews began ploughing at 'Afuleh last Friday is Jewish land belonging officially to the American Zionist Commonwealth, the Authorities have promised to take the necessary steps to render it possible for the Jews to resume work today.[196]

Bramley wrote that for several days following, 'the Jews were protected by the presence of the police, while the Arabs watched the Jews at work on the land prepared by them during the previous months'.

The importance which the Zionists attached to the 'Afuleh affair was described in an article in *New Palestine* on 19 December 1924 in which Bernard Rosenblatt wrote that after a 'long and arduous struggle' for 'Afuleh, it was finally won on 23 October 1924, and that on the same day there were celebrations in the Jewish settlement of Balfouria. The Zionist newspaper held that 'Afuleh was a 'small insignificant village' on the way between Haifa and Tiberias, but it was situated in such a strategic position that the Haifa-Damascus railway had established a station there. Rosenblatt claimed that as long as 'Afuleh remained Arab, 'the small Jewish colonies were cut off from possible growth to the south, east and west'. To the north, they were restricted by the ancient city of Nazareth. 'Afuleh was 'the spearpoint among the small but growing Jewish settlements ... With 'Afuleh in Jewish hands there is the possibility of consolida[ting] the entire region'.

Bramley asked: 'Can it be that the British people and the League of Nations will silently watch the Jewish National Home being built on the blood of the Arabs slain by Jewish bullets in the process?' He also drew attention to a large meeting which had been held in Liverpool on 7 December 1924, at which Dr Weizmann said that he was proud to say that in their work since the Balfour Declaration, it was 'impossible to find a single act committed which would or could be interpreted as damaging to the other peoples in Palestine'. Bramley ended his memorandum by asking: 'Did he not know of the Afuleh "incident" when he spoke?'[197]

Zionist discourse at that time insisted publicly that creating a national home for the Jews in Palestine did not imply that the Arabs would be dispossessed at any future date. However, as Caplan notes, in dealing with such a sensitive subject, 'the researcher is often faced with the problem of distinguishing between what was "really" believed and what was said or written for the requirements of good public relations'. True Zionist intentions were often deliberately concealed, accusations of dispossession and expropriation were emphatically denied, and Yishuv leaders often made reassuring statements that Jewish intentions were 'peaceful, constructive and would bring benefit to the Arabs'.[198] There were other occasions, however, when the Zionists revealed their true intentions in public. When Weizmann was asked at the Paris Peace Conference in 1919 what he meant by a Jewish national home, his frequently quoted reply was that there should ultimately be such conditions in Palestine that 'Palestine should be just as Jewish as America was American, or England was English'. Indeed, as Ronald Storrs noted: 'What was the Arab to believe?'[199]

In similar vein, the chairman of the political committee of the English Zionist Federation wrote to the Colonial Office in June 1924, drawing attention to 'certain inaccuracies and mis-statements' which he said had appeared in a memorandum circulated to members of parliament by the National Political League.[200] The Zionist leader stated that the covering letter of the National Political League began by declaring that 'the policy of giving up their country to become the national home of the Jews is in principle a grave injustice to the Arabs'. He went on to say:

> There is no such policy. No suggestion has ever been made that the Arabs should 'give up their country' or that they should be in any way dispossessed or disturbed for the benefit of the Jewish National Home.

Referring to the latest land sales in the Jezreel Valley, he claimed that: 'Such lands as have been acquired for Jewish settlements, have been acquired from willing sellers in the open market at exceptionally high prices, and with the fullest protection for any sitting tenants.'[201] However, because of the continuing evictions of Arab peasants during that year, an Arab company was established in 1924 to buy Arab land which would otherwise be sold to Jews.[202]

'ECONOMIC ZIONISM' AND ITS EFFECTS

That the battle between the Zionists and the Palestine Arabs was to a large extent an economic one had become increasingly evident by the mid-1920s. As early as 1920, the Palin Report claimed that it was as an economic competitor that the Jew really inspired the 'profoundest alarm' in the minds of the Arabs, who saw that 'where the Jew became a landed proprietor, the Arab and Christian *fellah* peasant proprietor was reduced to the position of a wage labourer. The prospect of extensive Jewish immigration fills him with fear.'[203]

The American consul in Jerusalem observed, in the aftermath of the Fifth Palestine Arab Congress in 1922, that not until the Arabs could get together on a sound economic basis, with capable leadership, could they ever hope to make their majority in numbers felt from a political point of view.[204] In the same month, a senior member of the Colonial Office, Eric Mills, remarked that the Jews

> inevitably had to face the problem of an Arab population the subjugation of which was not complete. In these days subjugation may be affected in many ways and I suppose it is ever-present to Zionists, professing a maximum programme, that economic means may effect what political means could not.[205]

Samuel confirmed to the Colonial Office that much of the industrial and agricultural development was being done by Jewish capital and labour, and 'almost all economic activity' was Jewish. For the Jewish community to grow, a growth which he believed was 'certain to take place in time, with the expansion of industry and the increase of cultivation', what was needed was capital, enterprise and additional supplies of labour. He emphasized that it was the Jews, 'and the Jews alone, who are able and willing to supply all three'.[206]

Towards the end of 1923, the district governor of Haifa, G. S. Symes, reported that a sense of 'despondency almost of despair in regard to the immediate economical outlook', especially in respect of agriculture, was growing in Palestine. With a few exceptions, the *fallahin* in his district were 'more indebted than ever', were finding it 'very difficult (sometimes impossible) to obtain cash' to pay their taxes, and could see 'no good prospects of easier, more prosperous times ahead of them'.[207] They had become convinced over the past few years that cereals—a staple cultivation in Palestine—was no longer profitable, and the question of what alternative crops should be introduced was 'beyond their own capacity and energy to solve'. A direct consequence of anti-government agitation was that the Arab population was being persuaded that its disabilities were 'remediable' and that if the government had not 'deliberately created' them, it was nevertheless disinclined to remove them for political reasons. Symes explained:

> To quote the propaganda in its crudest form 'the Arab population has been deliberately impoverished to serve the needs of Zionist policy and Jewish penetration into the country'. It will be said that a propaganda based on such false premises will fail in its effect. I agree that this is true ultimately; but immediately, and coinciding with a period of economic stress, it has affected the psychology of the people and their despondency is heavily saturated with suspicion of malign motives by the Government.[208]

The Arabic press also came to realize the key role of what it called 'economic Zionism' as a necessary precondition for Zionist political predominance in Palestine.[209]

Concern over the economic situation prompted an Arab Economic Conference in February 1923 to study the state of affairs and devise remedies.[210] The Conference passed 'moderate feasible decisions', which included, inter alia, the abolition

of the *werko* tax (the Ottoman tax on all immovable property), and the tithe (or
'ushur which was the tax on the gross produce of the soil), and demanded: the
establishment of an agricultural school; the reopening of the Agricultural Bank;
the improvement of roads; the prevention of land sales when the land in question
was less than 200 dunums; and the cessation of gambling, which had become widespread. The government, however, did nothing to alleviate the situation.[211] Jamal
al-Husseini pointed out in his speech that had the administration really been willing to consider the interests of the people of the country, it would have executed
these decisions and helped the conference. The government had merely sent a 'nonsensical' reply and even increased the taxes on some necessities. In Arab eyes, this
was only natural because the administration was applying a 'fixed policy based on
other than Palestine Arab interests'. The secretary of the Arab Executive Committee concluded: 'Should we pay taxes with the existence of this policy?'[212] (See
Appendix H)

How far, then, did Samuel's policy in Palestine honour the double pledge: that
of facilitating Jewish immigration and contributing to the development of the Jewish economy, while at the same time 'protecting' Arab rights? And how did he
actually translate these words in his policy? In his interim report on his first year
in office, Samuel had conceded:

> To install the Jews in Palestine might mean the expulsion of the Arabs. If there were
> an unlimited Jewish immigration and finally a Jewish majority in the population,
> how could the safeguards embodied in the second half of the Declaration be en-
> forced? ... This is not to say that Jewish immigration is to involve Arab emigration,
> that the greater prosperity of the country, through the development of Jewish en-
> terprises, is to be at the expense, and not to the benefit of the Arabs, that the use of
> Hebrew is to imply the disappearance of Arabic, that the establishment of elected
> Councils in the Jewish Community for the control of its affairs is to be followed by
> the subjection of the Arabs to the rule of those Councils. In a word, the degree to
> which Jewish national aspirations can be fulfilled in Palestine is conditioned by the
> rights of the present inhabitants.[213]

Eight years later, in the aftermath of the 1929 uprising, a commission of inquiry headed by Sir John Hope-Simpson looked into the economic consequences
of the Jewish national home policy and found that its impact had been detrimental
to the Arabs.[214]

To sum up, after making the necessary provisions for land and immigration, as
well as Palestinian citizenship, in order to give Jewish immigrants the right to vote
in the Legislative Council as well as in Municipal Councils, Samuel forged ahead
with promoting the economic development of Palestine through Jewish financiers.
In this preoccupation he had a single purpose: the promotion of the economy so
that the country could support an ever increasing number of Jewish settlers.

Conclusion

Herbert Samuel's understanding of the 'double pledge' contained in the Balfour Declaration and the Mandate for Palestine was shaped by his single-minded commitment to the Zionist cause which prevented him from interpreting and applying the pledge in a way that would have secured Arab rights. Samuel was not impartial, and his understanding of the establishment of a Jewish national home was neither moderate nor cautious, as implied in the wording of these two documents.

Samuel believed in the ultimate establishment of a Jewish state. He cooperated closely with Chaim Weizmann, the president of the Zionist Organization, and when he applied policies such as the temporary suspension of immigration following the 1921 disturbances in Jaffa, which caused an outcry among the extreme Zionists in Palestine, he did so in the best interests of Zionism itself. He was keenly aware that to attempt too much too soon might wreck the whole experiment in its infancy. Indeed his gradualist approach was itself a crucial element in the growth of the Zionist movement.

Samuel's one virtue, as this book has shown, was consistency. This can be seen in the 1915 Cabinet memorandum in which he advocated a Jewish state in Palestine under British protection; in his efforts to secure the Balfour Declaration in 1917; in his hostility to applying the principle of self-determination in Palestine (the King-Crane Commission of Inquiry in 1919), and in his hostile stand against Faisal, who at that time was a symbol of the emerging Arab nationalism.

Moreover, Samuel was directly involved in ending the military administration in Palestine, which was bound by the Hague Conventions of 1899 and 1907, and which had maintained the *status quo* of the country, thus blocking extreme Zionist interpretations of the Balfour Declaration. Knowing that the military administration could not be won to the Zionist cause, Samuel suggested that it be informed that the Balfour Declaration was a *chose jugée*, and that there was no way of reversing it. When Lloyd George offered him the post of high commissioner in Palestine during the San Remo Conference in April 1920, Samuel accepted after consulting with Weizmann, who strongly urged him to take the office on the

grounds that it was in the best interest of the Zionists that the military administration should be immediately brought to an end and replaced by a civil one. The
transition from a military to a civil administration with a sympathetic Zionist administrator was vital to the Zionist cause, still in its infancy.

Not only did the Mandate for Palestine incorporate the Balfour Declaration in
its text,[1] but also, by giving concrete meaning and direction to what was no more
than a letter of intent, it went far beyond it. Although Article 22 of the Covenant of
the League of Nations denied immediate independence to the people of Palestine
and other dependent territories by stipulating that they were 'not yet able to stand
by themselves under the strenuous conditions of the modern world',[2] it did recognize them as having an international status. Moreover, states administering those
territories bore certain responsibilities, and the condition of tutelage was only temporary. The League divided mandated territories into three classes. Class A mandates
were the closest to independence, and Class C were farthest from it. Former territories of the Ottoman Empire, including Palestine, were designated as Class A
mandates, which, according to paragraph 4 of Article 22 of the Covenant of the
League of Nations, were defined as those whose 'existence as independent nations
can be provisionally recognized'.[3] Furthermore, in 1947, the United Nations Special Committee on Palestine stated that the mandate system gave 'international
recognition' to self-determination. In 1971, the International Court of Justice asserted that the mandatory powers had no right of sovereignty but that people
under the mandate held ultimate sovereignty.[4] Therefore, from a legal standpoint,
the role of Britain was to prepare the people of Palestine for full independence.

The inclusion of the Balfour Declaration in the mandate was incompatible with
Article 22 of the Covenant of the League, and it changed its focus and goal away
from the principle of self-determination. The Palestinians thus never accepted the
mandate as it violated their national rights. It was also because of the Balfour Declaration that the phrase 'self-governing institutions' was made to apply only to
Jews, whereas, according to Article 22 of the Covenant, it was in fact meant to
prepare the Arab people of Palestine for independence.

This book has argued that Samuel's application of the mandate went even further than its declared aims and intentions. In the political sphere, Samuel's policy
was to block Palestinian Arab national aspirations for independence, first, by systematically refusing to recognize the elected representatives of the Palestine Arabs
(the Arab Executive Committee, and the Muslim-Christian Associations); second,
by taking advantage of their leaders' antagonisms, with the intention of weakening and dividing their nationalist movement, and third, by giving them control
only over their religious affairs by establishing the 'Supreme Muslim Council',
instead of preparing them for self-government, as the mandate stipulated.[5]

Official policy, both in Jerusalem and in London, was clearly to divide the Arab
front by encouraging a small faction to split the nationalists in such a way as to

enable Samuel and the Middle East Department to claim that the Arab Executive Committee did not represent the whole population. Samuel's manoeuvres also succeeded in calling into question the representative character of the Arab Delegation in London during 1921. This course of action did not differ from—in fact complemented—Zionist policy, which aimed at weakening the Arab movement from within. By promoting the 'Moderate Party', and thus exploiting family feuds and differences between the Arab political elite, Samuel played one side off against the other.

The founding of the new Arab National Party, and the schism in Arab ranks from late 1923 until the end of Samuel's term in 1925, weakened the Arab nationalist movement. Although 'nationalistic', the Arab National Party opposed the policies of the Arab Executive Committee as well as those of the Muslim-Christian Association, and sought to achieve its ends through co-operation with the government rather than opposition. This took place at a time when greater unity, not the formation of new parties, might have effectively challenged the Zionist threat. The new party was considered to be pro-British although its programme was similar to that of the Arab Executive Committee. Indeed, even some British officials in Palestine wondered why there should be two parties at all since both pursued the same objects.

By restricting the Palestinian Arab organization to religious affairs, Samuel prevented Arab leaders from exercising and developing their authority in the crucial political, economic and social fields. Throughout the rest of the British Mandate in Palestine, until 1948, and in the absence of any other officially recognized political authority, this institution eventually—as it was bound to—assumed a political role in the struggle against Zionism. The creation of the 'Supreme Muslim Council' as an alleged institution of self-government adds little to Samuel's credit, for two reasons: first, because he prepared the Jews for political ascendancy, and second, because he had no option but to recognize such a religious authority, for had he denied the Muslims this small measure of religious autonomy on *awqaf* and Muslim religious affairs, Samuel was well aware that he would have risked a full-scale revolt.

Conversely, to the Jewish community, which at that time constituted about 7 per cent of the population, Samuel offered wide powers of autonomy, including the power to levy taxes. This small community was, by such measures, given a 'juridical personality', while the Palestinian Arabs, the overwhelming majority in Palestine, were treated and referred to by Samuel as the 'non-Jewish inhabitants', and the 'other sections of the population', and thus dealt with as a minority. Moreover, Samuel fully recognized the Jewish National Assembly, the Va'ad Leumi—which later became the Israeli Knesset—as the official elected representative of the Jewish community. His most important and far-reaching contribution to the eventual political ascendancy of the Jewish community in Palestine was, however, the Jewish Community Ordinance, which although officially announced in 1928 was his brainchild. In laying plans for the Ordinance, he violated the clear instructions of the Colonial Office to the effect that the measure was unacceptable, and went ahead with his own agenda to further the Zionist cause. This was calculated to block the road to Palestinian self-determination, and to pave the way for Jewish political supremacy in Palestine once the Jews had achieved their numerical supremacy through organized immigration.

It can therefore be concluded that Samuel's understanding of the pledge in the mandate to develop the 'self-governing institutions' was one-sided: it was to be applied only in case of the Jewish minority. Jewish 'self-governing' institutions were encouraged and nurtured, and those of the Palestinians were obstructed and weakened.

In the economic sphere, Samuel pursued a policy which would have led only to the economic supremacy of the Jewish population. Even when he raised the slogan of 'economic absorptive capacity' in regulating immigration following the out-break of violence in Jaffa in May 1921, at a time when Jewish unemployment was rife, he meant the absorptive capacity of the Jewish community itself, and not the economic ability of the country as a whole to support the influx of immigrants.

There is no question that the ultimate aim of Zionism was to change the demo-graphic picture in Palestine so that, as Samuel had prophetically written in 1915, in the course of time, the Jewish inhabitants, grown into a majority, and settled on the land, 'may be given such degree of self-government as the conditions of that day might justify'. He saw that this could only be achieved through organized immigration, and the rules he set for organizing immigration were certainly in line with his original vision. When he was attacked by Zionists for imposing tem-porary restrictions on immigration in June 1921, (albeit for a period of one month), he himself declared that this was in the best interest of the Zionist cause, and that if he had not placed such restrictions, the Zionists would have borne the embar-rassment themselves and would have asked for restrictions on immigration.

In the sphere of land legislation, Samuel adopted all possible means to make 'state and waste lands' available to Jewish settlers. Since there was no vacant land in Palestine to support the influx of settlers, Samuel, with the help of his legal secretary Norman Bentwich, manipulated Ottoman land laws to achieve his goals. This policy contributed to the creation of a landless class of Palestinian tenant farmers who had clear legal rights under Ottoman law, but because of Samuel's land policy became liable to eviction from their land by court orders. Moreover, thousands of tenant farmers, who had worked on land owned by absentee land-lords, were evicted from their land during Samuel's term in office.

In order to implement his policies effectively in the political and economic spheres, not to mention those of land and immigration, Samuel chose his staff carefully. His administration was seen by the Palestine Arabs, and by many British officials on the spot, as well as the British Army in Palestine, as a Zionist administration camouflaged as British.

Together Samuel's measures reflect a remarkable degree of consistency in the pursuit of a single aim, namely to see a Jewish state established in Palestine, regardless of the interests and national aspirations of the Arab population, as well as a remarkable deviation from the so-called impartiality conventionally attributed to him. Samuel may have paid lip service to Arab rights, and was at times extraordinarily sensitive in his public statements to Arab criticism. His words, however, were not supported by his deeds.

On the other hand, when the Mandate for Palestine came under a heavy attack in the British parliament in June 1922 because of its strong Zionist bias, Samuel was instrumental in drawing up the policy of the White Paper in June 1922, which was the first official written interpretation of the Balfour Declaration. Although it did not meet Arab demands by reversing its pro-Zionist policy, the White Paper nevertheless asserted that the British government did not contemplate the disappearance of the Arabs, or their national or cultural existence in Palestine, and placed severe limits on what the national home meant, making it clear that a totally Jewish Palestine was out of the question. And yet, in order to allay Zionist fears, the White Paper 'reaffirmed' the Balfour Declaration, thus reaffirming the inherent ambiguity and ambivalence in that document. By asserting that Jews were in Palestine 'as of right and not on sufferance', Samuel went a further step in adopting Zionist arguments and gave them an additional powerful tool to further their most extreme interpretation of the Balfour Declaration.

Equally important, this statement of policy played the role of palliative to the British parliament itself, and was meant to pave the way, on the international level, for the ratification of the mandate by the League of Nations. The statement, furthermore, guided the British government until 1929, when Palestine witnessed another eruption of violence against the Jews. Samuel's statements to the effect that he was committed to the cause of protecting the welfare and the well-being of the Arabs were therefore no more than tactical manoeuvres designed, firstly, to conciliate the Arabs by making concessions over trifles in order to render them amenable in matters essential to the achievement of Zionist aims; secondly, to mislead the international community, and, thirdly, to pacify those British politicians who were opposed to Zionist policy in Palestine.

When the mandate was ratified by the League of Nations in July 1922, the Palestine Arabs rejected it, as well as the Constitution, (the Palestine Order-in-Council 1922), because it was based on the Balfour Declaration. In protest, the Arabs boycotted the elections to the Legislative Council, which the Order-in-Council had called for. By doing so, they made it clear that they had not made peace with Zionism, either directly or indirectly, and that to accept a Constitution based on the Balfour Declaration amounted to a sentence of death on the Palestinian people.

However, the boycott of the elections, a purely negative measure, was ineffective because it was not accompanied by other, more positive, actions such as civil disobedience and the non-payment of taxes. Measures of this kind had been contemplated by the Arab leaders, but could not be effectively carried out due to disorganization, as well as internal disagreements. At this juncture, and in desperation, a small section of Palestinian leaders turned to the Wahhabis of Najd, since they saw in this religious movement the only means left open to them against the Zionist threat. Just as the Zionist movement appealed to ancient religious sentiments as a propaganda weapon among world Jewry, so the struggle against Zionism re-ignited strong religious feelings among some Palestinian Muslims.

When, in July 1922, the Palestine Arabs rejected the mandate on the grounds that it was a danger to their national existence, their leaders missed an important opportunity by failing to submit their case to the Permanent Court of International Justice, as the Covenant of the League stipulated. Since the obligation of the mandatory was to supervise and improve the conditions and the material well-being of the mandated territories; since the British government was the trustee under the mandate 'for the happiness of the people of Palestine', and since the mandate was a *sacred trust* of civilization until such time as the mandated peoples were able 'to stand alone', any dispute arising over the application of the mandate could be submitted to an arbitral tribunal and might come before the Permanent Court of International Justice. Moreover, the Covenant of the League of Nations included a clear provision that the wishes of the people must be consulted in the selection of the mandatory power.

While the Arabs wrote protests and petitions, the Jews went ahead with the task of organizing an underground army. Even in this sphere, it has been shown that Samuel played a decisive role in allowing the arming and training of the Jewish community in Palestine without the knowledge of the international community under whose trust Palestine was placed, and in flagrant violation of the terms of the mandate itself.

Finally, in placing the onus of later developments in Palestine on British policy, it would be a mistake to consider this policy as having had at any point a monolithic structure. There were certain forces within the British government who were strongly opposed to official policy, and who consistently warned of the futility of such a pro-Zionist line. First, Lord Curzon, as a member of the British Cabinet, and later as foreign secretary, stood firmly against the Balfour Declaration and pointed out that the Mandate for Palestine was a Zionist document, written by Zionists and for Zionists, which would render the Arabs 'hewers of wood and drawers of water'. He made it clear to Balfour in 1920, during the San Remo Conference, that he would apply the Balfour Declaration in its most limited sense and he objected to the insertion in the draft mandate of the phrase concerning the Jewish 'historic connection' to Palestine, which, he declared, he would not be responsible for allowing. He admitted later that this phrase was nevertheless inserted without his knowledge. Second, the House of Lords strongly opposed the government's pro-Zionist policy, as did many Conservative MPs, especially in the period 1922–23. Third, the British press, throughout the period under study, strongly attacked Zionist activities in Palestine. Finally, the military establishment—before and after 1920—was strongly anti-Zionist, and frequently alerted the British government to the dangers of supporting the movement. However, these warnings went largely unheeded.

The decision to continue a pro-Zionist policy, regardless of the consequences for the Palestine Arabs, was the result of the efforts of a small number of officials in the Middle East Department of the Colonial Office, where Weizmann was a regular visitor, and where he exerted considerable influence. Whether this policy was in the best interests of Britain in the region is open to question. The answer may be seen, in the light of later developments, to be negative.

In his relations with the Middle East Department of the Colonial Office, Samuel was less amenable to guidance than an ordinary British colonial governor would have been. Considering Weizmann's special relations with the Middle East Department, Samuel's own relationship with it was in general harmonious. Nevertheless, on some occasions, when the Middle East Department thought Samuel's course of action went far beyond the policy of the mandate, he defied the clear instructions of the Colonial Office and acted on his own initiative. This can be seen from the way he dealt with the issue of the Jewish Community Ordinance which gave wide powers of representation to the Jewish community.

The transfer of responsibility for Palestine from the Foreign to the Colonial Office in 1921, at a time when the draft mandate was still being revised, proved to be detrimental for Palestine and had far reaching effects. Curzon, the foreign secretary, had always made clear that implementation of the Balfour Declaration would be as restricted and as limited as possible. By contrast, the Middle East Department solicited Weizmann's views on a regular basis, especially on matters of immigration and land, the two most important elements for the success of the Zionist project. On other important matters concerning the Jewish national home, Weizmann and Samuel acted as a team. In this way, the policy drawn up by Zionists was, in the final analysis, the one that bounced back to Samuel from the Middle East Department.

When Britain became increasingly cool towards Zionist aspirations, especially during 1922–23, after the fall of Lloyd George's government and the coming to power of a new Conservative government, Weizmann managed to convince British statesmen and politicians that the Balfour Declaration, which many had come to regard as a political mistake, meant much more than originally intended. Shuckburgh and the Middle East Department maintained this view and asserted that the Balfour Declaration was a closed issue, a *'chose jugée'*, a term first coined by Samuel.

Shuckburgh was convinced that Britain was bound to uphold the policy embodied in the Balfour Declaration, constantly insisting at the same time that this policy would *not* lead to a Jewish state. Though his beliefs were certainly genuine, for he was not a Zionist himself, Shuckburgh was without doubt manipulated by Weizmann, whose omnipresence at the Middle East Department promoted the Zionist cause and influenced British officials. Shuckburgh often commented that it was difficult to preserve a cool head 'in the face of Weizmann's pleadings and Stein's heroics'.

Among the tactics that the Middle East Department employed to keep Britain's pro-Zionist policy on course when domestic opposition to it was on the increase were: (i) it downplayed military reports from the British army in Palestine which warned of the futility of Zionist policy and directed attention to the injustice of this policy to Arabs; (ii) it refused to accept the representative character of Arab leaders and dealt harshly with them while, at the same time, there was a constant flow of information from the Middle East Department to Zionists; (iii) it prevented Arab leaders, upon Samuel's advice, from putting their case to the high level Cabinet Committee which met in June 1923 to decide the future of Palestine, and (iv) it made new interpretations of the Balfour Declaration, as well as McMahon's pledge to Sharif Hussein in 1915, which put both documents in a new light to suit Zionist interests. Thus, on the strength of the 'moral argument', that if Britain failed to honour its pledge 'we certainly should stand convicted of an act of perfidy from which it is hardly too much to say that our good name would never recover', and that the real alternative facing the government would then be between 'complete evacuation [from Palestine] or continuing to honour the Zionist pledge', the colonial secretary was convinced—in spite of the fact that imperial strategists had defined Palestine as of no strategic importance to the British Empire—that Britain should not abandon its pro-Zionist policy.

The Balfour Declaration was the main point of contention between Arab leaders and the British government throughout the period under study and beyond. Whenever this issue was brought up, the British government emphasized to the Arabs that there was a 'misunderstanding' as to what Zionist policy really meant. It did not mean, according to British officials who implemented the Balfour Declaration in the crucial years in the early 1920s, the establishment of a Jewish state; it did not mean 'making Palestine as Jewish as England is English'; it did not mean the extinction of Arab culture and political rights. That, in the end, it meant all these things combined, and more, attests either to a Machiavellian diplomacy, or to an unjustified British naivety about real Zionist intentions. In either case, the mandatory power over Palestine, entrusted by the international community to administer the country to promote 'the well being and development of such peoples' as a 'sacred trust of civilization', has yet to be held answerable.

Notes

PREFACE

1. See, for instance, CO 733/ 54, Imperial Conference 1923. Secret, E 2nd Meeting (1923), 'Stenographic Notes of the Second Meeting Held at 10 Downing Street, S.W., On Wednesday, October 3, 1923. At 11 A.M'.

2. Bernard Wasserstein argues that Samuel, while being a devoted Zionist, was also an impartial administrator: *The British in Palestine: the Mandatory Government and the Arab-Jewish Conflict, 1917–1929* (London, 1991). See also, Bernard Wasserstein, *Herbert Samuel: A Political Life* (London, 1992).

3. *Palestine Royal Commission Report. Presented by the Secretary of State for the Colonies to Parliament by Command of His Majesty, July 1937*, Cmd. 5479 (hereafter Peel Report).

HISTORICAL PROLOGUE

1. This is directly derived from the title of a pamphlet written by Chaim Weizmann entitled *Palestine's Role in the Solution of the Jewish Problem*, published by the Jewish Agency for Palestine (London, 1942), p. 14.

2. This is not the place to dwell on these issues, but the interested reader might want to explore two ground-breaking books that deal with them: Keith Whitelam's *The Invention of Ancient Israel, the Silencing of Palestinian History*, (London and New York, 1996), and David Myers' *Re-Inventing the Jewish Past. European Jewish Intellectuals and the Zionist Return to History*, (Oxford, 1995). Whitelam demonstrates how the history of ancient Palestine has been obscured by the search for Israel, arguing that biblical scholarship, through its traditional view of the region, has contributed not only to the dispossession of Palestinian land but of Palestinian history as well. On the other hand, David Myers shows how a group of European Jewish scholars who settled in Jerusalem in the 1920s and 1930s forged ahead with the task of inventing a new collective identity for the new nation. Their intellectual home was the Institute of Jewish Studies at the Hebrew University.

3. In Britain too, the influx of Jews from Russia and Rumania since the early 1880s caused the British government to introduce the Aliens Bill of 1904. This was heavily attacked

by leaders of Anglo-Jewry, and was replaced by the Aliens Act of 1905 under Prime Minister A. J. Balfour. This too was received by the Jews of England with resentment, and Balfour was attacked by the *Jewish Chronicle* and by the Seventh Zionist Congress and charged with 'open anti-Semitism against the whole Jewish people'. See Oskar K. Rabinowicz, 'The Aliens Bill and Jewish Immigration to Britain 1902–1905', in Walid Khalidi (ed.), *From Haven to Conquest: Readings in Zionism and the Palestine Problem Until 1948* (Beirut, 1971), pp. 108-9, 112. At about the same time (1903) as the controversy revolving around legislating against aliens was in process, the British colonial secretary under Balfour, Joseph Chamberlain, offered al-Arish (a coastal town in Egypt close to the border between Sinai and Palestine) to Theodor Herzl for Jewish settlement, but the project came to nothing because of the refusal of Lord Cromer, the viceroy of Egypt, to provide Nile water for irrigation. See *The New Standard Jewish Encyclopedia*, (7th ed., NY & Oxford, 1992), p. 295. Twelve years after the 1905 Aliens Act, Balfour was to endorse the Zionist cause with his 'Balfour Declaration'.

4. In November 1903, Weizmann summarized the problem of anti-Semitism in a speech in which he stated that there was 'no remedy' for the distress of the present situation of Jews: 'We must tell the people this. The Jewish people are sitting on a volcano, and this position will continue to exist until an appalling disaster takes place ... And then, ultimately, the solution to the Jewish Question will be found. This only, unique, solution is that given by National Zionism: The revival of Israel in its historic land!' See *Chaim Weizmann Decade, 1952–1962*. The Weizmann Archives (Rehovot, Israel), p. 7. From a speech delivered at a student's meeting in Berne after the Sixth Zionist Congress (The Uganda Congress), November 1903.

5. Chaim Weizmann, *Trial and Error. The Autobiography of Chaim Weizmann*. (4th ed., London, 1950), p. 402.

6. See *The New Standard Jewish Encyclopedia*, p. 437. For a different perspective, see the brilliant analysis in Jacques Kornberg's, *Theodor Herzl, From Assimilation to Zionism* (Bloomington & Indianapolis, 1993). In this book, Kornberg explores Herzl's intellectual development and the reasons that led him to 'suddenly' become the founder of Zionism in the 1890s having been thus far a totally assimilated German nationalist.

7. For more see, David Vital, *Zionism: The Crucial Phase*, (Oxford, 1987), pp. 5, 360.

8. A. L. Tibawi, *Anglo-Arab Relations and the Question of Palestine 1914–1921*, (London, 1978), pp. 18–19. For a brief exposition on how Herzl proposed to solve the 'demographic' problem in Palestine, by 'expropriating' land from rich landowners and driving the 'penniless' to 'transit countries', see Desmond Stewart, *Herzl*, (London, 1974), p. 192.

9. Vital, *Zionism: The Crucial Phase*, p. 31.

10. See Christopher Sykes, *Crossroads to Israel, 1917–1948*. (Bloomington & Indianapolis, 1973), pp. 10–11. Nordau gave the following account: 'I did my best to persuade the claimants of the Jewish state in Palestine that we might find a circumlocution that would express all we meant, but would say it in a way as to avoid provoking the Turkish rulers of the coveted land. I suggested *"Heimstatte"* as a synonym for "State"... This is the history of the much commented expression. It was equivocal, but we all understood what it meant. To us it signified *"Judenstaat"* then and it signifies the same now.' Christopher Sykes commented: 'Was this not proof of a duplicity that peculiarly and sinisterly marked a Jewish

search for power?' He added that, influenced by such statements, the Cabinet of 1917 was officially advised by Sir Mark Sykes that in asking for a national home the Zionists 'were not seeking a Jewish republic'. Christopher Sykes points out: 'That they were in fact seeking just that, is clear today.'

11. At the 8th Zionist Congress in 1907 at the Hague, Max Nordau raised the slogan 'Zionism or liquidation'. At the 9th Zionist Congress in December 1909, he told his listeners that the programme of the First Zionist Congress still applied, but did not mean, as some had thought at the first congress, that Jews would 'sneak' into Palestine under the auspices of a great power, but that they wished to enter the country only on the basis of expressly granted rights. See Vital, *Zionism: The Crucial Phase*, pp. 10, 31.

12. Yaacov Ro'i, 'The Zionist Attitude to the Arabs 1908–1914', *Middle Eastern Studies*, vol. 4 (October 1967), no. 3 pp. 204–6. The Palestine Office kept itself aware of Arab feeling by regularly translating from the Arabic press, and hence its archives are considered to be an important source on the Arabic press during that period.

13. Engeres Aktions-Comite (The Smaller Actions Committee).

14. Ro'i, 'The Zionist Attitude to the Arabs', pp. 2–6.

15. It is interesting to mention in this respect that Harold Nicolson, one of the Foreign Office officials charged with the drafting and redrafting of the Balfour Declaration, wrote many years later that the declaration was represented as a wartime measure to 'placate the denizens of Wall Street'. However, it was not of the 'strong Jews that we were thinking; it was of the millions of weak Jews who lived, not in Kensington Palace Gardens or on Riverside Drive, but at Cracow and Galatz'. See Vital, *Zionism: The Crucial Phase*, p. 371.

16. Ibid., p. 157. In 1917, Weizmann pleased the British government by helping to abort the attempted plan of Henry Morgenthau, former US ambassador in Constantinople, to negotiate terms on which Turkey would remove itself from the central powers and leave the war, a move which would have upset British and French plans for the Near East. When news of Morgenthau's mission reached London, Weizmann was rushed to Gibraltar to talk Morgenthau out of his plan; a task which he accomplished to everyone's satisfaction, especially Mark Sykes. For this see David Vital, *A People Apart. The Jews in Europe 1789-1939.* (Oxford, 1999), p. 691.

17. At Manchester University.

18. Vital, *Zionism: The Crucial Phase*, p. 158.

19. Ibid., p. 224.

20. Ibid., pp. 157, 161, 163. Se also Myers, *Re-Inventing the Jewish Past*, p. 47.

21. Neville Mandel, *The Arabs and Palestine Before World War I.* (Berkeley, 1976), pp. 34–6.

22. Amos Elon, *The Israelis. Founders and Sons* (New York, 1971), p. 162.

23. Mandel, *The Arabs and Palestine*, p. 224.

24. Ibid., p. 33.

25. Ibid., p. 39.

26. Ibid., pp. 43–4.

27. Ibid., pp. 223–4, 226, 229. It is estimated that the total Jewish population in 1919 was 9.7%. See, for instance, Walid Khalidi (ed.), *From Haven to Conquest*, p. 841.

28. Since the Zionist Organization was founded in 1897, it was not represented in Palestine

until the opening of the Palestine Office. This was taken over in 1918 by the Zionist Commission.

29. Ro'i, 'The Zionist Attitude to the Arabs', pp. 200–1.

30. Ibid., p. 205.

31. Alexandre Schölch, *Palestine in Transformation 1856–1882. Studies in Social, Economic and Political Development* (Washington D.C., 1993), p. 284.

32. R. W. Seton-Watson, *Disraeli, Gladstone and the Eastern Question.* (London, 1971), pp. 26–7.

33. *Atlas of World History* (Penguin), vol. 2., p. 97.

34. Rashid Khalidi, *British Policy Towards Syria and Palestine, 1906–1914. A Study of the Antecedents of the Hussein-McMahon Correspondence, the Sykes–Picot Agreement, and the Balfour Declaration* (London, 1980), pp. 1, 15.

35. Ibid., pp. 65–6.

36. David Fromkin, *A Peace to End All Peace. Creating the Modern Middle East 1914-1922* (London, 1991), pp. 280–1.

37. Wasserstein, *The British in Palestine*, p. 74.

38. Schölch, *Palestine in Transformation*, pp. 61–2. And for a detailed and in-depth study see Regina Sharif, *Non-Jewish Zionism. Its Roots in Western History* (London, 1983). Also See Mayir Vereté, 'The Restoration of Jews in English Protestant Thought 1790–1840', *Middle Eastern Studies*, vol. 8, no. 1. 1972.

39. Stewart, *Herzl*, p. 209. As Palmerston explained to the British ambassador in Constantinople: 'It would be of manifest importance for the Sultan to encourage the Jews to return to, and settle in Palestine, because the wealth which they would bring with them would increase the resources of the Sultan's dominions; and the Jewish people, if returning under the sanction and protection and at the invitation of the Sultan, would be a check upon any future evil designs of Mohammad Ali or his successor... .'

40. Schölch, *Palestine in Transformation*, p. 65.

CHAPTER ONE

1. See D. Edward Knox, *The Making of a New Eastern Question: British Palestine Policy and the Origins of Israel 1917–25* (Washington, 1981), p. 9.

2. The Foreign, India and War Offices, the Admiralty and the Board of Trade.

3. Vital, *Zionism: the Crucial Phase*, p. 98. Sykes' non-professional background, and the fact that he had his own ideas about the destinies of the people of the Near East, did not disqualify him, and it was upon Kitchener's advice that he was appointed to the committee.

4. Fromkin, *A Peace to End All Peace*, pp. 100–2.

5. Wasserstein, *The British in Palestine*, p. 74.

6. Fromkin, *A Peace to End All Peace*, p. 269. *Tancred* is a novel by Benjamin Disraeli in which he advocated a Jewish return to Palestine.

7. Fromkin, *A Peace to End All Peace*, pp. 196–7.

8. Samuel Papers, Middle East Centre, St. Antony's College, Oxford, DR 588.25 (244S), Sykes to Samuel, 26 February 1916. In November 1918, Sykes sent gloomy reports from Palestine of the considerable friction between Arabs and Jews, which took the form of street

fights and stone throwing. He telegraphed Ormsby-Gore in London stating that the 'non-Jews' want to know 'whether Zionist objective is an independent Jewish State'. See Doreen Ingrams, *Palestine Papers: Seeds of Conflict, 1917–1922* (London, 1972), pp. 42–3; Tibawi, *Anglo-Arab Relations*, p. 311.

9. Wasserstein, *Herbert Samuel*, p. 222.

10. Philip Kerr (later Lord Lothian) was editor of the *Round Table* magazine, founded in 1910 by Lord Milner and others. Its aim was to publish a quarterly and comprehensive review of imperial policies and developments. Kerr joined the Prime Minister's Secretariat and during 1917 had come to regard the establishment of a Jewish Palestine as a vital British imperial interest.

11. Chaim Weizmann, *The Letters and Papers of Chaim Weizmann* (Oxford, 1968–), vol. 7, p. 516.

12. David Gilmour, *Curzon* (London, 1994), p. 481.

13. See, for instance, Leonard Stein, *The Balfour Declaration* (London, 1961), pp. 196–7. See also Frank. E. Manuel, 'Judge Brandeis and the Framing of the Balfour Declaration', in Khalidi (ed.), *From Haven to Conquest*, pp. 165–72.

14. The letter was signed by A. J. Balfour, Foreign Office, and addressed to Lord Lionel Walter Rothschild at his home at 148 Piccadilly. The letter read: 'Dear Lord Rothschild, I have much pleasure in conveying to you, on behalf of His Majesty's Government, the following declaration of sympathy with Jewish Zionist aspirations which has been submitted to, and approved by, the Cabinet. His Majesty's Government view with favour the establishment in Palestine of a national home for the Jewish people, and will use their best endeavours to facilitate the achievement of this object, it being clearly understood that nothing shall be done which may prejudice the civil and religious rights of existing non-Jewish communities in Palestine, or the rights and political status enjoyed by Jews in any country. I should be grateful if you would bring this declaration to the knowledge of the Zionist Federation.'

15. It seems that Colonial Office officials dealing with Palestine each had his own understanding of the term. Indeed, the colonial secretary, the Duke of Devonshire, wrote in a secret memorandum on 17 February 1923: 'Prior to 1921, no authoritative explanation was ever given of what precisely was meant by a "National Home" for the Jews.' CO 733/58.

16. CO 733/35, Minute by Eric Mills, Acting Principal Colonial Office, 30 September 1922.

17. Israel Zangwill, 1864–1926, was a writer on Jewish themes living in Britain. He joined the Zionists in 1896 and after Herzl's death, between 1904 and 1911 devoted himself to the search for a home for the Jews, founding the unsuccessful Jewish Territorial Organization.

18. Ibid.

19. Edward Keith-Roach, *Pasha of Jerusalem: Memoirs of a District Commissioner under the British Mandate* (London, 1994), p. 96.

20. Ibid., pp. 92–3.

21. Peel Report, p. 24.

22. Ibid.

23. In an address to Congress on 8 January 1918, the US president Woodrow Wilson laid down the conditions of peace known as the Fourteen Points, on the basis of which Germany

agreed to surrender. Point 12 stated that the nationalities now under Turkish rule should be assured 'an undoubted security of life and an absolutely unmolested opportunity of autonomous development'. See E. Lipson, *Europe in the 19th and 20th Centuries 1815–1939* (London, 1940), pp. 302–3.

24. CO 733/52, 'Palestine's Protest Against the Balfour Declaration'. Proclamation by Musa Kazim al-Husseini, President of the Arab Executive Committee, 2 November 1923, submitted to the 'civilized world through its governments', in Samuel to Devonshire, Political Report for November 1923.

25. Norman Bentwich, *The Mandates System* (London, 1930), pp. 1–2.

26. On 28 June 1919 the Treaty of Versailles and the Covenant of the League of Nations were signed. Paragraph 4 of Article 22 of the Covenant reads: 'Certain communities formerly belonging to the Turkish Empire have reached a stage of development where their existence as independent nations can be provisionally recognized subject to the rendering of administrative advice and assistance by a mandatory until such a time as they are able to stand alone. The wishes of these communities must be a principal consideration in the selection of the Mandatory.' See *A Survey of Palestine: Prepared in December 1945 and January 1946 for the Information of the Anglo-American Commission of Inquiry* (Institute for Palestine Studies, Washington DC., 1991), vol. 1, p. 2.

27. Bentwich, *The Mandates System*, p. 3.

28. Ibid., pp. 12, 27.

29. Ibid., p. 23.

30. Born in Ta'if in 1885, Faisal was a son of Hussein ibn 'Ali, the Sharif of Mecca. He played a prominent part in the British-supported Arab revolt against the Turks during the First World War. On 3 October 1918, he entered Damascus with Arab forces on the same day as General Allenby's troops. Allenby was prepared to recognize an Arab administration under Faisal, as representing his father, Sharif Hussein, in occupied enemy territory east of the Jordan river, from 'Aqaba to Ma'an to Damascus. On 5 October, Faisal established in Damascus an 'Arab Military Government' for 'Syria', with the knowledge and permission of Allenby, and issued his first official proclamation addressed to the 'People of Syria'. He emphasized that his government was an Arab government 'based on justice and equality for all Arabs, who would enjoy the same rights, be they Muslim, Christian or Jew'. Zeine Zeine, *The Struggle for Arab Independence. Western Diplomacy and the Rise and Fall of Feisal's Kingdom in Syria*. 2nd edition (New York, 1977), pp. 29–34. Faisal was proclaimed King of Syria by the Syrian Congress in March 1920 but his rule was short-lived and he was deposed by the French when they took Damascus in July 1920. In 1921, he became King of Iraq under British auspices and remained in power until his death in 1933.

31. 'The American King-Crane Commission of Inquiry 1919' in Khalidi (ed.), *From Haven to Conquest*, pp. 213–18. (Henceforth King-Crane Commission).

32. It is interesting to note that the British government appointed Sir Henry McMahon, the negotiator with Sharif Hussein in 1915, and Commander D. G. Hogarth of the Arab Bureau in Cairo as British members of the commission. Arnold Toynbee was appointed as secretary. See Ingrams, *Palestine Papers*, p. 69; George Antonius, *The Arab Awakening* (Beirut, 1969), p. 288.

33. N. Harry Howard, *An American Inquiry in the Middle East: the King-Crane*

Commission (Beirut, 1963), pp. 236–7.

34. Ibid., p. 60.

35. Bayan Nuwayhid al-Hut (ed.), *Watha'iq al-haraka al-wataniyya al-filastiniyya 1918–1939: min awraq Akram Zu'aytir* (Beirut, 1984), p. 22 (henceforth Zu'aytir Papers).

36. Muhammad 'Izzat Darwazeh, *Mudhakkirat Muhammad 'Izzat Darwazeh, 1305 H–1404H/1887 M–1984 M: Sijill hafil bi-masirat al-haraka al-'arabiyya wa-al-qadiya al-filastiniyya khilala qarn min al-zaman*, vol. 1 (Beirut, 1993), pp. 345–7.

37. Bayan Nuwayhid al-Hut, *al-Qiyadat wa-al-mu'assasat al-siyasiyya fi filastin 1917–48* (Beirut 1986), p. 110.

38. Zu'aytir Papers, p. 27.

39. For example, the Acre delegation consisted of 6 Muslim religious leaders, 3 'ulama, 3 notables, 6 young men, 6 villagers, 6 Catholics, 6 Greek Orthodox, 1 Protestant, 1 Latin, 1 Maronite, 1 Druze, 1 Baha'i and one Jew.

40. Al-Hut, *al-Qiyadat*, p. 111.

41. According to George Antonius, Christians were represented in much higher proportion to their numerical strength; it was in his opinion a representative assembly in the true sense of the word. See pp. 440–2 for full translated text of resolutions of the Syrian Congress.

42. Zu'aytir Papers, 'The Resolutions of the Syrian Congress submitted to the King-Crane Commission, 3 July 1919', pp. 32–3.

43. Tibawi, *Anglo-Arab Relations*, p. 362.

44. Bentwich, *The Mandates System*, p. 13.

45. See Christopher Sykes, *Crossroads to Israel*, p. 37.

46. Bentwich, *The Mandates System*, p. 10.

47. Gilmour, *Curzon*, p. 521.

48. Vital, *Zionism*, pp. 325–6. The Sykes-Picot Agreement of 1916 had proposed placing Palestine under international trusteeship. However, by the end of 1918, the Sykes-Picot Agreement was being replaced by new post-war policies when the Versailles Peace Conference met to discuss the spoils of war.

49. On 22 April 1920, the prime minister received a letter signed by thirteen influential Zionists saying that there were strong rumours that the British government were hesitating to accept a mandate for Palestine; the signatories ventured to submit that 'Zionist opinion throughout the world regards a British mandate as essential to the effective fulfilment of the Balfour letter' and that they agreed with this and urged that the early settlement of this mandate question was 'vital to the pacification of Palestine'. The letter was signed, in addition to Lord Rothschild and William Ormsby-Gore, by the following: George N. Barnes, Robert Cecil, Martin Conway, Brunel Cohen, Ralph Glyn, Frederick Green, Raymond Greene, Walter Guinness, Arthur Murray, Josiah Wedgwood and W. Whitla [sic]. On 1 May, Lord Curzon reassured Lord Rothschild in a private letter: 'There was not, and never had been, any intention of placing Palestine under Arab suzerainty'. FO 371/5113, 22 April 1920.

50. Sykes, *Crossroads to Israel*, p. 38.

51. Ingrams, *Palestine Papers*, p. 98.

52. *Survey of Palestine*, vol. I, p. 3.

53. Malcolm E. Yapp, 'The Making of the Palestine Mandate' in Moshe Dayan Center for Middle Eastern and African Studies, Tel Aviv University, *Middle Eastern Lectures*

Number 1 (Tel Aviv, 1995), pp. 24–5. On the process of the four stages of drafting between 1918 and 1923, see ibid., pp. 15–16. The crucial stage was dominated by two young men, Eric Forbes-Adam, a junior Foreign Office official and a Zionist American lawyer, Benjamin Cohen. Yapp points out that 'Adam seems to have been left to his own devices with very little supervision'. Thus, when the fourth stage arrived, from March to December 1920, even though Britain's 'room for maneuver' was 'theoretically unimpaired', it was practically 'much reduced'. When Britain was awarded the mandate, and senior staff looked closely into the matter, there was 'horror when the depth of commitment to Zionism was appreciated'; ibid., p. 22–3.

54. Ingrams, *Palestine Papers*, pp. 94–5.

55. Ibid., p. 96. Curzon added: 'It is quite clear that this mandate has been drawn up by someone reeling under the fumes of Zionism. If we are to submit to that intoxicant, this draft is all right. Perhaps there is no alternative.'

56. Gilmour, *Curzon*, pp. 522–3.

57. Ingrams, *Palestine Papers*, p. 99.

58. CO 733/12, House of Lords Debate, 'Mandate for Palestine', 20 April 1921.

59. The agreement between the US and Great Britain regarding the Mandate for Palestine was eventually made in December 1925, and provided that the nationals of the US should enjoy all the rights and benefits secured under the terms of the mandate. See Bentwich, *The Mandates System*, p. 15.

60. Ingrams, *Palestine Papers*, p. 97.

61. CO 733/30, Balfour to Secretary of the Cabinet, 22 May 1922, Secret despatch, 13 May 1920. The original document does not elaborate on this point.

62. CO 733/30, Curzon to Churchill, 13 April 1922. Translation of a letter from the Vatican dated 6 March 1922.

63. Ibid.

64. Ibid.

65. Ronald Storrs, *Orientations* (London, 1945), p. 358, fn. 3 quoting J. M. Mackover, *Governing Palestine* (1936).

66. The draft mandate was submitted to the Council of the League of Nations in December 1920, but until July 1922 the Council was unwilling to take any definite steps. CO 733/35, 'Points for Introductory Speech by Balfour at the meeting of the Council of the League of Nations', 18 July 1922.

67. F. Kassim Anis, *The Palestine Yearbook of International Law*, vol. 1 (Cyprus, 1984), p. 21. Significantly, the high commissioner officially proclaimed that 6 August 1924 should be treated in the mandated territory of Palestine as the date of termination of war with Turkey. On the same day, the Treaty of Lausanne came into force. See the *Official Gazette for Palestine*, No. 125, 15 October 1924. Also on that date, Turkey agreed to the separation of Arab territories, including Palestine, from the Ottoman Empire.

68. Samuel Papers, Samuel to Churchill, 28 April 1921, Despatch no. 72, Reference no. Adm. 402.

69. Samuel was referring to a public loan which could not be given until the mandate was conferred. He needed the loan, as will be seen, to initiate public works for unemployed Jewish immigrants.

70. CO 733/6, Samuel to Churchill, 14 October 1921, Confidential.

71. CO 733/15, Translation of a petition to the High Commissioner signed by Jamal al-Husseini, 1 December 1921.

72. CO 733/33, 'Notes for Mr. Harmsworth', 6 January 1922.

73. CO 733/35, 'Points for Introductory Speech' by Balfour at the meeting of the Council of the League of Nations, 18 July 1922.

74. Ibid.

75. CO 733/66, Minute by Young, 3 May 1924.

76. See Peel Report, pp. 107–9.

CHAPTER TWO

1. *A Survey of Palestine*, vol. 1, p. 15.

2. FO 371/5121 E 9373, 'Enquiry into Rioting in Jerusalem in April 1920', submitted Port Said, August 1920, p. 41 (henceforth Palin Report).

3. Chapter 14, Articles 353 et seq., of the Manual of Military Law laid down the proper procedures for occupied enemy territories, including the principle of maintaining the status quo. Article 354 stated: 'it is no longer considered permissible for him [the administrator] to work his will unhindered, altering the existing form of Government, upsetting the constitution and domestic laws and ignoring the rights of the inhabitants.' (Ibid).

4. See for instance *Official Gazette for the Government of Palestine*, no. 2, 1 August 1919. Public Notice no. 115 on Transfer of Land, whereby the chief administrator, Major General Money, maintained previous proclamations on land transfers and announced that any such transactions 'will be null and void, and the person to whom such a note or instrument was given may further be liable to prosecution.'

5. FO 371/5114 E 7095, W. H. Selby to Sir W. Tyrell, 6 June 1920.

6. John McTague, *British Policy in Palestine 1917–22*, (Lanham, 1983), p. 83.

7. The Palin Report sets the date as 28 April 1920.

8. Gladys Skelton [John Presland, pseud.], *Deedes Bey* (London, 1942), p. 322. General Wavell, Allenby's biographer, explains why Allenby remained silent on the Balfour Declaration, censoring all mention of it as he launched his great offensive in 1918: 'with the entry into Palestine and capture of Jerusalem political as well as military problems began to occupy Allenby. Palestine presented some very thorny and difficult questions. The awkwardness of reconciling our pledges to the Arabs, our undertakings to our Allies (the Sykes-Picot Agreement), and the Balfour Declaration to the Zionists was already becoming evident to those who knew of them … He refused to allow the Balfour Declaration to be published in Palestine'. See Sir Archibald Wavell, *Allenby* (London 1940), pp. 236–7.

9. A few years later, J. M. N. Jeffries, the *Daily Mail* correspondent who reported on the situation from Palestine wrote: 'Now what does that mean, put into plain English? It means that the British Government has issued a Declaration so high-handed, unwarranted and dangerous that it was an impediment to the progress of the British Army, it had to be suppressed … has any British Government before been censored by its own forces in the field, as if its pronouncements had been written by the enemy? … It is a strange Magna Carta which cannot be published in Runnymede'. See CO 733/54, J. N. M. Jeffries, 'The

Palestine Deception—Tricks of the Balfour Declaration', *Daily Mail*, 10 January 1923.

10. CO 733/10, Colonel Richard Meinertzhagen, Egyptian Expeditionary Force, Cairo to Secretary of State, 26 September 1919.

11. CO 733/10, Telegram from Lord Curzon to Field Marshall Allenby, Cairo, 7 November 1919. Despite Meinertzhagen's efforts, the military administration resisted publication of Curzon's memorandum, with General Bols arguing that publication of the government's policy would do no good, but rather would create antagonism (McTague, *British Policy in Palestine*, pp. 89–92).

12. The Palin Report, p. 33.

13. Ibid.

14. McTague, *British Policy in Palestine*, p. 186. The *Morning Post* wrote on 22 September 1920, that the army of occupation, officers and men, sympathized with the people 'whom it is called upon to repress', and that outbreaks of violence in Palestine occurred more frequently than the public was allowed to know. FO 371/5123.

15. McTague, *British Policy in Palestine*, pp. 83–4.

16. Wasserstein, *The British in Palestine*, p. 25 and note 31.

17. The military governor of Jerusalem, Ronald Storrs, reveals that when Clayton read the telegram announcing the 'impending' arrival of the Zionist Commission, 'we could hardly believe our eyes, and even wondered whether it might not be possible for the mission to be postponed until the status of the Administration should be more clearly defined.' See Storrs, *Orientations*, p. 340.

18. By 1920, the military administration was referring to the 'intolerable' activities and 'indiscretions' of the Zionist Commission (Palin Report, p. 81).

19. According to Fromkin, the Zionist Commission's object was to prepare the way to carry out the Balfour Declaration. Fromkin, *A Peace to End All Peace*, pp. 323–4.

20. Vital, *Zionism*, p. 311 (Weizmann was President of the World Zionist Organization between 1920 and 1931).

21. The Palestine Office was the first institution founded by the World Zionist Organization in Jaffa in 1908 to supervise practical Zionist work in Palestine. *The New Standard Jewish Encyclopedia* (1970 edition), column 1490.

22. Ibid., column 2020.

23. Wasserstein, *The British in Palestine*, p. 29.

24. Storrs, *Orientations*, p. 341.

25. Darwazeh, *Mudhakkirat*, vol. 1, pp. 310–11.

26. This was to be the main theme in the 1922 Statement of Policy, drawn up by Sir Herbert Samuel, which formed the basis of British policy throughout the rest of the decade.

27. Several sources hold that the Muslim-Christian Association was founded in November 1918. See for example Wasserstein, *The British in Palestine*, p. 36; Yehoshua Porath, *The Emergence of the Palestinian-Arab National Movement, 1918–1929* (London, 1974), p. 32. Weizmann's meeting with Arab notables was held in Jerusalem on 27 April, after which the association was formed, giving a difference of seven months. *Al-Mawsu'a al-filastiniyya* (Encyclopedia Palestina) (Damascus, 1984), p. 65, vol. 2, maintains that the Muslim-Christian Association was officially registered in Jerusalem in June 1918 according to the Ottoman Law which was still in operation.

28. See Khalidi (ed.), *From Haven to Conquest*, pp. 189–90. Weizmann's reply in Paris in 1919 to the American secretary of state Lansing, asserted that the Zionist Organization did not want an autonomous Jewish government, but merely wanted to establish in Palestine under a mandatory Power, an administration 'not necessarily Jewish, which would render it possible to send into Palestine 70 to 80,000 Jews annually' (ibid. p. 191).

29. Zu'aytir Papers, p. 3. See also Ingrams, *Palestine Papers*, pp. 30–1 for the English version of Weizmann's speech and Shaykh Raghib's reply, quoting FO 371/3383.

30. Ingrams, *Palestine Papers*, p. 32.

31. Vera Weizmann, *The Impossible Takes Longer: The Memoirs of Vera Weizmann, Wife of Israel's First President, As Told to David Tutaev* (London, 1967), p. 277.

32. Vital, *Zionism*, p. 319. As Weizmann phrased it, 'c'est a prendre ou a laisser'.

33. Zu'aytir Papers, p. 5.

34. Ibid., p. 6.

35. 'Petition from the Moslem-Christian Association in Jaffa, to the Military Governor, on the occasion of the First Anniversary of British Entry into Jaffa', 16 November 1918, Zu'aytir Papers, pp. 7–8.

36. The Muslim-Christian Association also protested to General Allenby, through the military governor of Jaffa, that although Jaffa and Jerusalem were the two cities with the highest percentage of Jews, their numbers in Jaffa did not exceed 10,000, while the Arabs counted more than 70,000. Their real ratio in Palestine was 1:500. The memorandum claimed that the Arabs were apprehensive after reading a statement in the *Times* that Palestine was to become a 'Jewish Kingdom', and asked whether it was possible that the future of Palestine would be decided without the consent of its people (Zu'aytir Papers, pp. 1–2, 'Memorandum from the Moslem-Christian Association in Jaffa, to General Allenby in protest of Zionist ambitions and presenting Arab demands', November 1918).

37. This use is curious because, prior to that date, the term 'national home' was rendered more accurately as *al-watan al-qawmi*. This seems to suggest that there was still confusion as to the exact meaning of the term.

38. Vital, *Zionism*, pp. 314, 317.

39. Wasserstein, *The British in Palestine*, pp. 56–7.

40. FO 371/5117 E 3376, 16 April 1920. On 18 August 1920, Storrs wrote a personal letter to Samuel commenting on the Palin Report, and saying that with regard to the 'dismissal' of the mayor, the Mayoralty of Jerusalem 'is a two years office'; Storrs had appointed the ex-mayor in January 1918 and 'every consideration had been accorded him but there had never been any question of retaining him over the statutory period'. Storrs Papers, Pembroke College, Cambridge, Box no. III/2, Jerusalem 1920–1.

41. FO 371/5117 E 3142, 12 April 1920. The term 'riots' was often used by British observers to describe Palestinian demonstrations, uprisings or mini-revolts. It has, despite its indiscriminate application and somewhat judgmental overtones, for the most part been retained in this book because it is often hard to pinpoint the exact character of the incidents involved.

42. A delegation of Jerusalem Jews went to London to convince the British government of the need to change the regime in Palestine. Neil Caplan, *Palestine Jewry and the Arab Question 1917–25* (London, 1978), pp. 59–60.

43. FO 371/5117 E 3259, 15 April 1920. D. Yellin to the Prime Minister, 12 April 1920.

44. FO 371/5118 E 3580. Bols said he would welcome a Zionist advisory council consisting of about three members with a few clerks attached to him directly and under his control.

45. FO 371/5119 E 5237, 25 May 1920.

46. Ibid.

47. Ibid.

48. Ibid.

49. Ibid.

50. Wasserstein, *The British in Palestine*, p. 79.

51. The Commission of Inquiry was formed under Major General P. C. Palin as president, with Brigadier General G. H. Wildblood and Lieutenant Colonel C. Vaughan Edwards as members. By the time the commission submitted its report (on 1 July 1920, coinciding with Samuel's first day in office as high commissioner), the military administration had already ceased to exist. However, the findings of the report were not published. In the face of renewed Zionist attacks on the personnel of the military administration, Allenby had advised that the Palin Report should be published but in anticipation of Zionist objections, it was decided only to convey the gist of the report verbally to a 'responsible' Zionist leader.

52. Palin Report, p. 79.

53. Jargon (Yiddish) is a mixture of Hebrew, German and Slavic languages. After the First World War, Yiddish speakers who arrived in Palestine in greater numbers soon clashed with advocates of Hebrew revival who used the term 'Jargon' to highlight the purity of the ancient Hebrew tongue. David Myers, *Re-inventing the Jewish Past*, p. 77. It is curious that the report does not mention German.

54. Mr S. Alexander of the firm R. S. Devonshire & Co. Advocates, Cairo.

55. Palin Report, p. 184.

56. Ibid.

57. Ibid., p. 14.

58. Ibid., pp. 29–33.

59. Ibid., p. 80.

60. Wasserstein, *The British in Palestine*, p. 134.

61. This long delay in officially establishing the Jewish Agency was partly due to rivalries and complications within Zionist ranks, but, more importantly, it was a result of Weizmann's endeavours to transform the Jewish leadership in Palestine from a local party into something far more powerful: 'into an expression of the will of the whole Jewish people'. See, for instance, Sykes, *Crossroads to Israel*, p. 103.

62. Wasserstein, *The British in Palestine*, pp. 136–7.

63. Ibid., p. 24.

64. FO 371/5114 E 6982/61/44, Allenby to Lord Curzon, 10 June 1920. The letter was signed by Taher Aboul Seoud, Aref El Rigali [sic], and Ibrahim El Schakassi [sic]. The letter also alleged that the Zionist Committee, 'composed chiefly of Russian, American and German members, accustomed to revolutions, have jointly planned this programme so that news may reach Europe of the tyranny and bloodshed caused by the Arabs to the so called innocent Jews, and thus attaining their devilish aim'. The Muslim-Christian Association also asked that a commission be appointed to investigate the killing of Jews and Arabs in

the riots, since the Arabs claimed that 'most of the wounded Jews had wounded themselves to increase the number of the wounded'. This letter was among copies of protests presented by four Palestinian societies to the military governor of Jaffa, which Allenby was transmitting to the Foreign Office. Allenby had received them from the Comite Central [sic] du Parti de l'Union Syrienne in Cairo, relative to the British government's policy towards Zionism. In replying, Allenby confined himself to 'a bare acknowledgement of the receipt of these protests' and that he was communicating them to HMG 'as desired'.

65. The document merely mentions the 'said law' and gives no more details. It probably refers to martial law which was still in force at the time.

66. FO 371/5114 E 6982/61/44, Allenby to Lord Curzon, 10 June 1920.

67. Vladimir Jabotinsky (1880–1940) began his Zionist activities in Russia in 1903. During World War I he advocated the recruitment of Jewish regiments to fight with the British army in Palestine, leading to the formation of the Zion Mule Corps in 1915 and in 1917 to the formation of the Jewish battalion, in which Jabotinsky served. Having organized the formation of the Haganah in 1920, he joined the Zionist Executive in 1921 but resigned in 1923, accusing it of failing to attack British policy strongly enough. In 1925 he formed the World Union of Zionist Revisionists, and in 1935 the New Zionist Organization. He was the main influence behind the formation of Irgun Tzevai Leumi, and its nominal head.

68. An intelligence report, compiled in May 1922, gave the history of the movement, and asserted that the originator of the idea of Jewish 'self defence' organizations in Palestine 'in March or April 1920' was Vladimir Jabotinsky, aided by Rutenberg, who 'had some experience in this direction while a Commissioner of Police in Moscow or Petrograd during the Revolution'. The reason for the establishment of such a force was the refusal of OETA to allow a permanent Jewish battalion in Palestine and its 'alleged antipathy' to Zionist policy. The intelligence report drew attention to the fact that: 'It must be borne in mind that up to this time there had been no "pogroms"' in Palestine. CO 733/33, General Officer Commanding Palestine to Director of Military Intelligence, War Office, 'Notes on Jewish Self Defence Scheme', 23 May 1922.

69. Palin Report, p. 70.

70. Ibid., p. 71.

71. FO 371/5118 E 3478 20 April 1920. Secret.

72. FO 371/5118 E 3715, GHQ to War Office, Telegram, 23 April 1920, Secret. When news of Jabotinsky's conviction reached the Foreign Office, Osborne, an official, minuted on 24 April 1920: 'The severity of the sentences can only be explained on the supposition that the authorities discovered that Jabotinsky and his followers contemplated a serious disturbance of the peace—something in the nature of a Garibaldian coup d'état'. In the same context, Young wrote that a certain Dr Salaman had come to see him expressing 'great concern at the severity of the sentence on Jabotinsky, of whom he spoke as the Garibaldi of the Zionist movement'. Young adds that Salaman 'made no secret' of what he wanted: 'an independent enquiry into the whole administration of Palestine, not merely into the recent disturbances'.

73. In his inaugural speech upon his arrival in July 1920, Samuel publicly declared amnesty to Jabotinsky and the others as an act of clemency.

74. FO 371/5120, Allenby to War Office, 14 June 1920.

75. FO 371/5120 E 6714, 24 June 1920, marked No Distribution—Docketed.

76. Caplan, *Palestine Jewry*, p. 71.

77. FO 371/5122 E 11096, Allenby to Curzon, 5 September 1920.

78. Ibid. See chapter 2.

79. FO 371/5112, Minute by Gilbert Clayton, 9 September 1920.

80. Palin Report, pp. 52, 68.

81. Ibid.

82. Ibid., p. 69.

83. Sir Walford Harmood Montague Selby. Diplomatic Service. First Secretary, Cairo, 1919–22.

84. FO 371/5114 E 7095, Selby to Sir William Tyrell, 6 June 1920. It is interesting that it was Ronald Storrs, governor of Jerusalem, who depicted practical Zionism as 'Irredentism to the nth'. See Storrs, *Orientations*, p. 340. He later wrote in his memoirs: 'Zionism is admittedly a departure from ordinary colonizing processes; an act of faith. To this extent, therefore, impartiality is condemned by Zionists as anti Zionistic: he that is not for me is against me ... What is less justifiable (and much less helpful to the cause) is the assumption that the smallest criticism of any Zionist method or proposal is equivalent to anti-Zionism, even to anti-Semitism'. See McTague, *British Policy in Palestine*, pp. 48–9, quoting the *Memoirs of Sir Ronald Storrs* (New York, 1937).

85. 'Great Britain and Palestine', delivered by the Rt. Hon. Sir Herbert Samuel, GCB, CBE, University College, London, 25 November 1935. The Second Lucien Wolf Memorial Lecture (The Jewish Historical Society of England, London, 1935), p. 18.

86. FO 371/5118 E 3476/85/44, 19 April 1920, Minutes, 'Record of a Conversation at War Office on the Political Situation in Palestine'. Present were Major-General Radcliffe, director of Military Operations, Brigadier General Bartholomew, director of Military Intelligence (DMI) and, from the Foreign Office, Mr. Osborne and Major Young.

87. Meinertzhagen, an ardent Zionist sympathizer, did not 'see eye to eye' with General Bols, or the other officers in the administration who were inclined to be anti-Zionist. In March 1920, Meinertzhagen wrote to the Foreign Office describing the military administration in the following words: 'Its creed is stagnation, its object is to keep the peace and the *status quo ante bellum*. A continuation of such conditions, with a highly civilized, sensitive and idealistic community clamouring to be allowed to lay the foundations of their National Home after 2,000 years in exile, and a fanatical retrogressive and ill-civilized community equally anxious to prevent such a policy being put into execution, is becoming well nigh intolerable.' See FO 371/5034 E 3182, Meinertzhagen to Foreign Office, 31 March 1920.

88. Samuel, *Memoirs*, p. 150.

89. FO 371/5118 E 4077, 'Palestine Under the Mandate. British Policy Outlined', The *Times*, 1 May 1920.

90. FO 371/5119 E 4247, 3 May 1920, GHQ Egypt to War Office, Secret.

91. Vital, *Zionism*, p. 83. See also Knox, *The Making of a New Eastern Question*, p. 153, and Ingrams, *Palestine Papers*, p. 105.

92. Samuel, *Memoirs*, p. 152.

93. Ibid., p. 154.

94. Storrs, *Orientations*, p. 391. Ronald Storrs also relates the receipt incident on the

same page.

95. FO 371/5114 E 7573, 2 July 1920. Extract from Parliamentary Debates, House of Lords, 29 June 1920.

96. FO 371/5114 E 7573, House of Lords Debates, 2 July 1920.

97. Ibid.

98. Ibid., 29 June 1920.

99. FO 371/5204 E 6826, 21 June 1920.

100. FO 371/5123 183455, *Morning Post*, 13 September 1920.

101. Quoted in Ingrams, *Palestine Papers*, p. 106.

102. FO 371/5278, Intelligence Report, June 1920.

103. FO 371/5114 E 7276, 26 June 1920.

104. FO 371/5114 E 7095, Selby to Sir William Tyrell, 6 June 1920.

CHAPTER THREE

1. McTague, *British Policy in Palestine*, p. 38; Major Sir Hubert Young, *The Independent Arab* (London, 1933), p. 267.

2. Hubert Young states that the Middle East Department was inaugurated on 14 February 1921. Young, *The Independent Arab*, p. 325.

3. AIR 5/206 Part I, Weizmann to Samuel, 7 March 1921. It is ironic that British officials should have been informed of decisions by their own government through the leader of the Zionist Organization. On an earlier occasion, Hubert Young minuted that Dr Weizmann had telegraphed from San Remo to the effect that His Majesty's Government had decided to set up a civil administration in Palestine to replace the military administration. See FO 371/5139, Minute by Young, 27 April 1920.

4. Ibid. Weizmann also noted that Churchill's visit to Palestine filled the Zionists with great hope. The visit, in his opinion, formed 'an excellent basis for the policy of the newly established committee with regard to the welfare of Palestine'.

5. John Shuckburgh (1877–1953) began his career in the civil service in 1900, when he entered the India Office, where he stayed for the next twenty-one years. He was selected in 1921 by Winston Churchill, the colonial secretary, to be the first assistant under-secretary of state in charge of the new Middle East Department. Shuckburgh was apparently chosen for this post because of his long experience in India.

6. Young, *The Independent Arab*, p. 267. Other staff members included Reader W. Bullard from Mesopotamia, Eric Forbes-Adam from the Foreign Office, and Lieutenant-General Sir Geoffrey Howard from the War Office as principal officers. Gerald Clauson, a former army officer with a knowledge of Arabic, completed the staff.

7. Meinertzhagen, a passionate advocate of Zionism, saw the Middle East Department as the position from which he could best serve the Zionist cause. He admitted that he had turned down a number of offers from places outside the Colonial Office when the department was being set up, and he stayed in it until March 1924. Mark Cocker, *Richard Meinertzhagen: Soldier, Scientist and Spy*. (London, 1989), p. 151.

8. Palin Report, pp. 44–6.

9. Richard Meinertzhagen, *Middle East Diary 1917–1956* (London, 1959) p. 145.

10. McTague, *British Policy in Palestine*, p. 181. In his diary, Meinertzhagen wrote on 23 July 1921, 'I am rapidly infusing into Young and Shuckburgh some enthusiasm for the cause'. Meinertzhagen, *Middle East Diary*, p. 103.

11. Fromkin, *A Peace to End All Peace*, p. 524.

12. This step favoured the Zionists, in view of the military administration's hostility to the pro-Zionist policy of the British government.

13. McTague, *British Policy in Palestine*, p. 181, quoting CO 733/14/38372.

14. Ingrams, *Palestine Papers*, p. 151.

15. Jehuda Reinharz, *Chaim Weizmann: The Making of a Statesman* (New York, 1993), p. 381.

16. CO 733/86, Shuckburgh to Secretary of State, 24 July 1924.

17. Reinharz, *Chaim Weizmann*, p. 377.

18. Young, *The Independent Arab*, p. 325.

19. McTague, *British Policy in Palestine*, p. 140.

20. Ibid., p. 131.

21. Ibid., p. 186. The *Morning Post* wrote on 22 September 1920 that the army of occupation, officers and men, sympathized with the people 'whom it is called upon to repress', and that outbreaks of violence in Palestine occurred more frequently than the public was allowed to know. See FO 371/5123, *Morning Post*, 22 September 1920.

22. CO 733/3, General Commanding Officer, Egyptian Expeditionary Force to the High Commissioner for Palestine, 30 May 1921, Strictly Confidential.

23. CO 733/17, Letters from General Congreve and Air Marshal Salmond, through Air Marshal Trenchard, 'Situation in Palestine', 28 June 1921.

24. CO 733/17, Minute by Shuckburgh, 1 July 1921.

25. CO 733/17, Minute by R. Meinertzhagen, 29 June 1921.

26. CO 733/17, Minute by T. E. Lawrence, 29 June 1921.

27. McTague, *British Policy in Palestine*, p. 186.

28. CO 733/13, Minute by Meinertzhagen, 8 September 1921.

29. McTague, *British Policy in Palestine*, p. 181, quoting CO 733/14/38372.

30. CO 733/7, Samuel to Churchill, 10 November 1921.

31. CO 733/7, Minute by Shuckburgh to Sir J. Masterton-Smith, 1 December 1921.

32. Wasserstein, *The British in Palestine*, p. 107.

33. CO 733/17, Minute by Young, 29 June 1921.

34. Quoted in McTague, *British Policy in Palestine*, p. 165. However, it was not until many years later that Churchill openly admitted that he was 'not aware of the slightest advantage which has ever accrued to Great Britain from this painful and thankless task'. See, for instance, Leonard Stein, *The Balfour Declaration*, p. 619. Churchill suggested in 1945 that the policy in Palestine should be re-examined.

35. Quoted in Ingrams, *Palestine Papers*, p. 139.

36. When two members of the delegation approached him about a question regarding the Greek Orthodox Patriarchate in Jerusalem, he minuted that it would be worthwhile to convey the Arab suggestion privately to the civil secretary in Palestine, since 'If we can conciliate these people on minor points, so much the better'. CO 733/15, Minute by Shuckburgh to Clauson, 28 November 1921.

37. CO 733/15, Memorandum by Shuckburgh, 7 November 1921.

38. Ibid.

39. Suspicion fell upon Richard Meinertzhagen, though the latter wrote in his diary that he suspected a junior member of the Middle East Department, 'a Jew', whom he had 'seen leaving Weizmann's house', of being the source of the leak. However, at a meeting with Leonard Stein, the Secretary of the Zionist Organization, in the summer of 1923, Meinertzhagen did in fact reveal full secret details of a meeting of the Cabinet sub-committee on Palestine, at which doubts were expressed about the wisdom of continuing a pro-Zionist policy in Palestine. This revelation was so alarming to the Zionists that Weizmann was urged to return immediately from a visit to Europe. Cocker, *Richard Meinertzhagen*, pp. 151–2.

40. Meinertzhagen's biographer maintains that 'the flow of information between the military adviser and his close friend, Weizmann, was far greater' than Meinertzhagen was prepared to admit. Ibid. pp. 151–2.

41. Reinharz, *Chaim Weizmann*. p. 379. Reinharz notes that the 'relationship of trust that Weizmann had carefully nurtured with Shuckburgh paid off'.

42. Moshe Mossek, *Palestine Immigration Policy Under Sir Herbert Samuel* (London, 1978), pp. 45–8.

43. CO 733/16, Weizmann to Shuckburgh, 7 December 1921.

44. CO 733/86, Minute by Shuckburgh to Secretary of State, 24 July 1924.

45. Churchill rejected Shuckburgh's proposed statement of policy, and instead adopted the statement which was eventually drawn up with Samuel's assistance: the White Paper of June 1922.

46. CO 733/15, 'Summary of a Statement to be made by the Secretary of State', drafted by Shuckburgh in November 1921. Appendix to Shuckburgh's memorandum of 7 November 1921, op. cit.

47. Colonial Office officials noted that the Carlsbad Zionist Conference had announced publicly and in Weizmann's presence that the ultimate aim of Zionism was to establish a Jewish state. CO 733/35, Clauson, Memorandum on Immigration, 19 October 1921.

48. CO 733/15, 'Summary of a Statement to be made by Secretary of State', drafted by Shuckburgh in November 1921.

49. CO 733/15, Memorandum by Shuckburgh, 7 November 1921.

50. CO 733/17, to the Duke of Atholl, 27 October 1921.

51. CO 733/27, to the Rt. Hon. Lord Southborough of Southborough. The letter was signed by Eric Mills, 29 October 1921.

52. CO 733/15, The *Times*, 'Future of Palestine. Arab Plea for Fair Play', 16 November 1921.

53. CO 733/15, Minute by Meinertzhagen to Shuckburgh, 17 November 1921.

54. Ibid.

55. FO 371/5034 E 3182, 'Political Situation in Syria and Palestine', 15 April 1920.

56. *Daily Express*, 5 February 1921, 'In the Wilderness'.

57. Young, *The Independent Arab*, p. 325.

58. Fromkin, *A Peace to End All Peace*, pp. 524–5.

59. The *Times*, 8 February 1922, 'Lord Northcliffe in Palestine. Advice to Zionists. Visit

to Vineyard Colony'. In 1918 Lord Northcliffe was Director of Propaganda in enemy countries. He made use of the Balfour Declaration for propaganda purposes, but when the civil administration was set up he became an anti-Zionist and bitterly attacked the government's pro-Zionist policy. He died in 1922.

60. Quoted in Porath, *The Emergence*, pp. 137–8. Conversation between Milner and a delegation of the Muslim-Christian Society of Haifa.

61. CO 733/18, Churchill to Samuel, Telegram, Private and Personal, 25 February 1922.

62. United States, Department of State. *Records of the Department of State Relating to Internal Affairs of Turkey, 1910–1929. Telegram, Green to Secretary of State.* Record Group. Microcopy No. 353 Roll No. 80, National Archives.

63. CO 733/22, Minute by Young, 23 June 1922.

64. Fromkin, *A Peace to End All Peace*, pp. 525–6.

65. McTague, *British Policy in Palestine*, pp. 222–3.

66. Reinharz, *Chaim Weizmann*, p. 394.

67. Ibid., pp. 356–7.

68. Ibid. p. 357, quoting Central Zionist Archives (CZA) Z 4/16055, 'Notes of Conversation at Mr. Balfour's on 22/7/1921'.

69. Porath, *The Emergence*, pp. 166–7.

70. CO 733/28, Samuel to Devonshire, 15 December 1922, Personal.

71. CO 733/28, Samuel to Devonshire, 12 December 1922, Confidential.

72. Ibid.

73. Ibid.

74. FO 371/5139 E 3109/131/44, Samuel to Curzon, 2 April 1920, Confidential. See chapter 4.

75. CO 733/28, Samuel to Devonshire, 12 December 1922.

76. Ibid.

77. CO 733/28, Minute by Shuckburgh, dated 30 December 1922 on Samuel's report of 12 December 1922.

78. United Kingdom, *Parliamentary Debates*, (Lords) vol. 53, 13 February to 3 May, 1923, pp. 639–69.

79. CO 733/58, Secret, CP 106 (23), 'Policy in Palestine', 17 February 1923.

80. CO 733/54, Minute by Shuckburgh to Secretary of State for the Colonies, 8 January 1923. Interestingly, the arguments of those opposed to the Balfour Declaration mirrored Shuckburgh's exactly. Lord Sydenham, in the Debate in the House of Lords on 1 March 1923, declared that the Arabs had 'rendered us very great services during the war at a very critical time, and they certainly believed that the pledge to which I have referred was a real pledge that we should honour'. Charging that 'our pledge has been distinctly broken', he urged the government to restore its 'tarnished reputation for good faith'. He noted that before the armistice 'we were universally regarded as a straight-dealing people whose word was their bond', but that because of the Balfour policy 'our prestige in the Near East and far beyond it has undergone a very dark eclipse'. United Kingdom, *Parliamentary Debates*, [Lords] vol. 53, 13 February to 3 May, 1923, pp. 226–34.

81. Porath, for example, in *The Emergence* credits the department with Devonshire's decision to continue the policy of its predecessor, p. 168.

82. CO 733/35, Memorandum by Shuckburgh, 21 December 1922.

83. Ibid.

84. Porath, *The Emergence*, p. 168.

85. CO 733/ 58, CP 60 (23), 'History of the Negotiations Leading up to the Balfour Declaration'.

86. Ibid.

87. The full text of the note was included in CO 733/58, Secret Cabinet Paper CP 60 (23), 'Palestine and the Balfour Declaration', January 1923. The FO unofficial note added that 'little referring to the Balfour Declaration has been found among such papers as have been preserved'. Shuckburgh's memo asserts that 'as the official records are silent, it can only be assumed that such discussions as had taken place were of an informal and private character.'

88. William Ormsby-Gore had joined the Arab Bureau in 1916 as an intelligence officer, but was recalled to London in March 1917 to be parliamentary private secretary to Lord Milner. He later became assistant secretary to the Cabinet, assisting Mark Sykes. At this time he also established cordial relations with Chaim Weizmann. In 1918, he went to Palestine as British liaison officer with the Zionist Commission, and was a member of the British delegation to the Paris Peace Conference in 1919. From October 1922 until 1929, he was parliamentary under-secretary at the Colonial Office under Conservative governments.

89. Sir Maurice Hankey, Secretary, Committee of Imperial Defence, 1912–38; Imperial War Cabinet 1917–18. Hankey was known as the man of a 'million secrets'.

90. Ormsby-Gore's memorandum, dated 24 December 1922, was printed as part of the Secret Cabinet Paper CP 60 (23) (in CO 733/58). This version, however, omits the final handwritten paragraph. The facsimile of Ormsby-Gore's minute, with the handwritten paragraph, is in the file CO 733/35, 'Zionist Policy in Palestine'. For further discussion of this minute, see Sahar S. Huneidi, 'The Balfour Declaration in British Archives, 1922–1923: New Insights into Old Controversies' *Annals of the Faculty of Arts*, Kuwait University, vol. 19, 1999, Monograph no 136.

91. Colonel Amery was at that time one of the two political secretaries to the Cabinet, along with Mark Sykes.

92. In a minute to the Secretary of State of 8 January 1923, Shuckburgh wrote: 'We made our promise to the Jews at a time of grave national emergency, because we thought we might obtain some assistance from them. We induced our allies to become parties to the promise. Finally we had it formally ratified … It seems to me that, if we are to tear up our pledge … [we] should have to announce to the world that we had undertaken a task beyond our strength and that we have no alternative but to put it aside. In that event we must clear out of Palestine altogether …', CO 733/54.

93. CO 733/58, Minute by Shuckburgh to Ormsby-Gore, 10 January 1923.

94. CO 733/58, Secret Cabinet Paper CP 60 (23) 'Palestine and the Balfour Declaration', January 1923.

95. Knox, *The Making of a New Eastern Question*, pp. 163–4 quoting CAB 24/159 CP 106 (23).

96. CO 733/58, Secret Memorandum, CP 106 (23), 17 February 1923.

97. CO 733/54. See, for instance, *Daily Mail*, 9, 10, 11 January 1923.

98. CO 733/38, Forbes-Adam to Shuckburgh, 20 October 1921. Private.

99. India Office Records L/P&S/18/B 313. Peace Conference. Memorandum Respecting Palestine. Secret. P49. Printed for the War Cabinet, January 1919. The memorandum is written by Sir Erle Richards, submitted to Lord Curzon, 'and is now circulated, by his instructions, for the consideration of the Eastern Committee'.

100. Ibid.

101. Ibid.

102. McMahon's letter to Sharif Hussein on 24 October 1915 stated: 'the portion of Syria lying to the west of the district of Damascus, Hama, Homs and Aleppo, cannot be said to be purely Arab and should be excluded from the proposed limits and boundaries'.

103. CO 733/38, Shuckburgh to Hogarth, 12 October 1921. Private.

104. CO 733/38, Hogarth to Shuckburgh, 17 October 1921.

105. CO 733/8, Minute by S. M. Campbell, 6 January 1922

106. CO 733/8, Minute by Shuckburgh, 11 January 1922.

107. On 11 March 1922, Shuckburgh minuted that McMahon had come to see him the previous day and read to him his explanation of his intention, in which he had said that he meant 'to exclude the whole of Palestine from the area in respect of which the pledge of Arab independence was given', and that he was 'quite clear' on that point. CO 733/38, Minute by Shuckburgh, 11 March 1922. McMahon's letter to Shuckburgh is in the same file, and is, curiously, dated 12 March 1922.

108. Ibid. The Peel Report stated that the Palestine Arabs never accepted the interpretation of the McMahon letter set out in the government's Statement of Policy in June 1922. See Peel Report, p. 107.

109. CO 733/24, Samuel to Churchill, Political Report for July 1922.

110. CO 733/59, Minute by Eric Mills, the Acting Principal in the Colonial Office, 18 August 1922.

111. There had in fact been no such entity as the vilayet of Damascus, only a vilayet of Syria, with Damascus as its capital. Sykes, *Crossroads to Israel*, p. 63.

112. CO 733/39, Shuckburgh to Samuel, 7 November 1922, Private.

113. CO 733/39, Samuel to Shuckburgh, 17 November 1922.

114. CO 733/55, R. C. Lindsay to Shuckburgh, 19 February 1923.

115. CO 733/57, Minute by S. Moody, 21 February 1923.

116. CO 733/57, Letter from Bland to Shuckburgh, 28 February 1923. The letter was probably from John Otway Percy Bland (1863–1945), writer on China. Correspondent to the *Times* until 1910, then continued to write widely.

117. For the complete debate, see United Kingdom, *Parliamentary Debates*, (Lords) vol. 53, 13 February to 3 May, 1923, pp. 226–34.

118. Evyatar Friesel, 'British Officials on the Situation in Palestine, 1923' in *Middle Eastern Studies*, vol. 23, no. 2, April 1987, p. 200. This illuminating document, which Friesel reproduces in full, is the transcript of a conversation between the two men, written from memory by Moody, obviously not meant for publication. Friesel states that the conversation was very private; thoughts, doubts and hesitations were voiced that would not find expression in formal correspondence.

119. Ibid. pp. 200–1.

120. CO 733/83, Secret Cabinet Memorandum, CP 121 (24), 19 February 1924.

121. CO 733/57, Minute by Hubert Young, 22 February 1923.

122. The draft article, suggested for insertion in the treaty by Young, read: 'His Hashimite Majesty King Hussein hereby recognises the special position of His Britannic Majesty in Iraq, Transjordan and Palestine and undertakes that in such matters as come within the influence of His Hashimite Majesty concerning any or all of these countries, he will do his best to co-operate with His Britannic Majesty in the fulfilment of his obligations.' CO 733/43, 'Draft Article for insertion in Treaty with King Hussein', 23 March 1923.

123. CO 733/43, Minute by Shuckburgh, 23 March 1923.

124. CO 733/65, Samuel to J. H. Thomas, Political Report for January 1924, Secret.

125. Ibid.

126. CO 733/78, Memorandum by the Middle East Department, 12 February 1924. Printed for the Cabinet.

127. CO 733/78, Draft Telegram to High Commissioner for Palestine, Memorandum by the Middle East Department, Secret, CP 121 (24) Printed for the Cabinet, February 1924.

128. Porath, *The Emergence*, p. 182. See also Y. Porath, 'The Palestinians and the Negotiations for the Anglo-Hijazi Treaty 1920–1925', in *Asian and African Studies: Journal of the Israel Oriental Society*, vol. 8, no. 1, 1972, pp. 20–48.

129. See, for instance, H. St. John Philby, *Arabian Jubilee* (London, 1952), p. 73.

130. Sir Reader Bullard, *Two Kings of Arabia. Sir Reader Bullard's Letters from Jeddah 1923–5 and 1936–9*, ed. E. C. Hodgkin, (Reading, 1993), pp. 60, 62.

131. James Morris, *The Hashemite Kings* (London, 1959), p. 82.

132. CO 733/58, Secret Report, Cabinet Committee on Palestine, 'The Future of Palestine', 27 July 1923.

133. CO 733/54, Petition by Members of the House of Commons, 26 July 1923.

134. CO 733/54, Ormsby-Gore to Secretary of State, 19 July 1923.

135. CO 733/54, Minute by Shuckburgh to Masterton-Smith, Ormsby-Gore and the Secretary of State, 24 July, 1923.

136. CO 733/58, Minute by Shuckburgh, 27 July 1923.

137. Ibid.

138. CO 733/54, Memorandum by Meinertzhagen, 'Strategical Importance in Palestine', 14 May 1923. He argued that: firstly, the defence of the Suez Canal in any major war must depend on Palestine and not Egypt; secondly, Palestine's geographical position controlled Arabia; thirdly, the development of the trans-desert route to Iraq, whether by railway or by pipeline, depended on British retention of Palestine, or 'on at least a friendly Palestine'; and last, Palestine was a vital link with the British Far Eastern Empire and would increase in importance as time went on.

139. CO 733/54, Minute by Lord Devonshire, 19 May 1923.

140. CO 733/58, Minute from Shuckburgh to the Secretary of State, entitled 'Cabinet Committee on Palestine', 2 July 1923.

141. Cocker, *Meinertzhagen*, pp. 152–5.

142. CO 733/54, Shuckburgh to Secretary of State, Secret Minute, 25 July 1923.

143. Chaim Weizmann, *The Letters and Papers of Chaim Weizmann*, vol. XI, January 1922–July 1923, ed. Bernard Wasserstein (Jerusalem 1977), p. 350.

144. Wasserstein, *Herbert Samuel*, pp. 262–4. Wasserstein calls the Cabinet decision 'not the least of services rendered by Samuel to Zionism'.

145. CO 733/58, Secret Cabinet Report CP 351 (23) 23 July 1923.

146. Cabinet Committee on Palestine, 'The Future of Palestine', 27 July 1923, Secret Cabinet Paper CP 351 (23) in CO 733/58.

147. Knox, *The Making of a New Eastern Question*, p. 20.

148. Reinharz, *Chaim Weizmann*, p. 379.

149. CO 733/84, Minute by Shuckburgh to Marsh, 28 January 1924.

150. CO 733/84, Minute by Shuckburgh, 1 February 1924.

151. For instance CO 733/15, Minute by Shuckburgh, 7 November 1921.

152. For instance CO 733/54, Minute by Shuckburgh to Secretary of State, 25 July 1923, Secret.

153. Richmond to Samuel, 13 March 1924 (HS 11), quoted in Wasserstein, *The British in Palestine*, p. 146.

154. Knox, *The Making of a New Eastern Question*, p. 171, quoting a letter, FO 800/156, Clayton to Walford Selby, 3 March 1924.

155. CO 733/84, Letter from B. Jacobs, acting chairman of the London political committee of *Po'ali Zion* to Lord Arnold, 29 April 1924.

156. CO 733/84, Minute by Shuckburgh to Lord Arnold, 10 May 1924.

157. CO 733/86, Letter from Chaim Weizmann to J. H. Thomas, Secretary of State for the Colonies, 18 July 1924.

158. CO 733/86, Minute by Shuckburgh to Secretary of State. 24 July 1924.

CHAPTER FOUR

1. Sir Ronald Storrs, in his introduction as chairman at a lecture delivered by Sir Herbert Samuel in 1935, stated: 'In the building up of Palestine, the big four consisted of Theodor Herzl, who saw and imagined: Chaim Weizmann, who grasped the occasion and turned it to the right account: Lord Balfour, who embodied that occasion in history; and Sir Herbert Samuel who turned principle into practice, word into fact …' Sir Herbert Louis Samuel, 'Great Britain and Palestine', delivered in the Great Hall of University College, London, by the Rt. Hon. Sir Herbert Samuel, G.C.B., C.B.E., D.C.L., on November 25th 1935. The Second Lucien Wolf Memorial Lecture (The Jewish Historical Society of England, 1935), p. 26.

2. Samuel, *Memoirs*, pp. 139–40.

3. Wasserstein, *Herbert Samuel*, pp. 202–4. Wasserstein writes that only fragmentary evidence exists of Samuel's interest in Zionism prior to 1914. He draws attention to a letter which Samuel received in 1900 from an 88-year-old English lady congratulating Samuel's baby son Edwin on the signing of his first letter, and saying that perhaps one day he might be governor of the Holy Land, adding: 'I believe in the prophesies as much as you do that the country shall be restored to its owners.'

4. Samuel, *Memoirs*, p. 139. See also 'Great Britain and Palestine', p. 11.

5. John Bowle, *Viscount Samuel: A Biography* (London, 1957), p. 170.

6. Wasserstein, *Herbert Samuel*, pp. 404–5.

7. See, for example, the arguments in Weizmann's pamphlet, *Palestine's Role in the*

Solution of the Jewish Problem. However, developments on the European continent were far more important in shaping the Zionist movement than sentimental factors. In Eastern Europe, anti-Semitism was on the rise after the pogroms in Czarist Russia in 1881. There was also a trend of anti-Semitism in Western Europe, especially following the Dreyfus affair in France in 1894. In Britain, the influx of Jews from Russia and Rumania from the early 1880s led the British Government to introduce the Aliens Bill of 1904 and the Aliens Act of 1905 to control unrestricted immigration. The Bill recommended, *inter alia*, that an alien arriving in Britain might be required to furnish a certificate with respect to his character and antecedents, and that 'undesirables' might be refused entry to the country. The Bill was strongly attacked by the leaders of Anglo-Jewry who argued that it could be taken as a justification 'for every Jew-hater and persecutor' who might point to it and say 'if England had to legislate against the Jew, is it not proof that he is right in other circumstances to exercise towards him more violent methods?' The 1905 Act, though considered by its opponents to be an improvement on its predecessor, was still attacked on the grounds that it did not make any exception in the case of victims of religious persecution; that persons refused permission to land had no right of appeal to the ordinary courts of law; that the Act enabled the expulsion of persons on 'trivial' grounds, and that it placed the cost of returning expelled aliens on the shipping companies which had transported them, which was bound to affect the traffic in immigrants. Rabinowicz, 'The Aliens Bill and Jewish Immigration to Britain 1902–1905', pp. 100–10.

  8. His mother's family, called Yates, also belonged to the cousinhood.

  9. Samuel's emotional attachment to his mother continued and he wrote to her once a week, with unfailing regularity, until her death in 1920. See Wasserstein, *Herbert Samuel*, p. 9.

  10. Ibid., pp. 18–21.

  11. Ibid., pp. 372–3.

  12. 'Great Britain and Palestine', p. 10.

  13. Stuart Samuel.

  14. Wasserstein, *Herbert Samuel*, pp. 11, 16.

  15. 'Great Britain and Palestine', pp. 11–12.

  16. Samuel, *Memoirs*, p. 139.

  17. Wasserstein states that there is very little evidence of Samuel's interest in Zionism before 1914, but, according to Samuel's own account, it would appear that he became interested in the Zionist movement after having read Herzl's *Der Judenstaat*. Wasserstein speculates that Samuel must have read it soon after its publication in 1896. Wasserstein, *Herbert Samuel*, p. 202.

  18. 'Great Britain and Palestine', pp. 11–12.

  19. Samuel, *Memoirs*, p. 140.

  20. Wasserstein, *Herbert Samuel*, p. 198.

  21. CO 733/102, 'Palestine. Report of the High Commissioner on the Administration of Palestine 1920–1925', p. 33. Samuel referred to this report as the 'Book of Chronicles'. It was published as Great Britain, Colonial no. 15, *Palestine. Report of the High Commissioner on the Administration of Palestine 1920–1925* (HMSO, London, 1925).

  22. 'Great Britain and Palestine', pp. 12–13.

23. This view was said to have been conveyed to Weizmann and by him to the Zionist International. Robert John and Sami Hadawi, *The Palestine Diary, 1914–45*, vol. I (Beirut, 1970), pp. 60–1.

24. The same argument could have been used in regard to Palestine, where Jews were estimated to comprise only about 7 per cent of the population in 1914.

25. Samuel did not circulate this memorandum to the Cabinet immediately, he sent copies of it to the prime minister and two or three of his colleagues, in particular Grey, who, he later claimed, were 'sympathetic' to Zionist ideals, although not necessarily favouring a British protectorate. According to his own account, Samuel received letters of approval from Reading, Haldane and Grey. He was also keen to approach Lord Bryce, a former Cabinet member, because of the 'great weight' of his views on Middle Eastern matters. Samuel, *Memoirs*, pp. 142–4. Lloyd George also assured Samuel that he was 'very keen to see a Jewish State established in Palestine'. Knox, *The Making of a New Eastern Question*, pp. 15–16.

26. 'Great Britain and Palestine', pp. 13–14.

27. Samuel, *Memoirs*, p. 142. Samuel's comment on this famous and often quoted Asquithian remark, which he himself quoted in his memoirs many years later, is of special interest. He said that he was 'amused' to have read this note in Asquith's diary and wrote: 'With Disraeli's maxim I do not concur. If it were true, how is it that, in this very case, my cousin, Edwin Montagu, of precisely the same stock as myself, should have taken exactly the opposite view to mine on Palestine and Zionism?'

28. Wasserstein, *Herbert Samuel*, p. 209. For more details on anti-Semitism in Eastern Europe see I. M. Herrman, 'Anglo-Zionist Relations from Herzl to the Balfour Declaration, 1902–17', unpublished D.Phil. thesis, Oxford University 1971, pp. 93, 95.

29. CAB 37/126. Secret Cabinet memorandum, 'Palestine', March 1915. The full text is published in Bowle, *Viscount Samuel*, pp. 172–7.

30. CAB 37/126, op. cit.

31. Probably referring to some members of Anglo-Jewry who were hostile to Zionism in its initial stage.

32. Samuel Papers, Thames TV 1978, Box I, File II, DS 149.

33. Fromkin, *A Peace to End All Peace*, p. 270. Indeed, Asquith found it 'singular' that Lloyd George and Samuel should advocate a British protectorate for such different reasons.

34. High commissioner, South Africa, 1897–1905; member of the War Cabinet 1916–18; secretary of state for war 1918–19; secretary of state for the colonies 1919–21.

35. Wasserstein, *The British in Palestine*, p. 74.

36. Wasserstein, *Herbert Samuel*, p. 212.

37. Ibid., pp. 173–7.

38. Ibid., pp. 211–12.

39. Wasserstein, *The British in Palestine*, pp. 74–5.

40. Samuel, *Memoirs*, p. 148.

41. Wasserstein, *Herbert Samuel*, p. 239. Wasserstein does not explain how this came about. Samuel himself mentions in his memoirs that he acted as chairman of a committee which drew up a statement of political proposals for submission to the government, and of another committee on the future finances of the Zionist movement and the Jewish national

home, and that the Zionists benefited from advice from the economist J. M. Keynes. See Samuel, *Memoirs*, p. 148.

42. *Palestine: The Organ of the British Palestine Committee*, vol. 4, no. 13, 2 November 1918, p. 103.

43. Wasserstein, *Herbert Samuel*, p. 238.

44. British Zionist and industrialist. Secretary of the Zionist Commission in Palestine, 1918.

45. Wasserstein, *Herbert Samuel*, p. 239. The memorandum was entitled 'Memorandum of the Zionist Organization relating to the reconstruction of Palestine as the Jewish National Home', January 1919.

46. Wasserstein, *Herbert Samuel*, pp. 239–40.

47. Ibid., p. 239.

48. Ibid., p. 238.

49. Bowle, *Viscount Samuel*, pp. 183–4.

50. Ibid.

51. Wasserstein, *Herbert Samuel*, p. 241.

52. Wasserstein, *The British in Palestine* p. 76.

53. Bowle, *Viscount Samuel*, p. 184. Whether Samuel was in fact 'asked' by the Foreign Office is in question. See note 56 below.

54. *Palestine: The Organ of the British Palestine Committee*, vol. 6, no. 23, 17 January 1920, p. 180.

55. FO 371/5139 E 3594/131/44, Samuel to Allenby, Report on the Administrative and Financial Situation, 31 March 1920, Confidential.

56. FO 371/5139 E 3109/131/44, Samuel to Curzon, Report on the Political Situation, 2 April 1920, Confidential. However, Curzon, answering a parliamentary question on 29 June 1920 revealed that, up to that moment, he had 'no idea' that Samuel's report had any 'official' character at all. He also said that Samuel 'went out really in a private capacity to Palestine, at the suggestion of Lord Allenby', and that after going round the country, he wrote a report, which he later 'allowed' him [i.e. Curzon] to see, but that the report was not written for publication. FO 371/ 5114, House of Lords Debates, 29 June 1920.

57. Replacing the anti-Zionist officials of the military administration with the pro-Zionist personnel of the new civil administration was one of the most far-reaching measures in bringing the Balfour Declaration into effect.

58. FO 371/5139 E 3109/131/44, Samuel to Curzon, 2 April 1920.

59. Ibid., Samuel to Allenby, 31 March 1920.

60. Ibid. Compare this to the statement in 1905 by Israel Zangwill, an extreme Zionist and a strong advocate of removing the native population as a 'solution' to the demographic problem, who recognized that Palestine was 'already twice as thickly populated as the United States'. He wrote that the Zionists must be prepared 'to drive out by the sword' the Arab tribes in possession of the land. Nur Masalha, *Expulsion of the Palestinians: the Concept of 'Transfer' in Zionist Political Thought 1882–1948* (Washington, 1992), p. 10.

61. Throughout the Mediterranean plains, from Portugal to Lebanon, malaria is a disease that directly results from the geographical landscape; water from the mountains, barred from reaching the sea by the high line of sand dunes, flooded the plains, forming stretches

of stagnant water and marshes. The French historian, Fernand Braudel, points out that water, here, becomes 'synonymous with death'; Fernand Braudel, *The Mediterranean and the Mediterranean World in the Age of Philip II*, tr. Sian Reynolds (6th impression, London, 1990), pp. 62–3. Even today 'great tracts of land remain uncultivable and of little use'; ibid., p. 241. Braudel also describes malaria as 'the background to Mediterranean pathology'; ibid., p. 64.

62. Referring to what later became known as the Rutenberg Concession. See Chapter 9.

63. FO 371/5139 E 4347, Samuel to Curzon, 3 May 1920.

64. FO 371/5139 E 3594/131/44, Samuel to Allenby, 31 March 1920.

65. FO 371/5139 E 3109, Samuel to Curzon, 2 April 1920.

66. Wasserstein, *The British in Palestine*, p. 79.

67. FO 371/5139 E 3109/131/44, Samuel to Curzon, 2 April 1920.

68. Wasserstein, *Herbert Samuel*, p. 244.

69. Wasserstein, *The British in Palestine*, p. 79.

70. Wasserstein, *Herbert Samuel*, p. 226.

71. *Palestine: The Organ of the British Palestine Committee*, vol. 3, 30 March 1918, p. 64.

72. The address was entitled 'Zionism, its ideals and practical hope'.

73. ESCO Foundation for Palestine, *Palestine: a Study of Jewish, Arab, and British Policies*, (2 vols, New Haven, London and Oxford, 1947), vol. 1, p. 261.

74. Samuel, *Memoirs*, p. 168.

75. Wasserstein, *Herbert Samuel*, p. 240.

76. In fact, Faisal was proclaimed and accepted as King of all Syria by the people of Syria and Palestine, both Muslim and Christian.

77. FO 371/5139 E 3109/131/44, Samuel to Curzon, Report on the Political Situation, 2 April 1920, Confidential.

78. The British government implicitly recognized the competence of the Syrian Congress to deal with Palestine, and Allenby had clear and urgent instructions 'not to interfere in any way with the meeting of the Congress', asking him only to urge Faisal to moderation, and to assure the congress that the Allies had 'every intention' of fulfilling their promises to the people of Syria and Palestine. See Tibawi, *Anglo-Arab Relations*, p. 388, quoting FO 371/ 5032/ E 329, 19 February 1920.

79. FO 371/5034, Samuel to Curzon, 27 March 1920.

80. Wasserstein, *The British in Palestine*, p. 79.

81. Porath, *The Emergence*, p. 97.

82. FO 371/5200 E 920/920/44, Meinertzhagen to FO, 2 March 1920. Sir John Tilley wrote the next day that it was 'only natural that the inhabitants of Palestine should be anti-Zionist'.

83. FO 371/5139 E 3109/131/44, Samuel to Curzon, 2 April 1920.

84. Faisal had already been proclaimed 'King' of Syria by the Syrian Arab Congress when Samuel wrote his proposal; but Samuel ignored this, preferring to call him Emir instead.

85. FO 371/5139 E 3109/131/44, Samuel to Curzon, 2 April 1920.

86. Samuel Papers, JC 368.

87. Wasserstein, *Herbert Samuel*, p. 384.

88. Wasserstein, *The British in Palestine*, p. 81.

89. Bowle, *Viscount Samuel*, p. 189–90.

90. Wasserstein, *The British in Palestine*, pp. 82–3.

91. FO 371/5263 E 6878 and E 6786, Bols to War Office, 18 June 1920.

92. FO 371/5263 E 6786, Minute by Young, 21 June 1920.

93. FO 371/5120 E 7277, 24 June 1920, Secret.

94. Storrs, *Orientations*, pp. 336–7.

95. Wasserstein, *The British in Palestine*, p. 88.

96. Viscount Samuel, *Memoirs* (London, 1945), p. 168. Samuel lived long enough (he died in 1963) to see the birth of the Jewish State in 1948, and hence, the birth of the Palestinian refugee problem. However, he seems to have been silent on the mass exodus of the Arabs from their homes before and during the 1948–49 war.

97. Ibid., p. 144–5.

98. Wasserstein, *Herbert Samuel*, p. 269.

99. In June 1932, Chaim Arlosoroff, director of the Political Department in the Jewish Agency (who was assassinated the following year by a rival Zionist group) gave verbal expression to what was meant by gradualism in attaining Zionist objectives. Although lying outside the scope of this study, it is important to address this issue in as much as it throws light on the conflicting nature of the announcements made by Zionist leaders at different stages of the development of the national home, including the period under study. In what seems to have been the first open expression of this policy, Arlosoroff, writing to Weizmann, described his own memorandum as 'an abstract essay' on Zionist policy, basing his argument on the assumption that it was necessary to attain Zionism's aims 'gradually, step by step', and that it had become evident that this policy was 'the only correct one in the past'. He added that by referring to 'stages' in the development of the Zionist enterprise, he did not mean concrete situations that could be 'exactly defined statistically or by some diplomatic or legal formula'; what he had in mind was 'definite stages of development in the relationship of forces between the two peoples contending in the country'. The first stage (at the time of his memorandum) had already been attained by gradual development: the Arabs were no longer strong enough to destroy the Zionists' position but still considered themselves strong enough to establish an Arab state in Palestine, without considering Jewish political demands, whereas the Jews were strong enough to preserve their status quo without sufficient strength to ensure constant growth through immigration, colonization and the maintenance of peace and order. The second stage would be attained when the balance of power between the two communities would be such as to prevent any possibility of establishing an Arab state in Palestine, when the Jews would have acquired 'such additional strength as will automatically block the road for Arab domination'. The third stage would be attained when the Arabs were unable to frustrate the constant growth of the Jews through immigration and economic activity. This constant growth would influence the Arabs in the direction of 'negotiated accord'. The fourth stage would be attained when an equilibrium between the two peoples would be based 'on real forces and an agreed solution to the problem'. See Chaim Arlosoroff, 'The Stages of Zionism and Minority National Rule, June 30, 1932' in Khalidi (ed.), *From Haven to Conquest*, pp. 245–54.

100. Wasserstein, *The British in Palestine*, p. 88.

101. Samuel, *Memoirs*, p. 176.

102. Evyatar Friesel, 'Herbert Samuel's Reassessment of Zionism in 1921' in *Studies in Zionism*, vol. 5, no. 2, p. 217.

103. Great Britain, High Commissioner for Palestine, 'An Interim Report on the Civil Administration of Palestine during the period 1st July, 1920–30th June, 1921. Presented to Parliament August 1921', Cmd. 1499.

104. CO 733/52, 'Palestine's Protest Against the Balfour Declaration'. Proclamation by Musa Kazim al-Husseini, President of the Arab Executive Committee, 2 November 1923, submitted to the 'civilized world through its governments', in Samuel to Devonshire, Political Report for November 1923.

105. Norman Bentwich, *My 77 Years* (London, 1962), p. 65.

CHAPTER FIVE

1. FO 371/5205 E 7101/1136/44, 'Message from His Majesty the King to the People of Palestine'. Enclosure in Earl Curzon to Sir H. Samuel, Jerusalem, 19 June 1920.

2. Sykes, *Crossroads to Israel*, p. 42.

3. 'Interim Report on the Civil Administration of Palestine during the period 1st July, 1920–30th June, 1921', op. cit., pp. 6–7.

4. Ibid.

5. CO 733/15, quoted in *The British Cabinet and Zionism*, a pamphlet published by the British Committee of the Palestine Arab Delegation in November 1921.

6. Ibid.

7. According to the ESCO Foundation for Palestine, the official policy which guided the administration between 1922 and 1929 was 'worked out in the first two years of Samuel's administration and incorporated in the White Paper which was the 1922 statement of policy'. ESCO Foundation for Palestine, *Palestine. Jewish, Arab and British Policies*, New Haven, 1947, vol. 1, pp. 256, 259.

8. Sykes, *Crossroads to Israel*, p. 70.

9. FO 371/5113 E 1184, 2 March 1920.

10. *A Survey of Palestine*, vol. I, p. 17.

11. Bentwich, *My 77 Years*, p. 67.

12. *A Survey of Palestine*, vol. 1, p. 108.

13. Keith-Roach, *Pasha of Jerusalem*, p. 76.

14. Ibid., pp. 94, 214.

15. CO 733/24.

16. CO 733/66, Minute by Young, 3 May 1924. On many occasions, the Palestine Arabs requested the removal of Norman Bentwich from office. In May 1921, for instance, the people of Tulkarm district submitted a petition to the British government in which they asked for the removal of all Zionist officials from the Palestine administration, and in particular Bentwich, who, they asserted, was responsible for enacting legislation which was detrimental to Arab interests and favourable to those of the Zionists. Kayyali, *Watha'iq al-Muqawama*, p. 20. Petition by the people of Tulkarm dated 17 May 1921.

17. Deedes' relationship with his mother, Rosie Deedes, was a very close one and she lived with him in Jerusalem. She was the daughter of a Jewish doctor whose wife had been converted to Christianity. See Keith-Roach, *Pasha of Jerusalem*, p. 74.

18. Ben Zvi noted, 'no impartial historian can fail to acknowledge, in retrospect, that a series of important legislative measures dating from the first half of Samuel's term (which coincided, more or less, with Deedes' tenure of office as chief secretary) were constructive, and designed to implement the declared policy of the British Government. The Land Transfer Ordinance, the Immigration Ordinance, the Banking Ordinance, and many more prosaic Acts.' He affirmed that Deedes had richly earned the honourable and very rare designation of *Hassidei Ummot Ha-Olam* (pious ones among the nations of the world). Eliahu Elath, Norman Bentwich, Doris May (eds), *Memories of Sir Wyndham Deedes*, (London., 1958), pp. 28–9.

19. Albert Hyamson was a member of the Political Committee of the Zionist Organization, and was appointed in 1921 in the Immigration Department. British officials were at first reluctant to appoint a Jew to such a post, but finally decided to go ahead. Although he opposed the influx of destitute Jews from Eastern Europe, and was disgusted by the fact that they dominated the Yishuv, and opposed the concept of Jewish State, he nevertheless continued to call himself a Zionist. See for instance Wasserstein, *The British in Palestine*, pp. 210–12.

20. Bentwich, *My 77 Years*, p. 67.

21. Wasserstein, *The British in Palestine*, pp. 208–10. Kenneth Stein asserts that Nurock made the administration's reports on land issues readily available to the Jewish Agency. Kenneth Stein, *The Land Question in Palestine 1917–1939* (London, 1984), p. 94.

22. FO 371/6307, Despatch no. 232 E 6283, 18 July 1921.

23. FO 371/ 6370 E 8983, 5 August 1921.

24. FO 371/6370, Shuckburgh, Colonial Office, to the Under Secretary of State, Foreign Office, 6 December 1921.

25. Samuel, *Memoirs*, p. 155.

26. Storrs, *Orientations*, p. 340.

27. Ibid., p. 358.

28. John Richmond, 'Prophet of Doom: E. T. Richmond, FRIBA., Palestine 1920–1924' in *Arabic and Islamic Garland: Historical, Educational and Literary Papers Presented to Abdul Latif Tibawi* (London, 1977), pp. 189–96. This article contains highly revealing information and is based on records discovered as late as 1970 by E. T. Richmond's son. Unfortunately, very few of his father's letters from his first eight months in the Palestine administration have survived.

29. Ibid., p. 190.

30. Ibid., p. 191.

31. C. R. Ashbee, quoted in Knox, *The Making of a New Eastern Question*, p. 170.

32. Keith-Roach, *Pasha of Jerusalem*, p. 76.

33. Sir H. W. Richmond, Master of Downing College, Cambridge.

34. J. Richmond, 'Prophet of Doom', p. 191.

35. CO 733/84, Minute by Keith-Roach, 7 May 1924, denying Zionist charges that the Jewish position in Palestine was prejudiced by 'the largely anti-Zionist attitude of a number

of influential British officials' in Palestine, and that Richmond was the only opponent of Zionist policy who pointed out the possible dangers of the government's policy.

36. Richmond, 'Prophet of Doom', p. 194.

37. Ibid., p. 195. Richmond added in the same letter: 'Deedes goes in a month's time—a very good riddance. He is a fanatical little missionary with his Old Testament and other Hebraic furniture'.

38. Knox, *The Making of a New Eastern Question*, p. 170.

39. CO 733/17, Deedes to Shuckburgh, 2 December 1921, Personal and Confidential. Letter to introduce the bearer, Richmond.

40. Richmond, 'Prophet of Doom ', p. 195.

41. Ibid., pp. 195–6.

42. D. Edward Knox, 'The Development of British Policy in Palestine, 1917–1925: Sir Gilbert Clayton and the 'New Eastern Policy', PhD thesis, University of Michigan, 1971, p. 371.

43. Richmond, 'Prophet of Doom', pp. 195,196.

44. CO 733/67, Ronald Storrs, Political Resumé for Jerusalem–Jaffa District for period ending March 31st 1924, Secret, in Samuel to Thomas, Political Report for March 1924.

45. Porath, *The Emergence*, p. 173.

46. Quoted in Fromkin, *A Peace to End All Peace*, p. 317.

47. Knox, 'Development of British Policy', p. 350.

48. Ibid., p. 387.

49. CO 733/46, Press Comments, Samuel to Devonshire, Political Report for May 1923, Secret.

50. CO 733/48, Press Comments, Clayton to Devonshire, Political Report for July 1923.

51. Knox, 'Development of British Policy', pp. 386–7.

52. Ibid., p. 373.

53. The last letter in the Bramley Papers (Cambridge University Library: Royal Commonwealth Society Library), dated 14 January 1925, mentions his illness; correspondence was cut short by his death in 1925. See Jones, *Britain and Palestine*, p. 17.

54. Correspondence dated 8 November 1923 [to Colonial Secretary?].

55. Bramley Papers, MSS2 P.B. Papers on India and Palestine, To Secretary of State for the Colonies, 6 November 1923.

56. Bramley Papers, Bramley to the Secretary in Charge, Near East Department, Foreign Office, 'Memorandum re. the murder of Sir Lee Stack', Secret and Strictly Confidential, no date but probably written in November 1924. Bramley wrote: 'The Foreign Office is also, I believe, for the moment at all events, the least susceptible to political Zionist influence and therefore in the strongest position to deal independently with such questions as these.'

57. Colonel Stirling, governor of Jaffa District, served with T. E. Lawrence in the desert campaign and was sympathetic to the Arabs.

58. Palestine was divided into six administrative districts: Jerusalem, Lydda (headquarters Jaffa), Haifa, Gaza, Samaria (headquarters Nablus) and Galilee (headquarters Nazareth). Each district was under the control of a district commissioner, who reported to the chief secretary Wyndham Deedes (Gilbert Clayton after 1923). Each district commissioner was assisted by a deputy and one or more assistants. The district commissioner had no direct

specific authority over the local representatives of the professional and technical departments of the government who reported directly to their respective heads; his main responsibility was to maintain a liaison with them, coordinate their activities, and above all, keep public security. *A Survey of Palestine*, vol. 1, p. 112.

59. Lt-Col. W. F. Stirling, 'Palestine: 1920–1923' in Khalidi (ed.), *From Haven to Conquest*, p. 229.

60. Ibid., pp. 231–2.

61. Ibid., p. 232.

62. Ibid., p. 235.

63. Ibid. Stirling wrote his book, *Safety Last*, in 1953, five years after the Jewish state was established. He stated that 'it was clearly not right to inject a foreign state into the heart of a group of Arab countries; nor was it right to displace an existing population against its will in order to make room for migrants from abroad'.

64. CO 733/13, War Office to Churchill, 15 August 1921, Confidential.

65. CO 733/28, Samuel to Devonshire, 8 December 1922, Confidential.

66. CO 733/47, note by Samuel commenting on Sir Gilbert Clayton's despatch of 6 July 1923, 18 July 1923.

67. CO 733/54, Imperial Conference 1923, Secret, E. 2nd Meeting (1923), 'Stenographic Notes of the Second Meeting Held at 10 Downing Street, S.W., On Wednesday, October 3, 1923. At 11 A.M.'

68. CO 733/47, Political Report for June 1923. Clayton to Devonshire. Jamal al-Husseini's speech at the Sixth Arab Congress.

69. CO 733/78, Memorandum by the Middle East Department, Palestine, 19 February 1924. Circulated to the Cabinet, Secret. CP 121 (24).

70. Ibid.

71. Geoffrey Furlonge, *Palestine is My Country: The Story of Musa Alami* (London, 1989), pp. 88, 89.

72. Ibid., p. 78. However, it did not take long for the Palestine Arabs to become sceptical of Samuel's real motives. Musa al-'Alami, from his position as a government official in the legal service in Palestine, subsequently concluded that Samuel was dedicated to the success of the national home. He never saw the Arabs as having any real power, or as being politically equal with the Jews. He succeeded in outmanoeuvring the Arabs by 'making concessions over trifles', in order to make way for other matters which were essential to the achievement of Zionist aims.

73. FO 371/5121 E 8599/85/44, Samuel to Curzon, 12 July 1920, Confidential.

74. Ibid.

75. FO 371/512, Samuel to Curzon, 12 July 1920. Personal letter.

76. FO 371/5121 E 8599/85/44, Samuel to Curzon, 2 April 1920.

77. The frontier to the north was fixed later, in 1924, in accordance with an Anglo-French agreement of 1920. Until 1930, according to Bentwich, the frontier to the south-east with Hijaz and Najd was not finally demarcated, but was described in a British Note to King Ibn Sa'ud dated May 1927. Bentwich, *The Mandates System*, p. 22.

78. It is to be noted that when the British Cabinet approved the text of the mandate in December 1920, Maurice Hankey telegraphed to Balfour in Switzerland that the 'words

"national home" in the fourth paragraph of preamble of Palestine Mandate *should not* be written in capitals as in texts of November 29th'. (FO 371/5247 E 15030 1.12 1920). It is therefore safe to assume that Samuel's use of the term 'the National Home' was a deviation from official policy and intentions. Also, for an explanation of the difference between 'a' and 'the' national home, see ESCO Foundation for Palestine, *Palestine*, vol. 1, pp. 113, 266. The main issue 'was not the use of the term Jewish National Home versus the term Jewish State' and that the real compromise made by the Zionists was the acceptance of the phrase "a national home in Palestine" instead of their original suggestion "the recognition of Palestine as the Jewish national home"'.

79. FO 371/5121 E 8599/85/44, Samuel to Curzon, 12 July 1920.

80. Ibid. The Grand Mufti at the time was Kamil al-Husseini who was known for his British sympathies and who supported the anti-Zionist movement only after the riots of April 1920. See, for example, Porath, *The Emergence*, pp. 39, 187–8.

81. Porath, *The Emergence*, p. 305.

82. FO 371/5117 E 772, GHQ to FO, 13 February 1920, transmitting a copy of a translation of a petition from the Muslim-Christian Society.

83. FO 371/ 5033, 12 March 1920. Hardinge commented on this telegram: 'All we have to do is to keep cool and not be bluffed. Anybody with experience of the East knows the value of such demonstrations.'

84. The secret Arab society whose members were Muslims and Christians, which had led the movement for Arab emancipation against the Young Turks since 1908.

85. Darwazeh, *Mudhakkirat*, vol. 1, p. 202. Darwazeh records that a secret society (Jam'iyya Fata Filastin) had been set up in Damascus in mid-1920, to promote armed resistance against the British on the Palestine-Syrian borders, in order to impress upon the British that the Palestinian people were willing to adopt such methods in order to prevent Zionist-British designs in Palestine. Darwazeh was the secretary of this movement, and among its members were Hajj Amin al-Husseini, 'Aref al-'Aref, Shaykh 'Abd al-Qadir al-Muzaffar, Salim 'Abd al-Rahman, and Mu'in al-Madi. Darwazeh also reveals that this society received financial help from the central committee of al-'Arabiyya al-Fata (the secret organization which had formerly fought the Young Turks). However, the fall of Faisal's regime led to the collapse of this movement, as Damascus was its centre.

86. Knox, *The Making of a New Eastern Question*, p. 153.

87. Porath, *The Emergence*, p. 103.

88. FO 371/5123, Samuel to Curzon, 13 September 1920. It should be noted that, contrary to what Samuel suggested, the Arabs demanded in 1921, and even later, that Palestine should *not* be separated from her sister states.

89. Kamil Khillah, *Filastin wa-al-intidab al-baritani 1922–1939* (Beirut, 1974), p. 154.

90. Darwazeh, *Mudhakkirat*, vol. 1, p. 497. Darwazeh explains why this was called the 'Third' Palestine Arab Congress, while in fact it was the second. The First Congress was held in Jerusalem in 1919 and the Second Congress was supposed to meet in May 1920 to protest against the incorporation of the Balfour Declaration in the mandate, but the military administration prohibited it from convening.

91. Ann Mosely Lesch, *Arab Politics in Palestine, 1917–1939: The Frustration of a Nationalist Movement* (London, 1979), p. 91.

92. Porath, *The Emergence*, p. 110.

93. M. Y. Muslih, *The Origins of Palestinian Nationalism* (New York, 1988) pp. 207–8.

94. Porath, *The Emergence*, p. 274.

95. Darwazeh, *Mudhakkirat*, vol. 1, p. 498; Porath, *The Emergence*, p. 46.

96. Muslih, *The Origins of Palestinian Nationalism*, pp. 5–8.

97. Ibid., pp. 105–7.

98. FO 371/ 5121 E 8599/85/44, Samuel to Curzon, 12 July 1920, Confidential.

99. The other members were: the financial secretary, the governor of Jerusalem, the director of Public Works, the director of Health, the director of Education, the director of Commerce and Industry, the director of Customs and Revenue, and a governor according to roster. CO 733/22. Samuel to Churchill, 4 July 1922. 'Report on the Administration for the period 1st July 1920–31st December 1921'.

100. FO 371/5123 E 13008, Samuel to Curzon, 10 October 1920.

101. CO 733/22, 'Report on the Administration for the period 1st July 1920–31st December 1921', op. cit.

102. At the 12th Zionist Congress held at Carlsbad in 1921, for instance, David Yellin publicly stated that 'the Jews are ready to take Palestine by war, if the outflow of blood is necessary to establish their claim upon the land'. This was reported by the American Consul at Jerusalem, Addison Southard, on 22 October 1921. He added that the Arabs were distinctly annoyed with Yellin. Upon hearing his statement, they had filed a long complaint against him with the high commissioner demanding that he be expelled from membership of the Advisory Council and prevented from returning to Palestine in accordance with the deportation regulations for agitators drawn up as a result of the Jaffa riots the previous May. National Archives, Washington, Roll No. 79 (765).

103. H. M. Kalvarisky was a Russian-born land purchasing agent who emigrated to Palestine in 1895 and headed the Arab Department of the Zionist Executive. During the First World War, when Palestine was cut off from the source of funds from France (being an enemy country) which had come from Baron Edmond de Rothschild and the Jewish Colonization Association, the only progress made in colonization was solely the work of Kalvarisky. Acting on his own initiative, he borrowed money from local sources and purchased land on which he founded at least four collective settlements. See Anne Ussishkin, 'The Jewish Colonization Association and a Rothschild in Palestine', *Middle Eastern Studies*, vol. 9, no. 3 (1973), p. 352. From 1921 he was behind the organization of the Arab opponents of the Arab Executive Committee into a political framework with a programme favourable to Zionism. His tactics were aimed at 'proving' that the Arab Executive Committee was not representative of the whole nation. By setting up the National Muslim Association, which was inspired by him and financially supported by the Zionists, he aimed at denying that the Arab Delegation in London was representative of all the Muslims and Christians. See Porath, *The Emergence*, pp. 67, 215 and Caplan, *Palestine Jewry*, p. 4.

104. FO 371/ 5123 E 13008 /85/44, Samuel to Curzon, 21 October 1920, Confidential.

105. Ben Zvi was to be denounced by the Director of Public Security, Colonel Bramley, as the 'dictator of Jewish policy in Palestine'. Wasserstein, *The British in Palestine*, p. 138.

106. CO 733/22, 'Report on the Administration for the period 1st July 1920–31st December 1921', op. cit.

107. FO 371/5123 E 11947, *Morning Post*, 22 September 1920, 'The New Zion'.

108. Ibid. According to the *Morning Post*, the above opinions were expressed by the American archaeologist Professor Clay of Yale University who was acquainted with the country and who had spent some time in Palestine in connection with the foundation of the American School of Oriental Research.

109. Edwin Montagu was a chief opponent to the government's Zionist policy. During 1917 he was a Cabinet member and was outspoken in his criticism of the Balfour Declaration.

110. FO 371/5124 E 14973, Montagu to Curzon, Private letter, 26 November 1920.

111. Ibid., Young to Tilley, Minute, 29 November 1920.

112. Ibid. It is also interesting to note that when Curzon read Young's minute, he disliked the phrase 'constituting it a National Home for the Jewish People', and wrote in the margin 'NO'; and, correcting Young, he added 'Constituting a National Home *in* Palestine for the Jewish people—a very different proposition'.

113. Norman Bentwich, *Fulfilment in the Promised Land 1917–1937* (London, 1938), p. 17.

114. Porath, *The Emergence*, p. 140.

115. Bentwich, *My 77 Years*, p. 68.

116. Ibid.

117. CO 733/22, 'Report on the Administration for the period 1st July 1920–31st December 1921', op. cit.

118. FO 371/5123 E 13008/85/44, Samuel to Curzon, 10 October 1920.

119. Ibid.

120. Lesch, *Arab Politics*, p. 91.

121. Porath, *The Emergence*, p. 126.

122. Norman Bentwich, *Palestine* (London, 1934), pp. 206–8.

123. Wasserstein, *The British in Palestine*, pp. 92, 105, 137.

124. *A Survey of Palestine*, vol. 2, pp. 916–17.

125. FO 371/5124 E 13627/85/44, 2 November 1920.

126. Ibid. This issue came up again at a later date and official documents show that the Muslim-Christian Association intended in October 1925 to complain to the Permanent Mandates Commission with regard to the use of the words 'Eretz Israel' on the postage stamps of Palestine. See, for instance, CO 733/ 107, Weizmann to Under-Secretary of State, Colonial Office, 16 October 1925.

127. FO 371/5123 E 11947, Samuel to Curzon, 13 September 1920.

128. Zionist activists had long held the view that the Hebrew language was 'the thread which held together the national fabric of the Jewish people'. But this was by no means universal. Although the use of German was contemplated by some Zionists, the real threat to Hebrew as the national language was from Yiddish. During the 1920s, this war of languages was being fought inside the walls of the Hebrew University. Myers, *Re-inventing the Jewish Past*, pp. 76–7. However, in Britain, there was some opposition to Samuel's measure. The Hebrew language, as one parliamentary question showed in November 1920, was the language of less than 2 per cent of the small Jewish population in Palestine (which itself was a mere 7 per cent or less of the total population). Lord Treowen asked if this measure

was adopted at the instance of the Zionist Commission, and in the interest of recent immigrants from central Europe. After English had taken the place of Turkish as an official language equal with Arabic, he enquired, were there any special reasons which justified the expense, and inconvenience, of a third official language? FO 371/5124 E 14400, 19 November 1920.

129. FO 371/5123 E 11947, Samuel to Curzon, 13 September 1920.

130. Ibid., *Morning Post*, 13 September 1920.

131. FO 371/5123 E 12406, Deedes to Sir John Tilley, 8 October 1920.

132. FO 371/5124 E 14900/85/44, Samuel to Curzon, 8 November 1920. Confidential.

133. FO 371/5125 E 16185/85/44, Samuel to Curzon, Political Report for November 1920, 6 December 1920. Confidential.

134. CO 733/1, Deedes to Churchill, Political Report for February 1921, signed by Deedes 'for High Commissioner'.

135. Ibid.

136. Ibid.

137. CO 733/2, Deedes to Churchill, Political Report for March 1921. Deedes noted that discussions had begun in Haifa about the need to convey to Mr Churchill the views of the Muslims and Christians who looked with 'disfavour' upon the Balfour Declaration. The Arab-Palestinian Executive Committee decided that a deputation should proceed to Egypt to lay before Churchill the Arab grievances. Although the high commissioner advised them to save their 'time' and 'money' and await the arrival of Churchill in Jerusalem, for the Secretary of State might not 'find time to receive them' in Cairo, Arab leaders decided to send the delegation, which left for Egypt on 12 March 1921.

138. Tibawi, *Anglo-Arab Relations*, p. 447.

139. CO 733/2, Political Report for March 1921, op. cit. Tibawi, however, argued that this story was 'pure invention' and was part of Samuel's campaign to build up his popularity. Tibawi, *Anglo-Arab Relations*, p. 478.

140. The Arab Executive Committee submitted the following demands to the colonial secretary: (i) the principle of a national home for the Jews to be abolished; (ii) a national government to be created which would be responsible to a parliament elected by the Palestinian people who existed in Palestine before the war; (iii) a stop to Jewish immigration until such time as a National Government was formed; (iv) pre-war laws and regulations to be observed and all others framed after the British occupation to be annulled, and no new laws to be created until a National Government came into being; (v) Palestine should not be separated from her sister states. CO 733/13, 'Report on the State of Palestine presented to the Right Honourable Mr Winston Churchill P.C., M.P. by the Executive Committee of the Palestine Arab Congress', Jerusalem, 28 March 1921, p. 32.

141. Ibid, pp. 30–1.

142. Ibid. pp. 28–9.

143. Moshe Mossek, *Palestine Immigration Policy Under Sir Herbert Samuel* (London, 1978), p. 18.

144. *Filastin*, 23 March 1921. The bi-weekly Arabic paper *Filastin* had ceased publication in January 1915 when the Turks closed it down but resumed in March 1921 with English and French as well as Arabic versions.

145. On 21 April, the Colonial Office received a memorandum from a certain Mr Mohamed Osman, addressed to the colonial secretary, commenting on Mr Churchill's reply to the Muslim delegation during his visit to Jerusalem, which prompted G. L. M. Clauson in the Colonial Office to comment on 26 April: 'This is a remarkably well written document considering that it was apparently composed by a Palestinian Arab and puts the anti-Zionist case as strongly as it can be put.' However, Clauson commented that it 'hardly seems wise to take any notice of it, even by an acknowledgement'. Hubert Young suggested that it should be sent to Sir Herbert Samuel 'for perusal and return'. CO 733/17B, Memorandum by Mohamed Osman of Palestine to Winston Churchill, 'Comments on the Reply of Mr Churchill to the Moslem Delegation during his visit to Jerusalem', 9 April 1921, from Port Said. (See Appendix D for full text)

146. Darwazeh, *Mudhakkirat*, vol. 1, p. 497.

147. Ibid., p. 512.

148. CO 733/3, Deedes to Churchill, Political Report for April 1921, 9 May 1921.

CHAPTER SIX

1. Wasserstein, *Herbert Samuel*, p. 257.

2. CO 733/3, Samuel to Churchill, Report on the Political Situation in Palestine for May 1921.

3. CO 733/13, Secret Report by Captain Brunton of General Staff Intelligence to G.H.Q. Cairo, Jaffa, 13 May 1921.

4. CO 733/3, Report on the Political Situation in Palestine for May 1921, op. cit.

5. Ibid.

6. Martin Kolinsky, *Law, Order and Riots in Mandatory Palestine 1928–35* (London and New York, 1993), p. 32.

7. CO 733/13, Secret Report by Captain Brunton, 13 May 1921, op. cit.

8. Ibid. Churchill decided on 9 June 1921 to print Captain Brunton's intelligence report for circulation to the Cabinet. On 16 May, Richard Meinertzhagen had minuted that the report gives a 'wilfully distorted view of the situation in Palestine'. Meinertzhagen might have obstructed the circulation of this report had he had the chance to see it beforehand. He wrote: 'I wish I had seen this before the S of S [Secretary of State] decided to present it to the Cabinet. In the first place its value is largely detracted by the fact that the author is a notorious anti-Zionist and has openly criticised the policy of H.M.G.'

9. CO 733/3, Samuel to Churchill, Political Report for May 1921.

10. Ibid.

11. CO 733/3, signed by Musa Kazim al-Husseini, 8 May 1921.

12. Friesel, 'Herbert Samuel's Reassessment', pp. 213–37. Friesel argues that Samuel underwent a profound change of policy regarding Zionism after the riots of 1921, and that his original aim of the active development of the Jewish community through immigration and settlement, 'so that with a minimum of delay the country may become a purely self-governing Commonwealth with an established Jewish majority', was abandoned in 1921 (pp. 225–6). This seems somewhat overstated, for Samuel never really abandoned his vision of a Jewish state in Palestine with a Jewish majority.

13. CO 733/3, Samuel to Churchill, Telegram, 25 May 1921.

14. Porath, *The Emergence*, p. 133.

15. CO 733/3, Samuel to Churchill, Confidential despatch no. 82, 8 May 1921.

16. In September 1920, Samuel passed the Prohibition of Export of Cereals and Legumes Ordinance. The Arab leaders accused Samuel that this was intended to keep prices down for the benefit of Jews.

17. It had been proposed that a defence force be raised consisting of two battalions, one Arab and the other Jewish. The Jews had agreed to the scheme, while the Arabs totally opposed it on two grounds: its organization into separate units and that it would be equally divided between Arabs and Jews. After the Jaffa riots, feelings ran very high, and it was decided that the force would be composed of one third Jews, one third Palestinian Arabs and one third non-Palestinian elements, if they could be found. See Ingrams, *Palestine Papers*, p. 133, where a confidential letter from Deedes to Young on 2 August 1921 is quoted.

18. It is interesting to mention that neither the Balfour Declaration nor the Mandate for Palestine capitalized the words national home (see note 78 above). Yet, even when quoting the Balfour Declaration, Samuel seems to have deliberately changed the form in the original document.

19. CO 733/3, 'High Commissioner's Declaration. The King's Birthday Celebrations', Jerusalem, Friday 3 June 1921. Special supplement to the *Palestine Weekly*, vol. 11, no. 21. This part of Samuel's speech was quoted by the British delegate at the League of Nations when discussion of the Palestine mandate was under way, as being the declared intention of the British government. A Middle East Department note stated on 10 May 1922 that the British representative on the Council of the League of Nations said that this definition was endorsed by HMG 'through the mouth' of the secretary of state for the colonies in a speech he delivered in the House of Commons on 14 June 1921, and that this was 'the spirit in which the terms of the draft Mandate are being carried out in Palestine and will continue to be carried out'. CO 733/34. Therefore, Samuel's 'verbal' declarations that he was committed to the cause of protecting Arab rights played a useful role at this juncture and paved the way for the ratification of the mandate by the international community.

20. CO 733/34, Minute by Mills, 24 May 1922.

21. *Filastin*, 8 June 1921.

22. Ibid., 11 June 1921.

23. Ibid., 15 June 1921.

24. Reinharz, *Chaim Weizmann*, p. 355. See also Wasserstein, *The British in Palestine*, pp. 112–13. Wasserstein notes that Weizmann even discussed the idea with MacDonogh and with Shuckburgh at the Colonial Office. He does not, however, question why Weizmann believed he had the power to change the high commissioner of Palestine, and simply attributes the non-removal of Samuel to the fact that Weizmann realized that the resignation of the Jewish high commissioner, at a time when Samuel and the Zionists were under heavy attack by the British press, 'might have a fatal effect on the Zionist cause'. Wasserstein adds that Weizmann therefore defended Samuel 'vigorously' at the Zionist Congress at Carlsbad in September 1921.

25. CO 733/13, War Office to Colonial Office (41898 20. 8. 1921), 'Situation in Palestine 1921', 15 August 1921.

26. CO 733/10, *Morning Post*, 'Palestine To-Day: Under the Zionist Yoke. The Prince of Israel', 10 June 1921.

27. *Palestine: Disturbances in May 1921. Reports of the Commission of Enquiry with correspondence relating thereto*, Cmd 1540, London, 1921 (henceforth Haycraft Report). Muslims were represented by 'Aref Pasha al-Dajani, Christians by Ilyas Effendi Mushabbak and Jews by Dr Mordechai Eliash.

28. Haycraft Report.

29. Ibid.

30. Ibid.

31. Knox, *The Making of a New Eastern Question*, p. 158.

32. *A Survey of Palestine*, vol. 1, p. 19.

33. CO 733/7, Samuel to Churchill, Political Report for October 1921; CO 733/8, Samuel to Churchill, Political Report for November 1921.

34. McTague, *British Policy in Palestine*, pp. 154–5.

35. CO 733/5, Minute by Clauson, 2 September 1921.

36. CO 733/6, Minute dated 7 October 1921.

37. CO 733/6, Samuel to Churchill, Secret.

38. Wasserstein, *The British in Palestine*, p. 135, quoting a secret letter from Deedes to Shuckburgh, 22 November 1921 (CO 537/852).

39. Ibid.

40. Ibid.

41. CO 733/8, Samuel to Churchill, 15 December 1921.

42. Ibid.

43. Ibid.

44. ESCO Foundation for Palestine, *Palestine*, vol. 1, p. 323. The Va'ad Hahinuch (Jewish Board of Education) was established in 1914; see p. 393. The Kadoorie Agricultural School is an interesting case in point. Sir Ellis Kadoorie, a Jewish philanthropist from Iraq, had bequeathed a large amount of money for the purpose of setting up an agricultural school for the benefit of all inhabitants of Palestine, and with clear instructions that there should be no distinction as to race or creed. However, the Jews strongly objected, and after two years of unsuccessful negotiations, the government set up two schools, one for Jews and another for Arabs. See Barbara Smith, *The Roots of Separatism in Palestine: British Economic Policy 1920–1929* (London, 1993), p. 60.

45. Samuel Papers, Thames TV 1978, Box I, File II DS 149.

46. For example: CO 733/13, Colonel Commandant John Byron, Commanding Troops, Jaffa to GOC Palestine Command, Secret Report, 14 May 1921; CO 733/33, General Office Commanding Egyptian Expeditionary Force to the Secretary, Director of Military Intelligence, War Office, 'Importation of Arms into Palestine', 12 January 1922. Secret; CO 733/33. Secret Intelligence Report, 'Jewish Self Defence Organisation in Palestine', from General Officer Commanding, Egyptian Expeditionary Force to the Director of Military Intelligence, War Office, 23 May 1922.

47. For instance, AIR/5/206 Part II, Samuel to Churchill, secret telegram, 22 June 1921.

48. For instance, CO 733/22, Deedes to Churchill, Memorandum by Richmond, 'Note on the Present Tendencies and Dangers of the Jewish Labour Movement in Palestine', 30 June

1922. Secret Despatch.

49. CO 733/24, Samuel to Churchill, 11 August 1922; *Filastin*, 17 July 1921, 'Palestinian Gendarmerie', in CO 722/22, Political Report for May 1922.

50. Samuel offered the following explanation: 'The measure adopted, which had given rise to this story, is the placing in certain isolated Jewish Agricultural villages of a small quantity of arms for the protection of the inhabitants, to be used in case of attack by the neighbouring Arab villages, and then only with the permission of the governor of the district. This step was taken, after consultation with the military authorities of the country, and as a result of the unprovoked attack on Jewish agricultural villages by Arabs in May, 1921. It will be realised that it is not possible, immediately, to send Police or troops to each of the seventy agricultural villages in Palestine, some of which are very isolated, and until the relations of the two communities improve, the people threatened with attack must be given the means to defend their lives and their homes.' To further mislead British representatives in Muslim countries, Samuel stated that, 'similar provisions' had been made in the case of Muslim villages on the frontiers 'for defence against attack from raids from Trans-Jordania'. CO 733/24, Samuel to Churchill, 11 August 1922.

51. Wasserstein, *The British in Palestine*, p. 236.

52. CO 733/7, Secretariat Government House Jerusalem (signed Keith-Roach for Civil Secretary) to the Governors of Jerusalem, Phoenicia, Samaria, Galilee, Jaffa, Gaza and Beersheba Districts, 'Confidential Instructions for the use of Governors and Sub-Governors of Districts', 19 October 1921, Private and Confidential.

53. CO 733/4, Samuel to Churchill, Political Report for June 1921.

54. AIR 5/206 Part II, Samuel to Churchill, secret telegram, 22 June 1921.

55. Quoted in Ingrams, *Palestine Papers*, p. 132. Because of financial pressures, the garrison in Palestine was reduced from 25,000 at the beginning of Samuel's administration to 7,000 in May 1921. In 1925, it consisted of 450 British gendarmes, a regiment of cavalry, one squadron of aeroplanes, and one company of armoured cars. Samuel stated in his five-year report to the colonial secretary that the cost to the British taxpayer was £3,155,000. After the May riots, the proposal for a mixed defence force, Jewish and Arab, was dropped, and a new plan was adopted whereby the garrison was further reduced to 2,800 in December 1922, and two paramilitary forces under civil control (a British gendarmerie, consisting of the former Irish 'Black and Tans', originally numbering 762, and later reduced to 555, and a Palestinian mounted gendarmerie, consisting of 500 men, Jews and Arabs, with a large number of Circassians and minority groups). Control of the defence of Palestine was transferred from the War Office to the Air Ministry in December 1921. The Palestine gendarmerie was entrusted with the defence and policing of the whole eastern part of Palestine from north to south. See Wasserstein, *The British in Palestine*, pp. 158–9. See also CO 733/102, 'Palestine. Report of the High Commissioner ...' ('Book of Chronicles'), pp. 3–5. The high commissioner was commander-in-chief of the Armed Forces, and was responsible for policy but not for operational control. The Police Ordinance of 1921 provided for a force of 1,300; the Palestine gendarmerie of 500 men would be in principle composed of one-third Arabs and one-third Jews. See Kolinsky, *Law, Order and Riots*, pp. 7, 25.

56. Ingrams, *Palestine Papers*, p. 133, quoting a confidential letter from Deedes to Young, 2 August 1921.

57. *Filastin*, 17 July 1921, 'Palestinian Gendarmerie'.

58. Caplan, *Palestine Jewry*, p. 77. See also pp. 110–14. Another important by-product of the Jaffa riots, with far-reaching effects upon the Jewish 'self-defence' movement, was that, for the first time, the municipal police force of Tel Aviv became completely Jewish. Ibid., p. 202.

59. Wasserstein, *The British in Palestine*, p. 204.

60. CO 733/22, Political Report for May 1922.

61. Kayyali, *Palestine: A Modern History*, p. 110.

62. Koestler, *Promise and Fulfilment*, p. 69.

63. Ibid.

64. Sykes, *Crossroads to Israel*, p. 155.

65. Reinharz, *Chaim Weizmann*, pp. 356–7, quoting Central Zionist Archives, CZA, Z4 / 16055, 14 June 1921. See also Wasserstein, *The British in Palestine*, p. 138. Wasserstein, quoting the CZA document, mentions that the existence of this underground army was 'tacitly' approved by Churchill when he told Weizmann in July 1921: 'We won't mind it, but don't speak of it.'

66. Caplan, *Palestine Jewry*, p. 117.

67. CO 733/6, Samuel to Churchill, Political Report for September 1921, Secret Despatch.

68. Caplan, *Palestine Jewry*, p. 120.

69. CO 733/8, Deedes to Churchill, Political Report for December 1921, Secret Despatch.

70. CO 733/18, Keith-Roach (for High Commissioner) to Churchill, Political Report for January 1922, Secret Despatch.

71. CO 733/19, Deedes to Churchill, Political Report for February 1922, Secret.

72. Ibid.

73. One such incident was reported in April 1922; a certain Kastof David, employed as a storekeeper by the Haifa Jewish Co-operative Labour Association, had attempted to transfer a bag containing 135 kilos of gunpowder from Haifa to Tel Aviv, 'without notifying the Police or observing the proper formalities'. The licence granted to the Haifa Association was subsequently cancelled. CO 733/21, Political Report April 1922, Secret.

74. CO 733/33, General Officer Commanding Egyptian Expeditionary Force to the Secretary, Director of Military Intelligence, War Office, 'Importation of Arms into Palestine', 12 January 1922, Secret.

75. CO 733/33, Hammick to Director of Military Intelligence, War Office, 23 May 1922, Secret.

76. Quoted in Ingrams, *Palestine Papers*, pp. 161–2.

77. CO 733/22, Deedes to Churchill, Memorandum by Richmond, 'Note On The Present Tendencies and Dangers of Jewish Labour Movement In Palestine', 30 June 1922, op. cit.

78. Ibid.

79. Ibid.

80. Ibid.

81. CO 733/22, Minute by Meinertzhagen, 18 July 1922.

82. CO 733/33, Secret Intelligence Report, 'Jewish Self Defence Organisation in Palestine', 23 May 1922.

83. In 1930, the build-up of Jewish military strength in Palestine had become linked with a growing conviction that a 'fundamental Zionist solution' to the Arab 'demographic problem' was to be found in an ultimate military solution. As early as 1937, following the partition plans the Haganah did in fact prepare an actual plan for the conquest of Palestine (Caplan, *Palestine Jewry*, pp. 24, 26). In the mid-1930s the number of Jews serving in the Palestine police rose from 365 in 1935 to 682 in 1936, and by the end of 1936 approval was given for the recruitment of 2,863 Jewish police armed with guns. These provided, according to Ben Gurion's own account, an 'excellent framework for training the Hagana', adding that 'The appearance of thousands of Jewish young men with legalised arms immediately improved our defence position' (David Ben Gurion, 'Britain's Contribution to Arming the Hagana', in Khalidi (ed.), *From Haven to Conquest*, pp. 371–4, first published in the *Jewish Observer* and the *Middle East Review*, 20 September 1963). Thus with the aid of the British army hundreds of Haganah members received military training, and the lessons, according to Ben Gurion, 'were passed on in secret to thousands of others', and this continued till the final days of the mandate (ibid, pp. 372–3).

In the late 1940s, Palestine was described by an Anglo-American Committee of Inquiry as an 'armed camp'. The Haganah had been 'procuring arms over a period of years', and those arms and ammunition were kept and concealed 'in specially constructed caches in settlements and towns'. (*The Anglo-American Committee of Enquiry Regarding the Problems of European Jewry and Palestine*, Lausanne, April 1946, Cmd. 6808) By 1946, the Haganah had evolved into a 'completely organised' body, numbering 64,000 men under a central control and with subsidiary territorial commands 'in three branches': (i) a permanent force composed of settlers and townsfolk with an estimated strength of 40,000; (ii) a field army, based on the Jewish Settlement Police and trained in mobile operations counting 16,000 and (iii) a full-time force, the Palmach, 'permanently mobilised' and provided with transport 'with an estimated peace establishment of 2,000 and war establishment of some 6,000' ('The Zionist Military Organizations 1946' in Khalidi (ed.), *From Haven to Conquest*, pp. 595–600). According to Ben Gurion's war diary, in October 1948 the Jewish forces numbered 111,697, including an air force, navy, and a corps of engineers (David Ben Gurion, *Yawmiyat al-harb* (Beirut, 1993), p. 782. Arabic translation of *Yoman ha-milhamah*).

84. CO 733/3, Confidential Despatch no. 82, Samuel to Churchill, 8 May 1921.

85. Ibid., Shuckburgh to Secretary of State, Minute, 20 May 1921.

86. Ibid., Samuel to Churchill, Confidential Despatch, 8 May 1921.

87. Ibid., Confidential Despatch no. 82, 8 May 1921, Samuel to Churchill.

88. *Morning Post*, 'Palestine Today, Under the Zionist Yoke' 10 June 1921. National Archives, Washington, 79, no. 123.

89. Kayyali, *Palestine: A Modern History*, pp. 195–6. On 9 November 1920, Samuel summoned a conference of *muftis* and principal *'ulama*, as well as Muslim notables, to discuss questions related to the control of Muslim religious affairs and *awqaf*. *Official Gazette for the Government of Palestine*, no. 43, May 15 1921.

90. Ibid. See also Wasserstein, *The British in Palestine*, p. 132. Wasserstein describes the position which Samuel tried to give the Arabs as '*millet* status'.

91. Wasserstein, *Herbert Samuel*, p. 265.

92. Porath, *The Emergence*, pp. 199–200.

93. CO 733/6, Samuel to Churchill, 8 October 1921.

94. CO 733/3, Samuel to Churchill, Telegram, 25 May 1921.

95. CO 733/3, Samuel to Churchill, 24 May 1921.

96. See for instance Porath, *The Emergence*, p. 136, and McTague, *British Policy in Palestine*, p. 195.

97. CO 733/6, Deedes to Churchill, Political Report for August 1921, Secret.

98. CO 733/6, Samuel to Churchill, 8 October 1921.

99. Ibid.

100. Ibid.

101. The electors were Muslim secondary electors to the Ottoman Parliament of 1914 who were still alive and resident in Palestine. See, for instance, Wasserstein, *The British in Palestine*, p. 132.

102. CO 733/6, Samuel to Churchill, 8 October 1921.

103. Ibid.

104. CO 733/7, Samuel to Churchill, Political Report for October 1921.

105. CO 733/8, Deedes to Churchill, Political Report for December 1921.

106. Hajj Amin was chosen and supported by the government, despite strong opposition from his rival Raghib Bey Nashashibi. The Supreme Muslim Council was established by the government of Palestine after the riots of May 1921, but official acceptance of it came towards the end of that year. See Wasserstein, *The British in Palestine*, p. 132.

107. Porath, *The Emergence*, p. 135.

108. Following the death of the Mufti of Jerusalem, Kamil Effendi al-Husseini, on 21 March 1921, the high commissioner helped Hajj Amin al-Husseini assume the post. Samuel verbally informed Hajj Amin of his appointment on 8 May.

109. CO 733/18, Samuel to Churchill, 20 January 1922.

110. Porath, *The Emergence*, p. 202.

111. CO 733/18, Keith-Roach to Churchill, Political Report for January 1922.

112. CO 733/21, Samuel to Churchill, Political Report for April 1922.

113. Porath, *The Emergence*, pp. 199–200.

114. It was not until the late 1920s that the Supreme Muslim Council acted in open defiance of the British administration, when its opposition to immigration and land sales became more overt. During the 1930s, the question of land ownership had openly become the crux of the problem between the Zionists and the Palestinians. The Supreme Muslim Council, as the leading Palestinian institution, had no alternative but to treat the land issue in religious terms, and tried to obstruct the activities of the Jewish National Fund by various means and systematically campaigned to prevent land sales to Jews by extending the area of *waqf* land. Throughout the British mandate, the administration was always reluctant to use its administrative and financial powers to restrict the activities of the Supreme Muslim Council with regard to increasing Jewish immigration, settlement and land acquisition, and by doing so, the British government avoided further antagonizing the Muslim community. Indeed as Shuckburgh wrote in 1926: 'The institution of the Supreme Muslim Council in 1921 has, on the whole, been one of the most successful moves in Palestine. It practically gave the Mohammedans self-government in regard to Moslem affairs. This has worked smoothly and has no doubt done much to reconcile the Mohammedans to the Mandatory

regime with its unpopular Zionist flavour.' See Michael Dumper, *Islam and Israel: Muslim Religious Endowments and the Jewish State* (Washington DC., 1994), pp. 20–2.

CHAPTER SEVEN

1. In January 1919, the military authorities had prohibited a Palestinian delegation from proceeding to Paris to present its case to the Paris Peace Conference. A second attempt to send a delegation in March 1920 was similarly blocked. Lesch, *Arab Politics*, p. 158. In contrast, the Zionists were fully represented in the Paris Peace Conference and all subsequent international conferences concerning the future of Palestine.

2. Even before the riots, in April 1921, Wyndham Deedes wrote that the nationalist leaders were more determined than ever to attain their ends. On 2 April, Musa Kazim had gone to Haifa for a meeting of the Muslim-Christian Association to arrange for the immediate collection of funds. These were needed to pay the expenses of a delegation which would go to Europe and negotiate with the British government in an attempt to persuade it to reverse its Zionist policy, put an end to Jewish immigration, and constitute a national representative government. Deedes reported that considerable sums had actually been collected for this purpose. He also pointed to a 'firmer union' between the Muslims and the Christians than ever before; during the Nabi Musa festivals black banners had been raised bearing the slogans: 'Moslems and Christians are brothers', 'Down with Zionism', and 'Long live the Arab Congress'. CO 733/3, Political Report for April 1921, op. cit.

3. Lesch, *Arab Politics*, pp. 94–5.

4. Porath, *The Emergence*, p. 110. It is important to mention that due to the new political situation after the French occupation of Syria, the name Southern Syria, referring to Palestine, ceased to be mentioned.

5. Porath, *The Emergence*, p. 139.

6. The Arab Delegation consisted of Tawfiq Hammad, Mu'in al-Madi, Amin al-Tamimi, Ibrahim Shammas, Fu'ad Samad, Jamal al-Husseini, Ruhi 'Abd al-Hadi, and Shibli Jamal. Miss Newton, an English lady from Haifa, accompanied the delegation in a personal capacity. See Ingrams, *Palestine Papers*, p. 138.

7. CO 733/15, Memorandum by Shuckburgh, 'Palestine', 7 November 1921.

8. Lesch, *Arab Politics*, pp. 159–60.

9. Darwazeh, *Mudhakkirat*, vol. 1, p. 547.

10. CO 733/6, Political Report for August 1921, op. cit.

11. Ibid.

12. Ibid.

13. CO 733/6, Samuel to Churchill, Political Report for September 1921. Secret.

14. CO 733/6, Political Report for August 1921, op. cit.

15. CO 733/17 B, 'Shorthand Writer's Report of Conversation between the Right Hon. Winston Churchill, and members of the Palestine Arab Delegation', August 1921. President: Musa Kazim Pasha. Secretary: Shibli al-Jamal. Official delegates: Tawfiq Hammad, Amin al-Tamimi, Ibrahim Shammas, Mu'in al-Madi. Assistant Secretary, Dr Fu'ad Samad. Miss Newton accompanied the delegates at the request of the congress, as adviser. Hubert Young from the Middle East Department was also present. Churchill stressed that the 'chat'

was private, and that nothing should appear in the press.

16. In his 'Interim Report on the Civil Administration of Palestine', Cmd. 1499 (1921), Samuel had written that the aspirations of the fourteen million Jews 'have a right to be considered', and that those Jews asked for the 'opportunity to establish a "home" in the land which was the political, and has always been the religious, centre of their race'. The Jews and Zionists 'ask that this Home should possess national characteristics—in language and customs, in intellectual interests, in religious and political institutions'. The Arab Delegation answered this report with a long statement which posed the question: 'What do "political institutions" mean if not a state?'. Official Statement by the Palestine Arab Delegation, November 1921, 'The Moslem-Christian Case against Zionist Aggression' in *Zu'aytir Papers*, p. 177. In their letter to Samuel the delegation referred specifically to the 'recent Interim Report on the Civil Administration of Palestine', which means that they had seen the report.

17. CO 733/17B, 'Shorthand Writer's Report ... ' op. cit. Hubert Young pointed out to Churchill that in their translation of the term 'Jewish national home', the Arabs used a word which 'practically means their native country', and that it was 'impossible to translate it'. At this point, Miss Newton, who had accompanied the delegation, said that 'The word *watan* implies long ancestral residence', to which Young replied: '*Watan* is 'native country'. That is not the correct translation. I do not think your translation is really correct.'

18. Ibid. The Middle East Department maintained that Palestine 'was not yet ripe for full self-government'. Shuckburgh maintained that this could 'hardly' be questioned by any 'reasonable' person. For Shuckburgh's views see for instance CO 733/15, 'Summary of Statement to be made by Secretary of State', November 1921 and CO 733/34, Minute dated 24 May 1922.

19. CO 733/6, Minute by Shuckburgh, 2 October 1921.

20. Ibid.

21. CO 733/6, Samuel to Churchill, Confidential Despatch, 14 October 1921.

22. Reinharz, *Chaim Weizmann*, p. 356.

23. CO 733/6, Samuel to Churchill, 14 October 1921, Report on the Political Situation in Palestine, Confidential.

24. CO 733/16, Arab Delegation (Hotel Cecil) to Churchill, 24 October 1921.

25. Lesch, *Arab Politics*, p. 161.

26. CO 733/6, Minute by Shuckburgh, 2 October 1921.

27. CO 733/15, 'Petition sent to Sir Herbert Samuel Concerning the Recent Jerusalem Riots', November 1921, signed Jamal al-Husseini, The Palestine Arab Delegation, Hotel Cecil, London.

28. CO 733/8, Samuel to Churchill, Political Report for November 1921.

29. CO 733/8, Deedes to Churchill, Political Report for December 1921. Secret.

30. CO 733/15, Memorandum by Shuckburgh, 'Palestine', 7 November 1921.

31. So far, Shuckburgh noted, they had had two interviews with Churchill, as well as a number of less formal conversations with members of the department.

32. CO 733/15, Memorandum by Shuckburgh, 'Palestine', 7 November 1921.

33. Ibid.

34. Ibid.

35. Lesch, *Arab Politics*, p. 162.

36. CO 733/6, Political Report for August 1921, op. cit.

37. Sir George Sydenham Clarke (1848–1933) Secretary, Committee of Imperial Defence, 1904–7.

38. CO 733/15, *Morning Post*, 'Protest Against Zionism', 16 November 1921.

39. CO 733/36, Mills to Deedes, 30 March 1922.

40. Lesch, *Arab Politics*, p. 163. See also Wasserstein, *The British in Palestine*, p. 119, for more details about Samuel's visit to London in May 1922 during the stay of the Arab Delegation and about the White Paper.

41. The Order-in-Council was finally published in the Extraordinary Issue of the *Palestine Gazette*, 1 September 1922.

42. CO 733/24, Palestine Order-in-Council.

43. Porath, *The Emergence*, p. 144. For the full text of the Palestine Order-in-Council 1922, see Bentwich, *The Mandates System*, pp. 146–65.

44. McTague, *British Policy in Palestine*, p. 199.

45. CO 733/24, Palestine Order-in-Council.

46. Ibid., p. 15 of the Order-in-Council. The reasons for rejecting the Palestine Order-in-Council were given in a statement by the president of the Muslim-Christian Society, Hafiz Toukan, to the Chief Secretary, Wyndham Deedes, on 13 November 1922; CO 733/28.

47. Zu'aytir Papers, pp. 216–18.

48. CO 733/19, Deedes to Churchill, Political Report for February 1922.

49. Porath, *The Emergence*, p. 144.

50. CO 733/19, Political Report for February 1922, op. cit.

51. CO 733/38, Deedes to Young, 22 February 1922, Secret.

52. According to a confidential report in May 1922 the situation was 'profoundly unsatisfactory'. Owing to the 'mysterious' delay on the part of the League of Nations in confirming the Mandate, industrial enterprise was paralyzed, and feelings between Arabs and Zionists were becoming more bitter. British prestige had suffered a serious setback, and despite the efforts of the administration, 'a growing hatred of Britain's Palestine policy is apparent amongst the Arab and Christian population'. The report added that extreme Zionists were 'trying to compress the work of a century into a single decade and much chaos is resulting'. CO 733/35, Compiled by Tudor Pole, 'Note on the present political and economic conditions in the following countries visited between January and May 1922', submitted 29 May 1922. The report was not compiled for publication and expresses the writer's personal impression in summary form. He visited a number of countries in the Middle East, as well as France, Switzerland, Italy, Greece, Yugoslavia and Constantinople.

53. CO 733/21, Deedes to Churchill, Political Report for April 1922. Secret.

54. CO 733/19, Samuel to Churchill, Confidential Despatch, 9 March 1922.

55. Weizmann made this statement at the Paris Peace Conference in 1919 when asked what he understood the Jewish national home to mean.

56. CO 733/19, Samuel to Churchill, 9 March 1922.

57. Ibid.

58. Ibid.

59. Ibid.

60. Ibid., Minute, Shuckburgh to Masterton-Smith, 29 March 1922.

61. Ibid., Churchill to Samuel, 4 April 1922, Personal and Private.

62. CO 733/34, Minute by Shuckburgh to Masterton-Smith and Secretary of State, 24 May 1922.

63. Ibid. In May 1922, Deedes wrote from Jerusalem that the governor of Galilee—a district considered by many as being the most peaceful in Palestine—had expressed the opinion that no good was to be hoped for if the people lost faith in the Palestine Arab Delegation to London. The governor of Galilee told Deedes that the Delegation, 'Inadequate as it may be regarded, is ... the only effective constitutional means of expressing the political views of what is the most powerful body of opinion in the country. If the last hope of agreement fades away political agitation will be able ... to represent to the ignorant and the fanatical that peaceful non-violent methods do not pay.' See CO 733/22, Political Report for May 1922.

64. CO 733/34, *Morning Post*, 'Palestine. Sir Herbert Samuel Explains. A National Home', 24 May 1922.

65. CO 733/34, Minute by Shuckburgh, 24 May 1922.

66. Ibid.

67. The White Paper of June 1922 (The Churchill Memorandum) Cmd. 1700. 'British Policy in Palestine'.

68. Sykes, *Crossroads*, p. 66.

69. Lesch, *Arab Politics*, pp. 163–4, 180.

70. Wasserstein, *The British in Palestine*, p. 117.

71. Knox, 'Development of British Policy', p. 349.

72. Young speaks of an 'undertaking' which has been obtained from the Zionist Organization which he says 'may satisfy moderate opinion in Palestine', but gives no further details in this minute.

73. CO 733/22, Young's minute on Deedes to Churchill, Political Report for May 1922.

74. Knox, *The Making of the New Eastern Question*, p. 161.

75. Reinharz, *Chaim Weizmann*, p. 394. Congratulating Weizmann on his personal efforts in securing the mandate, Vladimir Jabotinsky, the Revisionist Zionist leader, wrote to Weizmann that his achievements, as a 'personal performance', were unparalleled in history. The document was 'colossal' and 'absolutely ineffaceable'. He added: 'Its failings you yourself know, but on the other hand there is nothing in it, not a single sentence which in a severe judicial analysis could exclude our most remote goal—even a Jewish State.' In July 1922, Weizmann wrote to his sister: 'You are right ... the Mandate was written for the great part with my blood'. Reinharz, *Chaim Weizmann*, p. 396.

76. CO 733/1, Political Report for February 1921, op. cit.

77. Lesch, *Arab Politics*, p. 164.

78. Porath, *The Emergence*, p. 145.

79. CO 733/6, Political Report for August 1921, op. cit.

80. 'Abd al-Wahhab Kayyali, *Palestine: A Modern History* (London, 1978), p. 121.

81. 'Official Statement by the Palestine Arab Delegation', London, November 1921, Zu'aytir Papers, p. 177.

82. CO 733/23, Samuel to Churchill, Political Report for June 1922.

83. The governor of Haifa reported that meetings had been held in the houses of a number of Muslim and Christian notables to discuss means of expressing popular dislike of the mandate; a three-day fast, cessation of work and assemblies in mosques and churches and public demonstrations had been suggested.

84. CO 733/23, Political Report for June 1922, op. cit.

85. CO 733/8, Samuel to Churchill, 29 December 1921, Confidential.

86. Lesch, *Arab Politics*, pp. 138–9.

87. CO 733/23, Report on the Political Situation in Palestine during the month of June 1922. See also CO 733/22, Political Report for May 1922.

88. Samuel wrote that this belief originated from a frontispiece in a Yiddish publication in New York, 'depicting a stream of Jews entering Jerusalem by one of its gates; in the background a building surmounted by a dome, from which waves a Zionist flag'. He noted that there was no reason for the Arabs to believe that this domed building was Haram al-Sharif.

89. CO 733/24, Samuel to Churchill, 11 August 1922.

90. Ibid.

91. CO 733/23, Statement by His Excellency the High Commissioner at meeting of Advisory Council, 17 July 1922.

92. Ibid.

93. Porath, *The Emergence*, p. 305.

94. Ibid., p. 147.

95. CO 733/24, Political Report for July 1922, op. cit.

96. Ibid.

97. Darwazeh, *Mudhakkirat*, vol. 1, p. 555.

98. 'Abd al-Wahhab al-Kayyali, ed., *Watha'iq al-muqawama al-filastiniyya al-'arabiyya didd al-ihtilal al-baritani wa-al-sahyunniyya (1918–1939)* (Beirut 1988), pp. 55–6. Among the other resolutions were the following: to send a delegation to the east; to open an office in London; to write the history of the Palestinian nationalist movement, and to appoint a committee for this purpose; to appoint a committee for the purpose of removing any misunderstandings among the ranks of the nationalist movement; and to boycott the Rutenberg project which was a monopoly granted in September 1921 to the Russian electrical engineer, Pinhas Rutenberg, for the exclusive right to produce energy by means of water power in the Jaffa district (see Chapter 9).

99. Darwazeh, *Mudhakkirat*, vol. 1, p. 558.

100. Ibid.

101. Kayyali, *Watha'iq al-muqawama*, p. 57.

102. Lesch, *Arab Politics*, p. 21.

103. Darwazeh, *Mudhakkirat*, vol. 1, p. 560. This shows that, to the Arab mind, the British members were on the same footing as the Jews.

104. They were Raghib al-Nashashibi (Jerusalem), Mu'in al-Madi (Haifa) and Shaykh 'Abd al-Rahman al-Khatib al-Bitawi (Nablus province). Darwazeh points out that Mu'in al-Madi's nomination was surprising and very curious since he was one of the members of the Arab Delegation in London who had also approved the resolution to boycott elections in the Fifth Palestine Arab Congress. Darwazeh does not question Madi's motives but notes

that it was a big mistake on his part. See Darwazeh, *Mudhakkirat*, vol. 1, p. 562.

105. Darwazeh, *Mudhakkirat*, vol. 1, p. 561.

106. Porath also maintains that the Supreme Muslim Council helped in boycotting the elections. See Porath, *The Emergence*, pp. 151, 154–5.

107. Darwazeh, *Mudhakkirat*, vol. 1, p. 563.

108. CO 733/28, translation, signed Hafiz Toukan, President of the Muslim-Christian Society, through the Executive Committee of the Fifth Palestine Arab Congress to the Chief Secretary, 13 November 1922.

109. Ibid.

110. Darwazeh, *Mudhakkirat*, vol. 1, p. 563.

111. The ten Arab members chosen by Samuel were: Raghib Nashashibi, 'Aref al-Dajani, Isma'il al-Husseini, Sulayman 'Abd al-Razzaq Bey Tawqan, Amin 'Abd al-Hadi, 'Abd al-Fattah al-Sa'adi, Mahmud Abu Khadra, Frayh Abu Midyan, and two Christians, Sulayman Nasif and Antun Jallad. See Darwazeh, *Mudhakkirat*, vol. 1, p. 564.

112. These were Raghib al-Nashashibi, 'Aref al-Dajani, Sulayman Bey Nasif and probably, according to Darwazeh, (ibid.), 'Abd al-Fattah al-Sa'adi.

113. Ibid.

114. Lesch, *Arab Politics*, pp. 94–5, 135.

115. Kayyali, *Palestine: A Modern History*, p. 119.

116. Knox, *The Making of the New Eastern Question*, p. 163.

117. Porath, *The Emergence*, p. 120.

118. Wasserstein, *The British in Palestine*, p. 125.

119. See, for instance, CO 733/54, Minute by Shuckburgh to Masterton-Smith, Ormsby-Gore and the Secretary of State, 24 July 1923.

120. Lesch, *Arab Politics*, pp. 136–7.

121. Kayyali, *Palestine: A Modern History*, p. 115.

122. Porath, *The Emergence*, p. 120.

123. Lesch, *Arab Politics*, p. 165.

124. Porath, *The Emergence*, p. 174.

125. Lesch, *Arab Politics*, p. 166.

126. CO 733/54, Minute by Shuckburgh, 24 July 1923, op. cit.

127. Ibid.

128. Porath, *The Emergence*, p. 174.

129. CO 733/54, Minute by Shuckburgh, 24 July 1923, op. cit.

130. See for instance, CO 733/58, Cabinet Committee on Palestine, 'The Future of Palestine', 27 July 1923, Secret Cabinet Paper CP 351 (23).

131. Porath, *The Emergence*, p. 176.

132. Lesch, *Arab Politics*, p. 167.

CHAPTER EIGHT

1. Kayyali, *Palestine: A Modern History*, p. 122.

2. CO 733/63, Political Report for December 1923, Samuel to the Duke of Devonshire, Secret. Moody further minuted: 'In the meantime the Jews have turned from general poli-

tics and are directing their attention to the development of their own institutions in an autonomous direction. The institutions in question are schools and municipal councils. They seem to have dropped the idea of the organisation of the Jewish community as such. This trouble will be specially reserved for the successor of Sir H. Samuel. The Christians are now as always in the cleft-stick. But they will be quite comfortable in that position so long as the Mandatory Power remains'.

3. Bentwich, *Palestine*, p. 145.

4. Kayyali, *Palestine: A Modern History*, p. 130. For more details on the reasons behind this 'lull' until the second major outbreak of violence in 1929 see pp. 130–51.

5. CO 733/63, Samuel to the Duke of Devonshire, Political Report for December 1923. Secret.

6. He was also the representative of the ICA (the Jewish Colonization Association) and a member of the Advisory Council. He was at this time active in forming the National Muslim Associations. He demonstrated the success of his endeavours by pointing out that in all the towns where there were National Muslim Associations, such as Haifa, Beisan and Nablus, there had been no disturbances, whereas in Jerusalem riots took place. See Caplan, *Palestine Jewry*, p. 121.

7. Porath, *The Emergence*, p. 215.

8. Darwazeh, *Mudhakkirat*, vol. 1, pp. 422–4.

9. The Zionist Organization spent considerable sums of money to establish two political parties: the National Muslim Association (1921–3), and the Agricultural Parties (1924–6). The members of the National Muslim Association were basically those who, for reasons of family feuds, opposed the Husseini leadership. Chief among them were members of the Nashashibi family. Other members who joined the leadership ranks of those parties were Shaykh Sulayman Taji al-Faruki from Ramleh, and Shukri al-Dajani. See Porath, *The Emergence*, p. 211, and Lesch, *Arab Politics*, p. 51. Members of the Agricultural Parties were village sheikhs, and the Zionists exploited differences between the village and the city as well.

10. Porath, *The Emergence*, p. 215.

11. CO 733/7 and CO 733/8, Samuel to Churchill, Political Reports for October and November 1921. Secret.

12. CO 733/18, Keith-Roach to Churchill, Political Report for January 1922.

13. CO 733/21, Samuel to Churchill, Political Report for April 1922.

14. Porath, *The Emergence*, pp. 219–20, 222.

15. Kayyali, *Palestine: A Modern History*, p. 116.

16. CO 733/28, Samuel to Devonshire, 8 December 1922, Confidential.

17. Ibid.

18. Ibid.

19. Kayyali, *Palestine: A Modern History*, p. 117.

20. CO 733/49, Political Report for August 1923. Press comments.

21. CO 733/50, Political Report for September 1923.

22. Ibid.

23. Ibid.

24. Ibid.

25. Porath, *The Emergence*, p. 219.

26. CO 733/52, Political Report for November 1923, op. cit.

27. CO 733/52, Minute by S. Moody commenting on Political Report for November 1923.

28. Porath, *The Emergence*, p. 226.

29. CO 733/51, Political Report for October 1923.

30. CO 733/63, Samuel to Devonshire, Political Report for December 1923. Secret. Appendix A, Ronald Storrs to Chief Secretary, 2 January 1924.

31. Ibid. Appendix A, District Governor of Gaza, A. Abramson to Assistant Secretary (Pol), Jerusalem, 20 December 1923.

32. CO 733/65, Political Report for January 1924, op. cit.

33. Porath, *The Emergence*, pp. 227, 229.

34. CO 733/65, Political Report for January 1924, op. cit.

35. CO 733/71, Clayton to J. H. Thomas, Political Report for June 1924. Secret; CO 733/73, Samuel to J. H. Thomas, Political Report for August 1924. Secret.

36. CO 733/73, Storrs to Chief Secretary 8 September 1924, Secret.

37. CO 733/74, Clayton to J. H. Thomas, Political Report for October 1924. Secret.

38. CO 733/71, Political Report for June 1924, op. cit.

39. CO 733/73, Political Report for August 1924, op. cit.

40. CO 733/75, Secret Political Résumé for the Jerusalem-Jaffa District for the last ten days of October 1924, written by Ronald Storrs.

41. CO 733/76, Secret Political Résumé for the Jerusalem-Jaffa District for November 1924, Ronald Storrs to High Commissioner.

42. A Muslim scholar from Tunis who attempted to arbitrate between the two opposing Palestinian camps; see Porath, *The Emergence*, p. 248.

43. CO 733/71, Political Report for June 1924, op. cit.

44. Lawyer and member of one of Palestine's aristocratic families in Nablus. Confidant of Amir Faisal since 1920.

45. CO 733/42, Samuel to Devonshire, Political Report for January 1923. Secret.

46. CO 733/43, Political Report for February 1923.

47. CO 733/49, Political Report for August 1923.

48. CO 733/75, 'Ali Tahir edited the newspaper *al-Shura* which appeared in Egypt in 1924. He was described as an 'ultra-extremist'.

49. CO 733/51, Samuel to J. H. Thomas, Political Report for October 1923. Secret.

50. The revivalist movement against foreign infiltration took three different forms: (i) a call for independence under a Turkish mandate; (ii) a return to the caliphate with King Hussein as caliph, and (iii) support from the Ikhwan of Najd.

51. CO 733/63, Samuel to Devonshire, Political Report for December 1923. Secret.

52. Lesch, *Arab Politics*, pp. 138–9.

53. Major General C. S. Jarvis, *Arab Command. The Biography of Lieutenant Colonel F. G. Peake Pasha* (London, 1943), p. 100.

54. CO 733/19, Deedes to Churchill, 9 March 1922, Secret.

55. CO 733/23, Political Report for June 1922, op. cit.

56. AIR 5/206 Part I, 185757, Samuel to Churchill, 29 July 1922, Secret.

57. CO 733/24, Political Report for July 1922, op. cit.

58. AIR 5/206 Part I, 185757, Samuel to Churchill, 15 August 1922, Secret.

59. Head of the Huwaytat tribe of Southern Transjordan. He was one of the leaders of the Arab revolt who fought alongside Lawrence in 'Aqaba, and entered Damascus victoriously in 1918. It is interesting to mention in this respect that on 8 May 1920, the shaikhs of the tribes and heads of clans residing beyond the Jordan River and the Dead Sea, sent a petition to 'H.E. the C.A.' O.E.T.A. South commenting on the declaration by the British government in the presence of notables of Jerusalem, on 28 April 1920, announcing the separation of Palestine from 'United Syria and making it a national home for the Jews'. The heads of tribes expressed their deep concern over Zionist policy in Palestine, and pledged allegiance to the Palestine Arabs, making it clear that 'we are prepared to shed our blood in guarding our country which is threatened by danger on all sides'. It was signed by: 'Audeh Abu Taih, Masshour El-Fayez, Hamad ibn Djazi, Humeid ibn Husein, Hamed El-Sharary, Geith ibn Hadaya, Husein El-Tarawney, Bedeiwy Mohamed Ali, Selim ibn Dumeik, Suleiman ibn Tureif, Salih El-Husein and Mutlak ibn Jumeian (FO 371/5114).

60. CO 733/25, Samuel to Churchill, 8 September 1922, Secret.

61. CO 733/25, 11 September 1922.

62. Fromkin, *A Peace to End All Peace*, pp. 150, 560.

63. Jarvis, *Arab Command*, pp. 105, 115.

64. CO 733/45, Samuel to Duke of Devonshire, 21 May 1923, Secret.

65. AIR 5 /206 Part I, Devonshire to Samuel, 14 June 1923, Confidential.

66. CO 733/45, Memorandum by Richmond, 5 May 1923.

67. CO 733/77, 29 September 1924.

68. CO 733/75, Secret Political Résumé for the Jerusalem-Jaffa District for the last ten days of October 1924.

69. AIR 5/206 Part II, TJ/30/3, 18 October 1924, Secret.

70. A Wahhabi raid in January 1925 did cause Samuel some anxiety. A report from the Air Ministry to the Colonial Office noted that 'very recently' a threat of attack by the Wahhabis on the eastern frontier, was 'averted only by air action in conjunction with Armoured cars'. The report pointed out that the recent Wahhabi successes in the Hijaz called for attention, and that repeated attacks would 'directly and vitally threaten the internal security' of Palestine itself. CO 733/100, Air Ministry to CO, 20 January 1925 CO 3140.

71. See, for instance, CO 733/66, CO 733/67 and CO 733/68 for Political Reports for February, March and April 1924, and CO 733/89 for the Political Report for January 1925.

72. Knox, *The Making of the New Eastern Question*, p. 168.

73. Ibid., p. 174.

74. Ibid., pp. 166. It was Curzon who suggested the Arab Agency, and Samuel approved the idea. After his return to Palestine in September 1923, Samuel made the announcement in public. See for instance Wasserstein, *The British in Palestine*, p. 128.

75. CO 733/58, Devonshire to Samuel, 4 October 1923.

76. Wasserstein, *The British in Palestine*, p. 130.

77. Ibid., pp. 128-9.

78. Knox, *The Making of the New Eastern Question*, p. 167.

79. Darwazeh, *Mudhakkirat*, pp. 564-5.

80. McTague, *British Policy in Palestine*, p. 238.

81. Porath, *The Emergence*, p. 177.

82. CO 733/51, Political Report for October 1923.

83. CO 733/73, Minute by Vernon, 18 September 1924.

84. Artas is a village south of Jerusalem near Bethlehem. In British documents its name appears as 'Urtas'.

85. CO 733/67, Minute by Shuckburgh to Secretary of State and to Lord Arnold, 23 June 1924.

86. CO 733/67, Memorandum by Keith-Roach, 'Organisation of the Jewish Community', 20 May 1924.

87. Ibid.

88. Ibid.

89. CO 733/67, Minute by Young, 22 May 1924.

90. CO 733/67, Minute by Vernon, 28 May 1924.

91. CO 733/67, Minute by Shuckburgh, 23 June 1924, op. cit.

92. Ibid.

93. Shuckburgh mentions that after the Secretary of State had seen Weizmann, the latter had written him 'a long letter' on affairs in Palestine.

94. CO 733/67, Minute by Shuckburgh, 23 June 1924, op. cit.

95. CO 733/67, attached to Shuckburgh's Minute, 22 July 1924.

96. CO 733/67, Minute by Shuckburgh to Secretary of State, 22 July 1924.

97. CO 733/67, Minute by Shuckburgh to Sir H. Lambert, Lord Arnold and Secretary of State.

98. Wasserstein, *The British in Palestine*, p. 137.

99. The Urtas Springs Ordinance No. 13 of 1925 was passed by Samuel on 25 May 1925. See The Law Society, *Palestine Ordinances 1923–1926* (Institute of Advanced Legal Studies, University of London).

100. Leopold Amery was one of the strong advocates of the Balfour Declaration in 1917, and was a consistent and active Anglo-Zionist.

101. Samuel Papers, DS 126, The Executive Committee of the Palestine Arab Congress Jerusalem, 31 May 1925 (signed by Jamal al-Husseini) to Secretary of State for the Colonies.

102. *Al-Karmel*, 10 June 1925.

103. Ibid., 1 July 1925.

104. Porath, *The Emergence*, p. 135.

105. *A Survey of Palestine*, vol. 1, pp. 22–3. This was Balfour's first visit to Palestine. The day he arrived there was declared a day of mourning; black flags were raised and a general strike was observed by all Muslims and Christians. Khalil Sakakini, a Christian educationalist, delivered a patriotic speech from the platform of Haram al-Sharif in which he invited Lord Balfour to 'leave the country which he had entered against the wishes of the inhabitants'. See Kayyali, *Palestine: A Modern History*, p. 134.

106. Bentwich, *Palestine*, pp. 115–16.

107. Knox, *The Making of the New Eastern Question*, p. 169.

108. Bentwich, *England in Palestine*, pp. 109–10.

109. Samuel Papers, DS 125, 3 S.

110. Ibid.
111. Wasserstein, *Herbert Samuel*, pp. 269–70.
112. This could be attributed to the fact that Samuel's term was initially intended to be four years which could be extended to a fifth; hence he was keen on laying all the necessary foundations of the Jewish national home within the original time limit.
113. Peel Report, p. 62.

CHAPTER NINE

1. Smith, *Roots of Separatism*, p. 64.
2. Ingrams, *Palestine Papers*, p. 87.
3. Mossek, *Palestine Immigration Policy*, p. 9.
4. Smith, *Roots of Separatism*, p. 76.
5. Khalidi (ed.), *From Haven to Conquest*, Appendix I, p. 841. The figures of 120,600 for the Jewish population in 1925 is given by the Jewish Agency. The Palestine Government mid-year estimate for 1925 was 121,725. Justin McCarthy, *The Population of Palestine: Population History and Statistics of the Late Ottoman Period and the Mandate* (New York, 1990), p. 220.
6. Malcom E. Yapp, *The Near East since the First World War* (London, 1991), p. 117.
7. Stein, *Land Question in Palestine*, p. 65. The population of Tel Aviv rose from about 2,000 in 1920 to about 10,000 in 1925. Bentwich, *England in Palestine*, p. 119.
8. Jacob Metzer, *The Divided Economy of Mandate Palestine* (Cambridge, 1998), p. 68.
9. Smith, *Roots of Separatism*, pp. 77–8.
10. CAB 37/126, Secret Cabinet memorandum, 'Palestine', March 1915.
11. Mossek, *Palestine Immigration Policy*, pp. 4–5.
12. Weizmann's proposal was as follows: 2,000 unskilled and 3,000 skilled immigrants for building dwellings, schools, hospitals and other public buildings; 1,000 skilled and unskilled for cement, tile, furniture and other building industries; 2,500 for afforestation of 50,000 dunums of land; 3,000 agricultural workmen; 2,000 road makers; 3,000 for drainage and irrigation. These figures did not include persons who were self-supporting, who belonged to religious associations, who were of professional classes or government services, or who were members of families of present residents in Palestine. FO 371/5184 E 8901, Weizmann to Samuel, 25 July 1920.
13. Smith, *Roots of Separatism*, p. 66.
14. Mossek, *Palestine Immigration Policy*, pp. 5–6.
15. Ibid., p. 6.
16. Ibid.
17. For the full text, see Mossek, *Palestine Immigration Policy*, pp. 157–61.
18. Smith, *Roots of Separatism*, p. 66.
19. CO 733/35, 'A Memorandum on Jewish Immigration into Palestine', 19 October 1921.
20. Smith, *Roots of Separatism*, p. 67.
21. Dr A. Sonne, reporting from Palestine on the activities of the Zionist Commission to the Political Secretary, Central Zionist Organization, 24 August, 1920, quoted in Mossek, *Palestine Immigration Policy*, p. 10.

22. Ibid.

23. Smith, *Roots of Separatism*, p. 67.

24. The main target of Arab hostility during the riots was the Immigrant Hostel in Jaffa. Smith, *Roots of Separatism*, p. 67.

25. CO 733/22, Samuel to Churchill, Report on the Administration of Palestine July 1920–December 31 1921', 16 June 1922.

26. CO 733/35, 'A Memorandum on Jewish Immigration into Palestine', 19 October 1921.

27. Smith, *Roots of Separatism*, p. 68.

28. Present were: Shuckburgh, Clauson, Meinertzhagen, Weizmann, Professor Cajes, Leonard Stein and Eric Mills.

29. CO 733/16, Minutes of a meeting held at the Colonial Office on 25 November 1921, drafted by Mills.

30. CO 733/22, 'Report on the Administration of Palestine July 1920–December 31 1921', op. cit.

31. CO 733/35, 'A Memorandum on Jewish Immigration into Palestine', 19 October 1921.

32. CO 733/8, Deedes to Churchill, Political Report for December 1921. Secret.

33. Mossek, *Palestine Immigration Policy*, p. 154.

34. CO 733/46, Political Report for May 1923, op. cit.

35. CO 733/48, Political Report for July 1923, op. cit. By December, a public meeting was called for by the executive of the Jerusalem Workmen's Council to discuss the problem of unemployment. It became plain that this situation had been going on for a year, without any hope of being solved, and that 50 per cent of the Jerusalem Jewish community was unemployed. CO 733/64, Samuel to Devonshire, Political Report for December 1923. Secret.

36. Samuel disagreed with Morris on the question of whether British consuls in the main centres of immigration in Eastern Europe should be instructed to refer every case to Jerusalem, which was Samuel's suggestion, or to leave control of immigration to the discretion of the Palestine immigration officers in the main centres. Mossek, *Palestine Immigration Policy*, p. 154.

37. CO 733/28, Samuel to Devonshire, 8 December 1922.

38. CO 733/43, Samuel to Devonshire, Press Comments from the Political Report for February 1923. Secret.

39. CO 733/54, Minute by Shuckburgh to Secretary of State, 25 July 1923.

40. CO 733/86, Minute by Shuckburgh, 24 July 1924.

41. Mills had a long career in the Administrative Service in Palestine, from 1917 to 1947. Serving under the OETA from 1917, he was military governor of Gaza, 1919, and assistant governor of Samaria in 1920. From 1920–25, Mills was acting principal at the Colonial Office. He was appointed assistant chief secretary to Lord Plumer, the high commissioner who succeeded Samuel in 1925.

42. CO 733/33, Eric Mills, Memorandum, 'Some Sociological Aspects of Jewish Immigration into Palestine', 20 February 1922. Secret.

43. See Khalidi (ed.), *From Haven to Conquest*, Appendix I, p. 841.

44. CO 733/33, Eric Mills, 'Some Sociological Aspects of Jewish Immigration into Palestine', op. cit.

45. CO 733/33, Minute by Mills, 21 February 1922.

46. CO 733/21, Minute by Young, 14 June 1922.

47. Sir Herbert William Malkin, a Foreign Office official.

48. CO 733/75, 19 November 1924. Keith-Roach went on to examine the length of residence needed to become a citizen in each of the following countries: Great Britain (5 years), the USA (5 years), Switzerland (20 years), Belgium (10 years), France (10 years) and Italy (5 years).

49. CO 733/75, 26 November 1924. In this particular case, the request was not granted by the Middle East Department for fear of 'creating an awkward precedent', and Samuel was informed accordingly. The minute went on to say that Chief Rabbi Kook had been created an Honorary C.B.E. the previous year, and that in acknowledgment of the honour, the Chief Rabbi 'wrote a very "flowery" letter to the King ... in the course of which he used some rather indiscreet language (from the political point of view) about the future of Zionism in Palestine.'

50. Bentwich, *England in Palestine*, pp. 146–7.

51. CO 733/27, Memorandum of a conversation between the High Commissioner, Musa Kazim Pasha al-Husseini and Shaikh Abdul Qadir al-Muzaffar, 30 October 1922. The Arabic newspaper *Bayt al-Maqdis* commented in November 1922 that in Palestine the Jews could have dual citizenship, and that the government intended that Jews should have as many votes as possible in the forthcoming elections (i.e. the Legislative Council elections), as most Jews in Palestine were of foreign nationality and had no right to vote. CO 733/28, Samuel to Devonshire, Political Report for December 1922. Secret. Appendix D.

52. Mossek, *Palestine Immigration Policy*, p. 155.

53. CO 733/47, Press Comments in Clayton to Devonshire, Political Report for June 1923. For instance, *La Palestine*, 19 June 1923.

54. FO 371/5117, Petition by the Muslim-Christian Society, signed by the Vice-President Hafez Toukan, transmitted to the Peace Conference through the Chief Political Officer, General Headquarters, Egyptian Expeditionary Force, 13 February 1920.

55. FO 371/5113, Weizmann to Vansittart, and Scott's minute, 25 February 1920.

56. FO 371/5123 E 13008/85/44, Samuel to Curzon, Proceedings of the First Meeting of the Advisory Council, 6 October 1920.

57. CO 733/35, 'A Memorandum on Jewish Immigration into Palestine', 19 October 1921.

58. Quoted in Ingrams, *Palestine Papers*, p. 122.

59. CO 733/15, Minute by Shuckburgh to Masterton-Smith, 22 November 1921.

60. CO 733/47, Political Report for June 1923, op. cit.

61. CO 733/13, 'Report on the State of Palestine ... ' op. cit., p. 21.

62. FO 371/5123, Samuel's speech at the first meeting of the Advisory Council.

63. FO 371/5123 E 11966, Samuel to Weizmann, 5 September 1920.

64. FO 371/5123, First meeting of the Advisory Council (6 October 1920).

65. Samuel Papers, DS 126, Confidential letter, unsigned and thought to be from Weizmann, 2 February 1920.

66. Smith, *Roots of Separatism*, pp. 32–3.

67. CO 733/13, Samuel to Curzon, 1 January 1921, Confidential.

68. CO 733/24, Political Report for July 1922, op. cit. See also CO 733/23, 'Statement by

His Excellency the High Commissioner at meeting of Advisory Council, July 17th, 1922'.

69. CO 733/24, quoting *Filastin*, 20 July 1922, in Political Report for July 1922.

70. CO 733/24, Political Report for July 1922, op. cit., Appendix C, Press Comments.

71. Although the Arabs frequently accused Samuel of initiating road building projects mainly to provide opportunities for unemployed Jewish settlers, and that these roads mainly connected Jewish colonies, they did ask the government to improve roads, especially between Jaffa–Tulkarm, Acre–Safad, Wadi Isma'il–Battir–Jerusalem, Jaffa–Gaza and Latrun–Ramallah. CO 733/43, Samuel to Devonshire, Political Report for February 1923, Secret. The fact that they had to demand the improvement of these roads which passed through Arab towns suggests that Samuel neglected such improvements.

72. CO 733/13, 'Report on the State of Palestine ... ' op. cit., p. 21.

73. Metzer, *The Divided Economy*, p. 178.

74. Nachum Gross, *The Economic Policy of the Mandatory Government in Palestine* (Jerusalem, November 1982), p. 20, fn. 19.

75. CO 733/102, 'Palestine. Report of the High Commissioner... ' ('Book of Chronicles').

76. The Economic Board for Palestine was a London-based independent Zionist body which was interested in private industrial enterprise.

77. CO 733/73, Minute by Vernon, 17 October 1924.

78. Smith, *Roots of Separatism*, pp. 24, 35.

79. CO 733/15, Minute by Shuckburgh to Secretary of State, 7 September 1921. As early as 1902, Theodor Herzl anticipated that hydro-electric power would be the economic basis of his 'New Society' in Palestine. Smith, *Roots of Separatism*, p. 118.

80. Smith, *Roots of Separatism*, p. 126.

81. Quoted in ibid., p. 117.

82. CO 733/15, Minute by Shuckburgh to Secretary of State, 7 September 1921.

83. Smith, *Roots of Separatism*, p. 121.

84. CO 733/15, Minute by Young, 10 September 1921.

85. CO 733/15, Minute by Shuckburgh, 17 September 1921. Rutenberg's letter to Shuckburgh on 16 September read: 'With reference to the various interviews at the Colonial Office and to the question raised by the High Commissioner as to possible local opposition in Palestine to my scheme or its details, I would point out that if there is real opposition it will be impossible for me to raise the necessary capital and it follows that in that event the scheme would have to be abandoned, or alternatively, its terms would have to be modified so as to meet the local objections.' On 17 September, Shuckburgh minuted that Rutenberg's letter 'may be regarded as sufficiently safeguarding their position' (i.e. that of the Arabs) and that there was 'no reason why we should not now proceed to the signature of the agreement'.

86. CO 733/15, Memorandum by Shuckburgh, 'Palestine', 7 November 1921.

87. CO 733/15, Churchill to Samuel, Telegram, 12 September 1921.

88. *Filastin*, 19 October 1921.

89. Kayyali, *Watha'iq al-muqawama*, pp. 55, 73.

90. Smith, *Roots of Separatism*, pp. 122–3.

91. Ibid., p. 125.

92. CO 733/101, Minute by Shuckburgh, 12 March 1925.

93. Smith, *Roots of Separatism*, pp. 11–12. The Jewish National Fund (Keren Kayemeth le-Israel) was created in 1901 as an instrument of national Jewish land policy in Palestine, aiming to buy all lands used for Jewish colonization into public ownership. In contrast to the JNF, the Jewish Colonization Association—ICA (from 1924, the Palestine Jewish Colonization Association—PICA), purchased land and allotted it to settlers in private ownership. See Granovsky, *Land Problems in Palestine* (London, 1926), pp. 2, 27.

94. Khalidi (ed.), *From Haven to Conquest*, Appendix I, p. 841.

95. Ibid., p. xxvi. It should be noted that these figures vary and are sometimes held at about 6 per cent of the land in 1948. See for instance Sami Hadawi, *Palestinian Rights and Losses in 1948: A Comprehensive Study* (London, 1988), p. 230.

96. Kayyali, *Palestine: A Modern History*, pp. 29–32.

97. CO 733/13, 'Report on the State of Palestine … ' op. cit.

98. *A Survey of Palestine*, vol. 1, p. 238.

99. Tibawi, *Anglo-Arab Relations*, pp. 282–3.

100. Ibid., p. 284.

101. Ibid., p. 310.

102. Stein, *Land Question in Palestine*, pp. 214, 242.

103. Hadawi, *Palestinian Rights*, p. 24.

104. Smith, *Roots of Separatism*, p. 112.

105. Ibid.

106. The Palin Report notes that 'the latter ground is interesting as showing that the Zionist Organization was ready to plead the 'Status Quo' when they thought it was in their interest to do so'.

107. In a speech delivered after the Sixth Palestine Arab Congress was held at Jaffa (16–20 June 1923), Jamal al-Husseini, secretary of the Arab Executive Committee, commented on the same subject, saying that after the war ended, the military administration started to help the people by way of agricultural loans, and continuing: 'we could see for some time the phantom of death disappearing. Soon after these loans were suspended and it was later that we knew that the Zionist Committee had demanded that. In other words the Zionist interests require the people of the country to be weakened'. CO 733/47, Political Report for June 1923, op. cit.

108. FO 371/5121, The Palin Report, pp. 25–7.

109. FO 371/5117, Chief Political Officer General Headquarters, Cairo to Secretary of State for Foreign Affairs, 13 February 1920.

110. FO 371/5139, Minute by Scott, 24 April 1920.

111. The Palin Report, p. 18.

112. CO 733/22, Samuel to Churchill, 'Report on the Administration of Palestine July 1920–December 31 1921', 16 June 1922.

113. Smith, *Roots of Separatism*, p. 109. See also Stein, *Land Question in Palestine*, p. 13.

114. Stein, *Land Question in Palestine*, p. 46.

115. Ibid., p. 44.

116. Norman Bentwich, compiler, *Legislation of Palestine 1918–25, Including the Orders-Council, Ordinances, Public Notices, Proclamations, Regulations, Etc.* (Alexandria, 1926),

vol. 1, pp. ix–xv. Other Land Ordinances were the Acquisition of Land for the Army (September 1920, repealed by that of 1925), the Land Courts Ordinance (April 1921), Correction of Land Registries Amendment Ordinance (September 1921), Transfer of Land Amendment Ordinance, (December 1921), the Land Valuer's Ordinance (1922), the Land Surveyor's Ordinance (1925) and the Expropriation of Land Ordinance (1924).

117. These have been dealt with by Stein, *Land Question in Palestine*, and Smith, *Roots of Separatism*. Smith shows that British economic policy provided the perfect environment for the growth of the Zionist programme. Samuel's economic policies are studied in great detail in this work.

118. Gross, *The Economic Policy of the Mandatory Government*, p. 54.

119. Later commissioner of lands.

120. Kalvarisky was chosen by Samuel to head the Land Commission in an official capacity, while at the same time representing Jewish land purchasing companies, in his capacity as manager of the colonies of the Jewish Colonization Association. This anomalous position was highly resented by the Arabs. See Smith, *Roots of Separatism*, p. 101.

121. FO 371/5123 E 11966, 5 September 1920.

122. FO 371/5140, Samuel to Weizmann, 19 December 1920.

123. CO 733/18, Samuel to Churchill, 'General Report of the Land Commission', 10 February 1922. *Waqf* lands were divided into two main types, *sahih* and *ghayr sahih*; both were administered by the Supreme Muslim Council during the mandate. It is estimated that under the mandate 15 per cent of the agricultural land was *waqf*. *Waqf sahih*, or privately owned property, was registered and documented in title deeds. As early as 1919, Weizmann realized that the Arabs might resort to the powerful weapon of converting their land into *awqaf*, a step which would have rendered such lands as were altered to this category inalienable, and for this reason he favoured the continued closure of land registries during OETA. See, for instance Stein, *Land Question in Palestine*, pp. 41, 43.

124. CO 733/18, Samuel to Churchill, 10 February 1922.

125. CO 733/28, Samuel to Devonshire, 8 December 1922, Confidential.

126. CO 733/102, 'Palestine. Report of the High Commissioner … ' ('Book of Chronicles'). Kabbara referred to an area of 18 square miles which the Palestine Administration leased to the Jewish Colonization Association for fifty years, renewable subject to certain conditions.

127. CO 733/33, Eric Mills, 'Some Sociological Aspects of Jewish Immigration into Palestine', 20 February 1922, op. cit.

128. Smith, *Roots of Separatism*, p. 86.

129. Stein, *Land Question in Palestine*, p. 13.

130. Smith, *Roots of Separatism*, pp. 98–9.

131. Stein, *Land Question in Palestine*, p. 13.

132. CO 733/18, Samuel to Churchill, General Report of the Commission to Enquire into the Conditions of Land Settlement in Palestine, 10 February 1922.

133. CO 733/18, Report of the Land Commission to Enquire into the Conditions of State Land, August 1920.

134. Smith, *Roots of Separatism*, p. 98.

135. Tibawi, *Anglo-Arab Relations*, pp. 469–70.

136. CO 733/23, Political Report for June 1922, op. cit.

137. Smith, *Roots of Separatism*, p. 92; Charles S. Kamen, *Little Common Ground: Arab agriculture and Jewish settlement in Palestine 1920–48* (Pittsburgh, 1991), p. 157.

138. Stein, *Land Question in Palestine*, pp. 45, 48.

139. Ibid., p. 48.

140. Kamen, *Little Common Ground*, p. 157.

141. Smith, *Roots of Separatism*, p. 103; Raya Adler Cohen, 'The Tenants of Wadi Hawarith: Another View of the Land Question in Palestine', *International Journal of Middle East Studies*. vol. 20 (1988), pp. 198–9.

142. Ibid., p. 198.

143. Smith, *Roots of Separatism*, p. 96.

144. Kamen, *Little Common Ground*, p. 157.

145. Cohen, 'The Tenants of Wadi Hawarith', p. 199.

146. Land companies often wrote clauses into sales agreements that land should be delivered free of tenants. See for instance Stein, *Land Question in Palestine*, p. 52.

147. Son of Faydi al-'Alami, former Mayor of Jerusalem.

148. Furlonge, *Palestine is My Country*, pp. 90–1.

149. CO 733/63, Political Report for December 1923.

150. Smith, *Roots of Separatism*, pp. 91–2. See also Stein, *Land Question in Palestine*, pp. 46–51

151. The Peel Report, p. 223. See also Boustany, *The Palestine Mandate, Invalid and Impracticable: A Contribution of Arguments and Documents towards the solution of the Palestine Problem* (Beirut, 1936), p. 88.

152. Kamen, *Little Common Ground*, pp. 192–3.

153. Ibid., pp. 242–6.

154. The Peel Report, p. 222.

155. Stein, *Land Question in Palestine*, p. 212; Kamen, *Little Common Ground*, p. 154.

156. The lands in Ghor Beisan were classified as *mudawwara* (also known as *jiftlik*). They were taken over from Sultan 'Abdul Hamid after the 1908 revolution, first by the Ottoman government, and then by the Palestine government. See Hadawi, *Palestinian Rights*, p. 42.

157. Smith, *Roots of Separatism*, p. 95–8.

158. For example, in 1921, 63,634 dunums were bought by Jewish land purchasing companies in a single transaction for 226,040 Egyptian pounds, at an average of 3.6 pounds per dunum, a much lower figure than that reported by the British authorities for this period. See Smith, *Roots of Separatism*, p. 95.

159. Boustany, *Palestine Mandate*, p. 88.

160. Smith, *Roots of Separatism*, p. 98.

161. CO 733/1, Political Report for February 1921, op. cit.

162. CO 733/3, Samuel to Churchill, Political Report for May 1921.

163. CO 733/13, Report from the War Office to the Colonial Office on the Situation in Palestine July 1921, Confidential.

164. Bentwich, *England in Palestine*, pp. 76–7.

165. Ibid., p. 77.

166. CO 733/3, Political Report for May 1921, op. cit.

167. CO 733/6, Deedes to Churchill, Political Report for August 1921.

168. *Filastin*, 19 October 1921.

169. Quoted in Smith, *Roots of Separatism*, p. 122.

170. CO 733/8, Political Report for November 1921. For a different view see Tibawi, *Anglo-Arab Relations*, p. 494, in which he describes how Samuel was met in Beisan with angry demonstrations by mistrustful Arabs with slogans such as: 'Down with Zionism' and 'Palestine is Arab and Ours'.

171. CO 733/8, Deedes to Churchill, Political Report for December 1921, Secret.

172. Until 1927 the currency used in Palestine was the Egyptian Pound, which was equivalent to 100 piastres.

173. CO 733/22, Samuel to Churchill, 'Report on the Administration of Palestine July 1920–December 31 1921', 16 June 1922.

174. CO 733/24, Samuel to Churchill, 11 August 1922.

175. Agreement Between the Government of Palestine and the Cultivators of the Ghor Lands, November 19th 1921, reproduced in Lewis French, *First Report on Agricultural Development and Land Settlement in Palestine*, (Jerusalem, December 1931), Appendix IIIB.

176. *Al-Karmel*, 4 April 1925. In 1928, a Statement of Policy on the Ghor Mudawwarah Agreement of 1921 indicated that the government was prepared 'under certain conditions' to waive the requirement that the whole transfer price must be paid before the transferee had the freedom to dispose of his surplus land. The conditions were: '(i) that surplus land be transferred to persons approved by the Government and having as their object the promotion of close settlement and the intensive cultivation of the land, and (ii) that in every case shall the transferee retain such extent of land in the area to which the Ghor Mudawwarah Agreement of 1921 applies or elsewhere as will in the opinion of the Government suffice for the maintenance of himself and his family.' Statement of Policy published in the Official Gazette on 16 September 1928, reproduced in French, *First Report on Agricultural Development*, Appendix IIIC.

177. *Al-Karmel*, 26 August 1925.

178. Smith, *Roots of Separatism*, p. 111.

179. CO 733/26, Samuel to Churchill, 25 October 1922.

180. Stein, *Land Question in Palestine*, p. 15.

181. Ibid., pp. 12, 64.

182. Ibid., p. 62.

183. Granovsky, *Land Problems*, p. 72.

184. The old Turkish dunum was equal to 919.3 square metres. The British administration adopted a metric dunum of 1,000 square metres, which is about a quarter of an acre. Barbara Smith notes that, in general, no distinction was made between the two measures despite the 8 per cent variation. See Smith, *Roots of Separatism*, p. xiv.

185. Stein, *Land Question in Palestine*, p. 48. The same area is sometimes estimated at about 700,000 *dunums*. See for instance Smith, *Roots of Separatism*, p. 96.

186. Stein, *Land Question in Palestine*, p. 59.

187. Smith, *Roots of Separatism*, p. 96. Colonel Bramley reported that the Turkish government had borrowed money at some previous date from a banking firm in Beirut, and in return for the loan, large tracts of land in Palestine had been mortgaged to this firm. After

the civil administration was set up, the Zionists saw a golden opportunity in these absentee landlords, who were only too willing to part with unwanted land in return for the money they had lent. Bramley Papers, 'Creating the Jewish National Home in Palestine: the five villages'.

188. Smith, *Roots of Separatism*, pp. 96–7.

189. Quoting his work 'Dynamics of land alienation' in Ibrahim Abu-Lughod, ed., *The Transformation of Palestine: Essays on the Origins and Development of the Arab-Israeli Conflict* (Evanston, 1971).

190. Smith, *Roots of Separatism*, p. 97.

191. CO 733/86, Weizmann to Thomas, 18 July 1924.

192. Stein, *Land Question in Palestine*, pp. 226–7.

193. CO 733/89, Ronald Storrs, Political Resumé for Jerusalem-Jaffa District for the month of January 1925, Secret.

194. In a letter of 22 November 1924 to 'Secretary in Charge, Eastern Department' at the Foreign Office, Bramley requested a 'confidential talk' with whoever was in charge of Middle Eastern Affairs. He explained: 'I have retired recently from service under the Palestine Govt. and may quite possibly be of some assistance to you in helping to get at the root of the mischief in respect to our present troubles in Palestine and Egypt. ... I was Director of Public Security in Palestine up to April 1923—when Gen. Tudor assumed full charge—and I have maintained touch with that country and Egypt since I returned home.' Bramley Papers, Cambridge University Library: Royal Commonwealth Society Library.

195. Bramley Papers.

196. A land purchasing agency established in 1914 by the Zionist Organization of America, it was responsible for developing Jewish settlements. It was dissolved in 1931 after transferring its properties to the Jewish National Fund and private individuals.

197. Bramley Papers.

198. Caplan, *Palestine Jewry*, pp. xvi, 4–5.

199. Storrs, *Orientations*, p. 358.

200. The anti-Zionist lobby in Britain.

201. CO 733/84, Letter from the Chairman of the Political Committee of the English Zionist Federation to the Colonial Office, 13 June 1924.

202. CO 733/74, Ronald Storrs, Political Resumé for the Jerusalem-Jaffa District for the period ending 20 October 1924, Secret. An important point to be mentioned is that when in 1929 the Jewish land companies' strategy was targeted at buying smaller pieces of land privately owned by individual Palestinians, Muslim scholars issued a *fatwa* (a religious dispensation) prohibiting the sale of land to Jews. Hajj Amin al-Husseini, head of the Supreme Muslim Council toured Palestine 'castigating' sellers and brokers, and the *imams* in local mosques took up the theme and preached the 'holiness of Palestine'. The Supreme Muslim Council moreover intended to take practical measures to counteract the activities of the Jewish National Fund by buying large portions of land, but failed to do so because of their very limited resources. The Supreme Muslim Council nevertheless tried to hamper the Jewish strategy of buying only in places where there was a possibility of expanding later on, by launching a counter strategy of scattering its own purchases over a wide area. See for instance Dumper, *Islam and Israel*, p. 21.

203. The Palin Report, p. 13.

204. National Archives, Washington, Microfilm Roll no. 79, No. 1019, 6 September 1922, American Vice Consul in Charge, George C. Cobb.

205. CO 733/35, Minute by Eric Mills, 30 September 1922.

206. CO 733/28, Samuel to Devonshire, 8 December 1922.

207. CO 733/63, 'Political Report on the Northern District' in Samuel to Devonshire, Political Report for December 1923.

208. CO 733/63, Samuel to Devonshire, Political Report for December 1923.

209. See, for instance, *al-Karmel*, 28 February 1925.

210. The Arab Economic Agricultural Conference held its first meeting on 1 February 1923. See Kayyali, *Palestine: A Modern History*, pp. 116–17.

211. Kayyali, *Watha'iq al-muqawama*, p. 67, 'The Decisions of the Economic Conference'.

212. CO 733/47, Speech by Jamal al-Husseini at the Sixth Palestine Arab Congress, June 1923, in Clayton to Devonshire, Political Report for July 1923.

213. *An Interim Report on the Civil Administration of Palestine*, Cmd. 1499.

214. Smith, *Roots of Separatism*, p. 15.

CONCLUSION

1. What Weizmann had failed in achieving in the Balfour Declaration, he succeeded in incorporating in the writ of the mandate, whereas recognition was given 'to the historic connection of the Jewish people with Palestine and to the grounds for reconstituting their national home in that country'.

2. The General Syrian Congress, with delegates from Syria, Palestine and Lebanon, denounced Article 22, stating that it 'relegates us to the standing of insufficiently developed races requiring the tutelage of a mandatory power'. John Quigley, *Palestine and Israel: A Challenge to Justice* (Durham NC, 1990), p. 14.

3. See *A Survey of Palestine*, vol. 1, p. 2.

4. Quigley, *Palestine and Israel*, p. 15. This principle was affirmed in 1970 in connection with the continued presence of South Africa in Namibia. Ibid., note 4, p. 237.

Appendix A

Excerpts from the Mandate for Palestine [For the full text see *A Survey of Palestine: Prepared in December 1945 and January 1946 for the Information of the Anglo-American Commission of Inquiry* (Institute for Palestine Studies, Washington DC., 1991), vol. 1, pp. 1-13]

Article 2

The Mandatory shall be responsible for placing the country under such political, administrative and economic conditions as will secure the establishment of the Jewish national home, as laid down in the preamble, and the development of self-governing institutions, and also for safeguarding the civil and religious rights of all the inhabitants of Palestine, irrespective of race and religion.

Article 4

An appropriate Jewish agency shall be recognized as a public body for the purpose of advising and cooperating with the Administration of Palestine in such economic, social and other matters as may affect the establishment of the Jewish national home and the interests of the Jewish population in Palestine, and, subject always to the control of the Administration, to assist and take part in the development of the country.

The Zionist Organization, so long as its organization and constitution are in the opinion of the Mandatory appropriate, shall be recognized as such agency. It shall take steps in consultation with His Britannic Majesty's Government to secure the cooperation of all Jews who are willing to assist in the establishment of the Jewish national home.

Article 6

The Administration of Palestine, while ensuring that the rights and position of other sections of the population are not prejudiced, shall facilitate Jewish immigration under suitable conditions and shall encourage, in cooperation with the Jewish agency referred to in Article 4, close settlement by Jews on the land, including State lands and waste lands not required for public purposes.

Article 7

The Administration of Palestine shall be responsible for enacting a nationality law. There shall be included in this law provisions framed so as to facilitate the acquisition of Palestinian citizenship by Jews who take up their permanent residence in Palestine.

Article 11

The Administration of Palestine shall take all necessary measures to safeguard the interests of the community in connection with the development of the country, and, subject to any international obligations accepted by the Mandatory, shall have full power to provide for public ownership or control of any of the natural resources of the country or of the public works, services and utilities established or to be established therein. It shall introduce a land system appropriate to the needs of the country, having regard, among other things, to the desirability of promoting the close settlement and intensive cultivation of the land.

The Administration may arrange with the Jewish agency mentioned in Article 4 to construct or operate, upon fair and equitable terms, any public works, services and utilities, and to develop any of the natural resources of the country, in so far as these matters are not directly undertaken by the Administration. Any such arrangements shall provide that no profits distributed by such agency, directly or indirectly, shall exceed a reasonable rate of interest on the capital, and any further profits shall be utilized by it for the benefit of the country in a manner approved by the Administration.

Article 22

English, Arabic, and Hebrew shall be the official languages of Palestine. Any statement or inscription in Arabic on stamps or money in Palestine shall be repeated in Hebrew and any statement or inscription in Hebrew shall be repeated in Arabic.

Article 23

The Administration of Palestine shall recognize the holy days of the respective communities in Palestine as legal days of rest for the members of such communities.

Article 24

The Mandatory shall make to the Council of the League of Nations an annual report to the satisfaction of the Council as to the measures taken during the year to carry out the provisions of the mandate. Copies of all laws and regulations promulgated or issued during the year shall be communicated with the report.

Appendix B

Extract from the Palin Report [FO 371/5121 E 9373, Enquiry into Rioting in Jerusalem in April 1920 (submitted in August 1920), Port Said]

Conclusions

69. The following are the considered opinions submitted by the Court:

1.   That the causes of the alienation and exasperation of the feelings of the population of Palestine are:-
(a) Disappointment at the non-fulfilment of promises made to them by British propaganda.
(b) Inability to reconcile the Allies' declared policy of self-determination with the Balfour Declaration, giving rise to a sense of betrayal and intense anxiety for their future.
(c) Misapprehension of the true meaning of the Balfour Declaration and forgetfulness of the guarantees determined therein, due to the loose rhetoric of politicians and the exaggerated statements and writings of interested persons, chiefly Zionists.
(d) Fear of Jewish competition and domination, justified by experience and the apparent control exercised by the Zionists over the Administration.
(e) Zionist indiscretion and aggression, since the Balfour Declaration aggravating such fears.
(f) Anti-British and anti-Zionist propaganda working on the population already inflamed by the sources of irritation aforesaid.
2.   That the Zionist Commission and the official Zionists by their impatience, indiscretion and attempts to force the hands of the Administration, are largely responsible for the present crisis.
3.   That the Administration prior to the riots on the whole maintained under

difficult circumstances an attitude of equal justice to all parties and that the allegations of bias put forward by both sides, Arab and Zionist, are unfounded.

4. That the Administration was considerably hampered in its policy by the direct interference of the Home Authorities, and particularly by the fact that the late Chief Political Officer, Colonel Meinertzhagen, acted as a direct channel of communication with the Foreign Office independent of the High Commissioner and submitted to the Foreign Office, advice, not only independent of the High Commissioner, but at times contrary to the latter's considered opinion.

5. That the non-publication of the Foreign Office declaration of policy, though rejected for serious reasons, was an error.

6. That although the deliberation over a policy of accepting the Emir Feisal as titular King of Palestine might have aggravated the local situation, had it become publicly known, there is not sufficient evidence to show whether it did so become known to other than the Zionists, who undoubtedly were alarmed at it.

7. That the Military Governorate of Jerusalem failed to make adequate preparations for a possible disturbance at the Nebi Musa Pilgrimage in spite of the receipt of warnings and ample knowledge of the situation, such failure being probably due to over confidence induced by the success of the police authorities in handling earlier demonstrations.

8. That in spite of the prohibition of political demonstrations no definite instructions were issued by the Military Governorate to the police to prevent the delivery of inflammatory speeches on the occasion of the Nebi Musa pilgrimage.

9. That the decision to withdraw the troops from inside the city at 6 a.m. on Monday, April 5, whoever was responsible for it, was an error of judgment.

10. That the Military were slow in obtaining full control of the city after Martial Law had been proclaimed.

11. That the situation at present obtaining in Palestine is exceedingly dangerous and demands firm and patient handling if a serious catastrophe is to be avoided.

(Signed) P. C. Palin, Major General, President
G. H. Wildblood, Brigadier General, Member
C. Vaughan Edwards, Lieutenant Colonel, Member
A. L. McBarnet, Judge Courts of Appeal, Egypt, Legal Adviser

Port Said.
1st July, 1920.

Appendix C

Memorandum by the Muslim-Christian Association of Nablus, submitted to the High Commissioner on 7 July 1922, containing their reply and observations on the White Paper [CO 733/24, Political Report for July 1922, Samuel to Churchill]

TRANSLATION
His Excellency
The High Commissioner
Thro' Governor

The Moslem Christian Society, Nablus, have read the official Communiqué published on the 6/7/22 on the Palestine cause and the Zionist policy. The Society being representative of the population of this district and speaking on their behalf decided in its meeting of 6/7/22 to submit the following reply and observations on this communiqué to His Excellency the High Commissioner for referring same to the British Government.

1. The declaration of 1917 which provides for the establishment in Palestine of a Jewish National Home is illegal and is based on no right whatever as it contradicts both the promises given in 1915 by the British Government to His Majesty the King of Hijaz and the desires of the Arabs who form the great majority of the population. These desires have since the Armistice been submitted to the British Government, to other Governments and to the official International bodies. The population in submitting these desires base their demands on the right given to them by the promise of Great Britain in 1915 to the King of the Hijaz and by the declaration of both Great Britain and France in 1918 and by the provisions in Article 22 of the Regulations of the League of Nations.
2. The Jews have no right whatever in Palestine, as it is not their original country. The Arabs are the owners of the country in beginning and end, the Jews being only a small minority. Therefore the Arab population of Palestine consider that

the right which it is intended to give to the Jews has a false basis and is nothing but the result of compulsion and ambitions. The Arab population therefore consider that they have the full right to refuse it and to demand its abolition and that it is susceptible of change.

3. The Society although noting that the British Government does not aim at making Palestine Jewish nor at causing the disappearance of both the Arab population and culture, it nevertheless believes that this will be an inevitable and natural result of the void policy of the Jewish National Home. Therefore we do not see in the Government's communiqué anything new that might call to rest and quietness.

4. Palestine is an Arab province in population, history, general and private manifestations of life and is connected with all other Arab countries. Therefore the society consider the word 'Palestinian status' harmful and unjust to the rights of the Arab Nationality and that it is the first step towards assimilating the Arab nationality into the coming Jewish majority.

5. In the para re the intention of the Government to foster self-government in Palestine the Society do not see anything to raise hopes that right will be attained, as this para lacks any guarantee that the establishment of self-government would not be postponed until such time when the Jews become the majority in the country. Such self-government would then be in the interests of the Jews and against the interests of the Arabs. This matter is aggravated by the fact that at present almost all the Departments of the Government are in the hands of foreigners many of whom are Zionists. Arabs do not hold important posts neither in the centre nor in the districts. The establishment of a Legislative Council falls within the same lines, because this Council will not have any power in the Administration and Government of the country. Moreover the Arabs who are the great majority will be represented by a minority in the Council, a minority which will not be able to protect the interests of the population against the Zionist policy. This is because the Government officials many of whom are Zionist Jews, and the Jews will together form the majority of the Council. There is nothing in such majority which will induce quietness and confidence.

6. In para 6 of the communiqué the Government acknowledge[s] the special position of the Zionist Executive. Although the Government intends to make this position of no direct influence on the Government of the country yet the Zionist Executive will continuously be in touch with the official authorities on economy schemes and schemes of public utility, especially as many of the principal official departments are at present in the hands of Zionists.

7. The assurance given in para 7 of the communiqué re immigration does not abolish any of the Arab fears and troubles. The Government is continuously giving such assurance but nevertheless Jews are continuously coming also, many of whom are a burden on the Government and the country and are moreover

competitors to native labour. This is besides the many principles brought in with them— principles which disturb peace and quietness.

8. The right of the religious communities and sections of populations to appeal to the League of Nations if the Government does not carry out the terms of the Mandate is noted with astonishment. The terms of the Mandate drawn up by the Government without the concurrence and consent of the population. The Mandate contains the terms that will naturally make the Arab Nationality disappear and be replaced by the Jewish nationality and Jewish Sovereignty. Since the Mandate is not based on the desires of the population and is not in accordance with Article 22 of the Rules of the League of Nations regarding Mandates is therefore illegal in the first instance and cannot also be legal in its results and consequences.

The assurance of the Zionist Executive that they will act in accordance with the statements does not alter anything in the Arab cause, for the Arabs being the legal owners of the country do not admit the rights of this Executive to utter an opinion on the policy of the country. After what was actually done and aimed at by the Official Zionist leaders, and after seeing so many principal departments in the hands of the Zionists who care for nothing [...?] out of their national aims the [...?].

In consequence of the aforesaid the Moslem Christian Society decide that this communiqué does not alter any of the clear Arab rights and does not prevent them from defending these rights or from rejecting the unfounded Zionist policy or from continuously endeavouring to abolish it. The Society throws off on the British Government, which still insists on carrying out the baseless and despotic policy, all blame and responsibility for any danger that might in future ensue from the friction and collision between the two nationalities.

Respectfully,
(Sgd) Hafez
Representative of the Moslem-Christian Society, Nablus, 7/7/22

Appendix D

Memorandum by Mohamed Osman of Palestine to Winston Churchill. Comments on the Reply of Mr. Churchill to the Moslem Delegation during his visit to Jerusalem [CO 733/17B, from Port Said, 9 April 1921]

'This is not a formal conference' Mr. Churchill says in the first paragraph of his reply and we are glad to see that this is so. By this he means to tell his audience that although he is the Secretary of State for the Colonies, what he says represents only his views and not necessarily those of the British Government or of the British Public. We earnestly hope that public opinion in England will take a different view of the case and look upon events in Palestine in their true light. The reply of Mr. Churchill is objectionable both in form and in spirit. The spirit shows a mighty man taking advantage of his adversary's weakness to intimidate and coerce him. The form is vindictive, contemptuous, and disconcerting. Whatever the terms of the memorandum of the Moslem Delegation may have been Mr. Churchill admits that he did not receive them in his official capacity but out of courtesy. In our opinion he ought to have completed his courtesy by maintaining an obliging attitude rather than cut them so bluntly and abruptly. In his very agreeable reply to the Jewish Deputation, Mr. Churchill says it was his duty to encourage both parties. Comparing the two replies together we are of opinion that he did not accomplish his admitted duty towards the party representing the 'overwhelming majority' in the country. His words are the words of a dictator and not of an adviser as he professes to have been.

Mr. Churchill says 'It is manifestly right that the scattered Jews should have a National Centre and a National home to be reunited, and where else but in Palestine'. To make Palestine a National Home for the Jews, two questions present themselves, (1) Is this geographically feasible, and (2) if so, is it the intention of all Jews to take advantage of this opportunity by relinquishing their present nationalities and citizenships? In our opinion the answer to both questions would be NO.

Speaking of round figures the Jews of the world amount to about 15 millions in number. Palestine is not calculated to absorb more than 1 1/2 million at the utmost. Six hundred thousand of these already form the present Arab inhabitants of the country. Assuming that the remaining vacancy is to be filled solely by Jews, this leaves about 14 millions of Jews still to be scattered. There is no reason in saying that it is manifestly right that a spot of land holding about one million of people should have the privilege of being a National Home for a race of about 15 millions scattered in all parts of the world in masses of about three of four millions in certain territories. This is no reason for the British Government enforcing the Zionist programme with such pressure and forcibility unless the intention is to introduce a foreign and powerful element among the Moslem Arabs in order to break up their political unity and we cannot see the wisdom of pursuing such a policy. This being the case there is no proof of the statement of Mr. Churchill in the same speech that the British Government is 'well disposed to the Arabs and cherishes their friendship'. Both as Arabs and as Moslems we are entirely opposed to the introduction of such an element and we shall do so to the last atom of our blood. Our being is in danger and so also are our homes. This policy is not calculated to bring peace and prosperity to the country and we cannot see that we are likely to benefit by Jewish immigration. Our country is our own and it is only legitimate that no foreign element should be forced upon us. We know the Jews' ancient history too well to be led by roses and kisses. Their treatment to 'Amalik' still rings in our ears and their disposition to their old neighbours only aggravates our apprehensions. We have had enough of them during the past two years and we are resolved to fight them to the last.

But supposing that Palestine is vast enough to support all the Jews of the world, would all the Jews in England, for instance, be willing to forego their English nationality in order to acquire a new one in Palestine? The answer to this is NO and it does not pay them to do so. If they do they will lose the market of the world which is almost in their hands already. They will find no body in Palestine but themselves to feed upon or suck his blood and undoubtedly, like creepers, they cannot feed on each other. The truth is that a new market has been opened in the East and a party of Zionist agitators, through the medium of Great Britain, are trying to hold its reigns under the guise of a National Home for the Jews. This could not be done without prejudice to the vital interests of the overwhelming majority in the country and we are prepared to oppose it with our tooth and main.

We have a natural right to our country and we are determined to keep this right. Our fathers and forefathers have acquired the same right before us and we have inherited it from them. It takes a man at least five years' actual residence in a foreign country before he can obtain naturalization papers but we have never heard of a country being given wholesale to a people who have never seen it or whose fathers never lived in it. It is true that the Jews have been associated with this country for three thousand years but this is only a sentimental consideration and should not go so far as to establish a civil or political right. We are also associated with it in the same sense and if the Jews exceed us in the number of years we have an overwhelming majority in the number of community— 400 million Moslems. History tells us that Judas sold Christ to the Jews for thirty pieces of silver; may we ask for how many pieces of gold did England sell the land of His Birth and Death to the children of those who crucified Him about 2000 years ago. History repeats itself and we can only hope that it will not share the same fate.

The King of England bears the title of 'Defender of Faith'. We presume this relates to the Christian faith and it is only right that His Majesty's High Commissioner for Palestine should be in a position to represent him in that capacity. Mr. Churchill says he has no doubt that the League of Nations will accept his views about Palestine. We dare say if the League of Nations does so it will be no longer a League of Nations but a second council of Pontius Pilate. Pilate gave Christ to the Jews to crucify him and the League of Nations will be giving the Church of the 'Holy Sepulchre' to the same race in order to change its name to the 'Church of the Nazarine' as an eminent Jew recently suggested to a formal body in Jerusalem for naming streets and places.

Mr. Churchill says 'Palestine should support a larger population than it does now'. In this connection, we may remind the Honourable speaker that under a proper administration, such as we expect from the British Government, the present Arab inhabitants of the country are sure to more than double in the course of a few years and it is a MANIFEST right that our posterity should be allowed to live and prosper in the land of their birth and the birth of their fathers and forefathers. Mr. Churchill says 'we cannot tolerate expropriation of one set of people by another'. What does this gigantic and systematic Jewish immigration mean but filling the vacancy which nature and residence have provided for our children. Where shall we go with them when they come and is it a MANIFEST right that they should be driven so forcibly and systematically out of their and their fathers' land immediately after their birth simply because the British Government has been so graciously pleased to replace them by others. The GATHERING OF THE JEWS should not mean OUR SCATTERING. The Jews should not build up their nation on the debris of our own. Our fathers' graves shall not be disturbed by a hostile race. We cannot tolerate an antagonistic race to inherit our land or to throw our children away. The Jews are not suffering in their present homes and their rights are respected wherever they are. We would certainly suffer by their immigration so immediately and in such a bulk. We cannot believe that the establishment of a National Home for the Jews is the nucleus of their case. There is something more under the current. We object to an immigration supported and backed by a powerful state like Great Britain. We want time to recover our past sufferings and losses. If the Jews want to stand they should stand on their own feet and not use Great Britain as an instrument for their own ends and purposes. It is a shame on Great Britain to take advantage of our weakness in order to satisfy the wishes of a merciless race.

Mr. Churchill says 'the establishment of a National Home does not mean a Jewish Government to dominate the Arabs'. There is nothing to show that this is so. On the contrary every thing goes to show the contrary. The appointment of a 'devoted Zionist' as High Commissioner is the first step in the direction of a Jewish Government. The appointment of a Jewish wholehearted Zionist as Legal Secretary is another proof of our argument. The authority given to the Zionist Commission in the Mandate not only creates a Jewish Government in Palestine but makes the British Government an automatic instrument in their hands. The recognition of Hebrew as an official language at a time when the Hebrew speaking people in the country represent only 1/10th of the whole population and the official substitution of Hebrew names for Arabic ones are nothing but a practical creation of a Jewish Government to dominate not only the Arabs of Palestine, but, if possible, of the whole East.

No country in the world can ever sustain three official languages in its administration, but Palestine seems to be the LAND OF WONDERS for all ages. The scheme in itself is too costly to be borne and on the face of it quite superfluous. The Jews in the country represent only a very small minority and in the proper sense of justice they cannot claim such a right. Those of them who were in the country before the war know Arabic too well to make this step a necessity for their sakes. In fact most of them came from other Arabic speaking countries and do not know Hebrew. Those who were forcibly introduced into the country after the war do not know Hebrew and by a general recent demonstration at Jaffa they have protested against Hebrew being made an official language. The cost of maintaining three official languages in a country is too obvious to be commented upon and Palestine is not in a position to bear such an expenditure. Is it a MANIFEST RIGHT also that the 'overwhelming majority' in the country should be made to pay for the revival of a dead language spoken by a very small minority in the country.

Mr. Churchill says that Sir Herbert Samuel is 'animated by strong principles of liberal and impartial justice'. At the same time he describes him as his friend and DEVOTED TO THE CAUSE OF ZIONISM. We cannot see how we can reasonably reconcile those two contradictory statements. Sir Herbert Samuel cannot be a devoted Jew and at the same time impartial to the cause of the Jews. No one can serve two masters at the same time. Every enlightened Arab in the country can, if allowed, point out a case in which justice has been violated in furtherance of the Jewish cause. British officials in Palestine are collapsing under the strain and pressure of this policy and had it not been for allegiance to their country they would have been more outspoken in this regard than the Arab inhabitants themselves. Is it an impartial justice to make the 'overwhelming majority' provide work for Jewish immigrants who invade the country with the ardent hope of supplanting us and our children. Road making on a very large scale has been in progress ever since the High Commissioner has been in office. Contracts of considerable magnitude have been concluded by private treaties with the Zionist Labour Organization exclusively for the purpose of employing Jewish immigrants at high rates. Local labour is very seldom resorted to and even then with the sole object of throwing ashes in our eyes and at a comparatively very low rates. It is no wonder that a large deficit was shown on our budget last year. We know to whose pockets did all the money go. Mr. Churchill says repeatedly in his speech that we ought to help the Zionists in their programme. May we here ask what schemes are on hand when the road making is over so that we may contribute more generously and liberally towards their cause. Is it impartial justice to prevent Arab officials from joining societies of a political character or take part in their proceedings or pecuniarily contribute towards their cause while Jewish officials are not only active members of their societies but are divulging official information in furtherance of their schemes

It is, in our opinion, a gross act of injustice on the part of England to place the Government of Palestine in the hands of an official who pronounces himself so openly and devotedly in favour of one cause against the other. If the Jews cannot accuse him of not being a devoted Zionist we certainly accuse him of being so. It is not enough to say that 'he cannot be accused by the Jews when not favouring them'. He should be able to say the same thing to the Arabs when not favouring them. Mr. Churchill appears to have looked at the case with a Jewish eye only and it is our earnest hope that he will now open his other eye to the case of the 'overwhelming majority' if not with the same 'warmest sympathies' he had for the Jews let it be with the same sympathy he ought to have for PUBLIC JUSTICE. If he does so we will not accuse him of being partial to the Jews.

Mr. Churchill seems to deny us the share we have taken in the defeat of the Turkish Army in Palestine and the sufferings and miseries we have been subjected to on this account. This is a very good reward and we deserve it. We may, however, remind Mr. Churchill that the Turks and their allies the Germans were not so fools as to bring upon themselves our hatred and dislike at a time when they were in most need of our co-operation. It was absolutely essential for their interests to take us to their side at any cost but in vain they tried and tried to do so. We have already decided to give our 'warmest sympathies' to the Allies and in consequence of this decision we adopted a policy of a wholesale desertion from the Army and acted as spies for the Allies. We honoured the Allies' dead and withheld our assistance from the Turkish Government. It is no wonder that the Turks ultimately started a campaign against us. Foodstuffs were confiscated and withheld from the public. Court Martials became quite the order of the day and men of all classes and ranks were condemned and executed. General starvation and deportation of both individuals and families were very common and lastly but not least, men in the fighting line threw their arms and surrendered. All this we did for the sake of the

Allies who now forsake us in the hour of need. We have now become perfectly [apprised?] that we have been most unwise in adopting such a policy and that had we behaved so loyally and sincerely to the Turks and their allies as we have done to the Allies during the War our state would have been much better off than we are now. An internal enemy, however weak he may be, is worth one hundred outside; but unfortunately, Mr. Churchill does not wish to recognize this. We hope, however, that British public opinion will not close their eyes to our cause.

We submit this memorandum under a registered cover to His Lordship the Secretary of State for the Colonies hoping that he will care to read it with some consideration. At the same time we apologize for trespassing upon his valuable time and we trust that he will sympathize with our cause.

Port Said, 9 April 1921—Mohamed Osman of Palestine and now in Egypt

Appendix E

Letter from the Palestine Arab Delegation [CO 733/16, 2 October 1921]

Hotel Cecil
London. W.C.
24th October, 1921

The Rt. Hon. Winston Churchill, M.P.,
Colonial Secretary.

Sir,
On behalf of the People of Palestine, whom we represent, we thank you for the opportunities which you have given us of stating their case to you.

We wish now to put before you briefly the salient points of the case, the presentation of which to the British Government was confided to us, and we request you to put it before the Cabinet and inform us of its views. We wish to impress upon you two points. First, that the case we put forward is supported by 93% of the People of Palestine, and, second, that the People of Palestine will endorse a settlement of their present grievances on the lines we now suggest.

1. The People of Palestine welcomed the victorious British troops believing that they had come to fulfil promises made to them during the war, and to safeguard their existence as a people and their right of self determination. The very serious and growing unrest among the Palestinians arises from their absolute conviction that the present policy of the [...?] their country in order to make it a national state for immigrant Jews. It is no answer to urge that this is not the intention of the British Government, and that the Zionist policy will be checked before it destroys our people, for the fact is that an administration is installed which is, as regards very many of its important officials, Zionist: it is also a fact that the ancient Hebrew language which, for centuries, has not been spoken in Palestine except by a very few scholars, is now recognised as one of the official

languages of the country: and it is also a fact that there has been and still is, against our will, a great influx of Zionist immigration, largely composed of those least likely to make good citizens. The policy of the British Government may be, in intention, as benevolent to the Arab population as you claim, but all its outward manifestations and results (by which alone the people of Palestine can judge) show that that policy will, in fact, develop into the displacement of the Palestine Arab from the control, and even from the occupation, of his own country in favour of foreign Jews.

2. The Balfour Declaration was made without our being consulted and we cannot accept it as deciding our destinies. We wish to point out that if that portion of the Declaration which stated that the rights of the Palestine people should be safeguarded were interpreted strictly, there would be at the present moment, no flood of Jewish immigration into Palestine, and no administration in that country which is predominantly Jewish.

In his Declaration of June 3rd, 1921, the High Commissioner recognised the political rights of Arabs in Palestine in the following words: 'For the British Government, trustee under the Mandate for the happiness of the People of Palestine, would never impose upon them (the People of Palestine) a policy which that people had reason to think was contrary to their religious, their political and their economic interests.'

The Colonial Secretary confirms the recognition of these rights by the High Commissioner when he said in the House of Commons on June 14th, that he was 'following with very great confidence Sir Herbert's actions and giving them all possible support.'

In his Yearly Report recently published, Sir Herbert Samuel says that the policy of His Majesty's Government guarantees 'the full protection of the rights of the existing population', and almost in the same breath he states that the Jews ask for a home in Palestine 'that should possess national characteristics— in language, in customs, in intellectual interests, in religious and political institutions.'

There is evident contradiction in these pronouncements: for while recognising on the one hand the political rights of Arabs, a national political home for the Jews in Palestine is also accepted, which makes the first recognition of no avail. Add to this the obvious tendency of the present Administration and the political existence of the Arabs is virtually destroyed.

The Declaration should be superseded by an Agreement which would safeguard the rights, interests and liberties of the People of Palestine, and at the same time make provision for reasonable Jewish religious aspirations, but precluding any exclusive political advantages to them which must necessarily interfere with Arab rights.

3. A constitution for Palestine should be framed to carry out the Agreement and should provide for the following points:-

a. Representative Government giving the inhabitants control of their domestic affairs, but acting with the advice of the helping Power.
b. Complete religious freedom and religious equality, safeguarded by some means so that this should be unalterable by the Palestine Parliament or any other authority.
c. The Holy Places in Palestine to be guaranteed absolutely to their present guardians, the Palestine Parliament or any other authority to have no power to alter their disposition in any way.
d. The security of Palestine, as regards Land Forces, to be entrusted to a national gendarmerie, thus saving the British taxpayer the present great expenditure on a large garrison.

We have outlined above a plan which, it seems to us, is fair both to the Palestine people and the Jews. This plan will leave the control of immigration in the hands of the People of Palestine. It is the claim of the Zionists that the People of Palestine, after practical experience, will recognise the advantages to the country of Zionist immigration. If that be so, the Jews may be confident that the future immigration policy of Palestine would not be unfavourable to them: but if the immigration policy of the Zionist Organisation proves detrimental to the Palestine people, this policy should be regulated, not in the interests of the Zionists, but of Palestinians. [...?] that some control of their own destinies will be given to them in the future, while the Administration in the present allows their country to be subjected to a flood of alien immigration and to be put largely under Zionist control.

The Palestine people will never admit the right of any outside organisation to dispossess them of their country, and to threaten their very existence as a people economically and politically.

We ask you, Sir, to put our views as herein set out before the Cabinet, to which we have sent a copy of this proposal. If these views are, in the main, favourable, we could discuss with His Majesty's Government the details of the scheme subsequently to be submitted to the People of Palestine.

We are, Sir
Yours faithfully,
Secretary, Shibly Jamal; President, M. Kazim El-Husseini

Appendix F

Letter from the Palestine Arab Delegation to Churchill, commenting on the draft Order-in-Council [Zu'aytir Papers, pp. 216–18]

February 21st, 1922.
The Right Honourable
Winston Churchill M. P.
Secretary of State for the Colonies

Sir,
We wish to express our thanks to the Right Honourable the Secretary of State for the Colonies, for his courtesy in allowing us to see the draft of a proposed Palestine Order in Council embodying a scheme of Government of Palestine, and to discuss the same in our capacity of representatives of the Arab people of Palestine.

We would, therefore, submit the following observations:

While the position in Palestine is, as it stands today, with the British Government holding authority by an occupying force and using that authority to impose upon the people against their wishes, a great immigration of alien Jews, many of them a Bolshevik revolutionary type, no constitution which would fall short of giving the People of Palestine full control of their affairs could be acceptable.

If the British Government would revise their present policy in Palestine, and the Zionist condominium, put a stop to all alien immigration and grant the people of Palestine—who by experience are the best judges of what is good and bad to their country—Executive and Legislative powers, the terms of a constitution could be discussed in a different atmosphere. If to-day the People of Palestine assented to any constitution which fell short of giving them full control of their own affairs they would be in the position of agreeing to an instrument of government which might, and probably would, be used to smother their national life under a flood of alien immigration.

We, therefore, hold that the proposed constitution is wholly unsatisfactory because:

a. In the preamble to the Palestine Order in Council 'the declaration of November 2nd, 1917, in favour of the establishment in Palestine of a national home for the Jewish people' is made a basis for this Order; the People of Palestine cannot accept this declaration as a basis for discussion.

b. In Articles 4–9 of the Order dealing with the manner of Appointment of the High Commissioner and his powers, Palestine is considered as a colony of the lowest order, whereas according to paragraph 4 of Article 22 of the Covenant of the League of Nations, Palestine comes under grade A, where 'certain communities formerly belonging to the Turkish Empire have reached a stage of development where their existence as independent nations can be provisionally recognised subject to the rendering of administrative advice and assistance by a Mandatory until such time as they are able to stand alone.'

c. The Executive, dealt with in Articles 10–16, is in no way responsible to the Legislative Council.

d. Articles 17–28 dealing with the Legislative Council prescribe that this Council 'shall consist of 25 members in addition to the High Commissioner'—'who shall exercise a casting vote, in case of equality of votes.' This brings the total number of votes to 27. Of these 10 shall be official members holding office under the High Commissioner, and two members shall be nominated by him. Thus the High Commissioner commands 14 out of the 27 votes. Of the 12 elected members there will probably be 10 or 11 that would represent the Arab majority, who would be unable to carry any measure against the official preponderance of votes.

It is thus apparent that too much power is given to a High Commissioner whom we will suppose is impartial. But when, as is the case with the present High Commissioner, he is a Zionist, i.e. a member of the organization which is prompting the flood of alien Jew immigration into Palestine, whose officials as well as those members appointed by him must, naturally, carry out his policy, and when one or two of the 12 elected members will most probably be Zionists, then the Zionist policy of the Government will be carried out under a constitutional guise, whereas at present it is illegal against the rights and wishes of the people, and maintained by force of arms alone.

Article 22 gives the High Commissioner the power at any time to prorogue or dissolve the Council, without the provision that he must call a new council within a stated time.

Article 23 gives the High Commissioner the right to veto any measure passed by the Council.

We further submit in this connection that it is not in keeping with the constitutional spirit to place the Head of the Executive at the head of the Legislature and to introduce into this latter, as members, officials of the State. This invariably leads to the Executive becoming arbitrary since it is placed in the position of accused and judge at the same time.

We also notice with astonishment that 10 members constitute a quorum. This is less than half the total number of Members, and makes it possible for the 10 official members to carry on the work of the legislation should circumstances, for any reason whatever, prevent the other members from being present. In which case the power of the Legislative Council becomes a mere shadow and not a reality.

e. By the provision of Articles 33, 46 and 67, Palestine is considered as a Crown Colony, and the High Commissioner as the Governor of the Colony or British possession with the rights of confirming sentences of death, of deporting any person without trial and without allowing that person the right of appeal against the order for deportation.

f. The recognition of Hebrew as an official language of the State as in Article 80 is another proof of the desire to foster Zionist Nationalism in Palestine, when only about 10% [1% rather] of the present Jewish inhabitants of the country speak that language. This innovation is wholly unwarranted and adds to the expenses of the State, which derives its main revenue from the Arab population.

g. The High Commissioner by Article 61, is given the power to obstruct any appeal to the League of Nations.

h. Lastly we read in Article 83 that the High Commissioner may, after obtaining the approval of the Secretary of State, vary, annul or add to the provision of this Order in Council. These powers of the High Commissioner render this Order in Council as if it had not been.

For these reasons we find that no useful purpose would be served by discussing in detail the draft of 'The Palestine Order in Council, 1922'.

The Delegation requests that the constitution for Palestine should:

1. Safeguard the civil, political and economic interests of the People.
2. Provide for the creation of a national independent Government in accordance with the spirit of paragraph 4, Article 22, of the Covenant of the League of Nations.
3. Safeguard the legal rights of foreigners.
4. Guarantee religious equality to all peoples.
5. Guarantee the rights of minorities.
6. Guarantee the rights of the Assisting Power.

The Delegation is quite confident that the justice of the British Government and its sense of fair play will make it consider the above remarks with a sympathetic mind, since the Delegation's chief object is to lay in Palestine the foundation of a stable Government that would command the respect of the inhabitants and guarantee peace and prosperity to all.

The Delegation would request, in conclusion, that the Secretary of State would be good enough to communicate to them his views on their remarks and the next step to be taken in the matter.

We have the honour to be, Sir,
Your obedient servants,
for The Palestine Arab Delegation

Appendix G

Proclamation by the Arab Executive Committee, July 1922 [CO 733/24, in Political Report for July 1922, Samuel to Churchill]

The League of Nations, has, as has been expected, ratified the Palestine Mandate and the decision has been passed of the Western Powers who turn a deaf ear to the call of right and heed nothing but what has some material benefit to them.

The Executive Committee have previously declared that these defrauding decisions will only contribute to the adhesion of the nation to its rights from which it will not deviate by a hair's breadth and will only redouble its efforts in its national movement which means nothing more or less than the defence of self, of property, of personal freedom and of national life.

The Executive Committee hereby confirms the firm intention of the Palestine nation to explicitly reject the Mandate and its determination to persevere in its political national movement in a better organised and active manner and with a firmer will. In declaring this, the Committee depends on the national feeling that has pervaded all classes of the population and the heartfelt aversion of every individual to lead a life of oppression and misery.

The Zionist bodies and Great Britain have made great efforts towards the ratification of the Mandate, believing that this will weaken the nation, disturb its lines, and mortify its national movement, when the country will become an easy prey to the newcomers from all parts of the world. The nation has to prove to the world that these bodies have committed an error by means of a better unison, organisation and resoluteness for defending its rights.

Let it be known to every man or woman who has experienced these difficult days that every one is under a responsibility towards one's self, one's sons and one's forefathers. Let us then remove this responsibility off our shoulders at this critical moment by putting aside despair and by firmly believing that perseverance is the only way towards the nation's attainment of its rights.

Soon will the Wafd, who have made efforts unprecedented by any delegation that has ever knocked at the doors of justice in London and failed, return. The Arab Palestinian Congress will be convened on the day of their arrival. Then will the nation decide on the policy to be adopted for attaining its national rights of which it has been deprived by the European powers. The Congress will take measures to multiply the Moslem-Christian Societies, their better organisation and the formation of Societies at the capitals of both the Moslem and Christian Worlds for the defence of the Holy Land vis a vis the Zionist peril. It will further look into the deputation of a special delegation to the Eastern countries. It will also pass important decisions to show that in Palestine there is a living nation that knows how to defend its honour, existence and rights by every legal means without its being effected by the European Powers' decisions which, as we have learned by experience, are nearer to annihilation than realisation.

Let it be known that the European nations, apart from their Governments, sympathise with our case and help us avert the Zionist peril. We are confident that we shall find in the Moslem and Christian worlds the greatest help and let us realise that these hardships that befell us from the Powers are but columns on which our nation will build up its national life and that the country will be threatened by no danger. Zionism will never prosper and the Mandate will have no effect so long as the national life throbs in our veins and so long as common interest is the goal of every one of us.

Long Live Palestine, Arab, Free and Independent.

Appendix H

Speech by Jamal Husseini, Secretary of the Arab Executive Committee delivered at the Sixth Arab Conference, Jaffa 16–20 June 1923 [CO 733/47, Political Report for June 1923, Clayton to Devonshire]

My suggestion is based on a British rule built on the skulls of persons such as you are, loyal to the nation which they served and for which they sacrificed their souls. No taxation without representation.

This is the fundamental rule on which was based the oldest and greatest constitution. This is the rule which is esteemed and sanctified by those who to-day shape the fate of this nation and administer this country. This is a rule dear to their hearts which they built on the skulls of their poor fathers. I do not recommend adopting it merely because it is English or because by its means we acquire the sympathy of the British public which strove for it and for the safety of which it was on the watch; I recommend its adoption because it is the very means by which we achieve our rights without bloodshed but rather we adhere thereby to our grotesque plan in claiming our rights through peaceful and legal means.

Governments exact taxes from the governed for the purpose of securing their lives and property and rights individually and collectively against interior and exterior mishaps. Do you think the Government is adhering to this principle? I say No and with all force. The British Government occupied the country when the war had exhausted its strength. The Administration has commenced helping the people by way of agricultural loans and we could see for some time the phantom of death disappearing. Soon after these loans were suspended and it was late that we knew that the Zionist Committee had demanded that. In other words, the Zionist interests require the people of the country to be weakened. Sir Herbert Samuel said in 1919 'The Zionist policy to which adheres every Zionist with all his strength requires that the country be placed in a position which would fit Zionist immigration and imperialism.' 'That public concessions be given to Jews, and that the country should enjoy self-government, to its extreme limits so that it will be possible at the end to form an independent Government under the control of a Jewish majority.' Is it by this policy that our rights individually and collectively would be preserved? Let us now turn to facts and see whether this Government should legally execute taxes. His Excellency the High Commissioner entered the country, with a policy which he declared and which is mentioned in the Mandate before his eyes. He who thinks that the High Commissioner is a statesman of the grade of Yellin, Eder, Usishkin, he is mistaken; he is a clever master who brings his thoughts and political aims into being as a master who walks in the sun light and not in a poor light.

He first dealt to the people the blow of an embargo on cereals and thus he paralysed the Nation's agriculture and commerce and found means for the livelihood of immigrants. He then proclaimed the liquidation of the Ottoman Agricultural Bank and the nation had arisen and appealed and shouted and invoked help any to gain a reduction of the debts. He then convened his Advisory Council and put into force the old Turkish law for encouraging the people to till their lands. By this law the High Commissioner will appropriate one third of the lands of Palestine and he has the right to confer these lands on whom he wishes—the Zionists. He then placed an iron band round the neck of our economical interests by giving a foreign Zionist whose feet have never trodden the country, the well-known concession. He sold us, and sold our rights to the Zionists, as slaves. These and tens of other blights have stimulated thoughts and the Economic Conference was called for and it studied the state of affairs and devised the remedy and passed moderate feasible decisions. I have no doubt that had the Government intended to consider the interests of the people of the country and their economic future life, it would have executed the decisions and helped that Conference. But it did not do that; it only sent a nonsensical reply and increased the dues on some necessaries. This is only natural as it is applying a fixed policy based on other than Palestine Arab interests. Should we pay taxes with the existence of this policy?

Let us turn to another side of the question. The executive power is in the hands of a staunch Zionist Jew. The constitutional power is in the hands of an extremist Zionist, Mr. Bentwich, another of the 'Jewish Palestine'. Another headed the Department of Commerce & Industry. Whatever be the status of the other officials they are bound to obey the heads. However, the Government does not take any important action without first consulting the Zionist Commission. The Zionist Committee of London is able to obtain further there what they cannot obtain in Palestine. Rutenberg's concession, the Barra-Caisaeria concession which deprives 170 families of the means of their livelihood and the concession of which we now hear for the salt in the Dead Sea, were secretly given. What concessions have been given to people of the country—the tax payers—many of whom were repulsed on application, save perhaps the concession of Advisory Council. Is it for that we pay taxes to the Government and is it in this manner that the Government preserves our rights?

We now turn to the policy which prepares the way to create a Jewish majority—Jewish immigrants were admitted without restraint and were allowed as soon as they trod on the land, all the rights which the people of the country enjoy. They were given more than that; they were given temporary Palestinian citizenship— The Government then strove to find work of which the country is not in need in order to sustain the immigrants at our expense and out of our blood. But even this has not appeased those who commenced disseminating Bolshevic doctrines and the communist life by proclamations and speeches and commenced disturbing the set social rules. Thus ensued the 1920 riots [1921 rather] which resulted in (a) restriction on immigration which was only imaginary as the number of these immigrants was on the increase and the type much the same; and (b) the arming of the Jews under the pretence of self-defence. The Jews commenced organising a disciplined force which they call Hagana with the knowledge of the Government in the face of which it stands inert. The Jews generally were encouraged to smuggle in arms for distribution with the connivance of the Government. We have reliable information that the Government directed some British Officers to proceed to Jewish Colonies and instruct the young men in military tactics and musketry. One of these retiring officers has publicly declared that. For whom they prepare their armies for us, we who obediently offer our money. Dr. Weizmann has recently declared that he submitted a petition to the British Government asking for unrestricted immigration, for handing over Miri and untilled lands which amount to half of Palestine and said that the British Government had accepted this petition.

But we, the taxpayers, who are encumbered with these loads, were given a deficient institution which we rejected and boycotted. We have thus displayed ability.

I have striven to show that the Government is not working for our welfare nor is preserving our rights and as long as she is like that, the payment of taxes which she uses as arms for destroying us, is illegal. We don't blame the British Government for application of this policy for it might be expedient to it, nor the High Commissioner who is serving his people but we blame the leaders of the nation the sacrifice of which they witness. This Government which acts thus lives on your money. The money which is spent to prepare the way for the torrent of immigration is yours. The arms which are being distributed among your adversaries are yours. Your country is being converted into a Jewish country at your expense. You are responsible for this before History and your sons. The Jews do not pay the Government which adopts this policy anything worth mentioning. The Zionist comes to the country, lives in it, enjoys more than the rights of its sons, tills your lands and does away with you, without paying anything. You pay in money for making fetters for you. Rutenberg paid nothing and yet he was granted what has been denied to those sons who pay thousands. What man says that the poor Palestine peasant pays his money to the Government to guard Morums' stores and Rutenberg's concession. What man says that the son of the country who serves and who spends out of his own pocket for the upkeep of the Government on him is applied the prevention of Crime Ordinance because he says "There is no God but God" whilst the foreign Zionist who disseminates nefarious doctrines and roams about the country for him are created projects, granted concessions, and places built at your expense. What constitution says that the robber should gain and the victim be fined. This is unbearable. It is beyond human bearing. He is wise who follows the footpaths of his predecessors and there is one plan before us, i.e., "No taxation without representation".

As long as it is we who pay the taxes we must supervise that manner they are spent, and as long as we have no representative Council which has power of supervision over the Government, the payment of taxes is illegal according to the oldest and greatest constitutions in the world. I suggest the non-payment of taxes. My recommendation which is based on the above principle is equally consistent with the motto of our conference in that we should claim our rights in legal peaceful means. I suggest that the Congress should decide on referring the question of non-payment of taxes to the Executive Committee to study it minutely and select the opportune time for proclaiming it and putting it into effect.

(Sgd) Jamal al Hussaini, Secretary of the [Arab] Executive Com.

Bibliography

1. ARCHIVES

The Middle East Centre, St. Antony's College, Oxford

Samuel papers; Philby papers; Bentwich papers; Deedes papers

Pembroke College, Cambridge

Storrs papers

Cambridge University Library: Royal Commonwealth Society Library

Bramley Papers

Public Records Office, London

FO 371 General Correspondence July 1920–March 1921.
CO 733/1–110 Original Correspondence 1921–1925.
AIR 5/206, Political Situation in Palestine and Transjordan and Question of Anglo-French Boundary.
AIR 5/586, Strategical Importance of Palestine 1923.
CAB 37, Photographic Copies of Cabinet Papers.
WO 106/189–209 (Arab questions arising in Syria, Mesopotamia and the Levant and the Zionist Movement in Palestine February 1919– May 1921.

2. OFFICIAL PUBLICATIONS

Great Britain. Cmd 1499. High Commissioner for Palestine. *An Interim Report on the Civil Administration of Palestine.* HMSO, London 1921.
Great Britain. Cmd. 1540. *Palestine Disturbances in May 1921: Reports of the Commission of Inquiry with Correspondence in Relation Thereto. Presented to Parliament by Command of His Majesty, October 1921* (Haycraft Report).
Great Britain. Cmd. 5479. *Palestine Royal Commission Report. Presented by the Secretary of State for the Colonies to Parliament by Command of His Majesty July 1937.* (Peel Report).

Great Britain. Cmd. 6808. *The Anglo-American Committee of Enquiry Regarding the Problems of European Jewry and Palestine*. Lausanne April 1946.

Great Britain. Colonial no. 15. High Commissioner for Palestine. *Palestine. Report of the High Commissioner on the Administration of Palestine, 1920–1925*. HMSO, London 1925.

Palestine. *Official Gazette of the Government of Palestine*. Jerusalem 1920–1932.

Palestine. *First Report on Agricultural Development and Land Settlement in Palestine* by Lewis French. Jerusalem 1931.

Palestine. *A Survey of Palestine. Prepared in December 1945 and January 1946 for the Anglo-American Commission of Inquiry*, 2 vols. Government Printer 1946 and reprinted by the Institute for Palestine Studies, Washington D.C. 1991.

United States. National Archives Microfilm Publications. Microcopy No. 353. *Records of the Department of State Relating to Internal Affairs of Turkey, 1910–1929*. Rolls 79 and 80.

3. NEWSPAPERS AND JOURNALS

Al-Karmel 1920–1925.
Palestine: The Organ of the British Palestine Committee 1917–1924.
Filastin 1921–1925.

4. BOOKS, ARTICLES AND THESES

Abu-Lughod, Ibrahim, ed. *The Transformation of Palestine. Essays on the Origin and Development of the Arab–Israeli Conflict*. Evanston 1971.

——Roger Heacock and Khaled Nashef, (eds). *The Landscape of Palestine: Equivocal Poetry*. Birzeit, 1999.

Adelson, Roger. *Mark Sykes: Portrait of an Amateur*. London 1975.

Allon, Yigal. *Shield of David: The Story of Israel's Armed Forces*. London 1970.

Amery, Leopold. *My Political Life*. 3 vols, London 1953.

Anderson, M. S. *The Great Powers and the Near East, 1774–1923*. London 1970.

Anon. 'Lord Balfour's Personal Position on the Balfour Declaration'. (Two personal letters from Balfour. Comment by Caroll Quigley.) *Middle East Journal*, vol. 22, no. 3 (Summer 1968).

Antonius, George. *The Arab Awakening*. Beirut 1969.

Atiyah, Edward. *An Arab Tells His Story*. London 1946.

Barbour, Nevill. *Nisi Dominus: A Survey of the Palestine Controversy*. London 1946.

Bayley, W. R. *Saudi Arabia in the Nineteenth Century*. London 1965.

Ben Gurion, David, *Yawmiyat al-harb*, ed. Gershon Rivlin and Elhanan Oren, translated from Hebrew by Samir Jabbur. Institute for Palestine Studies, Beirut 1993.

Bentwich, Norman. *The Mandates System*. London 1930.

—— *England in Palestine*. London 1932.

—— *Palestine*. London 1934.

—— *Fulfilment in the Promised Land, 1917–1937*. London 1938.

—— *My 77 Years*. London 1962.

—— compiler. *Legislation of Palestine 1918–25, Including the Orders-in-Council, Ordinances, Public Notices, Proclamations, Regulations, Etc.* Alexandria 1926.

Berkowitz, Michael. *Western Jewry and the Zionist Project 1914–1933.* Cambridge 1997.

Bermant, Chaim. *The Cousinhood.* New York 1971.

Boustany, W. F. *The Palestine Mandate Invalid and Impracticable: A Contribution of Agreements and Documents Towards the Solution of the Palestine Problem.* Beirut 1936.

Bowle, John. *Viscount Samuel: A Biography.* London 1957.

Bullard, Sir Reader. *Two Kings of Arabia. Sir Reader Bullard's Letters from Jeddah 1923–5 and 1936–9.* ed. E. C. Hodgkin. Reading 1993.

Caplan, Neil. *Palestine Jewry and the Arab Question, 1917–1925.* London 1978.

Cattan, Henry. *The Palestine Question.* Saqi Books, London, 2000.

Cocker, Mark. *Richard Meinertzhagen: Soldier, Scientist and Spy.* London 1989.

Cohen, Raya Adler. 'The Tenants of Wadi Hawarith: Another View of the Land Question in Palestine'. *International Journal of Middle East Studies,* 20 (1988), pp. 197–220.

Cornelius, John. 'The Balfour Declaration and the Zimmerman Note'. *The Washington Report on Middle East Affairs,* vol. XVI, no. 2, (August/September 1997), pp. 18–20.

Crossman, Richard. *A Nation Reborn: A Personal Account of the Roles Played by Weizmann, Bevin and Ben-Gurion in the Story of Israel.* London 1960.

Darwazeh, Muhammad 'Izzat, *Mudhakkirat Muhammad 'Izzat Darwazeh 1305 H1404 H/ 1887 M–1984 M: Sijill hafil bi-masirat al-haraka al-'arabiyya wa-al-qadiya al-filistiniyya khilala qarn min al-zaman.* 6 vols, Beirut 1993.

Davis, John H. *The Evasive Peace. A Study of the Zionist–Arab Problem.* London 1968.

Deedes, Sir Wyndham. *The Memoirs of Sir Wyndham Deedes,* ed. Eliahu Elath, Norman Bentwich and Doris May, London 1958.

Divine, Donna Robinson. *Politics and Society in Ottoman Palestine: The Arab Struggle for Survival and Power.* London 1994.

Dumper, Michael. *Islam and Israel: Muslim Religious Endowments and the Jewish State.* Washington D.C. 1994.

Egremont, Max. *Balfour. A Life of Arthur James Balfour.* London, 1980.

Eldar, Dan. 'French Policy towards Husayn, Sharif of Mecca'. *Middle Eastern Studies,* vol. 26, no. 3 (1990).

Elon, Amos. *The Israelis: Founders and Sons.* New York 1971.

ESCO Foundation for Palestine. *Palestine. Jewish, Arab and British Policies.* New Haven 1947.

Fisher, John. *Curzon and British Imperialism in the Middle East 1916-19.* London, 1999.

Friesel, Evyatar. 'British Officials on the Situation in Palestine, 1923'. *Middle Eastern Studies,* vol. 23, no. 2 (1987), pp. 194–210.

—— 'Herbert Samuel's Reassessment of Zionism in 1921'. *Studies in Zionism,* vol. 5, no. 2 (1984), pp. 213–37.

Fromkin, David. *A Peace to End All Peace: Creating the Modern Middle East, 1914–1922.* London 1989.

Furlonge, Geoffrey. *Palestine is My Country: The Story of Musa Alami.* London 1989.

Gilbert, Martin. *Exile and Return. The Emergence of Jewish Statehood.* London 1978.

Gillon, D. Z. 'The Antecedents of the Balfour Declaration'. *Middle Eastern Studies,* vol. 5, no. 2 (1969), pp. 131–50.

Gilmour, David. *Curzon*. London 1994.

Granovsky, Abraham. *Land Problems in Palestine*. London 1926.

Gross, Nahum. *The Economic Policy of the Mandatory Government in Palestine*. Jerusalem 1982.

Hadawi, Sami. *Palestinian Rights and Losses in 1948*. London 1988.

—— *Bitter Harvest: Palestine Between 1914–1967*. New York 1967.

Halpern, Ben and Yehuda Reinharz. 'The Cultural and Social Background of the Second Aliyah'. *Middle Eastern Studies*, vol. 27, no. 3 (1991).

Herrman, I. M. 'Anglo-Zionist Relations from Herzl to the Balfour Declaration 1902–1917', D. Phil. thesis, University of Oxford 1971.

Herrmann, Klaus, J. 'Political Response to the Balfour Declaration in Imperial Germany: German Judaism'. *Middle East Journal*, vol. 19 (1965).

Howard, H. N. *An American Inquiry in the Middle East: The King-Crane Commission*. Beirut 1963.

Hughes, Matthew. *Allenby and British Strategy in the Middle East 1917–1919*. London 1999.

Huneidi, Sahar S. 'The Balfour Declaration in British Archives, 1922–1923: New Insights into Old Controversies' *Annals of the Faculty of Arts*, Kuwait University, vol. 9 (1999), monograph no. 136.

al-Hut, Bayan Nuwayhid. *Al-Qiyadat wa-al-mu'assasat al-siyasiyya fi filastin 1917–1948*. Beirut 1986.

Hyamson, A. M. *Palestine Under the Mandate 1920–48*. London 1950.

Ingrams, Doreen. *Palestine Papers 1917–1922: Seeds of Conflict*. London 1972.

John, Robert and Sami Hadawi. *The Palestine Diary, 1914–1915*. Vol. 1, Beirut 1970.

Jones, A. Philip. *Britain and Palestine 1914–1948: Archival Sources for the History of the British Mandate*. Oxford 1979.

Kagedan, Allan L. *Soviet Zion: The Quest for a Russian Jewish Homeland*. New York 1994.

Kamen, Charles S. *Little Common Ground: Arab Agriculture and Jewish Settlement in Palestine 1920–48*. Pittsburgh 1991.

Kaufman, Edy. 'French pro-Zionist Declarations of 1917–18'. *Middle Eastern Studies*, vol. 15, no. 3 (1979).

al-Kayyali, 'Abd al-Wahhab. *Palestine: A Modern History*. London 1978.

—— ed., *Watha'iq al-muqawama al-filastiniyya al-'arabiyya didd al-ihtilal al-baritani wa-al-sahyuniyya (1918–1939)*. Beirut 1988.

Kedourie, Elie. *In the Anglo-Arab Labyrinth. The McMahon-Husayn Correspondence and its Interpretations 1914–1939*. Cambridge 1976.

—— 'Sir Mark Sykes and Palestine 1915–16'. *Middle Eastern Studies*, vol. 6, no. 3 (1970), pp. 340–5.

—— 'Sir Herbert Samuel and the Government of Palestine'. *Middle Eastern Studies*, vol. 5, no. 1 (1969), pp. 44–68.

Keith-Roach, Edward. *Pasha of Jerusalem: Memoirs of a District Commissioner Under the British Mandate*, ed. Paul Eedle. London 1994.

Khalidi, Rashid. *British Policy Towards Syria and Palestine, 1906–1914: A Study of the*

Antecedents of the Hussein–McMahon Correspondence, the Sykes–Picot Agreement, and the Balfour Declaration. Oxford 1980.

Khalidi, Walid. *Palestine Reborn.* London 1992.

—— *All That Remains: The Palestinian Villages Occupied and Depopulated by Israel in 1948.* Washington D.C. 1992

—— *Before Their Diaspora. A Photographic History of the Palestinians 1876–1948.* Washington D.C. 1984.

—— ed. *From Haven to Conquest: Readings in Zionism and the Palestine Problem Until 1948.* Beirut 1971.

—— and Jill Khadduri, eds. *Palestine and the Arab–Israeli Conflict: An Annotated Bibliography.* Beirut 1974.

Khillih, Kamil. *Falastin wa-al-intidab al-baritani 1922–1939.* Beirut 1974.

Khuri, Yusuf Q. ed. *Al-Sahafa al-'arabiyya fi filastin 1876–1948.* Beirut 1976.

Kimche, Jon. *The Unromantics: The Great Powers and the Balfour Declaration.* London 1968.

Knox, D. Edward. 'The Development of British Policy in Palestine, 1917–1925: Sir Gilbert Clayton and the 'New Eastern Policy', PhD thesis, University of Michigan 1971.

—— *The Making of a New Eastern Question: British Palestine Policy and the Origins of Israel 1917–25.* Washington 1981.

Koestler, Arthur. *Promise and Fulfilment: Palestine, 1917–1949.* London 1949.

Kolinsky, Martin. *Law, Order and Riots in Mandatory Palestine, 1928–1935.* London 1993.

Krogh, Peter F. and Mary C. McDavid, eds. *Palestinians Under Occupation: Prospects for the Future.* Washington 1989.

Lehn, Walter with Uri Davis. *The Jewish National Fund.* London and New York 1988.

Lesch, Ann Mosely. *Arab Politics in Palestine, 1917–1939: The Frustration of a Nationalist Movement.* London 1979.

Louis, Wm. Roger. *In the Name of God, Go! Leo Amery and the British Empire in the Age of Churchill.* New York and London 1992.

Ludendorff, Erich. *My War Memories. 1914–18.* (trans.) London n.d.

Mallison, W. T. *The Balfour Declaration: An Appraisal in International Law.* Evanston 1971.

Mandel, Neville J. 'Ottoman Policy and Restrictions on Jewish Settlement in Palestine:1881–1908, Part I'. *Middle Eastern Studies*, vol.10, no. 3 (1974).

—— 'Ottoman Practice as regards Jewish Settlement in Palestine:1881–1908'. *Middle Eastern Studies*, vol.11, no. 1 (1975).

—— *The Arabs and Zionism before World War 1.* Berkeley 1976.

Manuel, Frank E. 'The Palestine Question in Italian Diplomacy, 1917–1920'. *Journal of Modern History*, vol. 27 (1955).

Marlowe, John. *The Seat of Pilate: An Account of the Palestine Mandate.* London 1959.

Masalha, Nur. *Expulsion of the Palestinians: The Concept of 'Transfer' in Zionist Political Thought, 1882–1948.* Washington 1992.

Massey, W. T. *How Jerusalem Was Won. Being the Record of Allenby's Campaign in Palestine.* London 1919.

—— *Allenby's Final Triumph.* London 1920.

Massiri, Abdul Wahhab. *The Encyclopedia of Zionist Concepts and Terminology.* (Arabic).

Cairo 1974.

Mazzawi, Musa. *The Balfour Declaration: What Did Britain Promise in Palestine?* London 1967.

—— *Palestine and the Law.* London 1997.

McCarthy, Justin. *The Population of Palestine: Population History and Statistics of the Late Ottoman Period and the Mandate.* New York 1990.

McTague, John. *British Policy in Palestine 1917–22.* Lanham 1983.

Meinertzhagen, Richard. *Middle East Diary, 1917–1956.* London 1959.

Metzer, Jacob. *The Divided Economy of Mandate Palestine.* Cambridge 1998.

Monroe, Elizabeth. *Britain's Moment in the Middle East, 1914–1956.* London 1963.

Moore, John Norton, ed. *The Palestine Question. Seminar of Arab Jurists on Palestine, Algiers, July 22–27, 1967. Part One. Historical 'Rights'.* New Jersey 1974.

Morris, James. *The Hashemite Kings.* London 1959.

Mossek, Moshe. *Palestine Immigration Policy Under Sir Herbert Samuel.* London 1978.

Muslih, Mohammad Yousef. *The Origins of Palestinian Nationalism.* New York 1988.

Myers, David. *Re-inventing the Jewish Past: European Jewish Intellectuals and the Zionist Return to History.* Oxford 1995.

Najjar, Aida Ali. 'The Arabic Press and Nationalism in Palestine 1920–1948'. Ph.D. dissertation, Syracuse University 1975.

Öke, Mim Kemal. 'The Ottoman Empire, Zionism and the Question of Palestine (1880–1908).' *International Journal of Middle East Studies,* vol. 14, no. 3 (1982), pp. 329–41.

Ormsby-Gore, William. 'Great Britain, Palestine and the Jews'. *The XIXth Century,* vol. 88 (July–December 1920).

Penslar, Derek. *Zionism and Technocracy: The Engineering of Jewish Settlement in Palestine 1870–1918.* London 1991.

Philby, H. St. John. *Arabian Jubilee.* London 1952.

Porath, Yehoshua. *The Emergence of the Palestinian–Arab National Movement, 1918–1929.* London 1974.

—— 'The Palestinians and the Negotiations for the British–Hijazi Treaty, 1920–1925'. *Asian and African Studies,* vol. 8, no. 1 (1972), pp. 20–48.

Presland, John, pseud. [Gladys Skelton]. *Deedes Bey. A Study of Sir Wyndham Deedes, 1883-1923.* London 1942.

Quigley, John. *Palestine and Israel: A Challenge to Justice.* Durham, NC 1990.

Reinharz, Yehuda. *Chaim Weizmann: The Making of a Statesman.* Oxford 1993.

Rabinowicz, Oskar. 'The Aliens Bill and Jewish Immigration to Britain 1902–1905', in Khalidi, ed., *From Haven to Conquest,* pp. 97–114.

—— 'The Balfour Declaration in Historical Perspective', in *Essential Papers on Zionism,* ed. Y. Reinharz and A. Shapira. London 1996. pp. 587–616.

—— and Anita Shapira (eds). *Essential Papers on Zionism.* New York 1994.

Richmond, John. 'Prophet of Doom: E. T. Richmond, F.R.I.B.A., Palestine, 1920–1924', in A. L. Tibawi, *Arabic and Islamic Garland: Historical, Educational and Literary Papers Presented to Abdul Latif Tibawi.* London 1977.

Ro'i, Yaacov. 'The Zionist Attitude to the Arabs, 1908–1914'. *Middle Eastern Studies,* vol. 4, no. 3 (1967), pp. 198–242.

Rokach, Livia. *The Catholic Church and the Question of Palestine*. London 1987.

Rosen, Jacob. 'Captain Reginald Hall and the Balfour Declaration'. *Middle Eastern Studies*, vol. 24, no. 1 (1988).

Roskill, Stephen. *Hankey: Man of Secrets*. London 1972.

Roth, Cecil. *A History of the Jews*. New York 1961.

Ruedy, John. 'Dynamics of Land Alienation', in Abu-Lughod, ed., *The Transformation of Palestine: Essays on the Origins and Development of the Arab-Israeli Conflict*.

Said, Edward. *The Question of Palestine*. New York 1979.

Samuel, Edwin. *A Lifetime in Jerusalem*. London 1970.

Samuel, Herbert Louis, Sir. 'Great Britain and Palestine', delivered in the Great Hall of University College, London, by the Rt. Hon. Sir Herbert Samuel, G.C.B., C.B.E., D.C.L., on November 25th 1935. *The Second Lucien Wolf Memorial Lecture*. The Jewish Historical Society of England 1935.

—— (Viscount) *Memoirs*. London 1945.

Sanders, Ronald. *The High Walls of Jerusalem: A History of the Balfour Declaration and the Birth of the British Mandate for Palestine*. New York 1983.

Schölch, Alexander. *Palestine in Transformation, 1856–1882: Studies in Social, Economic and Political Development*. Washington D.C. 1993.

Seikaly, May. Haifa: *Transformation of an Arab Society 1918–1939*. London 1995.

Seikaly, Samir. 'Unequal Fortunes: The Arabs of Palestine and the Jews during World War I' in Wadad al-Qadi, ed., *Studia Arabica & Islamica: Festschrift for Ihsan Abbas on his Sixtieth Birthday*. Beirut 1981.

Seton-Watson, R. W. *Disraeli, Gladstone and the Eastern Question*. London 1971.

Sharif, Regina. *Non-Jewish Zionism: Its Roots in Western Diplomacy*. London 1983.

Shorrock, William. *French Imperialism in the Middle East. The Failure of French Policy in Syria and Lebanon, 1900–1914*. Madison 1976.

Smith, Barbara. *The Roots of Separatism in Palestine: British Economic Policy 1920–1929*. London 1993.

Smith, Pamela Ann. *Palestine and the Palestinians, 1876–1983*. London 1984.

Stein, Kenneth W. *The Land Question in Palestine, 1917–1939*. London 1984.

Stein, Leonard. *The Balfour Declaration*, London 1961.

Stevens, P. Richard. *Zionism and Palestine Before the Mandate: A Phase of Western Imperialism*. Beirut 1972.

Stewart, Desmond. *The Middle East: Temple of Janus*. London 1972.

—— *Theodor Herzl: Artist and Politician*. London 1974.

Storrs, Ronald. *Orientations*. London 1945.

Sykes, Christopher. *Crossroads to Israel*. Bloomington, Indiana 1973.

Taylor, A. J. P. *The First World War*. London 1966.

Taylor, Alan R. *Prelude to Israel: An Analysis of Zionist Diplomacy*. London 1959.

Teveth, Shabtai. *Ben-Gurion: The Burning Ground, 1886–1948*. Boston 1987.

Tibawi, A. L. *Anglo-Arab Relations and the Question of Palestine, 1914–1921*. Second edition, London 1978.

Toynbee, Arnold J. *A Study of History: Abridgement of volumes VII–X* by D. C. Somervell. Oxford 1957.

Tyler, W. P. N. 'The Beisan Lands Issue in Mandatory Palestine'. *Middle Eastern Studies*, vol. 25, no. 2 (1989).

—— 'The Huleh Lands Issue in Mandatory Palestine, 1920–34'. *Middle Eastern Studies*, vol. 27, no. 3 (1999).

Ussishkin, Anne. 'The Jewish Colonization Association and a Rothschild in Palestine'. *Middle Eastern Studies*, vol. 9, no. 3 (1973), pp. 347–57.

Vereté, Mayir. 'The Balfour Declaration and its Makers'. *Middle Eastern Studies*, vol. 6, no. 1 (1970).

—— 'Why Was a British Consulate Established in Jerusalem?' *English Historical Review*, vol. LXXXV (1970).

—— 'Kitchener, Grey and the Question of Palestine' in Norman Rose, ed. *From Palmerston to Balfour, Collected Essays of Mayir Vereté*. London 1992.

Vital, David. *Zionism: The Crucial Phase*. London 1987.

—— *A People Apart. The Jews in Europe 1789–1939*. Oxford 1999.

Wasserstein, Bernard. *Herbert Samuel: A Political Life*. London 1992.

—— *The British in Palestine: The Mandatory Government and the Arab–Jewish Conflict, 1917–1929*. 2nd edn, Oxford 1991.

—— 'The British Mandate for Palestine: Myths and Realities', in Moshe Dayan Center for Middle Eastern and African Studies, Tel Aviv University, *Middle Eastern Lectures Number 1*. Tel Aviv 1995.

Wavell, Archibald Percival, Earl of. *The Palestine Campaigns*. London 1928.

—— *Allenby, a Study in Greatness: The Biography of Field Marshal Viscount Allenby of Megiddo and Felixstowe*. London 1940.

Weisgal, Meyer W., ed. *Statesmen of the Jewish Renaissance*. Jerusalem 1975.

—— and Joel Carmichael, eds. *Chaim Weizmann: A Biography By Several Hands*. London 1962.

Weizmann, Chaim. *Trial and Error: The Autobiography of Chaim Weizmann*, London 1949.

—— *The Letters and Papers of Chaim Weizmann: Volume 7, August 1914–November 1917*. London 1975.

Weizmann, Vera. *The Impossible Takes Longer: The Memoirs of Vera Weizmann, As Told to David Tutaev*. London 1967.

Westrate, Bruce. *The Arab Bureau: British Policy in the Middle East, 1916–1920*. Pennsylvania 1992.

Whitelam, Keith W. *The Invention of Ancient Israel: The Silencing of Palestinian History*. London and New York 1996.

Wilson, Jeremy. *Lawrence of Arabia. The Authorised Biography of T. E. Lawrence*. London 1989.

Yapp, Malcolm E. *The Near East Since the First World War*. London 1991.

—— 'The Making of the Palestine Mandate', in Moshe Dayan Center for Middle Eastern and African Studies, Tel Aviv University. *Middle Eastern Lectures Number 1*. Tel Aviv 1995.

Young, Hubert, Sir. *The Independent Arab*. London 1933.

Zaid. 'Chaim Weizmann's Scientific Work: 1915–1918', in A. L. Tibawi, *Arabic and Islamic Garland: Historical, Educational and Literary Papers Presented to Abdul Latif Tibawi*.

London 1977.

Zeine, Zeine. *The Struggle for Arab Independence. Western Diplomacy and the Rise and Fall of Feisal's Kingdom in Syria*. Second edition, New York 1977.

Zionist Library. *Chaim Weizmann. Statesman of the Jewish Resistance. The Chaim Weizmann Centenary 1874–1974*. Jerusalem 1974.

Zu'aytir, Akram, *Watha'iq al-haraka al-wataniyya al-filastiniyya (1918–1939): min awraq Akram Zu'aytir*, ed. Bayan Nuwayhid al-Hut. Beirut 1984.

Index